# Pillars of Salt

# Pillars of Salt

## *An Anthology of Early American Criminal Narratives*

Daniel E. Williams

MADISON HOUSE
Madison 1993

Williams, Daniel E.
*Pillars of Salt, An Anthology of Early American Criminal Narratives*


Printed in the United States of America.



LIBRARY OF CONGRESS CATALOGING-IN-PUBLICATION DATA

Pillars of salt/an anthology of early American criminal narratives / Daniel E. Williams [compiler]. — 1st ed.
p. cm.
Contains articles previously published between 1699 and 1796.
Includes bibliographical references and index.
ISBN 0-945612-31-1 (alk. paper)
1. American prose literature—Colonial period, ca. 1600–1775.
2. Crime—United States—History—18th century—Sources.
3. American prose literature—1783–1850. 4. Criminals—United States—Biography.
PS648.C7P54 1992
810.9'355—dc20
92–25124
CIP

ISBN 0-945612-31-1 (HC)
ISBN 0-945612-37-0 (PBK)

Designed by William Kasdorf
Printed on acid-free paper by Edwards Brothers, Inc.

Published by Madison House Publishers, Inc.
P. O. Box 3100, Madison, Wisconsin 53704

FIRST EDITION

# *Contents*

# *Illustrations*

# *Preface*

My Heart seemed to be melted within me, and Sin appeared worse than Hell. I hated Sin, because God hated it: and I loathed my self for Sin, and for dishonouring God, more than I ever loathed a Toad, or a Rattle Snake.

—from *A Faithful Narrative of The Wicked Life and Remarkable Conversion of Patience Boston*, 1738

According to the narrative of her life, Patience Boston cheerfully participated in her death. After walking calmly to "the Place of Execution," and after acknowledging her guilt and calling for "the innumerable Spectators . . . [to] take Warning by her," she smiled as the rope was placed around her neck (139). Then, moments before "the Executioner did his Office," she uttered her last words, a prayer begging Christ for mercy. Her compliant behavior prompted one minister to conclude that "she behaved her self very decently" (140, 138). According to most eighteenth-century criminal narratives published in what eventually became the United States, Boston was not the only condemned prisoner to prefer death to life. Most of those who were "launched into eternity" participated in the carefully staged rituals of death, either actively performing the part of a penitent or passively allowing others to make use of them while waiting for the inevitable moment when life would cease. No one had to be dragged kicking and screaming to the gallows, and no one died cursing and struggling in final, futile gestures of defiance—at least according to the published narratives.

This project began several years ago when I became interested in the depiction of condemned criminals cheerfully participating in their executions. Not believing that the taking away of an individual life was an act of kindness, I became concerned with trying to understand how and why a person would cooperate with those intent on destroying that person's life. Such curiosity led to many other questions, most of which involved the depiction of the criminal character in life and in death. As they were brought from the prison to the gallows, condemned criminals engaged the attention of hundreds, and sometimes thousands, of spectators, and as they later were paraded before readers they continued to be the focus of close attention. This anthology attempts to return twenty criminal characters to the scrutiny that they originally compelled, and in returning these characterizations to the public eye I hope encourage further scrutiny of gallows literature in particular and of early American print culture in general. In order to understand why Patience Boston smiled as the rope was placed around her neck, or at least why she was so depicted, we have to understand first how criminal characterization functioned within early American culture.

Public execution was an elaborately staged ritual drama, and great care was taken in preparing the condemned criminals for their part. Those staging the executions, ministers and magistrates alike, knew that the condemned prisoners would be the focus of attention, and they exerted great effort in taking advantage of this popular curiosity. During their confrontation with death, and because of their proximity to death, condemned criminals were a figures of power and influence, and in the narratives printed before and after the executions their characterizations were adapted to extend their power and influence. As examples, they originally were used in person and in print both to give warnings and to offer encouragement, since death gave their words the conviction of profound truth. Those responsible for staging their deaths attempted to use the force of this truth to shape social behavior; similarly, those responsible for producing the first criminal narratives in America equally exploited the "dying words" of condemned prisoners to promote law and order.

In life, criminals were agents of disorder, but in death they became the opposite. When presented in popular narratives, criminal characters functioned in the same manner to reinforce civil authority and social conformity. Because of the selection and arrangement of materials, narratives established cause and effect relationships and thus provided readers with a perception of meaning. Gallows and text both made crime understandable, or at least located such acts of deviance and defiance in conventional contexts that rendered them understandable. By placing crimes and criminals in a linear progression of beginning, middle and end, narratives imposed a structure on socially disruptive experiences, and thus they negated the misrule inherent in unlawful action. Criminal narratives, at least as they originally were intended, not only were produced to reflect cultural values, but also to police these values (Miller 69).[1]

[1] For the most succinct and readable introductory analysis on the narrative, see J. Hillis Miller's essay, "Narrative," included in the Lentricchia and McLaughlin anthology. The literature on narrative is extensive, but for helpful introductions see the anthologies edited by Mitchell and by Phelan. In addition to narrative theory, I also have been

Yet not all of them did. Written for a popular audience, criminal narratives were more susceptible to the pressures of the marketplace than other literary forms, and both character and structure came to reflect the expectations of readers. While most previous work has concentrated on the similarities of narratives published during the eighteenth century, often claiming that the genre resisted change and development, I have found the opposite to be true.[2] Conventions and formulas certainly were well established, and these indeed were part of what readers appreciated. Nevertheless, beneath the outer rhetorical and structural levels change was drastic, particularly concerning the depiction of authority and defiance.

As recent work in the history of the book has demonstrated, the study of popular literature offers valuable insight into "the substance of perception and belief" generally shared among people (Hall, *Worlds* 18).[3] By examining the developments within the criminal narrative genre in light of the wider social, cultural, and political developments of eighteenth-century America, we not only can perceive how literary texts reflected the values and beliefs of readers, but also how they shaped them. Literary texts are cultural artifacts, and when carefully examined they can provide insight into the historical contexts in which they were produced. By discussing the twenty narratives in my introduction, I have tried to suggest the complex and reciprocal relationship between readers and texts and how both changed as the world they were a part of changed around them. Ironically, although first produced in the late seventeenth century to reinforce authority and conformity, criminal narratives of the late eighteenth century nearly accomplished the opposite.

I have received some strange looks and comments when asked about my work. Assuming the traditional prejudices of elite literature, not a few of my colleagues in literature have smiled when I have taken the time to explain my work. Sometimes, in order to avoid such smiles, I have evaded their questions, offering instead general comments about either early American literature or early narrative forms. At other times, if pressed by the question, "*Who* are you working on?" I have taken impish delight in throwing out names like Levi Ames and Thomas Powers and then referring to them as writers of significance and influence. And I confess that I have smiled, expressing slight disbelief, when those I was talking to admitted they had never heard of Ames or Powers. The reactions I have received

influenced by discussions in reader-response and reception theory. For helpful introductions here, see the anthologies edited by Suleiman and Crosman and by Tompkins.

[2] For work concentrating on the genre's resistance to change, see Bosco ("Lectures"), Masur, and Towner.

[3] I am indebted to Professor Hall for both his recent work and his efforts on behalf of the History of the Book Program at the American Antiquarian Society.

indicate our own critical and cultural conventions. Too often in the past we have focused attention on the productions of elite literary culture, paying critical homage to those writers enshrined in the traditional canon.

Readers in the eighteenth century, however, did not worship in the cult of great authors as we do, and in order to better understand them we need to gain a better understanding of what they read. Sometimes this requires putting aside the usual (and ideological) questions of what constitutes "good" literature. The criminal narratives discussed and presented in this book were written and published specifically for early American readers. What is significant about them is not that they are "good" literary productions but that they affected the imaginations and perceptions of countless readers. One might argue, in fact, that in 1773 Levi Ames had a greater impact on the people of Boston than Samuel Adams. Criminal narratives are not trivial, nor can they be dismissed as ephemeral. Some are crude and poorly written, and some are shallow, but all were an essential part of a consequential relationship between writers, printers, booksellers, and readers.

In order to suggest how the narratives originally were read, I have adopted an editorial policy that attempts to approximate the original texts as closely as possible. I have therefore made no corrections, not even to correct obvious printer's errors. The only time something has been added in brackets—whether a word, a letter, or a puncutation mark—has been for the sake of clarity, and these changes were made only after checking several copies and editions. Since many of these narratives were published in more than one edition, I always have used the first as the copy text, referring to subsequent editions when something in the primary source could not be read. In addition, in order to suggest how the narratives either altered or supported popular perceptions, I have included in the source notes a variety of accounts (letters, diaries, and especially newspapers) describing the criminals.

Obviously, any editorial process of selection and inclusion cannot be comprehensive. By including some narratives I have excluded others. Yet these twenty narratives offer a fair representation of the criminal narrative genre in eighteenth-century America. They have been chosen because of their social and cultural significance and because they represent various styles, developments, concerns, and character types. All of the twenty narratives were published in the mid-Atlantic and northern colonies and therefore were shaped specifically for colonial readers. Far from perpetuating a myth of New England ascendancy, this regional preponderance reflects the historical pattern of commercial presses and distribution routes. I have located only one criminal narrative published in the south, *The Confession and Declaration of George Burns*, a brief two-page narrative published in Charleston in 1766, and only one other, *The Vain Prodigal Life and Tragical Penitent Death of Thomas Hellier*, situated in the south. Although a long and fascinating early narrative, I chose not to include the Hellier text because it was published in London and intended for an English audience. My intention has been to focus on those texts printed in the colonies and later states in order to reveal how authority and deviance, crime and criminals, were depicted for a popular American audience.

In a recent essay, Victor Neuburg has demonstrated not only that there was a sizeable market in eighteenth-century America for popular literature but also that English presses primarily were responsible for meeting the demands of this market.[4] The broadsides and chapbooks that contained the narrative lives of American criminals, then, were an exception to the standard practice of importing English literary products. American printers invested their time, energy, and materials in publishing criminal narratives because they knew that readers, their customers, would buy what they produced. Public execution was a dramatic spectacle, and significant numbers of people flocked around the gallows to experience collectively the mysteries of death, hoping to comprehend that which lay beyond the realm of human comprehension. As the ultimate human drama, it was cheap, sensational, and profound. Today, in view of the popular attitudes towards capital punishment, and more recently in view of the movement to return death to the public stage, we must try to understand the social function of crime by examining how historical figures were turned into literary characters.

By focusing on the eighteenth century, however, I do not want to imply that the genre died out with the end of public execution. Stopping in the 1790s, for instance, at the beginning of early America's reading revolution, was arbitrary; but, due to the nature and number of nineteenth-century criminal narratives a fair representation would have been difficult, if not impossible. Criminal narratives thrived in the nineteenth century and easily adapted to the conventions and expectations of the twentieth century. Though, in slightly different forms, it continues to thrive today. We still are as interested in those who defy our boundaries as our ancestors were in the eighteenth century.

Daniel E. Williams
Oxford, Mississippi, June 6, 1991

[4] See Professor Neuburg's essay, "Chapbooks in America," included in Davidson's recent *Reading in America*.

# *Acknowledgments*

No book is the product of one person. In order to reach readers, all books are put together through a collaborative effort as ideas are shared and pages are proofed. Along the path from inception to completion, this book has received much help and support from numerous friends and colleagues, and the debt I owe them is great.

As a graduate student at the University of Denver, I received immeasureable assistance from the staff at Penrose Library, and I would like specifically to express my gratitude to Ms. Pat Fisher, director of Public Serivces, who was both tolerant and generous with all my requests. To Professor Robert D. Richardson, I owe a debt greater than I can ever repay, since I cannot even count the number of times he patiently advised and encouraged me. Simply, neither this project nor my career would have been possible without Professor Richardson's liberal support. After two decades he remians my ideal of a teacher and a scholar.

I also must acknowledge the invaluable support I received from my friends and colleagues at Die Universitaet Tuebingen. Taking a chance on a young American Ph.D., whose knowledge of German was barely enough to locate the town of Tuebingen, they sustained and nurtured me as I extended my scholarship in the narratives and my capacity in the classroom. I especially am grateful for the many instances of friendship and help I received from Professors Hans Borchers, Hartmut Grandel, Siegfried Neuweiler, Elsa Lattey, and Uwe and Traudel Moennich. Without the kindly assistnace of Ms. Zoe Pacquier and Ms. Sonja Haas-Grueber I indeed would have been lost. To Dennis Anderson and Klaus Lenk I owe an equally great debt of friendship; on countless Saturday nights they enriched my life. While in Tuebingen Professor Alfred Weber was my director, but he was far more than just this. With his help I received a faculty grant that enabled me to acquire invaluable photocopy and microfilm. With his support I was able to establish myself as a specialist in early American narratives. And with his hospitality I felt at home far away from home.

At the University of Mississippi I have been similarly fortunate to encounter ideal colleagues, whose support enabled me to complete this project. In particular, I must thank H. Dale Abadie, Greg Schirmer, and Gerald Walton, all three of whom provided financial assistance that allowed me to travel and to acquire scarce materials. While they might have been skeptical about my group of malefactors, they had enough confidence in me to sustain my work. I also received invaluable help from Sara Selby, Kristen Sulser, Kathy Williams, Sam Stott, Billie Trott, and Judy Curtis; they not only helped me but kept the English department running smoothly.

While working on my "Pillars" project, I received help from numerous scholars, librarians, and archivists. While attending an NEH summer seminar on "Classic Texts in Early American History" at the University of Connecticut, I received kindly support from Richard D. Brown and Karen Ordahl Kupperman, encouraging me to pursue my rather unclassical texts. A fellowship at the John Carter Brown Library allowed me the luxury of focusing on my work, and with the help of my friends at the JCB I discovered new materials and new significance in old materials. I especially am thankful for the support I received from Norman Fiering, director of the JCB, and for the friendship I had with Bill Wilkie, my "tablemate." At the American Antiquarian Society I also would like to acknowledge both the kindness and the aid I received from Marie Lamoureaux, Nancy Burkett, Joann Chaison, Gigi Barnhill, and John Hench. With regularity I appeared and reappeared at the AAS, and these people always made me feel welcome. Both Jill E. Erickson of the Library of the Boston Athenaeum and Karen Nipps of the Library Company of Philadelphia provided valuable help in times of need.

I have received incalcuable support from numerous friends and colleagues along the way. To Philip F. Gura and Everett Emerson I am particularly grateful; with their encouragement and assistance I was able to explore unknown literary territory in the pages of *Early American Literature.* In the beginning Ron Bosco's enthusiasm for criminal narratives ignited my own, and his original "Checklist" was a constant and inexhaustible resource. I have been enriched by the friendships that have grown through my activities in the American Society for Eighteenth Century Studies, and I am especially thankful for the congenial times I have shared with Frank Shuffelton, John Engell, and Rosalie Murphy Baum. David S. Shields has been more than a good friend; in addition to his warmth, he has offered generous assistance. Ken and Sarala Van Dover have been constant friends for over a decade, and I am thankful that we encountered each other as strangers in a strange land. While during a History of the Book seminar at AAS I encountered two other individuals who have contributed infinite amounts of cordial help: David R. Warrington and Boyd Childress. Both opened up their libraries and their resources, and both acted as detectives when I needed something tracked down. I am grateful for their friendship. I also am grateful for the friendship I have enjoyed with John Samson; our conversations and our collaborations have extended my work and enhanced my life. Finally, this book would not be possible except for the ample assistance of John Kaminski from The Center for the Study of the American Constitution and Greg Britton of Madison House—Thanks.

To my two ladies, Cynthia and Leah, I dedicate this book. You are the "Pillars" in my life.

[One final note of caution: Having brought myself to this shameful and ignominious conclusion, by my own wicked conduct and composition, I confess that all vicious practices and typographical errors are my own. Take warning by my example. Shun vice, follow virtue, and rely on the infinite mercy and merits of your editors.]

# *Introduction*

## I

> Sir, as for the pain that my body must presently feel, I matter it not: I know what pain is; but what shall I do for my poor Soul? I'm terrify'd with the Wrath of God; This, this terrifyes me, Hell terrifyes me.
>
> —James Morgan from *Pillars of Salt*, 1699

Unlike most people, James Morgan knew exactly when and how he would die. Condemned for murder, he spent the last months of his life in the Boston jail waiting for the moment when the ladder would be jerked out from under him and Death, the King of Terrors, would claim him. Yet Morgan was not left alone to confront the uncertainties of his life's end. His death in 1686 was a public event, a communal affair in which hundreds, even thousands, of people participated. Although unknown and unimportant throughout the thirty years of his life, he became a celebrity in death. Curious crowds flocked to the jail to converse with him or simply to observe him. As the date of his execution approached, people from as far away as fifty miles travelled to Boston to witness the spectacle. When he was paraded in public on March 7, the Sunday before his Thursday execution, "a vast Concourse of People" packed into the Second Church to hear Cotton Mather and Joshua Moody deliver sermons written especially for the condemned man, who sat in the congregation chained and penitent as a dramatic illustration of their lessons (C. Mather, *Diary* 122). When March 11 arrived, so many people crowded into the Second Church to hear Increase Mather deliver the final execution sermon that the "Gallery crack'd," and the immense throng then followed the minister and the murderer to the Third Church, where the condemned man again sat in chains as unmistakable proof of the minister's warnings (Dunton 419).[1]

[1] In his *Diary*, Samuel Sewall offered a somewhat different account of the exodus from the Second Church. According to Sewall, a momentary hysteria was caused when "a crazed woman cryed the Gallery or Meetinghouse broke" (I, 125–26). As a precaution, "for fear of the worst," the meeting was then moved to the Third Church (126).

After this last sermon, the crowd continued to swell, joining the procession to the gallows. In order to receive a few final words of comfort and instruction, Morgan walked his last mile with Cotton Mather, but the crush of people was so great that their progress was blocked and interrupted. At the place of execution, as many as five thousand were jammed around the gallows, trying to get as close as possible so that they could behold the condemned man's gestures and hear his dying words. For the first and only moment in his life, James Morgan was the most important man in Boston.

Morgan's confrontation with death was indeed a public event. Despite his obscurity, and despite the awkward violence of his crime, he attracted the attention of a remarkable number of people, touching the collective imagination in ways particular to the time and place. Yet what made Morgan so exceptional was not simply that he had stabbed a man during a drunken rage, but how his culture had responded.[2] At the simplest level, he became the focus of attention due to the infrequency of both his crime and his punishment. Since a public execution had not taken place in Boston for seven years, the curious populace gathered to witness the gruesome spectacle. For people of all cultures, death always has fascinated because it was unknowable and mysterious, and the ritual of public execution always has drawn crowds hungry for the sensations of collective death. Yet for early New Englanders death was not dissolution, the extinction of identity; rather, the destruction of the flesh represented the transition from a lesser to a greater world. Not only did their theology promote a constant awareness of death, but it also affirmed the belief that life was a pilgrimage to an ultimate, eternal state. Death led to Final Judgment, when God offered the rewards of salvation to a chosen few and the pains of damnation to all the rest. Consequently, for those who believed in innate depravity and in the necessity of conversion, death became the most significant event in life. When crowds of people jammed their way into the churches to catch a glimpse of Morgan, and when they pressed about him at the gallows, they watched to see how he would confront that most dreadful moment of divine decree.

But the people came not just to watch, they came to participate. It was not only the idle and the curious who gathered to witness a macabre and sensational spectacle; people from a variety of levels and areas assembled to experience a carefully staged public ritual, a ceremony of death that had been sanctioned and promoted by the most influential leaders of New

[2] Morgan's crime was rather crude and unpremeditated. During a drunken rage, he stabbed by victim "by running a spitt into his belly a little above the navell" (Powers 289). Both Increase and Cotton Mather offered details of the attack in their sermons. For a description of Morgan's arraignment, see Sewall's *Diary*, I, 111.

England. Morgan's execution was a drama intended for popular consumption, and from the moment of his condemnation to his last moments at the gallows, he had been prepared thoroughly for his part. Told that he could expect no mercy in this world but that, if he repented, God might grant him mercy in the next, he was rehearsed in a role of public penitence. Fully aware of the popular fascination with death, both sacred and secular authorities encouraged people to share emotionally in the drama by casting Morgan in scenes of dramatic encounter and by stressing, rather than by denying, the similarities between the spectators and the spectacle. His conflict—a desperate attempt to secure God's mercy by renouncing the sinful self—engaged all individuals. In order to reinforce the social order, in order to reaffirm the values that the capital crime had threatened, ministers and magistrates collaborated in presenting Morgan before as many people as possible, and through their direction the ritual of death dramatized the condemned man's struggles to escape the fires of hell.

Yet in death Morgan continued to struggle. His last months and moments of life survived long after he had been taken down and laid to rest. Shortly after his execution he was resurrected in print; not only were the three execution sermons published, but also his final confession and his dying speech. Within a year the sermons and speeches were reprinted, and to supplement his sermon, Cotton Mather also added a transcript of the dialogue he had held with Morgan as they walked to the gallows. Just as he had been paraded before the public in chains, his character was now presented, and readers could follow his movements and listen to his words as he confronted the certainty of death and the terrible uncertainty of Final Judgment. And just as he had attracted the attention of a large, curious audience, his literary self continued to draw people to his death scene, offering them a similarly dramatic experience. In order to reach an even larger number of people than the "vast Concourse" who had surrounded the gallows, in order to influence those who would not normally attend church or read sermons, these publications recreated the entire ritual of Morgan's execution.

James Morgan was one of the first criminal characters to be developed in early American literature, and the literary representations of his death scenes were intended to function much like the actual events. Similar to the spectacle of execution, the various Morgan texts were not simply intended to warn by striking fear in potential offenders but also to mark the borders of acceptable behavior and thus reinforce the collective social identity.[3]

[3] For a valuable discussion of how crime and criminal process function in society, see Kai Erikson's introductory essay, "On the Sociology of Deviance," in *Wayward Puritans* (3–29). Basing his work on the theories of Emil Durkheim and George Herbert Mead, Erikson described the public rituals of criminal procedure, especially trials and punish-

Moreover, they helped to shape the perception of deviance, allowing readers to perceive various acts of defiance and non-conformity in ways that were socially useful. Obviously, Morgan's execution vividly testified that the state possessed the ultimate power—the right to take a human life. But it also attempted to balance the scales of justice by demonstrating that this ultimate power was divine in origin. God, and not the magistrates, punished iniquity. Crime was merely another form of sin, the pitiful rebellion of mortals against the sacred order. Here, then, was Morgan's significance. In his drunken rage he not only broke civil laws; he also challenged God. And in the ritual drama of his execution the ministers and the magistrates emphasized the inevitable failure of such defiance. Instances of public punishment, both in actuality and in print, were used in early New England to assert simultaneously the extreme polarities of divine omnipotence and human impotence. According to those responsible for his final performance, Morgan, having wasted his life, was "turn'd off" by God.

## II

> It hath been Thought, that the *Dying Speeches* of such as have been Executed among us, might be of singular Use, to Correct and Reform, The *Crimes*, wherein too many do *Live*; and it is wish'd, that at Least, some Fragments of those *Dying Speeches*, might be preserved and published.
>
> —Cotton Mather from *Pillars of Salt*, 1699

American criminal literature began in the late seventeenth century when ministers, such as the Mathers, started to publish their execution sermons. Aware of the intense popular interest in condemned criminals, they introduced various texts that dramatized the conflicts and the conditions of those about to be executed. Intended as supplementary illustrations of the sermons, these texts—final confessions, dying speeches, and last prayers—attracted readers by developing a specific fictional identity during a period of extreme crisis. Such "warnings from the dead" reconstructed the spectacle of a miserable sinner encountering the immediacy of

---

ments, as "boundary-maintaining devices"(11). Both deviant behavior and the official responses of a society to such behavior "give the inner structure its special character and thus supply the framework within which people of the group develop an orderly sense of their own cultural identity" (13).

death and the probability of damnation. Readers were drawn into the criminal's spiritual crisis, encouraged to identify themselves with the individual who dangled before them. The crimes to which the condemned confessed, in public and in print, inevitably were sins that many found common in their own lives, such as lying, cursing, or Sabbath-breaking, and disobeying parents and masters; thus through shared guilt New Englanders were encouraged to partake in the humiliation of public execution.[4] An individual's capital crime, then, represented the collective crimes of everyone who defied the sacred order (as it was interpreted by New England's ministers and magistrates), and his or her desperate struggle to escape damnation through redemption reflected the larger drama of New England itself. Although condemned through human agency, those who mounted the gallows had been appointed by God to become "Monuments of divine justice," examples chosen to terrify and edify a populace in urgent need of reform.[5]

The gallows literature that emerged in print culture as a steady seller during the late seventeenth century was developed by New England's ministers to what many generally perceived as threats to their order. Worldliness, as it was perceived from the pulpits, was apparent everywhere in a culture that originally had been intended to manifest the visible effects of godliness, and religious practice had become more a matter of institutional custom than of individual conscience. A variety of changes and catastrophes, including sickness, shipwreck, crop failure, Indian war, sectarian conflict, and political upheaval, were interpreted as signs that New England was backsliding, and in numerous jeremiads the ministers railed at their congregations to return to the pious examples of the first generation.[6] In such a context of flux and anxiety, public executions provided

[4]In tracing capital crimes back to their sources, the ministers consistently cited disobedience as a sin that led to greater sins. According to Increase Mather, in *The Wicked mans Portion*, New England had "become degenerate" because "Inferiors rise up against Superiors" in disobedience (17, 16). Mather further stated: "If there by any prevailing iniquity in *New-England*, this is it. . . . If ever *New-England* be destroyed, this very sin of disobedience to the *fifth Commandment* will be the ruine of this Land" (17).

[5]The concept of capital criminals as "monuments" chosen by God was widespread during the late seventeenth and early eighteenth centuries. In *Impenitent Sinners Warned of Their Misery*, Samuel Willard explained that God chose condemned criminals to become "astonishing Monuments of his righteous severity" (iii). This same idea was repeated in *Warnings to the Unclean*, when John Williams stated: "whensoever God in his just Wrath leaves any to be monuments of shame and ignominy before the world, it is a loud call to all who lye under such guilt, to be speedy and thorough in repentance" (5). Condemned criminals, however, were not always examples of God's wrath. When repentant, they could also be described as "Monuments of Divine Mercy and Grace" (Checkly 13).

[6]Much attention has been given to the problems (real and perceived) of late seven-

convenient opportunities for identifying New England's collective transgressions and, more importantly, for proclaiming God's wrath if such transgressions were not corrected.[7]

In their terror at confronting the imminence of death and probability of damnation, however, condemned criminals were manipulated to convey messages of hope as well as fear. Although his fate was left in doubt, James Morgan died penitently, and the movement (both literal and rhetorical) from condemnation to execution provided a model of penitence for all New Englanders. The spectators who participated in his ritual death were told that salvation was never beyond reach; even murderers who had lived wicked, ungodly lives still could experience conversion—but only through complete and sincere repentance. Indeed, upon the occasion of public execution, the people of New England were exhorted to reach for redemption. The Mathers and Moody used Morgan to stress that salvation came to those who penitently prepared for it; the miracle of grace could transform the worst of sinners into saints, but only after such individuals had exhibited a sincere denial of self, surrendering themselves fully to God. Throughout the late seventeenth century, the ritual drama of execution was used to illustrate that redemption, both individual and collective, only could be achieved by rejecting ungodliness and by renewing the special covenant between God and his people.

teenth-century New England. In both several of his essays and his books, most notably "Errand Into the Wilderness" and *The New England Mind,* Perry Miller first focused attention on the shift in values away from the spiritual ideals of the first generation. Since his pathbreaking studies, much has been written disputing some of Miller's points but not altogether contradicting them. For other helpful discussions of New England's sense of "decline," see Morgan, Bercovitch, Pope, Elliott, Delbanco, and Hall.

[7]For a discussion of the execution sermon as a jeremiad, and the link between individual and collective transgressions, see Bosco, "Pillory."

## III

> Then she asked, whether there was any Time Left? And being told there was, she began to warn all, espcially Young People, against the Sins of Drunkenness, Lying, &c; but seemed to be faint, and a little confused, and so she was bid to sit down. Then a Paper, at her desire, taken from her Mouth was read, during which she sat down on a Board that lay across the Cart, and read in the Bible, with such composure and calmness of Mind, it was truly admirable.
>
> —from *A Faithful Narrative of the Wicked Life and Remarkable Conversion of Patience Boston*, 1738

Yet in his struggle to secure salvation James Morgan stumbled; both Increase and Cotton Mather included references to the incomplete state of his spiritual recovery as he approached death.[8] According to the elder Mather, although repentance is never too late, "Late repentance is seldom true." Consequently, Morgan's example attested to the difficulty as much as the possibility of achieving redemption through self-surrender. For New England, the message of the condemned man's spiritual struggle was clear: although possible, salvation only could be attained through the most strenuous and immediate effort. The ministers used Morgan's death to evoke a sense of urgency particular to their time and place. The spiritual state of God's kingdom was in peril; great things still were possible, but only through the greatest effort could they be achieved.

Fourteen years later, however, another minister, John Rogers, used the example of a young woman's execution to convey a more hopeful, evangelical message. According to the minister's characterization in *Death the Certain Wages of Sin* (Boston, 1701), Esther Rodgers had lived a thoroughly depraved life, having twice committed infanticide; nevertheless, she died a true saint, demonstrating the miraculous effects of grace. Although her life was "lewd and rude and wretched," her death became a triumph of Christian piety, a celebration of God's love ("To the Christian Reader"). In

[8]In his final comments to Morgan, Increase Mather stated: "And that which aggravates your guiltiness not a little is, that since you have been in prison, you have done wickedly; you have made your self drunk several times since your Imprisonment; yea, and you have been guilty of Lying since your Condemnation" (*A Sermon* 36). As related in *Pillars of Salt*, Cotton Mather admonished Morgan for losing his temper the night before his execution, when arguing over the plans for his burial. As Mather pointed out, it had been "outrageous *Passionateness*" that had brought Morgan to the gallows in the first place (79). Even at this latest of all dates, Morgan was described as still struggling with his "chief Sin" (79).

contrast to Morgan's terror, she approached death with confidence, expressing joy rather than fear, hope rather than dread, and once adapted to an evangelical framework, her life story presented readers with a model of repentance rewarded: "*thou mayst behold a Tragick Scene, strangely changed into a* Theater of Mercy, *a* Pillar of Salt *Transformed into a Monument of Free Grace; a poor wretch entring Prison a Bloody Malefactor, her Conscience laden with Sins of a Scarlet Die . . . . [after] the space of Eight Months she came forth sprinkled, Cleansed, Comforted, a Candidate of Heaven*" (95). In her movement towards spiritual rebirth, Rodgers—as she was described—dramatized the crucial steps in the redemption process, and her story offered the assurance that, if these steps were followed, anyone could be redeemed.

The Rodgers text indicated a new development in the criminal narrative genre. Unable to slow down the effects of secularization through jeremiads alone, New England ministers became increasingly involved with arousing a more personal, evangelical form of piety, and in their execution sermons they became less concerned with the excitement of terror and more concerned with the process of conversion.[9] Criminal characterization similarly reflected this evangelical fervor, and narrative emphasis shifted from the individual's desperate distress to his or her confident faith in Christ's merciful love. Throughout the first four decades of the eighteenth century, from "The Declaration and Confession of Esther Rodgers" to *A Faithful Narrative of the Wicked Life and Remarkable Conversion of Patience Boston* (Boston, 1738), the theme of miraculous conversion dominated the criminal narrative genre, and thus contributed much to the rise of evangelical excitement which resulted in the Great Awakening.[10] Condemned criminals were not presented merely as examples of God's wrath, but also of God's Grace. In effect, those hanging from the gallows were depicted not just as criminals, but also as martyrs, whose devotion in death glorified God. Rodgers, like those who were to follow her example, died well:

> THE manner of her Entertaining DEATH, was astonishing to a Multitude of Spectators, (being as was judged Four or Five Thousand People at least) with that Composure of Spirit, Cheerfulness of Countenance, pleasantness of Speech, and a sort of Complaisantness in Carriage towards the Ministers . . . that even melted the hearts of all that were within seeing or hearing, into Tears of affection, with greatest wonder and admiration. Her undaunted courage and unshaken Confidence she modestly enough expressed, yet steadfastly held unto the end (108).

[9] For works discussing the rise of evangelicalism, see Ahlstrom, Elliott, Hall, Lovelace, Stout, Hambrick-Stowe, Butler, and Heimert.

[10] For a discussion of how the criminal narrative genre contributed to the fervor of the Great Awakening, see Williams, "Behold a Tragick Scene."

Condemned criminals, of course, were not the most likely candidates for sainthood, and to encourage them to present an "Entertaining DEATH," the ministers stressed "that God does often make the chiefest of Sinners, Objects of his choicest Mercy" and "that great Sins are often made preparations to Conversions" (Rogers 71, 72).[11] Such comments not only offered comfort and hope to the condemned but also reinforced their sense of uniqueness, enabling them more readily to accept their assigned roles. During this period of rising evangelical expectations, criminal narratives described those awaiting execution as actually longing for death. When told that her execution had been postponed, Rodgers, for example, expressed regret, stating "I find . . . a willingness in me to accept the punishment of my sins, and a readiness to glorify God by suffering the Death I have deserved" (100). When asked how she felt the night before her execution, she exclaimed: "Oh! I have had the joyfullest day to day that ever I had in my whole life. I bless God that I ever came into this prison" (102). And when asked "whether her heart did not fail her" while walking to the gallows, she triumphantly replied: "No, but the nearer I approach, the more I feel my strength and joy increase" (105).

For Rodgers, and for those who were depicted similarly, death meant fulfillment, the ultimate test of devotion. Instead of viewing themselves as despicable and insignificant, condemned criminals were given the comforting chance to believe that they were chosen especially by God for martyrdom, and the piety of their deaths verified the sincerity of their spiritual rebirths. Despite all forms of degradation and humiliation, both past and present, these individuals displayed a sense of worth in death that they had lacked in life. Paradoxically, through self-abasement they established their own self-esteem, and the chains they wore, even the rope itself, signified their special status. To bring them to this point of active participation in their death scenes, the ministers exerted great pressure upon them to confess fully, emphasizing that God—and not the magistrates—had assigned them their death roles. Writing in the 1730s of New England, one minister stated: "It may be there is no Place in the World, where such Pains are taken with condemn'd Criminals to prepare them for their Death; that *in the Destruction of the Flesh, the Spirit may be Saved*" (Foxcroft I).[12]

[11] Rogers further stated that the greatest "standing miracles which God hath left in the World" were "the Extraordinary Conversion of the vilest of sinners" (73). Three decades later John Webb attempted to encourage another condemned criminal with the same thought: "The greater our Transgressions have been, the more will the Mercy of God be magnified in pardoning of them. . . . the Mercy of God never appears more illustrious than it does, in Rescuing the most miserable and unworthy Objects from Destruction" (18).

[12] In addition to Esther Rodgers and Patience Boston, a number of other condemned criminals were paraded before readers as examples of last minute conversions during the

Not all, of course, were saved, and certainly not all condemned criminals had narratives written about them. Only those who manifested a willingness to accept their roles were likely to receive the attention of presses still dominated by the clergy. In effect, only those who acted out the scaffold characterizations imposed upon them became characters in their own life narratives. There were, however, exceptions. In 1726 William Fly was executed for piracy, and from the moment of his capture to his last gestures at the gallows he continually refused to surrender himself either to God or to those entrusted with preserving God's holy order. Instead of embracing the humiliation of execution, Fly mocked the ministers and ridiculed the hangman. Yet even his defiant death was exploited to promote godliness. Having refused the role of a humble penitent, the condemned pirate could not escape its opposite, a depraved sinner destined for hell, and despite his acts of bravado on the scaffold, his public perception nevertheless was shaped by the ministers who attended him. Both Cotton Mather and Benjamin Colman carefully presented Fly as being blindly, stupidly wicked; his crimes, mutiny and murder, were a reckless rebellion against God, and the contempt he exhibited toward the earthly agents of God's authority was rendered more foolish than courageous, more damned than defiant. According to Mather, the stubborn pirate was "running on Headlong to *Hell*" (20).[13] Unable to control the character, the ministers set out to control the context, portraying Fly as a miserable sinner trapped in his own obduracy. The very acts of his defiance, then, provided proof of his

---

1730s and 40s. For further examples of criminal conversion, see Eliphalet Adams, *A Sermon Preached on the Occasion of the Execution of Katherine Garret, an Indian;* John Campbell, *After Souls by Death are Separated from Their Bodies;* Rebekah Chamblitt, *The Declaration, Dying Warning and Advice of Rebekah Chamblitt;* Thomas Foxcroft, *Lessons of Caution to Young Sinners;* Hugh Henderson, *The Confession and Dying Warning of Hugh Henderson;* William Shurtleff, *The Faith and Prayer of a Dying Malefactor;* John Webb, *The Greatness of Sin Improv'd;* and William Williams, *The Serious Consideration.* For an earlier account, see Cotton Mather and Benjamin Colman, *The Sad Effects of Sin.* Before collaborating with his son on Patience Boston's narrative, Samuel Moody also was responsible for *A Summary Account of the Life and Death of Joseph Quasson, an Indian.*

[13]For a discussion of the narrative strategies Mather used to shape Fly's defiance for popular consumption, see Williams, "Puritans and Pirates." For an earlier example of a recalcitrant pirate, see *An Account of the Behaviour and last dying Speeches of the Six Pirates.* This account described the final words of John Quelch and five of his pirate crew, who were executed in Boston on June 30, 1704. Like Fly, Quelch used the gallows as a "Stage" to perform his final act of defiance: "when on the Stage he pulled off his Hat, and bowed to the Specators, and [was] not Concerned, nor behaving himself so much like a Dying man as some would have done. . . . yet now being called upon to speak what he had to say, it was but thus much; *Gentlemen, 'Tis but little I have to speak: what I have to say is this, I desire to be informed for what I am here, I am Condemned only upon Circumstances.*"

damnation, and the more he refused to cooperate in the ritual drama of his death, the more he verified God's sovereignty and his own depravity. In life, Fly had rejected offers to attend church and hear his own execution sermons, declining to *"have the Mob to gaze upon him,"* a spectacle in chains; yet in death he became exactly the kind of terrible warning that he previously had rejected: "Fly's Carcase was hanged in Chains, on an Island, at the Entrance into *Boston*-Harbour" (114, 115). Even more ironic, by recreating the damned pirate's spectacle in print, Mather guaranteed that "Fly's Carcase" would continue to hang before the public.

## IV

> I am now tried, convicted and condemned, on suspicion of having counterfeited the currency of this province; but, if the word of a dying man can be taken, I am innocent of the crime imputed to me. I never did make, sign or pass counterfeit Bills. . . .
>
> — from *A Journal of the Life and Travels of Joseph-Bill Packer*, 1773

Throughout the late seventeenth and early eighteenth centuries, both sacred and secular authorities had intended to *"have the Mob to gaze upon"* condemned criminals in order to convey an officially sanctioned system of values. As a ritual drama produced by the ruling elite for mass consumption, public executions were important in spreading attitudes and ideas that reaffirmed the social order and reasserted the powers of government. As such, they were used to exert ideological control. The early rulers of New England believed that discipline and subordination were necessary in society, and they presented condemned criminals to the public in order to dramatize the terrifying effects of disobedience. Surrendering the self to God, after all, could not take place without surrendering to God's earthly representatives. The gallows was a symbol of order, and those who mounted it were there to legitimize the power of those who erected it. Public executions, then, were one of the most important colonial contact points between the elite and the non-elite, between the ministers and the magistrates on one side and "the Mob" on the other. Paradoxically, however, by trying to control "the Mob" through ritual and convention, the authorities actually created popular expectations that ran counter to their attempts at subordination. By presenting large numbers of people with spectacles that both titillated and inculcated, they empowered the people they were trying to control by indirectly promoting a popular demand for sensation. Ultimately, the imaginative appeal of their death dramas was too strong to repress.[14]

In the narratives produced throughout this period, criminal characters similarly were used as agents of ideological control, but those initially responsible for their characterizations were unable to retain sole control of their creations. At the most basic level, the narratives were commodities, and as such they were shaped by the demands and expectations of the consumers. Ultimately, it was "the Mob," and not the ministers, who decided upon the characterization of condemned criminals. Just as the executions had been produced through a collaboration between the sacred and secular authorities, the narratives originally were the result of a collaboration between ministers and printers, but this latter form of cooperation proved to be far more fragile than the former. During the last decades of the seventeenth century, the commercial book trade had become increasingly more active and more competitive, and in an effort to secure a profitable share of the market New England printers developed a greater sensitivity to their readers and, inversely, a greater resistance to clerical domination.[15]

From the beginning of the gallows genre, a profit-making motive had been evident. James Morgan would not have been paraded in print had he not been both commercially and spiritually profitable. Initially, printers and ministers were able to collaborate because their separate goals—commercial profit and spiritual gain—were not in conflict. Because of their preference for dramatic situations over abstract doctrine, godly writers proved to be popular and, consequently, marketable writers, and in a variety of genre types (particularly tales of wonder, martyrdom, and captivity in addition to execution accounts) they narrated the individual's spiritual progress through the temptations of sin and disbelief, often enhancing the terrors which surrounded the soul (Hall 52). Intended for wide audiences, their writings made use of familiar formulas that appealed to readers for non-religious as well as religious reasons. Regardless of the context, the self was presented in a desperate conflict, and readers were encouraged to

[14]For a discussion of how executions empowered spectators, see Foucault's "The spectacle of the scaffold," in *Discipline and Punish*. According to Professor Foucault, "in the ceremonies of public execution, the main character was the people" (57).

[15]For a discussion of the development of New England print culture, especially concerning the expectations of readers and how printers responded to these expectations, see Hall, *World of Wonder*. Stressing that books must be considered as commodities, Professor Hall stated that a printer's "decision to print a specific book [was] based on expectations of demand" (48). Moreover, in order to respond to popular expectation, "printers in New England were alert to steady sellers," such as criminal narratives. As an example of reader demand, Professor Hall quoted an English minister in 1692: "the people expect a confession always at the time of any man's execution" (183).

believe that they too were engaged in similar conflicts. Whether writing or preaching, ministers drew their audiences into the greatest of all battles, good against evil, God against Satan, and through imaginative involvement they demonstrated that every individual was a part of this eternal spiritual war and that every soul was at stake (Hall 57).

Although the battle continued, the number of those actively committed to taking part in this spiritual war declined during the eighteenth century. Despite the evangelical fires they ignited during the Great Awakening, the ministers were unable to stem the tide of worldliness that washed over New England. Inevitably, as religion settled down to become more a matter of social observance than of individual experience, ministerial influence declined. Those in New England's pulpits could no longer control the popular tastes of their congregations nor, in turn, those who were in business to cater to these tastes. Printers, whose livelihoods depended on an assessment of reader expectation, responded to the changing interests and perceptions of their consumers, and while steady sellers continued to sell, their content and emphasis began to shift according to marketplace pressure. By mid-century, the most obvious shift in the gallows genre was a change in narrative focus from the criminal's spiritual state after condemnation to his or her crimes before condemnation. While maintaining the same basic formulas, particularly the rhetorical framework of penitential confession, the narratives portrayed criminal characters whose spiritual anxiety was more a matter of convention than of conviction.

During the decades between the Great Awakening and the Revolution, most of the criminal narratives published still followed the fall, repentance, humiliation, and redemption pattern; nevertheless, they exhibited a much greater concern for the imagination than they did for the conscience. Ironically, the lurid material ministers first appended to their sermons as illustrations of divine justice in order to terrify their audiences now became the primary text. Far more "Lives," "Accounts," and "Dying Speeches" were published separately than before, and the narratives generally were more detailed and more sensational. Significantly, emphasis shifted from the spiritual struggles of the criminals to their more worldly conflicts. No longer were they depicted as the archetypical sinner fallen from God but as distinct personalities moving about in a recognizable world. Crime was no longer presented as the inevitable outcome of sin, and criminals were no longer portrayed as examples of an unregenerated spirit. The ministers began the gallows genre in order to make crime understandable, and to accomplish this they imposed a rhetorical structure of sinful rebellion upon the criminal life, but as New England developed a more complex and commercial culture, depravity alone was no longer enough to account for the existence of crime. For the first time criminals referred to the motivations behind their transgressions and to the contexts that shaped their characters; more important, for the first time they began to confess an interest in worldly—rather than spiritual—wealth.

Both *A Short Account of John ********** Alias Owen Syllavan* (Boston, 1756) and *A Brief Description of the Life and Abominable Thefts of the Notorious Isaac Frasier* (New Haven, 1768), for example, illustrate the reversal in importance of the sacred and secular functions. Both texts generally follow the ritualized pattern of repentance through confession, but the sincerity and the extent of both confessions fail to fully convince. Even when confronted with "the King of Terrors," neither Syllavan nor Frasier demonstrated the same kind of humiliation and self-loathing as had Rodgers and Boston before them. When he was about to be "turned off," Frasier confessed his sins, thanked the judges, warned others not to follow his example, and prayed for his salvation, but before this declaration of faith he had demonstrated little interest in, or even knowledge of, religion. Moreover, his descriptions of the difficulties and setbacks he encountered allowed readers the opportunity to comprehend the social forces that compelled him to crime, encouraging at least the possibility of sympathy.

Raised "in the most abject conditions," Frasier was "often induced by hunger to take provisions to satisfy the cravings of this nature" (152). Furthermore, after having been sold into apprenticeship by his widowed mother, and then resold several times, theft became the only means he had of exercising his right of self-determination. His one attempt to "live by honest industry" ended in failure when his "intended wife" and friends learned of his disreputable past and refused to have anything to do with him. Once rejected, he declared: "I abandoned myself to my former course of wickedness, and having no restraints of character, I gave rein to my covetous disposition, being extremely desirous to be rich" (153). Frasier indeed substituted money for wife and friends, and for the next five years he robbed hundreds of shops, sometimes as many as three or four in one night. He was caught, jailed, and escaped more than a dozen times, and even escaped several times from the same jail and jailer. His relentless pursuit of money became so obsessive that, after he was eventually caught and condemned, he escaped only to begin robbing the same shops all over again. When he finally was led to the gallows in Fairfield, Connecticut, he—according to his narrative—declared: "the love of money, the ruling principle of my mind, has brought me to the grave in the flower of life, when my sun is scarce risen; at the age of 28, I am going down into the house of silence, to be numbered with the dead" (159). Despite his conventional pieties, Frasier's dying speech revealed far more of the printer's sense of melodrama than of the actual criminal's state of mind. The Frasier presented to readers in the narrative was a character intentionally shaped out of the raw materials that the original thief provided, and unlike previous examples, the characterization was created primarily for diversion rather than instruction.

All of the narratives, of course, offered characterizations of actual individuals, and what is remarkable about the gallows genre is that the individuals often were asked or even forced to validate their own characterizations. Having accepted their roles in the execution ritual, people like Morgan and Rodgers acted out their parts hoping to receive a spiritual, if not a worldly, reprieve. Similarly, Frasier, who acknowledged his total illiteracy and who obviously would never have conceptualized himself as passing from the "flower of life" into the "house of silence," supposedly legitimized his narrative by signing it with an "X," which was then duplicated and printed with the text. The difference here, however, is that the character expressed great interest in the affairs of this world during his life and little interest in anything during his death. The narrative commented that, contrary to the craving of the spectators for a sensational farewell, Frasier said nothing at the gallows. Unwilling to risk a similar disappointment, the writer of the Frasier narrative offered his readers a "dying speech" filled with the appropriate conventions and rhetoric. Moreover, since "the love of money" indeed was portrayed as his "ruling principle," the Frasier character was shaped to represent a much different system of values and perceptions than previous examples, one more reflective of the more worldly concerns and expectations of mid-eighteenth-century readers.

Owen Syllavan was an even more secularized example of a character shaped for a popular audience. Overtly, the structure resembled previous examples. A rebellious youth, Syllavan early began to throw off the yoke of discipline, first running away from home and then later from a succession of masters. For those readers seeking a purely spiritual justification for his crimes, the narrative described an early series of encounters between Syllavan and an "evil Spirit" who repeatedly appeared before him, calling his name (143). Consequently, his later crimes as an adult could then be perceived as the inevitable outcome of his youthful wickedness. Possessed by an "evil Spirit" at a young age, he could not avoid committing evil himself. Also, the narrative imitated the structure of previous texts in that the Syllavan character offered his life account as a confession and, once on the scaffold, he prayed, begging God for mercy. Yet between youth and death he manifested the antithesis of either humility or submission. Not only did he also exhibit a "covetous disposition," he became one of New England's most notorious counterfeiters, and instead of expressing the usual self-loathing, the Syllavan character freely recounted his successful exploits, ultimately creating an ambivalent, if not sympathetic, view of himself.

According to Syllavan, counterfeiting was simply "an easy way of getting Money," and once driven away by his wife's "Aggravating Tongue," he dedicated himself to his lucrative business (146, 145). During his career, he copied nearly every form of New England currency and succeeded in flooding the entire region from Maine to New York with his homemade specie. In one day alone he passed twelve thousand pounds worth of counterfeit, and at one time he had four different gangs under him distributing his product. Punishment and jail not only failed to reform him, but failed even to interfere with his productivity. In the narrative he stated: "during my Confinement, I engraved three sorts of Plates, two of *New Hampshire* Money, and one of *Boston* currency, and for want of a Rolling Press, struck it off by Hand, sign'd it in Goal and gave it out by Quantities to my Accomplices" (146).

Syllavan did not fit the pattern of fall, repentance, humiliation, and redemption. More proud than ashamed, he described the events of his life as exploits of craft and courage. Sheriffs and jailers became opponents in a contest for autonomy, a contest in which Syllavan had a clear edge. Moreover, after his final arrest in New York, he refused to confess fully and thus incriminate his accomplices. When listing the various currencies he copied, he stated: "all my Accomplices deserv'd the Gallows, as well as myself; but I will not betray them, or be guilty of shedding their Blood" (147). This failure to confess continued on the scaffold; instead of the usual dying speech, the only thing he confessed was "*that he was not willing to die*" (148). His final warning was not for youth to obey their parents and masters but for his accomplices to "*burn and destroy all the Money, Plates, and Accoutrements, that they have by them, and that they may not die on a Tree as I do*" (148). Syllavan even went so far as to caution the executioner: "*don't pull the Rope so tight, it is hard for a Man to die in cold Blood*" (148).

Although he acknowledged his guilt, Syllavan refused to acknowledge his iniquity. As the crucial step in the conversion process, confession required that individuals not only reveal their crimes but also reveal their baseness, thus humbling themselves before God and man. As the *Notorious Money-Maker and Cheat*, Syllavan did the opposite, and the reason for this reversal was directly related to changes in colonial readership. The printer who published the first of the two Syllavan editions was trying to capitalize on the counterfeiter's existing notoriety. His task was not to create a character but to satisfy readers by conforming his text to the popular image already in circulation. By the time he was brought to the gallows, Syllavan already was the subject of narratives, as many of those who gathered to witness his death knew of his crimes and escapes. In effect, once touched by the sensations of hearsay and rumor, they became willing participants in the Syllavan narrative, especially in its conclusion, and their version of the counterfeiter was not required to fit a theological model. Consequently, instead of stressing his depravity in life and his terror at death, Syllavan was characterized as defiant, clever, and even courageous. While condemned to die "on a Tree," he was not damned, and this textual ambivalence represented a wider ambivalence about the nature of his criminal activity. At the most basic economic level, his "money-making" skills demonstrated the same desires of his society; everyone was looking for "an easy way of getting Money."

Frasier and Syllavan were the first in a series of criminals whose activities in life and in death aroused a mixture of pity and outrage. Counterfeiters, the earliest of colonial con men, especially became popular narrative subjects, and like Syllavan, they were condemned but not damned. In *The Confession and Dying Warning of John Jubeart* (New York, 1769), for example, the protagonist was presented as more a victim than a criminal. According to his broadside narrative, Jubeart lived a stable, unexceptional life until well into his sixties when his wife died. Thrown into "a deep melancholy" by her death, he grew distracted, becoming "quite unsettled, and even . . . a little delirious" (163). In a Lear-like gesture, he then "settled his Estate, which was not inconsiderable, upon his Children," and left to travel about the country (164). He turned to counterfeiting only after poverty "had reduced him so low that he was greatly in want of linen and several other necessaries" (164). Caught and condemned, he was executed at the age of sixty-eight.

In *The Life and Confession of Herman Rosencrantz* (Philadelphia, 1770), the protagonist counterfeiter was depicted as equally pathetic. Having embraced the standard colonial dreams of opportunity, Rosencrantz purchased a tract of land in northeastern Pennsylvania, married into an "honest, reputable family," and for nine years prospered as one "blest with *the dew of heaven and the fatness of the earth*" (167). Yet prosperity was not long maintained, and after suffering "many losses and misfortunes" he chose counterfeiting as the fastest possible means of recovering what he had lost: "I gave myself over to an uneasy and restless mind, with an undue desire of gaining riches" (167). Ironically, Rosencrantz's dreams of "gaining riches" brought him to further suffering and eventually to the gallows, but he never relinquished his "undue desire." After having been arrested once, he was again seduced into counterfeiting when one of his confederates promised "that we all might live a gentleman's life" (169). In order to demonstrate the danger of such dreams, the narrative drew attention to the weaknesses of Rosencrantz's character, but at the same time it offered an ambivalent reading of this character. After being acquitted in a New Jersey court for counterfeiting, Rosencrantz declared his intention of "becoming a new man," but soon returned to counterfeiting *"like the dog to its vomit"*

(170). In explaining his return, he stated: "But that fatality which always attended me, or the evil disposition of my own heart, still pursued me on to my ruin" (170). According to their perspective, readers could attribute Rosencrantz's "ruin" to either one of the two extremes, the doctrinal certainty of an "evil disposition" or the far more ambiguously identified "fatality." In refusing to choose between the opposite poles of depravity and fate, the narrative revealed a more general hesitancy to impose a traditionally authorized framework of meaning on its story. There were no absolutes to clearly define the source of the counterfeiter's evil. Even his "disposition" did not necessarily result from depravity. Earlier in the text, when describing how his "uneasy and restless mind" had developed into "an undue desire of gaining riches," Rosencrantz had referred to this "disposition" as a "distemper of mind" (167). Not only was this a secular sickness (an indisposition) for which there was no sure cure, it was also an affliction to which nearly everyone was susceptible.

Much like Jubeart and Rosencrantz, Joseph-Bill Packer was executed for counterfeiting late in life, but unlike these two, he never acknowledged his guilt. In fact, Packer made use of the narrative opportunity his execution provided to document his virtues rather than his vices. Significantly, although the genre was clear, the conventions were reversed; instead of being labeled as either a "confession" or a "last dying speech," it was presented as *A Journal of the Life and Travels of Joseph-Bill Packer* (Albany?, 1773), and throughout the text Packer was displayed as compassionate and clever but never as corrupt. Moreover, in recounting his life he offered examples to demonstrate generosity rather than cupidity. Rather than "gaining riches," he (according to the narrative) devoted most of his life to an extraordinary medical practice: "The principal part of my business was curing cancers; of this art I may justly call myself master, as I have cured every species of them" (207). He not only cured his patients, but he took little or no money for his efforts. Although he became associated with a group of counterfeiters, he claimed he was innocent of their particular branch of science. Because he was anxious to pursue "philosophic studies, naturally inclined to learning, [and] remarkably inquisitive about the secrets of nature," Packer set up a "shop" to conduct his experiments, but his efforts were misinterpreted, and a rumor was spread that he was counterfeiting money (211). In response, he stated: "I declare, before God! that the said report, was *false*! for I did not make nor offer to pass any bad money, nor never had any thoughts on that subject" (211). In his final statement, he repeated his denial, using his last words, not to confess, but to protest: "I am now tried, convicted and condemned, on suspicion of having counterfeited the currency of this province: but, if the word of a dying man can be taken, I am innocent of the crime imputed to me" (212).

Without either acknowledging his guilt or communicating his "recipe for curing cancers," Packer went to his death as an "*Escape Goat*," dying in place of his more guilty associates (212).[16]

## V

> When I have Asked, as I have often Asked, the *Criminals, For what Sin, do you think, the provoked God of Heaven, gave you over to the Sins, for which you are now to Dy . . . ?* The common Answer which they have made, has been, *Oh my Disobedience to my Parents, my Disobedience to my Parents, and my Ungovernableness, under such Parents and Master, as God had given me!*
>
> —from *Pillars of Salt*, 1699

The depiction of such figures as Jubeart, Rosencrantz, and Packer tended to complicate the representation of authority.[17] These three mid-Atlantic narratives reflected legal systems incapable of responding to individual contexts at the same time they particularly dramatized these contexts. Indirectly, but inevitably, such dramatizations focused attention on the nature of authority, raising previously unexamined issues concerning power and privilege. Once depravity had been abandoned as the catch-all cause for crime, questions arose over motivations, and once the narratives began to examine individual explanations and to present individualized characterizations, the traditional foundations of authority were subverted. The condemned criminal, regardless of guilt, was no longer just another hellbound sinner whose personality had been effaced for ideological reasons. Through narrative progression, readers became involved in the per-

[16]The depicion of Packer in the newspapers contradiced that of the narrative, acknowledging his guilt rather than his innocence. The narrative, then, refuted both official and popular views of the counterfeiter and thus presented readers with a multivalent interpretation while undermining the authority of the courts and the newspapers to account for crime. For a full discussion of Packer, see the source note following his narrative.

[17]For a discussion of the representation of authority in early America, see Patterson. According to Professor Patterson, "the principle problem of the colony and nation" was the location and character of authority (xvi). Exploring the different possibilities of representation, "the first works of American fiction" provided readers with "important models for the definition of authority" (xvi). Because of their widespread popularity, and because of their obvious dramatization of conflicts between individual autonomy and social authority, criminal narratives were significant vehicles for transmitting the changing cultural perceptions of state power. Increasingly, the subtexts of later eighteenth-century narratives encouraged readers to distrust authority.

sonalities of the criminal characters, and their involvement contributed to a distrust of authority, if not outright sympathy for the condemned. Crime became contextual. But the changes in the representation of authority that took place within the criminal narrative genre were neither isolated nor random; at the same time criminal discourse became secularized, profound political, theological, and cultural changes were taking place within American society.

The American Revolution altered the relationships between people and authority on a variety of levels. Most obviously, the war itself raised the issue of political representation to a national level, not only breaking apart British systems and conventions but also entirely reversing the traditional hierarchy of descending authority. By challenging King George III, the American people in effect challenged traditional patriarchal perceptions of power, replacing them with new Enlightenment concepts of popular sovereignty.[18] During the Revolution and its aftermath, a cultural climate evolved that generally distrusted any expression of absolute or unmediated authority. Traditional figures of authority were left either to discover new means of sanctioning—and expressing—their power or face a loss of power. The republican rhetoric and egalitarian ideology of the Revolution had a far greater impact on the American populace than many of the social elite had intended.[19] Empowered by their belief in the ideals of democratic representation and individual rights, people from a variety of levels entered into a national debate over the organization and application of authority. At the same time, as new opportunities developed for financial gain and social advancement, people from a variety of levels competed for profits and positions within the new order. Perhaps at no other time in American history was there greater social turbulence than the critical decades during and after the Revolution.[20]

[18] In addition to Patterson's discussion of authority and representation, see Fliegelman's *Prodigals and Pilgrims* for a valuable analysis of changing attitudes towards patriarchal authority in early America. For the best overviews of political, cultural, social, and economic changes taking place as the colonies evolved into states, see Henretta, Wiebe, and Brown *Modernization*.

[19] In his analysis of post-Revolutionary confusion, Professor Wiebe stated: "During the 1770s the resistance to Britain and then Revolution had unleashed a great range of popular assertions, triggering protests among hitherto passive farmers and townspeople and elevating a number of their spokesmen to office. . . . the ferment of popular politics continued to bubble in public gatherings and state legislatures after the war" (22).

[20] In addition to the discussions of social and political turbulence found in Fliegelman, Henretta, Wiebe, and Brown, see also Elliott and Davidson. In *Revolutionary Writers*, Professor Elliott drew attention to the "crisis of culture that occurred during the early national period" (6). Such social instability was most evident in changes in form and expression of authority. In *Revolution and the Word*, Professor Davidson traced the impact

In the midst of such turbulence, as the colonies evolved into states, major transformations took place not only within the various colonial systems of justice but also in the very conceptualizations of crime and punishment. Part of a more pervasive shift in penal reform throughout the western world, the changes affected both the way figures of authority responded to lawbreaking and to the way people generally perceived lawbreakers.[21] By the beginning of the nineteenth century, most European societies had abandoned public punishment, including humiliation and torture, in favor of private alternatives. As one of the most visible symbols of public order, the gallows became the focus of an impassioned debate over the justification and function of capital punishment; many argued that the public ritual of execution was barbarous, while some even argued that the death penalty itself was barbarous.[22] According to Enlightenment theory, individuals were determined by their environments, and therefore, by carefully cultivating their surroundings, individuals thus could improve the quality of their lives. Such confidence in human capacity led to a nearly boundless faith in progress and, once focused on crime and criminals, to new concepts of reformation. In the nascent United States, the movements towards penal reform became particularly urgent. Those who had adopted the rhetoric of liberty and justice to justify their own defiance of British authority could not overlook the inconsistencies and cruelties within their own judicial systems. As the United States experimented with new political structures, it also experimented with new penal concepts. While reformers mounted opposition to the death penalty, state governments gradually abolished the public ritual of execution, moving the gallows behind prison walls. At the same time, a new penal institution, the penitentiary, was developed as an alternative to humiliation and execution. Providing discipline instead of punishment, the penitentiaries attempted to reform criminals by controlling their environments and altering their habits. Although among the most spectacular of American failures, the prisons of the Early Republic originally were intended as "houses of correction."

---

of the Revolution upon the print culture of the Early Republic, demonstrating that literary texts, especially novels, reflected—and explored—the young nation's "crisis of authority" (13).

[21] Professor Foucault's *Discipline and Punish* still is the most provocative yet perceptive analysis of the changes that took place in western judicial systems during the seventeenth and eighteenth centuries. For other valuable discussions, especially concerning the United States, see Rothman, Hirsch, and Masur.

[22] For the most recent and reliable discussion of the debate over capital punishment in the Early Republic, see "The Opposition to Capital Punishment" in Masur's *Rites of Execution.* In addition to the work of Masur and Foucault, see David J. Rothman's recently updated *The Discovery of the Asylum,* particularly his chapters "The Challenge of Crime" and "The Invention of the Penitentiary."

As the different American states gradually shifted from public physical punishment to private psychological discipline, the criminal narrative genre continued to develop greater complexity of character. Since the gallows was no longer a universally accepted symbol of order, gallows speeches tended either to become reactionary, attempting to justify both the specific execution and the more general issue of capital punishment, or to sensationalize, even to romanticize, the criminal, providing not moral lessons but lurid entertainment for popular audiences. Yet the most reactionary of narratives nevertheless expressed a "double discourse," a dialogical utterance that simultaneously contained the ideological intentions of the elite and the popular perceptions of general readers (Davis 123).[23] Throughout the eighteenth century, both gallows and narratives had been subjected to two different acts of interpretation, one from above and one from below. What people received from the execution experience, whether as witnesses or readers, was not always the same as what the authorities originally had intended them to receive. Early on, when the ministers and the magistrates held their greatest influence, they generally were able to foist their official conceptualizations on spectators and readers alike. But as their influence waned their views were countered by more popular notions and assumptions. During the Revolutionary period the division between official and popular perceptions increased, breaking apart the original connection between execution sermons and final confessions, between ministerial and criminal discourses. Fewer ministers were depicted as heroically rescuing the criminal's soul from the fires of hell. As pressures from the marketplace altered the relationship between those who wrote and those who read, as the importance of the hero-minister declined, the narrative conflict shifted from a clearly drawn issue of good versus evil to more complicated issues of individuals versus authority. Once secularized, crime was no longer "Rebellion against the Lord" but against the state (Mather, *Folly* 13).[24]

[23] In his chapter, "Criminality and the Double Discourse," Lennard Davis stated that the "double discourse" of criminal narratives "embodies opposing political and moral functions" (136). While acting as cultural agents of repression, criminal narratives nevertheless threatened social stability by popularizing examples of lawlessness. The perception that criminal narratives were "read as two-sided discourses" was first explored by Foucault in *Discipline and Punish* (68).

According to Foucault, although criminal narratives "were expected to have the effect of an ideological control" they provided readers with "not only memories, but also precedents" (67,68). Regardless of their guilt, criminal characters could be easily transformed into heroes by readers who identified with their struggles against state sovereignty. For an earlier but still interesting discussion of how criminal narratives were read, see Richetti.

[24] The view that crime was rebellion against God was widespread among early New

## VI

> The loss of body and soul made me tremble . . . I thought that if I should be executed in this condition, I must be dragged like a bullock to the slaughter.
>
> —from *The last Words and dying Speech of Levi Ames*, 1773

The more authorities attempted to exploit criminals at the gallows, the more attention they focused on them. During the Revolutionary period they increasingly discovered that, though they could control the criminal, they no longer could control the attention excited by their execution rituals. Such was the case with Levi Ames. During the fall of 1773, as English tea waited in Boston harbor to be unloaded, the people of the city turned their attention to a twenty-one year old burglar. From the moment of his arrest on August 29 to his execution on October 21, Ames became the center of intense attention. Not only did "seven or eight thousand persons" witness his execution, but Ames also became the most widely publicized criminal in early America.[25] During the final months of 1773, as Boston patriots prepared for their tea party, the city's printers produced eighteen Ames editions. Death had transformed an insignificant individual into a marketable commodity.

The attention Ames received was related directly to his historical context. Overall, as notions of economic, political, and social stability were shaken up during the Revolutionary period, judicial systems in general became more concerned with crimes against property. Not only did the number of executions increase during the 70s and 80s, but far more thieves and burglars filled the ranks of the condemned than formerly. In response to the anxieties of those who feared a redistribution of wealth, or any disruption of the status quo, the number of prosecutions against property crimes increased while certain other crimes, such as moral offenses, decreased.[26] As a thief with no employment other than crime, Ames repre-

---

England ministers. After describing sin as rebellion in the quoted passage, Increase Mather added that "Sinners make an Insurrection against Heaven" (*Folly* 13). In *Impenitent Sinners Warned of their Misery*, Samuel Willard similarly stated: "every sin is an act of disobedience to . . . God . . . it is an act of rebellion" (4).

[25] In addition to the notices carried in Boston's newspapers, thirteen separate Ames publications appeared before the end of the year, two of which were published a second time while a third was published three times.

[26] For a discussion of the decline in prosecution for moral offenses and the increase in prosecutions for property crimes, see Dargo, "The Privatization of Public Law" in *Law in the New Republic*. For other discussions of the changes that took place in American law during the Early Republic, see Horvitz, Nelson, Friedman, Schwartz, Gilmore, and Hindus.

# THEFT and MURDER!

## A POEM on the Execution of

# Levi Ames,

Which is to be on Thurſday, the 21ſt of October inſt. for robbing the Houſe of Mr. *Martin Bicker*, and was convicted of

## BURGLARY.

COME, ye ſpectators, and behold,
And view a doleful ſcene to day;
My tender fainting heart grows cold,
And I am fill'd with ſore diſmay.
Behold, a Man condemn'd to die,
For ſtealing of his Neighbour's goods:
But Murder doth for Vengeance cry,
But where's th'Avenger of the blood?
'Tis a great Crime to ſteal from Men,
And Puniſhment deſerves indeed;
But Murd'rers have releaſed been;
Who made our friends promiſcous bleed.
Oh! how the voice of Murders ring,
And ecchoes from the mournful ground:
But MURDER is a *little thing*,
And no Avenger can be found.
Oh! what a doleful time appears,
When Murderers are clear'd by Law;
How ſad and gloomy are the years;
Such times before I never ſaw.
The Life of Man is more than gold,
Or any other earthly good:
But Thieves are hang'd, while Murderers bold,
Are freed, who ſhed our precious blood.
Look back to FIFTH of MARCH, and ſee
The ſcarlet Murders! bloody ſtains!
What peace, think you, now can there be
In ſuch a Land where Guilt remains.
The crimes of Thieves, are great, I own;
But let me aſk one queſtion further,
Will this Thief's blood, think you atone
For that inhuman, barb'rous Murder?

Muſt Thieves who take men's goods away
Be put to death? While fierce blood hounds,
Who do their fellow creatures ſlay,
Are ſav'd from death? This cruel ſounds.
But GOD the Murderers will curſe,
On their curs'd heads will vengeance fall;
And whether Theft or Murder's worſe
I leave it to my brethren all.
But, ah! Alas it ſeems to me,
That Murder now is paſſed by
While Prieſts and Rulers all agree
That this poor Criminal muſt die.
What can they no compaſſion have?
Upon the poor diſtreſſed Thief,
Will none appear his life to ſave
Or pray that he may have relief?
Oh no! The Miniſters they ſay,
For him there can be no reprieve;
He muſt be hang'd upon the day,
And his juſt puniſhment receive.
The great corruptions of this day,
They fill my mournful heart with grief;
Murder is pardon'd, but they ſay,
There's no redemption for this Thief.
Oh! ſhocking, ſtrange! Can this be borne?
How can the people bear to ſee
Such things which make our land to mourn!
Lord look on this iniquity!
Dear countrymen now think I pray,
Upon theſe things which do appear;
It is a dark and gloomy day
And heavy woes will come I fear.

Sold near the MILL-BRIDGE, and at the Printing Office near the MARKET.

sented the fears of many property owners. Yet quite possibly he aroused as much sympathy as he did anxiety. At least part of the focus on him was caused by the larger controversy over capital punishment. Because of his youth, and because his accomplice was not condemned, he stirred the emotions of some who felt that death was too harsh a penalty. Moreover, regardless of his crimes, he was an unlikely candidate for the gallows, a fact obvious to the thousands who witnessed his death. According to the most recent statistical surveys, condemned criminals in all probability were "outsiders" of some sort, not only individuals of marginal social status but also those whose cultural or racial background easily identified their lack of social membership.[27] But Ames was an exception. In both the newspapers and in the various publications, he was presented to readers as being "born at Groton, [Conn.], of a credible family" (177).

The authorities of Boston undoubtedly were disturbed by the popular interest taken in Ames, and part of their collective response was to accelerate the judicial process.[28] Yet the celerity of official response might have backfired by keeping Ames too much in the public eye. Perhaps fearful that he would become too much of "a man of the people," the authorities exerted great pressure upon him to acknowledge not only his crime but also his sinful character (Foucault 69).[29] In order to justify the execution process, and thus themselves, the social and political leaders of Boston needed Ames to perform openly in a role of contrition. Evidence suggests, however, that the condemned criminal at first was less than willing to comply.[30]

[27] In "True Confessions and Dying Warnings in Colonial New England," Lawrence Towner found that, of eighty-five executed between 1702 and 1776, "sixty-six were outsiders" (537). From his analysis Masur concluded that of all criminals executed between 1776 and 1812 for whom biographical information was available "at least half were not born in the United States. Of twenty-five men and women for whom the place of birth is known, thirteen had immigrated to the United States. Of these thirteen, eight arrived from Ireland. Of the twelve born in the United States, six were black and one was an Indian. Only two of the twelve were executed in the same state in which they were born" (39).

[28] A little more than a week after his arrest, Ames was tried and convicted on September 7; three days later he received the sentence of death. Instead of receiving several months to prepare for his execution, he was scheduled to die on October 14, and as this date approached he was given a reprieve of only one week.

[29] According to Foucault, public execution always ran the risk of encouraging what they were intended to repress. Not only were people empowered through their participation in the ritual, but they also sometimes sympathized with the condemned criminals. Those in power were afraid that executions could be turned into "carnivals, in which rules were inverted, authority mocked and criminals transformed into heroes" (61). Aware of the sensation caused by Ames's condemnation, the leaders of Boston realized that, unless they strictly controlled the ritual of death, they risked fostering greater "solidarity" among the lower classes (63).

[30] In addition to his own comments referring to his "secret hopes of escape" and the suddenness of his eleventh hour conversion, several of the pre-execution texts commented

Consequently, since the person hesitated to perform in public, a character was appropriated to perform in print.

During the month or so between his conviction and his execution, five separate Ames broadsides appeared, and in four of these publications the thief was presented, either directly or indirectly, as a sincere penitent. In *A few Lines wrote upon the intended Execution of Levi Ames* the figure of the Penitent Thief who died next to Christ was described as a model for Ames to emulate. Using the same strategies of persuasion that ministers used at the beginning of the century, both this and the other three attempted to manipulate Ames by trading salvation for submission.[31] Yet while these publications attempted to quell all controversy surrounding him, the fifth, *Theft and Murder! A Poem on the Execution of Levi Ames*, probably created as much agitation by questioning the fairness of his condemnation. Whereas the previous four sought to vindicate the authorities by depicting Ames submitting to his penitential role, *Theft and Murder!* used him for a more subversive form of political propaganda. The broadside, in fact, had as much to do with the trial of Captain Thomas Preston and his eight soldiers for their part in the Boston Massacre as it did with Ames. Published by patriots attempting to incite further anti-British sentiment, the broadside challenged the justness of executing Ames while Preston and his men were acquitted:

> But, ah, Alas it seems to me,
> That Murder is now passed by
> While Priests and Rulers all agree
> That this poor Criminal must die.

Regardless of whether the pre-execution broadsides used Ames to vindicate or to agitate, all heightened the drama of death, anticipating the moment when the thief would be "turned off." Such publicity naturally would have aroused even more curiosity about the thief, as people hungered to know what was his state of mind as he approached the end. Certainly Boston's printers were aware of this curiosity and exploited it; the eight post-execution publications were printed, in part, to satisfy this hunger, offering readers various reflections of Ames in life and in death. For example, in publishing the two sermons he preached on Ames, Samuel

---

on Ames's initial lack of concern. When he first visited the condemned man, Stillman stated: "I went to see him; and found him seemingly stupid, with but little to say. Nor did he appear to me to be so much affected with his condition as a condemned malefactor, as one would reasonably have expected" (57).

[31]The other three pre-execution Ames texts referred to are *A Prospective View of Death*, *A Solemn Farewell to Levi Ames*, and *The dying Penitent; or, the affecting Speech of Levi Ames*.

Stillman conspicuously advertised the thief on the title page as "A Penitent Thief." According to the popular "Account" Stillman appended to his sermons, Ames thoroughly fulfilled the role of repentance imposed on him by the authorities. Remaining in a "distressed state of mind" until a few days before his first execution date, he suddenly experienced a conversion, after which he manifested the necessary signs of hope and remorse, including self-loathing (58). Yet the thief's personality was not obliterated by the model of the Penitent Thief that Stillman had placed before readers, offering them at least a glimpse of the man as he confronted death. While walking to the gallows, Ames pressed the minister for information concerning what he was about to experience. Evidently, he was not satisfied with the answers he received. Upon nearing the place of execution, he exclaimed: "There is the gallows; and I shall soon know, dear sir, more than you" (64).

With the possible exception of *Theft and Murder!*, all of the Ames publications attempted to respond to two different sets of expectations. The authorities expected a remorseful character who not only would justify their actions but who also would assist them in staging the ritual drama of execution. They wanted a humble but active participant in their spectacle of death. A more popular audience, however, expected a story of sensation and transgression. These people wanted to know the criminal's state of mind before as well as after condemnation. They wanted a character who defied, rather than submitted to, laws and conventions. Both elite and nonelite wanted to hear the criminal's voice, but what they wanted to hear differed drastically. Ultimately, the expectations placed upon the condemned man were in conflict, and the more printers attempted to respond to their general audience, the more they subverted the intentions of the authorities. Perhaps the best example of this narrative division was *The last Words and dying Speech of Levi Ames.*

Ames's broadside confession was printed directly after his execution, and its three columns of small, single-spaced print offered views of the thief before and after condemnation. Half of the narrative, in fact, covered his crimes, and half his preparations for death. But the balance only existed in the columns of print, as the personality of the sinner overwhelmed that of the saint. According to the saintly half, Ames stated that, once condemned, he became fearful at the prospect of damnation: "I thought I had been so wicked that I should certainly go to Hell. . . . And I seemed to have such an awful sight of Hell and the Grave, that I was very much terrified indeed—I then took to drinking strong liquor in order to drown my sorrow" (182). In such an unstable condition, he was visited by several ministers (including Stillman), who appealed to his "wounded conscience" (182). Their assurances that "the blood of Christ was sufficient to cleanse" even the worst of sinners had the right effect (182). In his own words, Ames renounced himself: "I now began to understand something of that law of God which I had broken. . . . I saw that I was undone, that my heart and life were bad beyond all account" (182) Once he had surrendered himself, Ames was ripe for conversion, and after finding an appropriate Biblical passage, he embraced "God's gracious promise" of a new heart (182). Thus the penitent thief became The Penitent Thief. He concluded his narrative warning youth not to follow his bad example and thanking both "the good ministers of the town" and "Mr. Otis, the goal-keeper [sic]" (185).

Yet even the conventions of his sainthood drew attention to his preconversion personality. For example, in addition to warning young people to resist "*disobedience to parents*" and "*profanation of the Lord's day*," in his final warning he cautioned them not to consort with "*bad Women*, who have undone many, and by whom I also have suffered much" (183). Such indirect references suggested a more sensational story underlying the conventional narrative, inviting readers to imagine what could not be written. Also, at the same time he warned youth to refrain from "*gaming*" and "*drunkenness*," he advised property owners "to keep your doors and windows shut on evenings, and secured well to prevent temptation. And by no means use small locks on the outside, one of which I have twisted with ease when tempted to steal. Also not to leave linnen or clothes out at night, which have often proved a snare to me"(183). While indirectly revealing his methods, again encouraging readers to imagine his criminal life, he offered advice, not to sinners to stop sinning, but to property owners to accept the realities of crime and thus take preventive measures. Moreover, his final warning was more petition than admonition, begging readers not to ridicule his "poor dear Mother, or Brother" because of his "shameful and untimely death" (183). Ames's final plea placed him in a world of family relations, forcing readers to view him in the context of his connections, not in terms of his otherness.

The accumulated details about his life depicted a human character whose emotions the readers easily could identify, if not identify with. As he listed his crimes, Ames added information about his life, not only creating a somewhat sympathetic portrait of himself but also contradicting previous accounts. After stating that his father died when he "was but two years old," he confessed his first attempts at "*Thieving*": "My first thefts were small. I began this awful practice by stealing a couple of eggs, then a jack-knife, after that some chalk" (177). Being "reproved" for his petty crimes, he attempted to "repent and reform" but was "powerfully urged to repeat this wickedness, by the temptations of the devil" (177). As he presented his life, Ames was caught between the devil on one side and his mother on the other, who "often pleaded and entreated" with him to turn away from "such horrid courses" (177). Like Syllavan and his "evil Spirit," Ames provided those readers who wanted a purely religious reason for his crimes with a plausible explanation ("the devil"). For such people, there was good, and there was evil, and nothing in between. Yet for others he offered a middle ground. As he listed his thefts, he depicted himself as being blind to all laws of property, yet not blind to all laws. When "an Irishman" proposed to rob the governor's house "well armed with swords and pistols," he declined, stating: "this I absolutely refused, because I never thought of murdering any man" (180).

In setting a limit to his iniquities, Ames invited readers to limit their condemnation, encouraging them to consider the distinction between being guilty and being evil. In a rhetorical appeal begging Christ for forgiveness, he called himself "the worst of sinners," but his narrative presentation of self was less severe (185). In fact, by calling himself "the worst of sinners," an act of public humiliation, he proved that he was not. Moreover, against the context of the previous publications, his narrative even moderated the harsh descriptions of his character and his crimes. The writer of *A Prospective View of Death*, for instance, assured readers that Ames already was "remarkably addicted" to theft "when he was scarcely arrived to the age of seven years." Although the thief refused to provide any details, the broadside writer nevertheless asserted that "a full relation of the life and actions of this young man . . . would open such a scene of iniquity to view as was never perpetrated by any one man in America." Concerning the crime for which Ames was condemned, the writer agreed with the judges, describing the thief as the actual perpetrator and his accomplice as merely a watchman. According to this account, after plying him with plenty of liquor, Ames asked his accomplice (Atwood) "if he would watch for him" while he burglarized the house of a local merchant. He then robbed the house alone, and once outside again he dismissed his accomplice with "a handful of money." In his final confession, his last chance to reveal the truth, Ames contradicted this account. According to his narrative, the theft had been his accomplice's idea; he merely had helped carry out the plan. His accomplice, and not he, had taken most of the money. As a dying man, Ames forgave the man both for cheating him out of the the money they stole and for swearing false testimony against him at the trial. More than simply offering a counter narrative that diminished the severity of public disapproval, his confession challenged the court's official judgment, and thus questioned its capacity for discovering the truth. Not only had the judges failed in their responsibility to uncover the facts, but they had condemned the wrong man, or at the very least they had condemned only one of two who equally deserved the same fate. Although overtly intended to justify the structure of authority that took away his life, Ames's *last Words and dying Speech* subverted the notion that the state was the sole guardian of truth and justice. Published in an atmosphere charged with political tension, his narrative suggested that the "power-knowledge relations" of the state were neither exclusive nor protective (Foucault 27).

In responding to the expectations of two different audiences, the Ames publications relied on genre conventions to provide readers with inimical perspectives. These and similar texts used familiar structures and styles to address as many readers as possible while the didactic impulses that originally had motivated criminal narrative composition began to break down. Certainly, the intention to edify through terror was not lost, but as the narratives focused more attention on the criminal lives the impact of the death spectacle was altered, becoming more a sensational melodrama than a spiritual drama. In *An Authentic and Particular Account of the Life of Francis Burdett Personel* (New York, 1773), the condemned criminal's spiritual awakening was traced from his capture to his death, a progression that resulted in conversion shortly before execution. Like Ames's *last Words and dying Speech*, in fact, the Personel text balanced between sinful action and saintly preparation. After narrating his life and crimes, particularly the murder for which he was executed, Personel abruptly shifted his rhetoric and focus:

> Thus you may have read how great a sinner I have been. I have provoked God times without number, procured his wrath daily, served the Devil faithfully, deserved nothing . . . but everlasting damnation . . . and yet, after serving the Devil so long, having been guilty of so many crimes of the deepest dye, yet God was pleased to draw me from the mouth of the pit . . . and to receive me even at the eleventh hour (194).

Here the narrator turned reader attention away from a lesser to a greater story, and while telling this story he followed the same steps that Rodgers, Boston, and others had covered decades before. After civil conviction, Personel experienced a more terrifying spiritual conviction in which he embraced his corruption: "my conscience was a hell to me, and witnessed against me: I then saw hell open . . . to receive me, and could then see no way of escape, for I was almost in despair" (195). In such an "almost" desperate state, he was visited by several ministers, who called his attention to the "great sinners whom the Lord had made monuments of his mercy" (195). Encouraged by their counsel, he "prayed earnestly to God," surrendering his vanities and begging for forgiveness (195). According to the narrative, his repeated entreaties soon were answered: "I prayed him to be merciful to me . . . desired him to save me, else I perish, importuning him constantly until he was pleased to hear me and grant my request" (195).

Despite a life wasted in sin, and despite the all too obvious suddenness of remorse, Personel indeed became one of God's merciful "monuments," or so he was depicted.

Addressing his final words "To The Public," Personel preached on the uncertainty of life and the certainty of death. In order to glorify God, the condemned convert urged readers to consider their eternal state:

> Whatever you are, whither rich or poor, learned or not, that read this, be assured that you must taste death as well as I, and in a short space of time. Your delicate bodies must be meat for worms, must lay rotting in corruption as well as mine. You are all certain of death, but uncertain when you must die; and there is nothing more sure, than that you must appear before the judgment-seat of the Lord Jesus Christ, to give an account of the deeds done in the body. (196–97)

While contemplating death, Personel exhibited a spiritual awareness that he had lacked in life. This transformation of perspective, of course, emphasized the fullness of his conversion. The saint could now perceive—and express—what the sinner could not. For example, in exhorting readers to imagine the "worms" and "corruption" of death, he remarked: "Consider, you are ever dying while in the body, still drawing nigher the grave; therefore, you should be always ready" (198). Obviously, Personel had lacked this double awareness (death in life, life in death), as his story illustrated. Yet the contrast between sinner and saint also contributed to an equally apparent contrast between the narrative's levels of discourse. Once the drama of spiritual redemption had been conventionalized, becoming more a structural framework than a dynamic force, readers were left to encounter a melodrama of murder.

Personel's *Authentic and Particular Account* was one of the most emotive of criminal narratives. The basic story of the Personel's life, as related in the first part, was sensational and pathetic. Born in Ireland in 1747, he was raised by an overbearing mother: "my mother being a passionate woman, could never be content with me; do what I could, I might have done it better" (189). After having experienced physical pleasure in the company of a "lewd woman," Personel left home and surrendered himself to sin: "I left my mother's house to be at liberty. While from under her eye, I was guilty of pleasing the sinful appetites of the flesh many times"(189). His mother, however, pursued him, returning him to her home and her supervision. In order "to get out of her reach," Personel then fled to America but returned after little more than a year in a "very much distressed" condition (190). Fearing that her son would leave again, the mother conspired to keep him by marrying him to a local woman. Personel, however, refused to obey:

"Thinking the young woman not handsome enough, nor fancying her in the least . . . I resolved not to have her, let what would happen" (190). His refusal resulted in a final break between mother and son: "through disobedience I came off to America a second time, and have never since returned" (190).

Up to his final crime, Personel's life was marked by a similar series of evasions. To pay for his voyage, he was indentured to a planter in Maryland but soon ran away. He then ran away from several other positions until he ultimately arrived in New York, where he suddenly married a woman his mother certainly would not have approved: "After I came to New-York, I took a wife; and notwithstanding I knew she had followed a loose way of life, I loved her" (192). Immediately after declaring his love, he added: "In short the next morning after I had been married and beded to her, I consented to her going to her old habitation, till she could pay some debts which she said she owed" (192). Emphasized by the curious transitional phrase, "in short," Personel—as he was presented—loved his wife so much that he allowed her to return to prostitution, supposedly to pay off several debts for which he might be held accountable. Caught between the conflicting impulses of possession and devotion, however, he soon retrieved his wife: "she was not long there before I took her away, as I could not bear to think of her following that course any longer" (192). But the wife—with the husband's blessing—soon returned to "that course": "I had not been long married before I was taken so ill, as to be unable to work; and, as we saw no other way, rather than be beholden to the people we lived with, we concluded unanimously, that we must either perish, or she take to her old course; accordingly, she prostituted her body as usual" (193).

Personel, however, again "could not bear to think" of his wife prostituting herself, despite encouraging her: "Sometime after I was ill, she went out every night she could, to which I encouraged her, even so much as to go with her some nights part of the way . . ." (193). When she did not return one night, he went in search of her and found her locked in a "bad house" with two "Gentlemen." After watching and waiting, and after "hearing her laugh," the voyeuristic husband suddenly became incensed when, instead of leaving, "the Gentlemen took her one by the one arm, and the other by the other arm, and so went away" (193). Thinking that if he attacked the two men, in an empty gesture of honor, he could convince his "neighbors" he was "an honest man, and innocent of her doings," Personel searched for a weapon (193). Appropriately, he picked up "the wooden bar of the door," the same that had barred him from his wife, and with his phallic club he pursued and attacked his wife's customers, striking one man in the head hard enough so that he later died (193–94).

After the attack, presented as the culmination of his sins, the narrator said little about his attempts to evade justice, sacred or secular. His remaining task was to verify his spiritual transformation by denying what he formerly had embraced. Adopting the language of damnation, he ridiculed those whose lives resembled his own:

> Thou drunkard, thou bold blasphemer, thou thief, thou whoremaster, thou Sabbath breaker, thou adulterer, thou fornicator, thou extortioner, thou unjust dealer, thou liar, and thou daughters of hell, that are bond slaves . . . to the Devil; you, I say, that take delight in prostituting your bodies as common whores, rather than work for an honest living; do any . . . of you . . . think that you are Christians? . . ." (197)

In order to demonstrate the power of grace to convert all sinners, even the most corrupt, the writers of the Personel text necessarily separated the discourses of the sinner and the saint. Not only did the latter have to utterly renounce the former, but the two also had to exhibit antithetical habits of mind. Yet to accomplish their task the writers ran the risk of creating two unrelated characters. During the earlier part of the century, when readers were more willing to accept the mystical realities of conversion, this risk was lessened; Rodgers and Boston were different, but the same, since both stories of sinner and saint were told from the same sanctified perspective. But the Personel and Ames texts offered two narratives—not just stories of before and after, but two tales, one sensational, and one formal. Within the conventions of conversion, all saints spoke alike; having surrendered the vanities of self, they offered a tale of divine universality, resistant to particularity. But the sinners told a tale of lurid, vivid specifics, and the specificity of their detail marked the emergence of a more realistic level of discourse, a narrative language free of the authorized rhetoric and ideology. Those responsible for shaping the narratives knew, as Milton had discovered, that in the epic struggle between good and evil, Satan was the most compelling character.

## VII

William Brooks went out and stood within the small gate leading to the kitchen, and as Mr. Spooner came past him he knocked him down with his hand. He strove to speak when down, Brooks took him by the throat and partly strangled him. Ross and Buchanan came out; Ross took Mr. Spooner's watch and gave it to Buchanan; Brooks and Ross took him up and put him in the well head first; before they carried him away, I, Buchanan, pulled off his shoes.

—from *The Dying Declaration of James Buchanan, Ezra Ross, and William Brooks*, 1778

The criminals who became characters during and after the Revolution were selected because they were "monuments," not of grace, but of vice. Although more often than not they were depicted as dying within the conventions of repentance, the criminals narrated their crimes, not their conversions. In *The Dying Declaration of James Buchanan, Ezra Ross, and William Brooks* (Worcester, 1778), for example, the three criminals related their crime of murder without specifically acknowledging their iniquity until the final paragraph of their narrative. Presented as both a final statement and a postscript, the paragraph combined the three voices into a generalized "We," offering readers familiar phrases of contrition. After glorifying God and begging "compassion, through the atoning blood of his son Jesus," the three desired "earnestly to warn all, especially young people . . . [to] avoid bad company, excessive drinking, profane cursing and swearing, shameful debaucheries, disobedience to parents, the prophanation of the Lord's day, &c" (224).

An ampersand? Here the warning, the most crucial narrative element at the beginning of the century, was relegated to a voiceless "and such." And even what was articulated had more to do with titillating readers than warning them. Aside from the conventional "disobedience to parents" and "prophanation of the Lord's day," what the three warned readers to beware of, particularly drinking and debauchery, reflected back on their own "heinous wickedness," reemphasizing the sensational parts of their story. Moreover, as readers were aware of by the time they encountered this rather sudden final warning, the only blood the three had been concerned with throughout the narrative belonged to their victim, Joshua Spooner, not to Christ.

*The Dying Declaration of James Buchanan, Ezra Ross, and William Brooks*, along with its several versions, related one of the more notorious murders in eighteenth-century America.[32] As was often the case with sensational crimes, readers generally knew enough of the story to know something of its structure and its elements before they read the texts. In this particular case, readers from Boston to Worcester might well have heard that during the winter of 1778, a bleak period of the war, the daughter of a wealthy Tory, herself a Tory, had hired two British soldiers to murder her husband. Some even might have heard enough to imagine the motives behind the murder; the woman not only wanted to be free from "Domestic dissentions" but also free to pursue her love affair with a younger man (Maccarty 36). Isaiah Thomas, the foremost printer of his age, certainly was aware of this notoriety and, realizing the market potential for a fuller relation, responded to it by publishing the *Dying Declaration*, supplying readers with details for a story they already possessed.

At the center of the crime was Bathsheba Spooner, a thirty-two year old woman characterized by various sources as "attractive, intelligent, and imperious" (McDade 266). Although raised in wealth and luxury, Spooner experienced a loss of both prestige and stability when her father's property was confiscated at the outbreak of hostilities and when he, a former general who had served under Lord Amherst, was forced to flee to Nova Scotia. Spooner remained with her husband in Brookfield but complained that "her match . . . was not agreeable to her," and consequently she "meditated his destruction" (Maccarty 36). According to the *Dying Declaration*, Buchanan and Brooks (who formerly had served under Burgoyne) were travelling through Worcester when they passed the Spooner farm by chance. Invited in to warm themselves by the kitchen fire during a snow storm, the two soon were given an even warmer reception by Spooner, who not only offered them breakfast but also "desired [them] to go into the sitting-room" (219). Surprised by such generosity, the two gladly traded the space of servants for that of family, and, when offered the chance to remain until the weather cleared, they again gladly accepted. Buchanan stated: "I am not positive whether it was the first or second day, she told me . . . that she and her husband did not agree—that he was gone a journey . . . and that he would not be home soon—that we should not go from thence until the weather was fair" (219). Such unexpected invitations and revelations continued, as Spooner, "getting very free in discourse," soon told the soldiers that "she never expected Mr. Spooner to return, as there was one Mr. Ross

[32]In addition to its sensational elements, the Spooner case also is significant as the first murder trial and executions to be held under American jurisdiction in Massachusetts courts.

gone with him, who had an ounce of Poison, which he had promised her he would give to Mr. Spooner the first convenient opportunity" (219).

The poison plot, however, was only the first of several plans, and readers in search of lurid details were provided with an insider's view of the murder. They learned, primarily through Buchanan's voice, how the two soldiers were lured into the intrigue with promises of money and clothes in addition to all the food and the liquor they wanted. When Spooner and Ross eventually returned, the latter having failed to find a "convenient opportunity" to dispatch the former, the two soldiers remained, enlisting in the bloody campaign. Readers could follow the movements of both murderers and victim as they moved towards the point of their violent confrontation. Along the way, pathetic scenes were depicted—the murderers drinking at taverns at the expense of their victim, and he, banished from his own bed, sleeping on the floor with his money box as a pillow. The murder itself received close attention, obscuring the line separating reader and voyeur. On Sunday evening, March 1, Buchanan and Brooks returned to the Spooner house to find Ross already there, waiting for the victim with "a brace of pistols loaded" (222). The three conferred on how best to kill Spooner and, fearing that the pistols "would alarm the neighbours," decided to throw him down the well (222). The three then sat down to "some supper," and when the hapless Spooner arrived he was knocked down, strangled, and beaten at his doorstep while his wife waited in the sitting room (223). After he was thrown "head first" down the well, the murderers returned to the house to divide up his money and his clothing (223). Aside from the final paragraph warning readers to "avoid bad company . . . &c.," the narrative ended with the murder, leaving readers with the scene of the criminal's bloody violence ironically juxtaposed to a non-scene of conventional contrition.

Little was said about their capture, only that they were seen in the taverns the next day with Spooner's watch and silver buckles. As soon as "news of the murder" began to spread, they were taken up and arrested along with Bathsheba Spooner (224). Significantly, the wife gave no "dying declaration" about her involvement in her husband's death. Only later, indirectly through the voice of the attending minister, were readers provided with an account of her behavior, but even here little was said. According to the minister, Thaddeus Maccarty, "she was not very free to converse upon the subject" (37). Although admitting that initially she "*had planned the matter*," the condemned woman insisted that "*she never thought it would be executed; that she relented.*" And although she supposedly "did not blame the judges or jurors or the Attorney-General," she "often declared that the witnesses wronged her." For readers hungering for details of the condemned woman, Maccarty merely stated that "she was a person of uncommon fortitude of mind," adding that "her behavior to all was very polite and complaisant" and that she was "a person naturally of a kind, obliging, generous disposition" (38). Readers expecting a murderous fiend were disappointed. While Buchanan, Ross, and Brooks declared themselves, recreating their crime through the act of confession, Spooner remained an enigma. But her silence did not hurt the marketing of her crime. During a six-month period from her execution (ironically July 2) and to the end of the year, fourteen Spooner texts and editions were published in at least three different cities.[33]

As commodities marketed for a popular audience, criminal narratives of the late-eighteenth century reflected the strategies used by printers and writers to capture reader attention. The further the narratives moved away from the authorities who first sanctioned them, the clearer their marketing strategies became. Some narratives, particularly those created specifically to sell copy rather than to save souls, went so far as to emphasize, and thus advertise, their most sensational elements. In the first criminal magazine published in the United States, *The American Bloody Register* (Boston, 1784), the printer's strategies to attract readers shaped the entire structure of the text. In addition to three different wood cut engravings (a skull and crossbones, a robbery, and a triple hanging), several stern Old Testament quotations demanding punishment for sinners, and numerous titles in bold face announcing the crimes of robbery, piracy, and murder, the text included advertisements for coming issues. Following the title page, which promised *A true and complete History of... the most noted Criminals that have ever made their Exit from the Stage*, the text announced that

> If Encouragement is given to this REGISTER, the other Numbers will contain (with the Assistance of several Gentlemen of the Cloth and Bar) a select and judicious Collection of the the most remarkable Trials for Murder, Treason, Rape, Sodomy, High-way Robbery, Piracy, House-breaking, Perjury, Forgery, and other Crimes and Misdemeanors committed in ENGLAND and AMERICA; from 1760 to 1784 inclusive. Also the LIVES, LAST WORDS and DYING CONFESSIONS of the most noted CRIMINALS that can be obtained (233).

In all probability, few readers would have paused to appreciate the irony of a "select and judicious Collection" made up of the most injudicious and notorious of crimes. Their expectations still controlled by didactic conventions, readers assumed that every narrative of crime offered a moral lesson and that, through "the Assistance of several Gentlemen of the Cloth

[33] For a full list of the various Spooner texts and editions, see the source note included after *The Dying Declaration of James Buchanan, Ezra Ross, and William Brooks*. Note: Bathsheba Spooner is sometimes referred to as Bathshua Spooner.

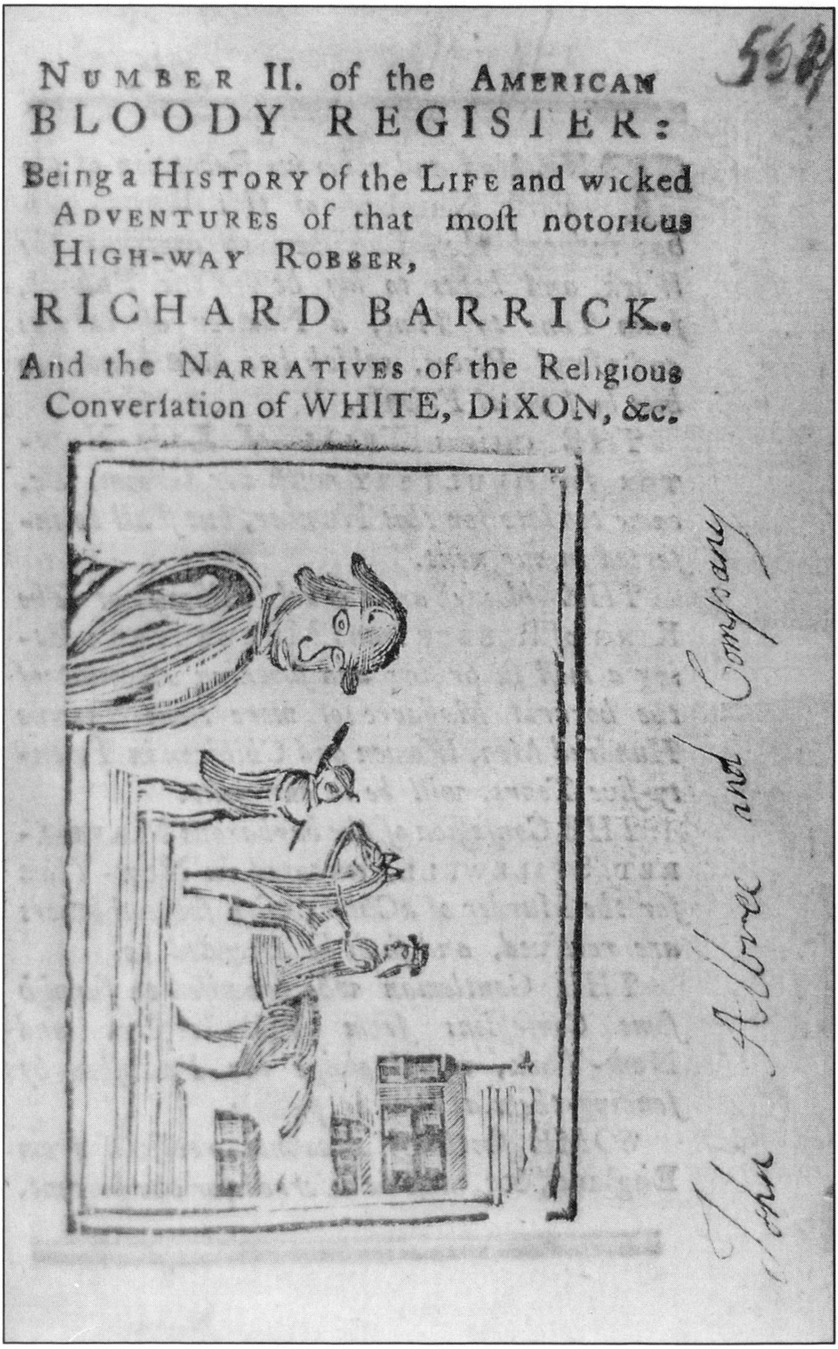

NUMBER II. of the AMERICAN
BLOODY REGISTER:
Being a HISTORY of the LIFE and wicked
ADVENTURES of that moſt notorious
HIGH-WAY ROBBER,
RICHARD BARRICK.
And the NARRATIVES of the Religious
Converſation of WHITE, DIXON, &c.

and Bar," these lessons would be made apparent. Yet obviously the *Bloody Register* writer[s] intended to advertise a series that would be "inclusive" rather than selective. Here inculcating lessons were not as important as arousing sensations.

In reading the first of three segments, each offering a criminal life, readers might have paused to consider just what sort of warning was intended. Beneath the crude but ominous skull and crossbones engraving, "The Life and Dying Confession of Richard Barrick, High-way Robber" began with the familiar references to early childhood that quickly shifted from innocence to corruption. After stating that he was "born in *Ireland*... in the year 1763, and brought up in the Foundling-Hospital," Barrick announced that he apprenticed to a silk weaver at the age of ten (234). The bonds between master and apprentice, however, were not long maintained, and once broken Barrick began to teach himself a less useful (but more profitable) craft: "he [his master] starved and froze me almost to death, for which I left him, and roved through the streets, and frequently stole small things from shop-windows" (234). His roving soon led him "before the Lord Mayor of *London*" for stealing a handkerchief, but Barrick's first encounter with judicial authority, instead of a repentant relation, was offered in the form of a joke: "I was tried and found not *innocent*; was complimented with thirteen stripes, *which is Continental colours*, signifying, that I should be honoured in *America* with the *Hibernian* coat of arms, i. e. two sticks *rampant*, one couchant, a string *pendant*, and an *Irishman* at the end of it" (234).

Confounding expectations of humble penitence, Barrick continued to employ irony and drollery to narrate his life. After a couple more arrests, he finally was pressed into naval service but deserted as soon as his ship arrived in New York. Escaping to Long Island during the early years of the Revolution, he affirmed: "*I was as honest as the times would allow*" (235). Implying that the "times" allowed little honesty, he then described his involvement with a gang of robbers who operated between the coasts of Long Island and Connecticut, variously posing as either cowboys or refugees. Most of the narrative, in fact, was made up of Barrick's descriptions of the raids his gang committed upon houses and farms at night. But the narrative once more confounded expectations; instead of the long anticipated closure, the wryly described *Hibernian* coat of arms, readers encountered an abrupt non-ending. After describing his capture by the British forces in New York, Barrick's narrative voice simply stopped, and in its place another advertisement was inserted: "*For the remainder of* BARRICK'S *Life (which contains a series of heinous crimes perpetrated in* Philadelphia, New-York, Hartford, New-Haven, in Boston *Market, at the vendues and on*

Winter-Hill) *we must refer our Readers to the Second Number of our* REGISTER, *which we shall publish immediately*" (237).

As one of the earliest and crudest cliffhangers in American literature, the openendedness of the Barrick narrative frustrated those readers expecting to follow the robber to the gallows. But the strategy was clear. Following the non-ending still another conspicuous advertisement was placed: "in a few Days will be published, A excellent SERMON . . . Delivered at *Cambridge* . . . immediately preceding the Execution of ALEXANDER WHITE, RICHARD BARRICK and JOHN SULLIVAN, the former for Piracy, the latter for High-way Robbery. With an APPENDIX, exhibiting some Account of their Conversation and Behavior in Prison, &c." (238). Readers wishing to experience Barrick's story, then, were obliged to purchase both "Number II" and the execution sermon. The textual order of sermon followed by supplementary confession not only had been reversed, but had been broken up for better marketability.

The second section, "The Life and Dying Confession of John Sullivan," furnished a more conventional structure in terms of closure but lacked a sense of progression. After stating that he was born in Ireland and eighteen years old, Sullivan's "voice" merely listed his crimes, offering little indication of development or motivation. Yet while the disjointed narrative lacked sequential continuity, it expressed textual relations through a succession of outrages. During this period of fiercely contested loyalties, Sullivan's narrative was remarkable for its disloyalties. His list of eleven crimes (including two labeled "Crime 9") began with a series of enlistments and desertions, a journey of sudden turns and reverses demonstrating a refusal to accept any sort of allegiance. As the ultimate rejection of social connections, highway robbery became the inevitable culmination of Sullivan's peripatetic life. His path eventually crossed with Barrick's, and readers were provided with at least a glimpse of their final robbery. Roaming around Cambridge during "Commencement," the two encountered "one Mr. *Baldwin*," whom they robbed "of his watch and money" (241). But Sullivan's confession was also a denial; introducing a third accomplice, he stated: "but *Poor* was the man that abused [Baldwin] and gave him heavy blows" (241).

In concluding his narrative, Sullivan declared: "These are the most capital crimes I have committed, and I sincerely wish that others may avoid the rock I have split upon" (241). To confirm that these were the young robber's words, the narrative stated that it was "Compiled from the Prisoner's mouth by ELISHA BREWER . . . [and] Transcribed by WILLIAM BILLINGS"; their efforts in turn were verified by the stamp of authority: "Attest, ISAAC BRADISH, Goaler" (241). Contemporary readers would not have questioned the accuracy of either the compilation or the transcription, especially when the cooperative acts of composition were witnessed by the jailer.[34] But Brewer, like so many others who acted in the same capacity, was no mere amanuensis. His discourse, and not that of the illiterate robber, was used both to describe the crimes and to provide the appropriate ideological perspective. Sullivan, who might have wondered on what specific "rock" he was "split upon" (had he the chance to hear his own narrative), had his characterization shaped by the perspectives of his compilers.

In a similar fashion, Brewer, Billings, and Bradish acted as agents of social control in the third section, "The Confession of Alexander White, Pirate," fitting the criminal's life into a suitable narrative structure. With their help, White confessed that his unchecked ambition led him to the gallows. Also born in Ireland, he asserted that, his mind "being inclined to see strange countries," he defied his "Parent's will and went to sea" (242). Readers, however, were not presented with a list either of White's iniquities or his travels. Since the intention was to narrate his vices, and not his voyages, he stated: "It is needless for me to give an account how I spent my life: for I have been in many parts of the world, but never did anything that would cause me to blush" (242). What was offered was his desire for status: "I still followed the occupation of a Mariner, and improved my education 'till I thought myself fit to take the command of a vessel" (242). But instead of social progression, White experienced moral regression. When describing his "heinous crime," he related how he had surrendered to ambition and greed in the pursuit of love, thus reinforcing a standard, conservative lesson of hierarchy and stability.

> MY mind being very uneasy on account of a young lady who I proposed to marry, and only the want of money prevented our being married. Being below her degree, and being ashamed to own my necessity, prolonged our being joined in wedlock. But Love began to burn my poor and wounded heart; and being resolved to go through any difficulty that might impede us, I intended to take the life of my fellow-creature. (242)

Burning with "Love," White explained how he picked up an ax and murdered his captain "and attempted to murder the passenger also" (242).

[34] The act of printing tended to valorize a subject, and readers were likely to accept the authority of the printed word, especially since colonial writers originally were made up of ministers and other members of the elite. The use of a witness's name added further weight to the text's verisimilitude. For insightful recent discussions concerning literacy and the reading experiences of early Americans, see Richard D. Brown's *Knowledge Is Power,* Cathy Davidson's *Reading in America,* William J. Gilmore's *Reading Becomes a Necessity of Life,* and David D. Hall's *World of Wonder,* especially his chapter "The Uses of Literacy."

According to the narrative, when he could not accomplish the second murder, he surrendered. After stating that he was "condemned to die" by his own confession ("chusing rather to die than to live"), he curiously commented that "Time wou'd fail me to give a particular account of this affair" (243). Yet a confession, by definition, was intended to disclose "a particular account" of the sinner's life. Clearly, the principles that informed the structure of White's confession had more to do with dollars than with souls. Humbling the self had less to do with the narrative than with inciting reader curiosity. Immediately after the confession (and the assistance provided by Brewer, Billings, and Bradish), readers were informed—once again—where they could turn for "a particular account." Their curiosity, however, would only be satisfied if those involved in the production of the narratives received "*suitable encouragement.*"

> *For a concise and accurate Account of the behavior and conversation of the Prisoners (particularly of* White *the Pirate) while in prison and in their last moments; also a pathetic and affectionate Address to the Prisoners, we must refer our Readers to Number II. of this* REGISTER, *or to the* APPENDIX *of* an excellent SERMON, *preached at their Execution . . . We should have readily gratified our Readers with the above interesting particulars, but it was out of our power, as the copy was handed to us but hours before this Publication. We shall endeavour (on suitable encouragement to this infant Work) to furnish Number II. with an elegant copperplate engraving, executed by an ingenious Artist* (243).

In helping to produce the *Bloody Register*, Billings, Brewer, and Bradish fulfilled both social and literary conventions. The form was familiar enough so that their actions satisfied a general expectation that condemned criminals confess before execution. Thus, by transcribing, compiling, and attesting, the three discharged a duty that most felt should be done. Yet this social service also was performed for literary incentives and, perhaps too, monetary considerations. The printer, Ezekiel Russell, was marketing a product, and the confessions were vital to the product's completion. Using the pretext of the social convention, Russell, or someone acting as his agent, approached Billings, Brewer, and Bradish, and while there is (at present) no record of their transaction, it seems highly likely that this meeting took place before the three acted to take down the confessions and that Russell or his agent not only encouraged the three to help assemble the literary product but also paid them for their services. Billings, Brewer, and Bradish functioned the same as Russell's "*ingenious Artist,*" helping to promote and market a literary product.

## VIII

> Thus have I given a history of my birth, education and atrocious conduct, and as the time is very nigh in which I must suffer an ignominious death, I earnestly intreat that all people would take warning by my wicked example.
>
> —from *The Life and Confession of Johnson Green*, 1786

Given the popular interest in capital crime and in the spectacle of execution, and as well the increased competitiveness of printers, the commercialization of criminal characters was inevitable. From the beginning they had been shaped specifically for audience consumption, but gradually the forces that shaped the characters shifted from the pulpit to the market. The type of character produced for readers during the post-Revolutionary period, more often than not, only nominally answered the expectations of the ministers and the magistrates, who assumed that the criminals would repent their crimes and justify their deaths. Aware of the possibilities for profit, printers such as Ezekiel Russell or Isaiah Thomas published narratives that maximized the sensational aspects of the criminal's life and minimalized the functions of repentance and justification. Such was the case with *The Life and Confession of Johnson Green* (Worcester, 1786). Another product from the press of Isaiah Thomas, this broadside presented a character who was both particularized, in terms of the specifics of his life, and conventionalized, in terms of the commercial motives that conditioned his characterization.

That Green was marketed for a popular audience was evident in the extended title, which declared that he was *to be Executed this Day, August 17th, 1786, for the Atrocious Crime of Burglary.* An obvious strategy, the broadside (technically the cheapest narrative form) was published to coincide with the climax of Green's drama, in effect as a program for the play about to be performed. As the people gathered to witness the execution, or as they departed, they could purchase the Green broadside, an exchange intended to deepen their execution experience. Through imaginative involvement with the narrative, they could become more engrossed in the figure who stood, or dangled, before them. Blurring the lines between reality and text, the figure thus advertised the character, while his death promoted his *Life*.

The broadside's title additionally announced Green's *Last and Dying Words,* but the actual words used in narrative were anything but the spontaneous expression of his final thoughts. His opening statement, for example, revealed more about the writer's sense of genre than about the figure's sense of himself: "I *Johnson Green*, having brought myself to a shameful and ignominious death, by my wicked conduct, and as I am a dying man I leave to the world the following History of my Birth, Education, and vicious Practices, hoping that all people will take warning by my example, and shun vice and follow virtue" (259). As the illiterate son of a Black man and an Irish woman, Green hardly would have conceived of himself in such conventional terms, even if he had the faintest idea what the word, "ignominious," meant. And even if contemporary readers assumed the act of transcription, caring not so much about the words but more about the facts, they still would have discovered little of the thief's personality. There was a nearly endless stream of facts, as Green listed the names, places, and objects of his thefts, but little insight into his motivations or his beliefs. Shaping the self in order to satisfy the expectations of readers, and thus suppressing alternative storylines, the narrative exhibited an incorrigible character whose life justified his "ignominious death."

Adhering to the standard conventions, Green was presented as a disobedient youth, rejecting both "the principles of Christian Religion" and his mother's "good advice" (259). His propensity for theft began when the twelve-year-old boy stole "four cakes of gingerbread and six biscuit, out of a horse cart" (260). Once begun, this "practice of stealing" continued nonstop until Green, at the age of twenty-nine, was brought to the gallows (260). Along the way, he was often caught and corrected, but, as he (and the writer) stated, "not so severely as I deserved" (260). Aside from the exhaustive list of cakes, cheeses, blankets, shoes, stockings, and silver buckles he stole, little was said about his personal life, but what was offered was sensational. While cataloguing his early thefts, Green remarked: "I would just observe to the world, that my being addicted to drunknenness, the keeping of bad company, and a correspondence that I have had with lewd women, has been the cause of my being brought to this wretched situation" (259).

These casual references were enough to indict the thief for defying moral as well as legal boundaries, teasing readers with the outlines of a highly salacious story. Directly after mentioning his "correspondence . . . with lewd women," he abruptly introduced his marriage: "In March, 1781, I was married at Eastown, to one Sarah Phillips, a mustee . . . She has had two children since I was married to her, and I have treated her exceeding ill" (260). Later, while summing up his iniquities, he returned to the subject of his lewd correspondences: "I have had great dealings with women . . . I often too easily obtained my will of them . . . I have had a correspondence with many women, exclusive of my wife, among whom were several abandoned Whites, and a large number of Blacks; four of the whites were married women, three of the blacks have laid children to me besides my wife, who has been much distressed at my behaviour" (264).

As a character, Green was presented as being unable to refrain from taking both property and women. Although ostensibly executed for one specific burglary, he rather was condemned for a corrupt self-indulgence. And while stressing this unrestraint, the narrative deemphasized all possibilities of self-sacrifice. At the outbreak of hostilities, Green "inlisted into the American service, and remained in the same for the duration of the war" (259). Yet instead of being commended for serving his country, he was condemned. Because he joined the army "contrary to . . . [his] mother's advice" and because he was caught stealing while a soldier, his enlistment was presented as rather being spent in "the Devil's service" (259). Even though he admitted that he stole food because he and his comrades "were extremely pinched for the want of provisions," he nevertheless was portrayed as being unable to resist "the old Tempter" (260). Through the narrative arrangement of sensational details, then, Green was shaped to dramatize his vices.

But why was he so shaped? As with the Spooner narratives and the *Bloody Register*, the convention of offering a warning remained, although it thinly masked more monetary motives. Just as he began the narrative, the Green narrator concluded with another rhetorical flourish, warning people "to shun vice, follow virtue, and become . . . victorious over the enemies of immortal felicity" (264). In the long ballad which followed the narrative (supposedly "*written at the request of Johnson Green*" and "*added to his Life and Confession, as a Part of his Dying Words*") the persona also offered a warning:

Repent, ye thieves, whilst ye have breath,
Amongst you let be wrought
A reformation, lest to death,
You, like myself, be brought. (266)

Not only were "ye thieves" unlikely to "shun vice" after reading the broadside, they equally were unlikely to read it. And if this warning was purely for the sake of convention, so was the persona's more general warning:

I hope my sad and dismal fate
Will solemn warning be
To people all, both small and great,
Of high and low degree. (266)

For warnings to be effective, terror—the threat of retribution—was needed, but more often than not the commercialization of these later narratives insulated readers from experiencing the panic that accompanied the criminal's death.

In the narratives of two women, Rachel Wall and Elizabeth Wilson, death similarly was rendered more a dramatic element of plot than an occasion for awe. Although conforming to the expected genre conventions, these narratives titillated rather than intimidated, especially since they (like Green text) focused attention on the link between sexuality and crime. In offering readers a means of comprehending their crimes, both Wall and Wilson referred to their (and their gender's) inability to resist the temptations of corrupt company.[35] Despite good parents and religious training, both women succumbed to the evil influences of men, and in succumbing they indirectly destroyed themselves. But readers were not presented with simple morales of sin and destruction; rather, in order to arouse emotions, and thus promote sales, the narratives complicated the issues of innocence and guilt. While acknowledging their general corruption, Wall and Wilson went to their deaths asserting their innocence regarding the particular crimes for which they were condemned.

In the *Life, Last Words and Dying Confession of Rachel Wall* (Boston, 1789), readers learned less about Wall's crime than about her criminality. After making the customary references to her "honest and reputable parents," Wall alluded to her rejection of both them and their "good advice": "I left my parents without their consent when I was very young, and returning again was received by them, but could not be contented; therefore I tarried with them but two years, before I left them again, and have never seen them since" (283–84). Without revealing much else about her personality and motives, she attributed her running away to the man who eventually caused her destruction. stating that she "came away with one *George Wall*," she avowed: "if I had never seen him I should not have left my parents" (284). Wall—as a woman—was depicted as weak, susceptible to corruption, and unable to resist the will of an evil man. All her later crimes, then, could be perceived according to this point in the narrative progression, when she was lured away from the security of her family.

After a quick marriage, Wall followed her husband to Boston, where he soon abandoned her, but this abandonment nearly saved her. As an "entire stranger" in a strange city, she stated: "I went into service and lived very contented, and should have remained so, had it not been for my husband; for, as soon as he came back, he enticed me to leave my service and take to bad company, from which I date my ruin" (284). Yet Wall, by current standards of revelation, said little about the specifics of her "ruin"; instead, she generalized her iniquity, embracing all manner of corruption

[35] For a recent discussion of female criminals, see Hull's *Female Felons*. For the best overviews of women in early New England, see Ulrich's *Good Wives*, Kerber's *Republican Mothers, and* Norton's *Liberty's Daughters*.

through rhetorical acts of self-humiliation. Reaching back to an older ministerial convention, she conflated sacred and secular deviations when offering examples of her wickedness: "I acknowledge myself to have been guilty of a great many crimes, such as Sabbath-breaking, stealing, lying, disobedience to parents, and almost every other sin a person could commit, except murder" (284). Stressing the susceptibility of her character, a frailty attributed to her gender, the narrative placed Wall's downfall within scenes of "bad company," prompting readers to imagine both her moral and physical seduction.

But perhaps Wall, or more likely whoever "took" her words, anticipated that readers wanted the sensational specifics of crime. She—the narrative voice—expressed an unusual awareness of the structure that ordered (and confined) her experiences, and whatever specifics she expressed she related through this awareness. Earlier, when referring to her leaving home, she remarked: "without doubt the ever-curious Public, (but more especially those of a serious turn of mind) will be anxious to know every particular circumstance of the Life and Character of a person in my unhappy situation," but when speaking of her parents she only commented: "with regard to my Parents, I have only room in this short Narrative to observe, that my father was a farmer, who was in good circumstances when I left him" (283). Similarly, when describing her guilt, she stated: "in short, the many small crimes I have committed, are too numerous to mention in this sheet, and . . . a particular narrative of them here would serve to extend a work of this kind to too great a length" (284). But both the narrator and "the ever-curious Public" knew what to expect from "a work of this kind," and immediately following her refusal to "extend" the narrative Wall nevertheless offered "the particulars" of three short episodes.

The first two were burglaries Wall committed on board ships docked along Boston's wharves, incidents that satisfied some of the readers's imaginative hunger for sensation while justifying her execution. The third, however, was almost comic, involving a loaf of bread baked with "a number of Tools, such as a saw, file, &c." inside. In an attempt to help her husband (her destroyer) break out of jail, Wall baked the curious loaf and presented it to the jailer, "who little suspected the trick" (285). Moreover, what makes this episode even more singular was Wall's (the writer's) continued sensitivity to her genre and to her readers. When introducing her loaf of bread, she stated: "I would beg the patience of the public for only a few minutes, while I relate another adventure" (285). In order to refute the potential protest that the "adventure" was "too trifling to mention," she insisted that she narrated the story "with a view of gratifying the curiosity of some particular friends" who supposedly pressed her for details. One easily can imagine that among these "particular friends" was the writer of the Wall text.

After depicting her general guiltiness, Wall denied her specific guilt: "As to the crime of Robbery, for which I am in a few hours to suffer an ignominious death, I am entirely innocent" (285). (Was the word, "ignominious," part of the "good education" she had received from her parents?) Possibly Boston readers already were familiar with the details of the "Robbery," and possibly too some knew of the sworn testimony that had convicted Wall, but in one of her final statements she persisted in stating that "the witnesses . . . are certainly mistaken" (286). Such a statement, given as a "dying confession," could not be taken lightly. As in all gallows speeches, death verified the narrative, especially since it was "taken from the prisoner's mouth, a few hours before her execution." By the time readers encountered the text, Wall herself was no more, and consequently her "last words" complicated an issue that officially had been resolved. As with the Ames narrative nearly two decades earlier, her denial challenged her judges, at least concerning the specific "Robbery." To assuage this challenge she concluded the narrative thanking (and thus absolving) "the Hon. gentlemen who were my Judges" and the "several Ministers" who attended her during her confinement (286). Similar to other narratives of the period, the Wall broadside compromised the expectations of two different audiences: the elite who demanded justification, and "the ever-curious Public" who desired sensation.

And did Wall envision her death as "ignominious?" Perhaps, but perhaps she was no more familiar with it than Johnson Green. Such rhetoric was used to heighten the drama, enhancing its literary effect. While satisfying the requirements of the genre, this stylization of rhetoric revealed an impulse to engage readers aesthetically. Style, along with plot, setting, character, and theme, became another narrative element available to writers increasingly aware of their popular audiences. When introducing one of her burglaries, for example, Wall suddenly broke into an effusion of stylistically enhanced rhetoric: "In one of my nocturnal excursions, when the bright goddess Venus shined conspicuous, and was the predominant Planet among the heavenly bodies, sometime in the spring of 1787 . . . I happened to go on board a ship" (284). Obviously, this is less a lesson in astronomy than an attempt to elevate the rhetoric, and by such rhetorical inflation to increase the scene's dramatic suspense. Once free of the restrictions imposed by ministerial discourse, criminal narratives began to explore the possibilities of literary experience. In the *Faithful Narrative of Elizabeth Wilson* (Philadelphia, 1786), an awareness of authorial manipulation of the text, and thus of readers, was particularly evident.

Early in January 1786, Elizabeth Wilson was executed at Chester, Pennsylvania, for the murder of her twin ten-week-old infants, and shortly thereafter the first of several narrative editions was published in Philadelphia, supposedly "drawn up at the request of a friend unconnected with the deceased" (title page). Sensational from the start, the story was a likely choice for narration, regardless of who the "friend" was and what his or her connection was with Wilson (and with the printer). Yet the narrative, however "faithful" in detail, was no mere relation of facts. Combining both third and first person narrations, the text was structured to achieve the greatest effect on readers by carefully controlling the devices of disclosure and progression. What readers were told and when they were told were manipulated to intensify the literary experience of the text, increasing the potential for imaginative involvement. Intended to arouse feelings of sentiment rather than a sense of justice, Wilson's narrative portrayed the shocking double murder as a melodramatic confrontation between innocence and iniquity.

The narrative began with a blunt third person statement of facts: "Was found, by a person with a dog, crossing the fields . . . two dead infants" (271). Wilson, the mother, was arrested, and without further delay or description she soon was convicted and condemned. Then, in a paragraph placed in obvious juxtaposition to the preceding, the narrative negated the reader's sense of conviction: "Before, at, and after her trial, she persisted in denying the fact: her behaviour was such, in general, as gave reasons to conclude she was innocent of the murder of which she was charged" (271). By the time they encountered Wilson's actual voice, readers already had been provided with the story's two most dramatic points, the deaths of the two infants at the beginning and the death of the mother at the end. As the line of progression between these two points, the narrative offered readers a means of discovering how the deaths were connected, a textual journey that promised to separate the innocent from the guilty as well as answer the morbid (but inescapable) questions of how, when, and why the murders occurred.

After the suspenseful build up, Wilson, speaking in her own voice, quickly disclosed the sensational details of the crime. Because of "*the subtilty of Satan and the corruptions of nature,*" she declared that she had been "*led away to the soul-destroying sin of fornication,*" and as evidence of this "*predominant evil*" she stated that she previously had given birth to "*three children in an unlawful way*" (272). But her corruption stopped at sexual promiscuity. Similar to many of the heroines in the newly developed genre of the novel, Wilson claimed she was the victim of a cruel seduction.[36]

[36] For the best recent discussion of the seduction motif in eighteenth-century fiction, see Davidson. For other valuable discussion of fiction during the early republic and the nineteenth century, see Baym, Tompkins, and Spengemann. For earlier but still interesting discussions, see Herbert Ross Brown, Cowie, Losche, and Petter. For a helpful reference guide, see Parker.

Twice stating that she "fell" into the company of Joseph Deshong, she confessed: *"he [Deshong] insinuated himself into my company, under pretence of courtship . . . and by repeated promises of marriage deceived and persuaded me to consent to his unlawful embraces"* (273). As soon as she became pregnant, her seducer "dropt entirely his purpose of marriage" and abandoned her, leaving her "in great want of money" (273). Five weeks after giving birth to the twins, she set out to find her deceiver and confronted him, demanding that he either *"do something . . . by fair means"* or she would "apply to the law" (273). But Deshong again played the deceiver, seeming to sympathize with her and agreeing to meet her again with the children in order to provide for them. When they met on the *"fatal appointed day,"* he still masked his intentions, treating Wilson with kindness, until he lured her into the woods and murdered the infants (273).

One of the more pathetic murder scenes in the criminal genre, the entire sequence exonerated Wilson while indicting her evil lover. But even afterwards the narrative continued to emphasize the elements of pathos, following the woman as she moved towards her death. Not only was her behavior described on "the morning of her execution," but also readers were given further description of her at the gallows and during her "last moment[s]" (274). An instant before she was "turned off," she was asked "if with her dying breath she sealed the confession she had made," and in her final words she affirmed that it was "the truth" (276). Offering her life as proof of her innocence, Wilson "quickly left the world" (276).

Yet death was not conclusion. In order to further arouse reader sentiment, the text revealed its final irony. Directly after Wilson's death, the narrative flow was interrupted, a rhetorical pause that invited readers to experience still greater pathos.

> But here we must drop a tear! What heart so hard, as not to melt at human woe!
>
> Her brother came in all haste from Philadelphia, with a respite or letter from the Honorable the President and Council, to delay the execution, but through unexpected and unavoidable hindrances on the road, did not arrive until twenty-three minutes after the solemn scene was closed. When he came with the respite in his hand, and saw his sister irrecoverably gone, beheld her motionless, and sunk in death,—who can paint the mournful scene?
>
> Let imagination if she can! (276)

Certainly the scene was pitiful—the brother arriving minutes too late to save his sister, but the narrative, through the sentimentalization of its style, attempted to increase the scene's literary effect. Dared to imagine the "mournful scene," readers were urged to indulge their emotions by envisioning the brother encountering the still dangling body of his sister.

Wilson's narrative, along with those of Wall, Green, and others from the period, reflected a tendency to pursue readers through the use of literary techniques, a marketing strategy that closed the gap between the realms of fact and fiction. These narratives, however, did not abandon their ideological functions of reinforcing the cultural framework. Overall, the narratives still made crime understandable, offering readers socially useful (or at least expedient) ways of comprehending conflicts between laws and lawbreakers. But while the task of explaining crime remained unchanged, the explanations themselves had shifted, adapting to the new cultural context of revolution and republicanism. Without depravity, criminal narratives had become individualized, presenting readers with intriguing specifics of crime and criminal personality. As the religious drama of sin and salvation gave way to melodrama, criminals were no longer depicted as stock representative figures, and their crimes no longer proclaimed the larger collective transgressions of their society. Yet the causes of crime were never completely contextual.

## IX

> Here about 7 o'clock in the evening I met a gentleman who appeared an object of plunder. I asked him the time of night; he drew his watch, and told me the hour. I observed "You have a very fine watch. . . . Sir, 'tis too fine for you—you know my profession—deliver." He drew back; I caught his bridle with one hand, presented a pistol with the other, and said, "Deliver, or I'll cool your porridge:" He handed me a purse of eight guineas, and a gold watch valued at 30 l. sterling. To compleat the iniquity, and exhibit the extent of my villainy, I then took a prayer-book from my pocket, and ordered him to swear upon the solemnity of God's word, that he would make no discovery in twelve hours: He took the oath.
>
> —from *Sketches of the Life of Joseph Mountain*, 1790

If the fallen state of human nature was no longer adequate to explain crime, still other generalized "causes" were possible. Increasingly, the narratives promoted criminal types, groups whose basic characters were weak and easily corrupted when removed from supervision and when surrounded by temptation. As women, both Wall and Wilson were characterized as succumbing to the weaknesses of their sex, falling prey to the influences of evil men. In expressing the sources of her destruction, Wilson referred to the "subtilty of Satan and corruption of nature," but in the context of the narrative her "corruption" had been more a matter of gender than of religion; female "nature," not human nature, provided readers with the means of perceiving her story. In a similar fashion, all of the criminal characters since mid-century can be separated into groups that in various ways reinforced predominant ideological beliefs. Two of the more obvious were age and class. With one or two exceptions (Jubeart and Packer), all were relatively young, and all lacked the privileges and power reserved for members of the elite. The narratives situated crime among lower class youth, setting in place perspectives that reinforced hierarchal prejudices. But the most obvious shared characteristic was that all of the criminals were portrayed as The Other, the outsider whose differences distinguished the cultural and social identity of the dominant group.

The most commonly identified criminal types were the most obvious—and therefore the most vulnerable—cultural and racial groups. Consistently, the narratives dramatized the lives of capital offenders who were either Irish or black. Barrick's joke about the "*Hibernian* coat of arms" being a gallows was unfortunately appropriate. A significant number of those who marched to the gallows began their journeys in Ireland, and in the criminal narrative genre their cultural character was used to explain their crimes. A prejudice transplanted from England, "Irish" served as a convenient label to identify those who were naturally disposed to vice. Once a criminal had been so identified, readers no longer were taxed with finding more complicated causes for the crimes; questions of social, political, and economic injustice did not need arise. In the same way, blacks provided expedient explanations for crime. Sharing the belief that blacks were racially inferior, readers used their own prejudices to account for the crimes committed by those with dark skin.[37] Like the Irish, and to a lesser extent the Indians, blacks were portrayed as being naturally inclined to vice; lacking self-discipline and foresight, they required supervision and discipline, or else they could not refrain from falling into sinful self-indulgence.

Johnson Green was an obvious example. The son of a black father and Irish mother, he combined the weaknesses of the two, unable to resist the evil enticements of alcohol, theft, and sex. In the same fashion, Joseph Mountain and Thomas Powers, both blacks executed for rape, could not resist taking whatever they wanted. In both their narratives, once they had evaded the control of their masters, they succumbed to the weaknesses of their race, thus presenting readers with lessons of racial prejudice. Theft and rape represented the same vicious impulse to defy the boundaries set by

[37]For the best discussions of slavery, blacks, and prejudice in early America, see Jordan and Genovese.

the social hegemony; disdaining the laws of ownership, including those that regarded women and blacks as property of the patriarchal order, Mountain and Powers were characterized as surrendering to the worst tendencies of their race. Dominated by a thoughtless process of constant gratification, they were reduced to a brutish reflex of wanting and taking.

In the *Sketches of the Life of Joseph Mountain* (New Haven, 1790), Mountain was presented to readers in contradistinction to their own beliefs, as the blackness of his skin served as a convenient symbol for the antithetical values he represented. As soon as he had escaped from the social hierarchy that ordered his life, running away from the merchant ship on which he served, Mountain immediately began to exhibit his contrary qualities, illustrating the dangerous correspondence between liberty and licentiousness. Instead of returning to Philadelphia and reassuming his "proper" place, he jumped ship and soon "was strolling the streets of London in quest of amusements," where he "speedily [was] initiated in practices disgraceful to human nature, and destructive to every moral virtue" (289). As the text revealed, such a narrative descent into disgrace and destruction was partly the result of his own vicious inclinations and partly the result of his corrupt environment. Being "susceptible" to vice, he fell in with two highway robbers, and after "becoming a companion in their iniquity" he fully demonstrated an inherent talent for wickedness (290).

Mountain and his companions began a cycle of robbery and debauchery, a cycle that led him to discover a counter system of values in the English underworld. Immersed in a criminal culture where robbery became a "profession," he was trained in an alternative social hierarchy where muggers aspired to be highwaymen and where esteem was awarded for vice rather than for virtue. Readers could not fail to notice the perverse contrast between the highborn gentlemen victimized by the robberies and the dissolute robbers cavorting in taverns as *"gentlemen of pleasure"* (291). Nor could they fail to recognize Mountain's desire to rise within this inimical society: "The business which now seemed most alluring to me, was that of *highway-men*. Considering myself at the head of foot-pads [those who robbed on foot], I aspired for a more *honorable* employment" (293). Free from all restraints, he pursued his adverse ambitions until, "notwithstanding the darkness of his complexion, he was complimented as the first of his profession" by his fellow highwaymen (295).

Inhabiting a world where racism was a social convention, eighteenth-century readers would not have so easily dismissed the "darkness of his complexion," and they would have perceived both the robber's ambitions and achievements as subversions of their natural order. Refusing to accept either his base social position or the baseness of his racial character, Mountain defied the standard conceptions that shaped the lives of those who read his narrative. Yet, as readers knew all too well, it was a safe defiance; given the requirements of the genre, they knew where, when, and how his defiance would end. Despite his bravado, Mountain inhabited two antithetical worlds, and continually his narrative focused on the contrast between the two. In one he was celebrated, while in the other he was condemned, and no matter how great a highwayman he was, readers experienced his accomplishments through the narrative conventions that ultimately would take the robber to the gallows. From the outset, they knew that their world would be affirmed, not his, and that Mountain, regardless of his criminal success, would return in death to his original base position.

In his own world, Mountain achieved spectacular success. After robbing in England, France, Holland, and Spain, he acquired enough booty to become part owner of a tavern outside London. According to this progression, then, the highwayman, by robbing people of their property, had passed from being property to owning property. But, in view of the racial and structural boundaries that shaped the characterization, this progression was presented as a travesty of self-determination; ironically, the more he achieved, the closer he approached the point where his worlds collided. Unable to remain in England because of his many iniquities, he returned to the sea, and in the spring of 1790 he made his last voyage to Boston. While travelling through Connecticut on his way to New York, the highwayman was whipped for a petty theft, and it was here, at the whipping post, where Mountain's counter world collapsed: "No event [the whipping] in my antecedent life produced such mortification as this; that a highway-man of the first eminence . . . should be punished for such a petty offence, in such an obscure part of the country, was truly humiliating" (299).

Although wearing the painful label of petty thief on his back, Mountain refused to accept his humiliation and set out immediately to reaffirm his status as a "highwaymen of the first eminence" by seizing whatever he wanted. Yet rather than plundering gold and watches, he assaulted a young woman. Consequently, as it was presented to readers, the crime of rape—the taking of a female body—was merely another form of robbery. Mountain wanted revenge against the social structure that had humiliated him, and as a material object, indeed as property, his victim represented this social structure. As forced sexual intercourse, rape was the medium through which he reasserted his contempt for the laws that denied him the privileges of ownership. His actions after the attack, as significant as the rape itself, confirmed this; instead of running away afterwards, he stated: "I still continued my barbarity, by insulting her in her distress, boasting of the fact, and glorying in my iniquity" (300). Having been humiliated, he felt the need to reclaim his status by humiliating a meaningful symbol of the order that challenged his exulted self-conception.

Throughout a century of criminal narrative production, readers had never before encountered a character like Mountain. He was the first English highwayman specifically shaped for an American audience, and he was the first to so clearly embrace his outsider status. The narrative, in fact, offered Mountain one last chance of "glorying in . . . iniquity." Throughout the text, his character had been created through the collaboration of two authors, a balancing of the experiences provided by the historical figure and the words provided by the ghostwriter. Imprisoned within a hostile environment and confronted with death, Mountain, the man, might have told a different story, one more appropriate for a sinner struggling for salvation, but he made use of the narrative opportunity to fashion a far more sensational tale, boasting of, rather than confessing, his accomplishments. Those involved in the process of turning the narrative into a commodity also might have told a different story, one less scornful of their own social codes and customs, but they too chose to present the alterity of their character's life, at least up until the final paragraph of contrived contrition. More interested in promoting readership than righteousness, they crafted a narrative that stressed Mountain's more marketable irreverence.

Although less exotic than the black highwayman, Thomas Powers was a more disturbing character. Unlike Mountain, he never openly challenged the boundaries of his social community, even when confronted and accused. More deceitful than defiant, he remained within the hierarchy that oppressed him, concealing his inherent wickedness beneath a pose of docile servility. Published in order to satisfy—and exploit—public curiosity, *The Narrative and Confession of Thomas Powers* (Norwich, 1796) exposed the sinister reality behind the character's passive pretences. Aside from acknowledging his crimes, Powers confessed little in his *Confession*, offering factual information without spiritual revelation, yet this lack of disclosure ironically revealed a capacity to commit evil unreconciled by either conscience or cognizance. Powers was a more disturbing character not only because he dissembled, but also because he was unthinking. Moreover, since he overtly remained within his community, and thus supposedly within the sphere of proper ideological influence, his narrative raised issues of how to identify, and guard against, such evil, issues that ultimately it answered by popularizing racist stereotypes.

On both the title page and headnote, Powers was identified as "A NEGRO," a label that not only allowed readers to place him at the bottom of his social environment but also suggested the base proclivities of his racial character.[38] Within the first paragraph, the narrative promptly con-

[38] The identification of Powers as "A Negro" was not unusual in early American narratives. As a rhetorical strategy intended to provide white readers with an appropriate ideological context to view the characters, racial epithets were commonly used on title pages. Mountain had been similarly identified.

firmed both his low status and fallen nature. Rejecting the moral lessons of both parents and masters (according to convention), he stated: "I was naturally too much inclined to vice . . . for I was very apt to pilfer and tell lies" (343). Confounding individual and racial nature, the narrative stressed that Powers was naturally weak and undisciplined, more disposed to corruption than to correction. The sequence that eventually led him to the gallows, in fact, began when the nine-year-old boy first surrendered to his evil inclinations. After he "was put out to live" with a new master, he symbolically "began the practice of villainy and debauchery" on a Sabbath while his (master's) family was at church: "being one Sunday at home from Meeting, with nobody but a young Negro woman . . . she, enticing me to her bed, where she was sitting, soon taught me the practice of that awful sin, which now costs me my life" (343). Commenting on his initiation into iniquity, he declared: "it was here I began my career in the gratification of that corrupt and lawless passion" (343).

Throughout the narrative, incontinence and disobedience were linked; not only was the former a form of the latter, but sexual excess, as a lack of restraint, also represented an inability to restrain the self in all areas of social participation, especially within the family. Self-gratification dominated all motivations. Without constant moral training, Powers could not help surrendering to his nature:

> being naturally vicious I improved my talents . . . to very bad purposes. I used to make a point of pilfering whenever I could; for when I saw an opportunity, the devil, or some other evil spirit, always gave me a strong inclination. I suppose it was because I was naturally inclined to be light-fingered; for I never hesitated to touch anything that came my way (343–44).

By referring to his natural inclinations, Powers (the character) encouraged readers to use their prejudices not only to attribute the causes of his crimes to his nature, both ethnic and personal, but also more generally to reinforce the link between criminality and iniquity. Lacking a moral awareness, Powers was evil, and the sources of his evilness belonged to his race. This narrative mixture of racial and literary character was reinforced by the sensationalized connection between lewdness and lawlessness. After the above passage, he added: "Here too I played my pranks, with young black girls about the streets; and indulged myself as freely as I could" (344). Indeed, as the narrative emphasized, Powers "never hesitated to touch anything," whether object or person, that he desired. Living in a world where the repression of the self was an essential part of the social contract, the character's acknowledgment of his unrestrained self-indulgence thus identified him as a dangerous element that could not long be tolerated.

When describing the actual rape, Powers presented his crime as a similar impulse of wanting and taking. Previous to the attack, he had neither forethought of what he was about to do nor malice towards his victim, and as it was described the rape was a random, spontaneous event, the result of a rash, vicious reflex. When riding along a road one evening, he encountered his victim by chance:

> I overtook a young woman . . . I passed on by her . . . till after a little querying with myself, and finding nothing to oppose, but rather the devil to assist me, I determined to make an attempt on her virgin chastity. —So I waylaid her . . . I threw her on the ground, and in spite of her cries and entreaties, succeeded in my hellish design (344).

The description itself was brutal enough, but the lack of premeditation, the sudden surrendering to an evil inclination, made Powers appear all the more perfidious. Yet this lack of intention was surpassed by an appalling lack of guilt. Describing his actions following the rape, he stated: "Then I left her, and . . . I returned to my master's house and sat down, as usual, to play chequers with the children" (344).

Such a graphic account of a black slave raping a white virgin would have shocked the sensibilities of most readers, but by describing the rapist soon sitting down "as usual" to play checkers with his master's children, the narrative revealed a more alarming level of evilness. Powers threatened readers not only because he was naturally wicked, but also because he so easily masked his wickedness behind a deceptive pose of docility. And since he was portrayed as a creature of reflex rather than of reflection, he presented readers with problems of distinguishing such evil. Without either deliberation or contrition, he committed his outrage, and then to conceal his crime he appeared to be the opposite of what he was. In order to arm readers with adequate ideological precaution, the narrative, while reinforcing the racist stereotype of the oversexed black, promoted still greater racial distrust by depicting deviousness as an element of blackness. Since no one possibly could anticipate a sudden "hellish design," and since no one could see behind a mask of docile submission, readers were encouraged to perceive all blacks as "being naturally vicious."

After his arrest, Powers "denied every syllable of the truth," and throughout his imprisonment he continued attempting to evade "the truth" (345). For those who gathered at the gallows, his execution, whether voluntary or involuntary, acted as his fullest confession. For readers, however, "the truth" came prepackaged; the character's guilt and deceit were part of the genre's conventions. Before becoming engaged in the narrative, readers encountered the linking of the character's name, crime, and execution on the title page. In substituting literary experience for historical occurrence, the Powers text offered readers an unequivocal—and univocal—reading of the rapist's nature that both sanctioned and popularized the official conviction. At the same time, it provided them with a means of perceiving the sources of crime (racism). But the narrative also inculcated a specific ideological lesson in how to overcome the corrupt tendencies of minorities. Like Green, Powers had been caught and punished for theft at a young age, and in describing his punishment he stated: "I was forced . . . to take a few stripes on my back; but if I had received my just deserts I might possibly have escaped the fate, that now awaits me" (344).[39] Given the innate weaknesses of his character, Powers needed his master's discipline, and although his example was extreme, his capacity to transgress and to deceive implicated all blacks. His plea for "just deserts" represented an ideological imperative for masters to subject those under them to strict control and even stricter discipline.

## X

> When I look back upon a company of thieves, with their whores, met after some house or shop-breaking match, full of plunder, and recollect the scenes of cursing, singing, dancing, swearing, roaring, lewdness, drunkenness, and every possible sort of brutish behaviour, I detest myself for having so often been one in such companies.
>
> —from *The Confession &c. of Thomas Mount*, 1791

By the end of the eighteenth century, the criminal narrative genre had developed into a popular print medium, a standard, pervasive form through which a series of cultural, political, and financial exchanges took place between writers, printers, and readers. Ironically, what the ministers had first introduced continued to engage readers long after ministerial influence had declined, nearly accomplishing the exact opposite of what the Mathers had first intended with James Morgan. Reversing its original priorities, the genre became more concerned with readers as consumers than as parishioners. Intended to stop the tide of secularism from sweeping over New England, the genre ultimately promoted secular concerns by removing the criminals from a drama of salvation and placing them in more

[39] Powers's remark about not receiving his "just deserts" closely resembles a remark made by Johnson Green concerning the punishment he received from his master for stealing "two shillings." He stated that "he discovered what I had done, gave me correction, but not so severely as I deserved."

individualized dramas of civil defiance. Although the conclusion was never in doubt, the presentation still popularized the criminal's worldly conflicts. Early America's "revolution in words" had moved the genre further into the marketplace.[40]

One of the more obvious results of this movement was the continued sensationalization of the narratives. The depiction of crime, including violent scenes, became more graphic and thus more shocking. Ironically, as the narratives moved readers closer to the scenes of the crimes, the more they came to resemble their English counterparts; the genre that had been developed carefully by New England ministers to combat worldliness eventually returned to Grub Street, where truth was less an eternal verity than a commercial commodity (Faller 69).[41] Both the Wilson text, by confronting readers with the violent details of the double murder, and the Mountain text, by offering them glimpses of the criminal underworld, demonstrated narrative tendencies that came to characterize English texts earlier in the eighteenth century. Similarly, both *The Confession, &c. of Thomas Mount* (Newport, 1791) and *The Confession and Dying Words of Samuel Frost* (Worcester, 1793) also reflected English textual characteristics.

As indicated in the conventionalization of the title (*&c.*), the Mount text revealed more sin than sincerity. A thief executed in Rhode Island, Mount—as he was depicted—made use of his narrative opportunity to document the development of a criminal underworld in colonial America, a world complete with its own culture and language. Similar to Joseph Mountain, Mount abandoned all loyalties and relations and, once immersed in an antithetical society of thieves and pickpockets, he expressed a determination "to arrive at the head of . . . [his] profession" (311). Arriving at the gallows instead, he expressed the usual fears of an "ignominious death," but instead of grasping at the conventions of a last minute conversion, he stated that "nothing can cure . . . [thieves] but the gallows.—I

[40] In *Revolution And The Word,* Cathy Davidson described the "revolution in words" as one of the primary social, cultural, and political transformations that took place during the late eighteenth century. In addition to Davidson's study, see William J. Gilmore, Richard D. Brown (both *Modernization* and *Knowledge Is Power*), and Hall *World of Wonder.*

[41] For a recent discussion of English criminal narratives, see Lincoln Faller's *Turned to Account.* According to Professor Faller, criminal characters were depicted as "either of two myths of crime": "where the one myth was in fact a species of spiritual biography, the other imitated the picaresque novel" (2, 3). In the former the character was presented as a sincere convert, and the narrative related the familiar story of the struggle for salvation; while in the latter he or she concentrated on the more sensational story of survival in a corrupt, competitive world. When New England ministers first began to shape criminals for American readers, the first of Faller's "myths" obviously dominated narrative strucure. Criminals told the story of their spiritual lives. But as the culture developed along more secular lines, the second "myth" came more to be articulated.

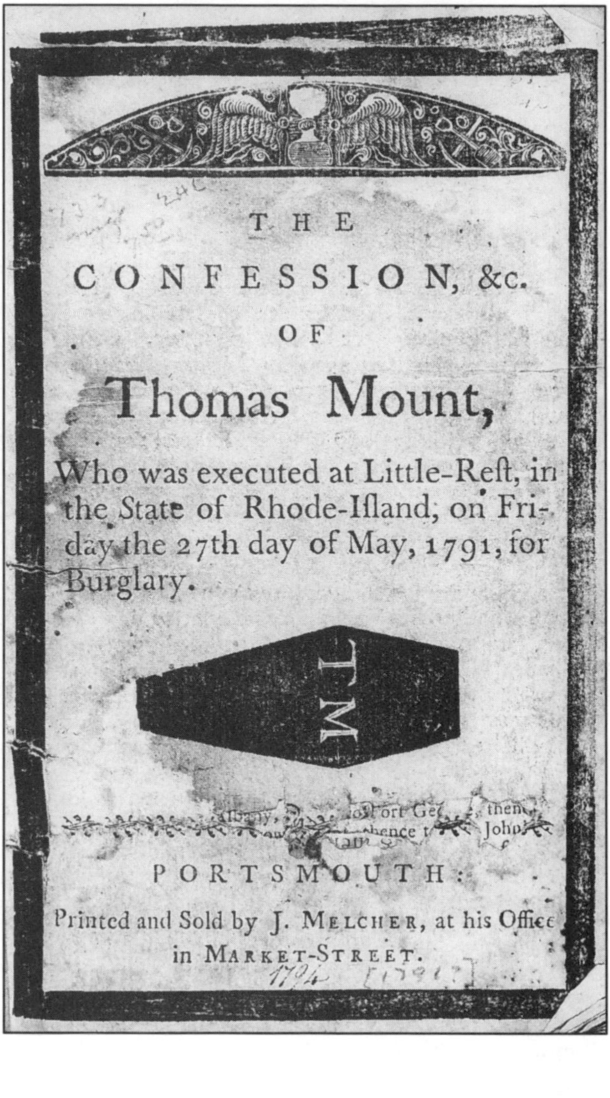
THE

CONFESSION, &c.

OF

Thomas Mount,

Who was executed at Little-Reſt, in the State of Rhode-Iſland, on Friday the 27th day of May, 1791, for Burglary.

TM

PORTSMOUTH:

Printed and Sold by J. MELCHER, at his Office in MARKET-STREET.

never heard of a thief that was reclaimed but one, and that under such circumstances as never can be the lot of any other thief to the end of the world" (323–24). Rather than submerging the self within the trope of the Penitent Thief, Mount denied the possibilities of repentance, and after affirming his wickedness, he used his "last words" to titillate readers with "the language and songs of the American Flash Company" (322). At the same time, he aroused both fear and fascination by claiming that this criminal underworld "if suffered to remain would destroy the rising crop of young fellows throughout the continent" (322). Not only did the narrative conclude with this wild alarm, but it also stirred up such anxiety in the beginning. While justifying his participation in the production of the text, William Smith, the Newport minister who visited the condemned criminal during his final confinement, engaged reader attention by declaring that Mount and his partner, both "noted villains," alone "were sufficient to contaminate all the unwary youth upon the continent" (309).

In the Frost text, readers encountered a murderer who not only destroyed life but who also destroyed the most sacred of family bonds. Not once, but twice Frost committed patricide, murdering first his father and then later his guardian. In the first paragraph of his broadside, he bluntly admitted his first breaking of kindred ties and skulls. Stating that his father abused his mother, he declared: "this induced me to kill him, which deed I executed . . . as we were digging a ditch together; I knocked him down with a handspike, and then beat his brains out" (337). Believing that he was being treated "as a slave," Frost repeated the same bloody attack on his guardian a decade later (338). While in the garden planting cabbages, he waited until his victim was "stooping to fix a plant" and then "gave him a blow with the hoe on his head, and repeated it" (338). Despite the pleas of his guardian, he "continued repeating the blows" until the man was dead (339). Emotionless, he added: "I had beaten his head so as it had made a large hole in the ground and his brains came out" (339). The narrative, however, did not simply present the gruesome details of the patricides; in order to satisfy readers who hungered for a closer view of murderer, a separate "ACCOUNT" was added after the condemned man concluded his confession.

Intended to shock readers further, the supplement stated that "Frost was certainly an extraordinary character—his mind was evidently not formed like those of other persons" (339). The primary reason for separating him from the rest of humanity was his total lack of recognition that murder, indeed patricide, was wrong: "he thought it no great crime to kill such as he supposed treated him ill" (339). As evidence of this "savage heart," the text stated that "he would talk with the same calmness and composure of the horrid Murders he had committed, as though the persons who fell sacrifice to his fury, had been of the brutal creation" (339). Yet the narrative emphasized that Frost, and not his father-victims, belonged to "brutal creation." In concluding the "Account," and thus leaving readers with a final, definitive perspective, the text offered:

> On the whole, as a man, he was savage—void of all the finer feelings of the soul, and destitute of the tender affections of filial love and grati-

> tude—He appears to have been cast in a different mould from those of mankind in general, and to be the connecting grade between the human and brutal creation (340).

Such a depiction stressed that Frost, a mere brute, was not even remotely aware of the bonds that held his society together. By spilling the blood of his blood relations, he destroyed the foundations of his social order, and consequently his crimes carried sensational significance for readers, since both they and he inhabited a patriarchal world where the authority of fathers represented all power structures. Frost relativized his world; after deciding for himself what was right and what was wrong, he passed judgment and exacted the ultimate penalty. No wonder the narrative commented that "he was a most dangerous person to society."

By bringing to life the dying words of such "extraordinary" criminals, the genre began to develop an entirely new set of conventions. Established by popular taste, these new conventions required figures larger than life, stressing the dissimilarities—and not the similarities—between readers and transgressors. Whereas the ministers in the early narratives emphasized the convergence between the condemned and the living in universal sin, the later narratives dramatized the distance between the two. For the most part, criminal characters were still evil, but evilness became both a marginal and racial attribute, and what compelled readers to keep reading was the defiant strangeness of the figures. As the genre spread throughout the new regional and cultural landscape of the United States, as both the number of texts and sources of publication increased, criminal characters continued to challenge traditional conceptions of order and authority, and their challenges offered readers the thrills of vicarious (and safe) defiance.

In his analysis of the complex social functions involved in rituals of execution, Foucault commented that capital punishment "did not reestablish justice; it reactivated power" (49). The most crucial part of this reactivation was demonstrating "the dissymmetry between the subject who has dared to violate the law and the all-powerful sovereign who displays his strength" (49). Yet the culture of Revolutionary America had defied this concept of "dissymmetry," not only reducing "the irreversible imbalance of forces" between subjects and sovereigns but also undermining the whole notion of political sovereignty (50). In order to justify its opposition to a king, God's chosen representative on earth, American patriots altered traditional perspectives, transforming sovereignty into tyranny and privileging defiance as a socially useful act. What was traditionally the most egregious of crimes, treason, became a test of loyalty once the new lines were drawn—or rather blurred.

The representation of criminal characters reflected the blurred lines between the condemnation and celebration of defiance. Just as the relationship between those who ruled and those who were ruled became destabilized, so too did the literary absolutes of crime and punishment. What Foucault called "an equivoval attitude" always had been inherent in the gallows speeches of condemned (65). By advertising his or her crimes, by raising mundane antisocial acts to "epic proportions," criminal narratives risked transforming the condemned into heroes (66). In early America, where a cultural ambivalence wavered between deference and defiance, this risk was even greater. The ministers themselves had converted malefactors into martyrs and had presented them to readers as protagonists of a heroic struggle. Once secularized, the same rhetorical framework was used to dramatize crime as a conflict of the individual against society, and at times the narratives specifically stated that society was not always right. Reflecting much wider cultural uncertainties about authority, criminal narratives became a textual battleground where differing conceptions of crime competed for the attention of readers, and at the center of this battle, in effect the territory to be conquered, was the criminal character.[42]

[42] In addition to those works previously cited, the following texts are recommended for those interested in the critical discussion of crime and criminal literature: Bethke, Botein, Burke, Chandler, Chapin, Cockburn, Cohen, Davis, Elliott, Faber, Franklin, Ferguson, Fitzroy, Greenberg, Harris, Haskins, Hay et al., Hibbert, Hobsbawm, Konig, Lane, Lazenby, McDade, Macfarlane and Harrison, Marcus, Minnick, Murrin, Nelson, Neuburg (both *Popular Literature* and "Chapbooks"), Powers, Scott, Sharpe (both *Crime* and "Last Dying Speeches"), Slotkin, Smith et al., Walker, and Zanger. I have found Louis P. Masur's *Rites of Execution* to be especially helpful.

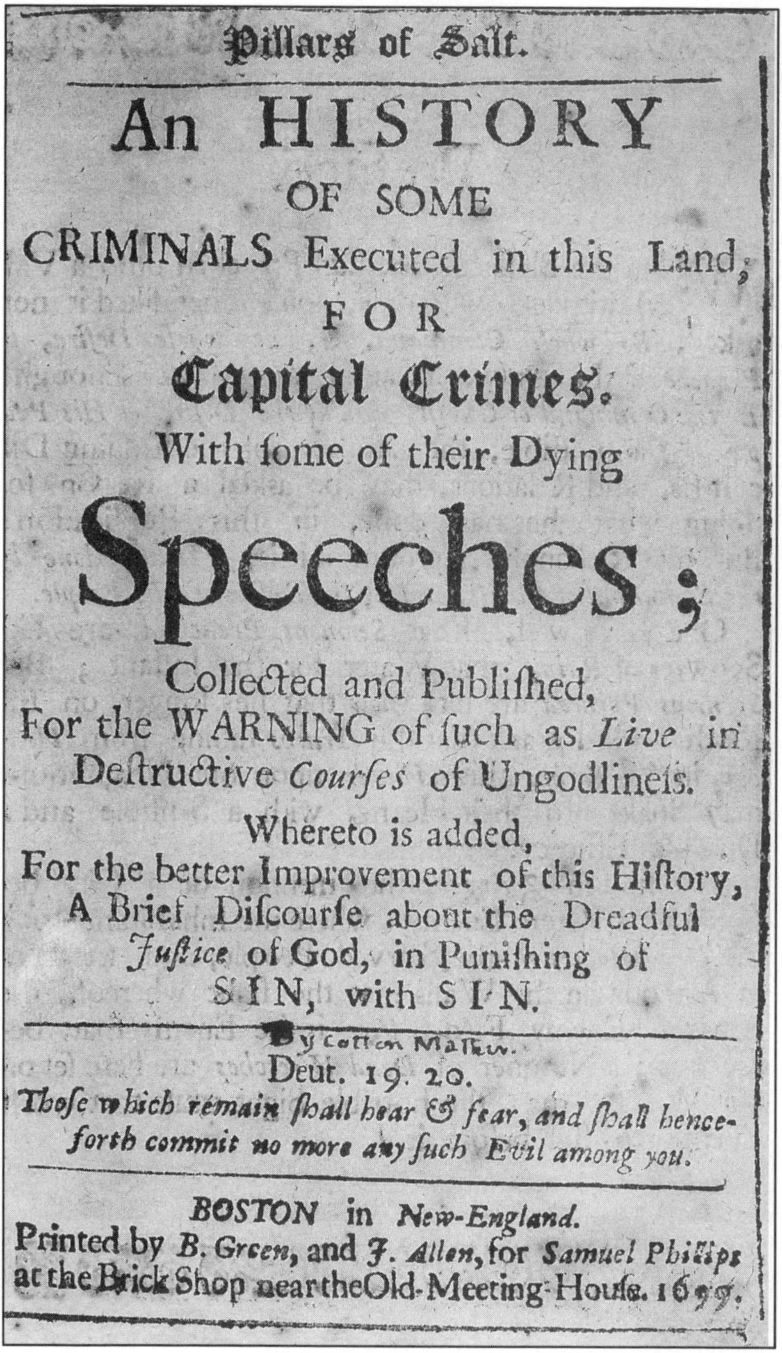

Pillars of Salt.

An HISTORY
OF SOME
CRIMINALS Executed in this Land,
FOR
Capital Crimes.
With some of their Dying
Speeches;
Collected and Published,
For the WARNING of such as *Live* in
Destructive *Courses* of Ungodliness.
Whereto is added,
For the better Improvement of this History,
A Brief Discourse about the Dreadful
*Justice* of God, in Punishing of
SIN, with SIN.

By Cotton Mather.

Deut. 19. 20.
*Those which remain shall hear & fear, and shall henceforth commit no more any such Evil among you.*

*BOSTON* in *New-England.*
Printed by *B. Green*, and *J. Allen*, for *Samuel Phillips*
at the Brick Shop near the Old-Meeting-House. 1699.

# [ COTTON MATHER ]

# *Pillars of Salt*

## [ 1699 ]

It hath been Thought, that the *Dying Speeches* of such as have been Executed among us, might be of singular Use, to Correct and Reform, the *Crimes*, wherein too many do *Live*; and it has been wish'd, that at Least, some Fragments of those *Dying Speeches*, might be preserved and published. Upon this Advice, from some *Good Persons*, I have Stollen an Hour or Two, wherein I have Collected some Accounts, of several *Ill Persons*, which have been Cut off, by the Sword of *Civil Justice* in this Land: and this Collection, I suffer to go abroad, in Hopes, that among many other *Essayes* to Suppress *growing Vice*, it may signifie something, with the Blessing of Heaven thereupon, to let the *Vicious* understand, what have been the Cries of our Miserables, when passing into another World. Behold, an *History of Criminals*, whom the Terrible Judgments of God have *Thunder struck*, into PILLARS OF SALT.

### I

About the Year, 1646, here was one *Mary Martin*, whose Father going from hence to *England*, Left her in the House of a Married Man, who yet became so Enamoured on *her*, that he attempted her Chastity.

Such was her Weakness and Folly, that she yielded unto the Temptations of that miserable man; but yet with such horrible Regret of Mind, that begging of God, for Deliverance from her Temptations, her plea was, *That if ever she were Overtaken again, she would Leave herself unto His Justice, to be made a publick Example.*

Heaven will convince the Sinful Children of men, that the *Vowes*, which they make, Relying on the Stability and Resolution of their own Hearts, are of no Significancy. A *Chain* of *Hell* was upon her, and the forfeited *Grace* of *Heaven* was witheld from her; She fell a *Third Time*, into the Sin, against which her *Vowes* had been uttered.

Afterwards, going to Service in *Boston*, she found her self to have Conceived: But she Lived with a favourable Mistress, who would admit and allow no suspicion of her *Dishonesty*,

A Question, Like that Convincing One, of our Saviours unto the Woman of *Samaria*, was once oddly put unto her; Mary, *Where is thy Husband*? And One said also; *Did I not think, thou wer't an honest and sincere Creature, I should verily think, thou wer't with Child*! These passages, which were warnings from God, unto her guilty Soul, did serve only to strike her with *Amazement*, not with any true *Repentance*.

She concealed her Crime, till the Time of her Delivery; and then, being Delivered alone, by her self in a Dark Room, She Murdered the harmless and helpless *Infant*; hiding it in a Chest, from the Eyes of all, but the Jealous GOD.

The *Blood* of the Child Cried, when the Cry of the Child it self were thus cruelly stifled. Some circumstance quickly occurr'd, which obliged her Friends to charge her with an *Unlawful Birth*. She Denied it Impudently. A further Search confuted her Denial. She then said; *The Child was Dead Born, and she had Burnt it to Ashes*. With an Hypocritical Tear, she added, *Oh! that it were True, that the poor Babe were any where to be seen*! At Last it was found in her Chest; & when she Touch'd the *Face* of it before the Jury, the *Blood* came fresh into it. So She confessed the whole Truth concerning it.

Great Endeavours were used, That she might be brought unto a True Faith in the *Blood* of the Lord Jesus Christ, for the pardon of her *Blood guiltiness*; and it may be, none Endeavoured it more, than that Reverend man, Old Mr. *Wilson*, who Wrote several Sheets of pathetical Instructions to her, while She was in Prison. That Renowned Man, Old Mr. *Cotton* also, did his part in endeavouring that she might be Renewed by Repentance; and Preached a Sermon, on Ezek. 16. 20, 21. *Is this of thy Whoredoms a small matter, That thou hast Slain my Children*? Whereof great Notice was taken. It was hoped, that these Endeavours were not Lost: Her Carriage in her Imprisonment, and at her Execution, was very *Penitent*. But there was this Remarkable at her Execution: She acknowledged, her *Twice* Essaying to Kill her Child, before she could make an End of it; and now, through the Unskilfulness of the Executioner, she was turned off the Ladder *Twice*, before She Dyed.

## II

There was a miserable man, at *Weymouth*; who fell into very ungodly practices: but would particularly Signalize his ungodliness, by flouting at those *Fools* (as he call'd 'em) who would ever *Confess* any Sins, laid unto their Charge.

This man lived in abominable *Adulteries*; but God at len[g]th smote him with a *Palsey*. His *Dead Palsey* was accompanied with a *Quick Conscience*, which compelled him to Confess his Crimes: But, he Confess'd them so Indiscreetly, that by their Divulgation, they reach'd the Ears of the Authority: And in this Confession, there was involv'd and concern'd, the Wretched Woman, who chiefly had been concern'd with him in the Transgression.

By the Law of this Country, *Adultery* was then a *Capital* Transgression, as it hath been in many other Countrys: and this poor *Adulterer*, could not escape the Punishment which the Law provided.

## III

On *June* 6. 1662. At *New-haven*, there was a most Unparallel'd Wretch, One *Potter*, by Name, about Sixty years of Age, Executed for Damnable *Bestialities*; although this Wretch, had been for now Twenty years, a Member of the Church in that Place, and kept up among the Holy People of God there, a Reputation, for Serious Christianity. It seems that the *Unclean Devil*, which had thc possession of this Monster, had carried all his Lusts with so much Fury into this One Channel of Wickedness, that there was no Notice taken of his being Wicked in any other. Hence t'was, that he was *Devout* in Worship, *Gifted* in Prayer, *Forward* in Edifying Discourse among the Religious, and *Zealous* in Reproving the Sins of the other People; Every one counted him, *A Saint*: And he Enjoy'd such a *Peace* in his own mind, that in several Fits of Sickness, wherein he seem'd *Nigh unto Death*, he seem'd *Willing to Dy*; Yea, *Death* (he said) *Smiled on him*. Nevertheless, this Diabolical Creature, had Lived in most infandous *Buggeries* for no less than Fifty years together; and now at the Gallows, there were killed before his Eyes, a *Cow*, Two *Heifers*, Three *Sheep*, and Two *Sowes*, with all of which he had Committed his *Brutalities*. His *Wife* had seen him Confounding himself with a *Bitch*, Ten years before; and he then Excused his Filthiness, as well as he could, unto her, but Conjured her to keep it Secret: but he afterwards Hanged that Bitch himself, and then Returned unto his former Villanies, until at last, his *Son*, saw him hideously conversing with a *Sow*. By these means, the burning *Jealousy* of the Lord Jesus Christ, at Length *made the Churches to know*, that He had all this while seen the Covered Filthiness of this Hellish Hypocrite, and Exposed him also to the Just Judgment of Death, from the Civil Court of Judicature. Very Remarkable had been the Warnings, which this *Hell-Hound*, had Received from Heaven, to Repent of his Impieties. Many years before this, he had a Daughter, who Dreamt a *Dream,* which caused her, in her Sleep, to cry out, most Bitterly; and her Father, then with much ado obtaining of her, to tell her *Dream,* She told him, she Dream't, that she was among a great Multitude of People, to see an *Execution*, and it prov'd her own *Father* that was to be hang'd, at whose Turning over, she thus cried out. This happened before the Time, that any of his Cursed Practices were known unto her! At another Time, when there was a Malefactor adjudged in those parts to Dy, for the very same Transgressions, which this Rotten Fellow was guilty of, the Governour, with some of the Magistrates, most unaccountably, without any manner of Reason, for their so doing, turn'd about unto this Fellow, and said, *What think You? Is not this man worthy to Dy?* He now Confessed, That these Warnings did so awaken his Conscience, as to make him, for a Time, Leave off his Infernal Debauches; and so, he said, *He thought all was Pardoned, all was well with him*. Nevertheless, he Return'd unto his *Vomit*, and his *Quagmire*, until the Sentence of Death, at last fell upon him; and then he acknowledged, That he had Lived in the Sin of *Bestiality*, ever since he was Ten years Old, but had sometimes Intermitted the Perpetration of it, for some years together. During his Imprisonment, he continued in a *Sottish*, and *Stupid*, frame of Spirit, and marvellously *Secure* about his Everlasting *Pardon* and *Welfare*: but the Church whereto he belonged, kept a Solemn Day of *Humiliation* on this Occasion, wherein Mr. *Davenport* Preached on Josh. 22. 20: *Did not Achan Commit a Trespass, in the Accursed Thing, and Wrath fell on all the Congregation of Israel?* And in the close of the *Fast*, that Faithful People of God, Excommunicated this *Accursed Achan*, from their own Society. But as I have seen *Bewitched Self Poisoners*, under a Singular Energy of some *Devil*, obstinately Refuse all offered Relief, until the Poisons had prevailed so far, that all Relief was too late, and then with roaring Agonies they would have given Ten Worlds for it; So this *Bewitched Beast*, that had not been afraid of Dying, till he came to the Place of Execution, when he came *There*, he was Awakened into a most Unutterable and Intolerable Anguish of Soul, and made most Lamentably Desperate Out cries; Among which Out cries, he warned men, particularly, to *Take heed of Neglecting Secret Prayer*; which he said, *had been his Bane*. He said, he never used *Secret Prayer* in his Life, and that he frequently omitted *Family Prayer* too; Yet, he said, he had *Prayed* and

*Sinned*, and *Sinned* and *Prayed*; namely, by *Ejaculations*, with which he contented himself, throwing *Set Prayer* aside. But so he Perished!

## IV

An English Ship, (in the year 1673) Sailing from somewhere about the Mouth of the *Streights*, was Manned, with some Cruel Miscreants, who quarrelling with the Master and some of the Officers, turn'd 'em all into the *Long-Boat*, with a Small Quantity of Provisions, about an Hundred Leagues, to the Westward of the *Spanish Coast*.

These Fellows, in the mean while, set Sail for *New England*: where, by a Surprizing providence of God, the Master, with his Afflicted Company, in the Long-boat, also arrived; all, Except one who dyed of the Barbarous Usage.

The Countenance of the *Master*, was now become Terrible to the Rebellious *Men*, who, though they had *Escaped the Sea*, yet *Vengeance would not suffer to Live a Shore*. At his Instance and Complaint, they were Apprehended; and the Ringleaders of this Murderous Pyracy, had a Sentence of Death Executed on them, in *Boston*.

Under that Sentence, there was heard among them, a grievous Lamentation for This; *Their Education had been under the means of Grace, and the faithful Preaching of the Gospel in* England; *but they had Sinned against that Education*.

And one of them sadly Cryed out, *Oh! 'Tis my Drunkenness, 'Tis my Drunkenness, that hath brought me to this Lamentable End*!

The Horrors, which attended the Chief of these Malefactors (one *Forrest*) in the last Hours of his Life, were such as Exceedingly astonished the Beholders. Though he were a very stout man; yet now his Trembling Agonies and Anguishes, were inexpressible. One Speech let fall by him, was, *I have been among drawn Swords, flying bullets, roaring Canons, amidst all which, I knew not what Fear meant*; *but now I have Apprehensions of the dreadful wrath of God*, *in the other World*, *which I am going into*, *my Soul within me*, *is amazed at it*.

## V

On *March* 18. 1674. two men, (whose Names were *Nicholas Feavour*, and *Robert Driver*) were Executed at *Boston*. The Crime for which they were Executed, was, the Murther of their Master; whom, upon the Provocation of some Chastisement, which he had given them, they knock'd on the Head, with an Axe, in their Bloody Rage.

After they were Condemned, they bestow'd their Lamentations not only, on the *Particular Crime*, which had now brought them, to their *Untimely End*, but also on some *Others*, for which their Consciences told them, that the Righteous God, had left them unto *This*.

One of them, said, His *Pride* had been his *Bane*; For, he thought much of it, that such a one as *he*, should be a *Servant*; and he would sometimes utter such words as these, *I am Flesh and Blood, as well as my Master, and therefore I know no Reason, why my Master should not obey me, as well as I obey him.* And now, said he, *See what my Pride has brought me to*!

One of them also, said, That his *Idleness* had Ruin'd him: He would not Industriously follow his Calling, but Live an Idle, Slothful, Vagrant Life. *This*, he said, had undone him.

And one of them, said, That his *Disobedience to his Parents*, had brought this misery upon him. His *Father*, he said, gave him Good Instructions, when he was a Child: but he Regarded them not. He would not go to a *School*, when his *Father* would have sent him to it. He would not go to a *Trade*, when his *Father* would have put him to one. After his *Father* was Dead, he would not be Subject unto them that had the Charge of him; he ran away from *Them*; and after that, he ran away from several *Masters*. Thus he *Ran* into the Jaws of Death.

These things are particularized, in the Sermon Preach'd just before their Execution; and afterwards Printed under the Title of, *The Wicked mans Portion.*

## VI

On *Sept.* 22. 1681. One *W. C.* was Executed at *Boston*, for a *Rape* committed by him, on a Girl, that Lived with him; though he had then a Wife with Child by him, of a Nineteenth or Twentieth Child.

This man, had been *Wicked Overmuch*. His *Parents*, were Godly Persons; but *he* was a *Child of Belial*. He began Early, to Shake off his Obedience unto *Them*; and Early had *Fornication* laid unto his Charge; after which, he fled unto a dissolute Corner of the Land, a place whereof it might be said, *Surely, the Fear of God, is not in this Place*: He being a Youth, under the Inspection of the Church at *Roxbury*, they, to win him, invited him to Return unto his Friends, with such Expressions of *Lenity* towards him, that the Reverend Old Man, their Pastor, in a Sermon, on the Day when this man was Executed, with Tears bewayled it.

After this, he Lived very Dissolutely, in the Town of *Dorchester*; where, in a Fit of Sickness, he *Vow'd*, That if God would Spare his Life, he would Live as a *New Man*: but he horribly forgot his *Vows*. The Instances of his Impiety, grew so Numerous and Prodigious, that the wrath of God could bear no longer with him: he was *Ripened* for the Gallows.

After his Condemnation, he Vehemently Protested his *Innocency*, of the Fact, for which he was Condemned; but he Confessed, *That God was Righteous, thus to bring Destruction upon him, for Secret Adulteries.*

A *Reprieve* would have been obtained for him, if his foolish and froward Refusing to hear a *Sermon* on the Day appointed for his Execution, had not hardened the Hearts of the *Judges* against him. *He*, who had been a great *Scoffer* at the *Ordinances* of God, now Expos'd himself, by being Left unto such a Sottish Action!

He had horribly slighted all calls to *Repentance*, and now through some Wretches over-perswading of him, that he should not Dy, according to Sentence & Order of the Court, he hardened himself still, in his *unrepentant* frame of mind.

When he came to the Gallowes, and saw *Death* (and a Picture of *Hell* too, in a *Negro* then *Burnt* to *Death* at the Stake, for *Burning* her Masters House, with some that were in it,) before his Face, never was a Cry, for, *Time*! *Time*! *A World for a Little Time*! *the Inexpressible worth of Time*! Uttered, with a more unutterable Anguish.

He then Declared, *That the greatest Burden then Lying upon his miserable Soul, was his having Lived so unprofitably under the Preaching of the Gospel.*

## VII

On *March* 11. 1686. was Executed at *Boston*, one *James Morgan*, for an horrible *Murder*. A man, finding it necessary to come into his House, he Swore he would *Run a Spit into his Bowels*; and he was as bad as his word.

He was a *passionate* Fellow; and now, after his Condemnation, he much bewayl'd, his having been given to *Cursing*, in his passions.

The Reverend Person who Preached, unto a great Assembly, on the Day of this poor mans Execution, did in the midst of his Sermon take occasion, to Read a Paper, which he had Received from the Malefactor, then present in the Assembly. It was as followeth.

I *James Morgan*, being Condemned to Dye, must needs own to the glory of God, that He is righteous, and that I have by my sins, provoked Him to destroy me before my time. I have been a great Sinner, guilty of Sabbath-breaking, of Lying, and of Uncleanness; but there are especially two Sins whereby I have offended the Great God; one is that Sin of Drunkenness, which has caused me to commit many other Sins; for when in Drink, I have been often guilty of Cursing and Swearing, and quarrelling, and striking others: But the Sin which lies most heavy upon my Conscience, is, that I have despised the Word of God, and many a time refused to hear it preached. For these things, I believe God has left me to that, which has brought me to a shameful and miserable death. I do therefore beseech and warn all persons, young men especially, to take heed of these Sins, lest they provoke the Lord to do to them as He has justly done by me. And for the further peace of my own Conscience, I think my self obliged to add this unto my foregoing Confession, That *I own the Sentence* which the Honoured Court has *pass'd upon me*, to be exceeding just; inasmuch as (tho' I had no former Grudge and Malice against the man whom I have killed, yet) my Passion at the time of the Fact was so outragious, as that it hurried me on to the doing of that which makes me justly now proceeded against as a Murderer.

After the Sermon, a Minister, at his Desire, went unto the place of Execution with him. And of what passed by the way, there was a Copy taken; which here Ensueth.

## *The DISCOURSE of the* MINISTER *with* JAMES MORGAN, *on the way to his Execution.*

MIN. I'm come hither to answer your desires which just now you exprest to me in the Publick, that I would give you my company at your Execution.

MOR. *Dear Sir, how much am I beholden to you! you have already done a great deal for me. Oh who am I that I have been such a vile wretch, that any Servants of God should take notice of me!*

MIN. I beseech you to make this use of it, I believe there is not one Christian this day beholding you, who would not willingly be at the greatest pains they could devise to save your precious Soul: How merciful then is that *Man* who is *God* as well as man! how unspeakably ready is the Lord Christ to save the Souls of sinners that affectionately *Look* unto him! The goodness and pitifulness of the most tender-hearted man in the world is but a shadow of what is in *Him*. The compassions of any man compared with the Bowels of a merciful *JESUS* are but as the painted Sun, or the painted Fire in comparison of the real.

MOR. *Oh that I could now look unto Him as I ought to do! Lord help me.*

MIN. Well, you are now a dying man, the last hour or two of your life is now running. You know your self now to stand just on the brink of Eternity; you shall presently be in a state of wonderful happiness or of horrible misery which must endure forever: which of those estates do you now count yourself stepping into?

MOR. *Oh Sir, I am afraid, but I am not without hope that God may have mercy on me.*

MIN. What's your ground for that hope? O see that your confidences been't such as God will by and by reject.

MOR. *I don't know well what to say, but this I hope is a good sign, I have lived in many grievous sins, in* Lying, Drinking, Sabbath-breaking, and *evil* Company-keeping; *God has made now these so bitter to my soul, that I would not commit them again, might I have my life this afternoon by doing it.*

MIN. That's a great word, God grant it may not be a word only, the good word of a good pang, without such a thro' change of heart, as you must have if you would not perish everlastingly. You are not like to have any longer time in this world to try the Sincerity of your Profession.

MOR. *I know it, and I beseech you Sir to help me what you can: I hope the means used with me since my Condemnation ha'n't been lost.*

MIN. I would not have the sence of the pain and shame which your body is about to undergoe, any ways hinder your mind from being taken up about the Soul matters which I shall endeavour to set before you.

MOR. *Sir, as for the pain that my body must presently feel, I matter it not: I know what pain is; but what shall I do for my poor Soul? I'm terrify'd with the Wrath of God; This, this terrifyes me, Hell terrifyes me: I should not mind my Death, if it were not for that.*

MIN. Now the Lord help me to deal faithfully with you, and the Lord help you to receive what he shall enable me to offer unto you. Mark what I say: You were born among the enemies of God, you were born with a soul as full of enmity against God, as a Toad is full of poison. You have liv'd now, how many years?

MORG. *I think about Thirty.*

MIN. And all these thirty years have you been sinning against the Holy God. Ever since you knew how to do any thing, you have every day been guilty of innumerable sins; you deserve the dreadful wrath and curse of the infinite God. But God has brought you here, to a place where you have enjoy'd the means of Grace. And here you have added unto your old Sins, most fearful Iniquities: you have been such a matchless, prodigious Transgressor, that you are now to Dy by the stroke of civil Justice; to *Dy before your time, for being wicked overmuch.* There is hardly any sort of Wickedness which you have not wallowed in. That Sin particularly which you are now to Dy for, is a most monstrous Crime. I can't possibly describe or declare the sins whereby you have made your self an astonishing Example of Impiety and punishment.

MOR. *O Sir, I have been a most hellish Sinner. I am sorry for what I have been.*

MIN. Sorry, you say: well, tell me, which of all your sins you are now most sorry for, which lies most heavy.

MOR. *I hope I am sorry for all my sins, but I must especially bewail my neglect of the means of Grace. On Sabbath dayes I us'd to lye at home, or be ill imploy'd elsewhere when I should have been at Church.* This has undone me!

MIN. And let me seriously tell you, your despising of Christ is a most dreadful sin indeed. You have for whole years together had the Call of Jesus Christ to seek an Interest in him, and you would now give all the world for that Interest, but you would take no notice of him. The Jews of Old put him to a worse death than yours will be this afternoon; and by your contempt of Christ you have said, the Jews did well to do so. How justly might he now laugh at your Calamity? And for these sins of yours, besides the direful woes and plagues that have already come upon you, you are now expos'd unto the Vengeance of eternal fire. You are in danger of being now quickly cast into those exquisite amazing Torments, in comparison of which, the anguishes which your body ever did feel, or shall feel before night, or can ever feel, are just nothing at all; and these dolorous torments are such as never had an End; as many sands as could lie between this earth and the Stars in Heaven would not be near so many as the Ages, the endless Ages of these Torments.

MOR. *But is there not Mercy for me in Christ?*

MIN. Yes, and its a wonderful thing that I have now further to tell you. Mind, I entreat you. The Son of God is become the Son of Man; the Lord Jesus Christ is both God & Man in one Person, and he is both sufficiently able & willing also, to be your Saviour. He lived a most righteous life, & this was that such as you and I might be able to say before God, *Lord, accept of me as if I had lived righteously.* He dyed at length a most cursed death, and this was that we might be able to say unto God, *Lord, let me not dye for Sin, since thy Son has dyed in my room.* This glorious Redeemer is now in the highest Heaven, pleading with God for the Salvation of His Chosen ones.—And he pours out his Spirit continually upon them that do believe on him: might you then be enabled by his Grace to carry your poor, guilty, condemned, enslaved, ignorant Soul unto Jesus Christ, and humbly put your trust in him for deliverance from the whole bad state which you are brought into. Oh then his voice is to you the same that was to the penitent Thief, *This day shalt thou be with me in Paradise.*

MOR. *Oh that I might be so! Sir, I would hear more of these things: I think, I can't better fit my self for my Death than by hearkening to these things.*

MIN. Attend then: The never-dying Spirit that lodges within you, must now within a few minutes appear before the Tribunal of the Great GOD; in what, or in whose Righteousness will you then appear? will you have this to be your Plea, *Lord, I experienced many good Motions & Desires in my Soul, and many sorrows for my sin before I dy'd*: or will you expect to have no other Plea but This, *Lord, I am vile, but thy Son is a Surety for the worst of Sinners that believe on Him*; *for his sake alone, have M E R C Y on me* .

MOR. *I thank God for what He has wrought in my Soul.—*

MIN. But be very careful about this matter: if you build on your own good Affections instead of Jesus Christ the only Rock, if you think they shall recommend you to God, *He that made you will not have mercy on you* .

MOR. *I would be clothed with the Righteousness of J E S U S C H R I S T.*

MIN. But you can't sincerely desire that Christ should justify you, if you don't also desire that He should sanctify you: those two always go together. Is every lust that has hitherto had possession of your heart become so loathsome to you, that it would fill your Soul with joy to hear Jesus Christ say, *I will subdue those Iniquities of thine*; *I will make a holy, an heavenly, a spiritually minded person of thee.*

MOR. *I would not Sin against God any more.*

MIN. But I must deal plainly with you: You have made it sadly suspicious that your repentance is not yet as it ought to be: when men truly & throughly repent of sin, they use to be in a special manner watchful against that Sin which has been their chief Sin: one of your principal sins which has indeed brought you to the Death of a *Murderer*, is *Passion*, unmortifi'd and outragious *Passionateness*: Now I have been this day informed, that no longer since than the last night, upon some Dissatisfaction about the place which the Authority hath ordered you by and by to be buried in, you did express your self with a most unruly Passionateness.

MOR. *Sir, I confess it, and I was quickly sorry for it, tho' for the present I was too much disturbed*: '*Twas my folly to be so careful about the place where my body should be laid, when my precious Soul was in such a Condition.—*

MIN. Truly you have cause to mourn for it. Secure the welfare of your soul, and this (now) pinion'd, hang'd, vile body of yours will shortly be raised unto glory, glory for evermore. And let me put you in mind of one thing more, I doubt you han't yet laid aside your unjust Grudges against the Persons concerned in your Conviction and Condemnation: You have no cause to complain of them: and you are not fit to pray, much less are you fit to dye, till you heartily wish them as well as your own soul: if you dy malicious, you die miserable.

MOR. *I heartily wish them all well, I bear Ill-will to none. What a lamentable thing is this*? *Ah this is that which has brought me hither*!

MIN. What do you mean?

MOR. *I over heard a man mocking and scoffing at me when I stumbled just now, he does very ill. I have done so my self. I have mock'd and scoff'd like that man, and see what it hath brought me to; he may come to the like.*

MIN. The Lord forgive that foolish hard hearted creature. But be not too much disturbed.

MOR. *Yonder! I am now come in sight of the place where I must immediately end my days.* Oh *what a huge Multitude of people is come together on this occasion.* O *Lord,* O *Lord, I pray thee to make my Death profitable to all this Multitude of People, that they may not sin against thee as I have done.*

MIN. Amen, Amen, ten thousand times; the Lord God Almighty say Amen to this Prayer of yours! It would indeed be an excellent thing if you would now come to receive your death with some satisfaction of soul in this thought, That much Glory is like to come to God by it: I am verily perswaded God intends to do good to many souls by means of your Execution: This a greater honour than you are worthy of.

(After the Discourse had been intermitted about a minute or two by reason of the miery way.)

MOR. *I beseech you Sir speak to me. Do me all the good you can: my time grows very short: your discourse fits me for my Death more than any thing.*

MIN. I am sorry so small a thing as a plashy Street should make me loose one minute of this more than ordinary precious time; a few paces more bring you to the place which you have now in your eye, from whence you shall not come back alive. Do you find your self afraid to dy there?

MOR. *Sir, if it were not for the Condition that my Soul must by and by be in, I should not fear my death at all; but I have a little comfort from some of Gods promises about that.*

MIN. And what shall I now say? These are among the last words that I can have liberty to leave with you. Poor man, thou art now going to knock at the door of Heaven, and to beg & cry, *Lord, Lord open to me*! The only way for thee to speed, is, to open the door of thy own soul now unto the Lord Jesus Christ. Do this, and thou shalt undoubtedly be admitted into the Glories of His Heavenly Kingdom: You shall fare as well as *Manasseh* did before you: leave this undone, and there's nothing remains for you but the *Worm which dyeth not, and the Fire which shall not be quenched.*

MOR. *Sir, shew me then again what I have to do.*

MIN. The voice, the sweet voice of the Lord Jesus Christ, (who was once hang'd on a tree, to take away the Sting and Curse of even such a Death as yours) unto all that close with him, His Heavenly voice now is, O that I and my saving work might be entertained, kindly entreated, in that poor perishing Soul of thine! Are you willing?

MOR. *I hope I am.*

MIN. His Voice further is, If I am lodged in thy Soul, I'le sprinkle my blood upon it, and on my account thou shalt find Favour with God. Do you consent to this?

MOR. *This I want.*

MIN. But this is not all that he saith, His Voice further is, If I come into thy Soul, I will change it, I will make all sin bitter to it, I will make it an holy heavenly soul. Do you value this above the proffers of all the World?

MOR. *I think I do,—and now Sir, I must go no further, Look here—what a solemn sight is this! Here lyes the Coffin which this Body of mine must presently be laid in. I thank you dear Sir, for what you have already done for me.*

MIN. When you are gone up this Ladder, my last Service for you, before you are gone off, will be to pray with you: but I would here take my leave of you. Oh that I might meet you at the Right Hand of the Lord Jesus in the Last Day. Farewell poor heart, Fare thee well. The Everlasting Arms receive thee! The Lord Jesus, the merciful Saviour of Souls take possession of they Spirit for himself. The Great God, who is a great Forgiver, grant thee Repentance unto Life; and Glorify Himself in the Salvation of such a wounded Soul as thine for ever. With Him, and with His free, rich, marvellous, Infinite Grace, I leave you. *Farewell.*

Being Arrived unto the place of Execution, his *Last Speech* upon the Ladder, then taken in Short-Hand, was that which is here inserted.

I Pray God that I may be a warning to you all, and that I may be the last that ever shall suffer after this manner: In the fear of God I warn you to have a care of taking the Lords Name in vain. Mind and have a care of that Sin of Drunkenness, for that Sin leads to all manner of Sins and Wickedness: (mind, and have a care of breaking the sixth Commandment, where it is said, *Thou shalt not do no Murder*) for when a man is in Drink, he is ready to commit all manner of Sin, till he fills up the cup of the wrath of God, as I have done by committing that Sin of Murder. I beg of God, as I am a dying man, and to appear before the Lord within a few minutes, that you may take notice of what I say to you. Have a care of drunkenness, and ill Company, and mind all good Instruction, and don't turn your back upon the Word of God, as I have done. When I have been at meeting, I have gone out of the Meeting-house to commit sin, and to please the lust of my flesh. Don't make a mock at any poor object of pity, but bless God that he has not left you as he had justly done me, to commit that horrid Sin of Murder. Another thing that I have to say to you is to have a care of that house where that wickedness was committed, and where I have been partly ruined by. But here I am, and know not what will become of my poor soul, which is within a few moments of eternity. I have murder'd a poor man, who had but little time to repent, and I know not what is become of his poor soul; Oh that I may make use of this Opportunity that I have! O that I may make improvement of this little little time, before I go hence and be no more. O let all mind what *I* am a saying now, I'm going out of this world. O take warning by me, and beg of God to keep you from this sin which has been my ruine. (His last words were) *O Lord, receive my Spirit, I come unto thee, O Lord, I come unto thee, O Lord, I come, I come, I come.*

## VIII

One *Hugh Stone*, upon a Quarrel, between himself & his Wife, about Selling a piece of Land, having some words, as they were walking together, on a certain Evening, very barbarously reached a stroke at her Throat, with a Sharp knife; and by that *One Stroke* fetch'd away the Soul, of her, who had made him a Father of several Children, and would have brought yet another to him, if she had lived a few weeks longer in the world. The wretched man, was too soon Surprised by his Neighbours, to be capable of Denying the Fact; and so he pleaded, *Guilty*, upon his Tryal.

There was a *Minister* that walk'd with him to his *Execution*; and I shall insert the principal Passages of the Discourse between them; in which the Reader may find or make something *useful* to himself, what ever it were to the Poor man who was more immediately concerned in it.

MINISTER. I am come to give you what Assistance I can, in your taking of the Steps, which your eternal *Weal* or *Woe*, now depends upon the well or ill taking of.

HUGH STONE. *Sir, I Thank you, and I beg you to do what you can for me.*

MIN. Within a very few Minutes your immortal Soul must appear before God *the Judge of all.* I am heartily sorry you have lost so much time since your first Imprisonment: you had need use a wonderful Husbandry of the little piece of an *Inch* which now remains. Are you now prepared to stand before the Tribunal of God?

H.S. *I hope I am.*

MIN. And what *Reason* for that *Hope*?

H.S. *I find all my Sins made so bitter to me, that if I were to have my life given me this Afternoon, to Live such a Life as I have Lived heretofore, I would not accept of it; I had rather Dy.*

MIN. That is *well*, if it be *True*. But suffer me a little to search into the Condition of your Soul. Are you sensible, That you were *Born* a Sinner? That the Guilt of the *First Sin* committed by *Adam*, is justly charged upon *you*? And that you have hereupon a *Wicked Nature* in you, full of Enmity against all that is *Holy, and Just, and Good*? For which you deserved to be destroyed, as soon as you first came into this world.

H.S. *I am sensible of this.*

MIN. Are you further sensible, that you have lived, a very ungodly Life? That you are guilty of thousands of *Actual Sins*, every one of which *deserves the Wrath and Curse of God, both in this Life, and that which is to come?*

H.S. *I am sensible of this also.*

MIN. But are you sensible, That you have broken *all* the *Laws* of God? You know the *Commandments*. Are you sensible, That you have broken every one of *Them*?

H.S. *I cannot well answer to that. My Answer may be liable to some Exceptions.—This I own, I have broken every Commandment on the Account mentioned by the Apostle* James; *that he who* breaks one is Guilty of all. *But not otherwise.*

MIN. Alas, That you know your self no better than so! I do affirm to you, that you have particularly broken *every one* of the Commandments; and you *must* be sensible of it.

H.S. *I cann't see it.*

MIN. But you must Remember, *That the Commandment is Exceeding Broad*; it reaches to the *Heart* as well as the *Life*: it excludes *Omissions* as well as *Commissions*, and it at once both *Requires* and *Forbids*. But I pray, make an experiment upon any *one* Commandment, in which you count your self most *Innocent*: and see whether you do not presently confess your self *Guilty* thereabout. I may not leave this point slightly passed over with you.

H.S. *That Commandment*, Thou shalt not make to thy self any Graven Image; *How have I broken it*?

MIN. Thus: You have had undue *Images* of God in your *Mind* a thousand times. But more than so; that Commandment not only *forbids* our using the *Inventions* of men in the worship of God, but it also *requires* our using all the *Institutions* of God. Now have not you many & many a time turned your back upon some of those glorious *Institutions*?

H.S. *Indeed, Sir, I confess it: I see my sinfulness greater than I thought it was.*

MIN. You ought to see it. God help you to see it! There is a *boundless Ocean* of it. And then for that SIN, which has now brought a shameful Death upon you, 'tis impossible to Declare the Aggravations of it; hardly an Age will show the like. You have professed your self *Sorry* for it!

H.S. *I am heartily so.*

MIN. But your Sorrows must be *after a Godly Sort*. Not meerly because of the miseries which it has brought on your *outward Man*, but chiefly for the *Wrongs* and *Wounds* therein given to your own Soul; and not only for the *Miseries* you have brought on your self, but chiefly for the *Injuries* which you have done to the Blessed God.

H.S. *I hope my Sorrow lies there.*

MIN. But do you mourn without Hope?

H.S. *I thank God, I do not.*

MIN. Where do you see a Door of Hope?

H.S. *In the Lord Jesus Christ, who has died to save Sinners.*

MIN. Truly, *There is no other Name by which we may be saved*? The Righteousness of the Lord Jesus Christ, is that alone, in which you may safely anon appear before the Judgment Seat of God. And that Righteousness is by the marvellous and infinite Grace of God, offered unto you. But do you find, that as you have no Righteousness, so you have no Strength? that you cannot of your self *move* or *stir*, towards the Lord Jesus Christ, though you *justly* perish if you do not *Run* unto Him? that it is the Grace of God alone which must enable you to accept of Salvation from the Great Saviour?

H.S. *Sir, my Case, in short, is This, I have laid my self at the Feet of the Lord Jesus Christ for my Salvation; and had it not been for His meer Grace and Help, I had never been able to do That. But there I have laid and left my self; I have nothing to plead, why he should accept of me. If He will do it, I am happy, but if He will not, I am undone for ever; it had been good for me that I never had been Born.*

MIN. And you must justifie Him if He should Reject you. You surprize me, with at once giving me so much of the Discourse, which all this while I have been labouring for. I can add but this: *The good Lord make you sincere in what you say*! —Your Crime lay in *Blood*; and your Help also, That lies in *Blood*. I am to offer you the *Blood* of the Lord Jesus Christ, as that in which you may now have the Pardon of all your sins. Now you may try the sincerity of your *Faith* in the Blood of the Lord Jesus for a Pardon, by this. Have you an *Hope* in that Blood, for all the other living effects of it? shall I explain what I mean?

H.S. *Do Sir.*

MIN. The Blood of the Lord Jesus is not only *Sin Pardoning* Blood, but also *Soul purifying*, and *Heart softening* Blood. It embitters all Sin unto the Soul, that it is applied unto, and mortifies every lust in such a Soul. Are you desirous of this?

H.S. *With all my Heart?*

MIN. The Lord make you so. The Lord *Seal* your *Pardon*, in that *Blood*, which is worth ten thousand Worlds! But what will you do for that God, who has given you these hopes of a *Pardon*? you must with a holy ingenuity

# Preface.

WHen the Bleſſed *Farel*, had Preached unto a Vaſt Multitude of People, ſome that liked it not, asked, *By whoſe Command, or, at whoſe Deſire, he Preached?* He Anſwered, and it was Anſwer Enough; *By the Command of Chriſt, and at the Deſire of His People.* 'Tis poſſible, the Author of the Enſuing Diſcourſes, and Relations; may be asked a Reaſon for doing what he has done, in this Publication: But his Reaſonable Account of it is, *'Tis all done by the Command of Chriſt, and at the Deſire of His People.*

One ſayes well, That *Sermons Preached*, are like Showres of *Rain*, that Water for the Inſtant; But *Sermons Printed*, are like *Snow* that lies longer on the Earth. God grant that the *Truths* falling from *Heaven*, in this *Form*, this *Winter* upon our Neighbours, may Soak into their Hearts, with a Senſible and a Durable Efficacy.

We find in *Zuinger*, the mention of a City beſieged by a Potent Enemy; where the Inhabitants took the *Dead Bodies* of the Starved People, and ſet them in Armour on the Walls; at the ſight whereof, the Amazed Enemy Fled. *Vice* is the Enemy that beſeiges us; a Number of *Dead Wretches* are here ſet on our Walls; may the horrible Sight cauſe that worſt Enemy to fly before it!

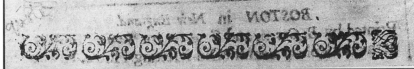

now do something for the Honour of that God, whom you have sinned so much against.

H.S. *What shall I do?*

MIN. Why, Confess and Bewail the Sins that have undone you, and publickly Advise, and Exhort, and Charge all that you can, to take heed of such evil ways.

H.S. *I will endeavor to do it as God shall help me.*

MIN. I pray tell me plainly what *special Sin*, do you think it was, that laid the first Foundation of your Destruction? where did you begin to leave God, and Ruine your self?

H.S. *It was Contention in my Family. I had been used unto something of Religion: and I was once careful about the Worship of God, not only with my Family, but in secret also. But upon Contention between me and my Wife, I left off the Wayes of God and you see what I am come to.*

MIN. I would pray you to Vomit up all Sin with a very hearty detestation. You are going (if I may so speak) to disgorge your Soul; if you do not first cast up your Sin, if your Soul and your Sin come away together, you cannot but know something of the dismal condition which it must pass into. O, what cause have you to fall out with Sin for ever? it has been your only Enemy. Here is the only Revenge which you may allow in your self. You must not now bear any Malice against any one man in the World, but forgive even those that have done you the greatest Injuries. Only upon Sin be as revengeful as you can; I would have you, like *Sampson*, so to Dy, taking of a just Revenge.

H.S. *I hope I shall.*

MIN. Well, we are now but a very few paces from the place, where you must breathe your last. You are just going to take a most awful Step, which has this most Remarkable in it, *That it cannot be twice taken.* If you go wrong now, it cannot be Recalled throughout the Dayes of a long Eternity. I can but commit you into the Arms of a Merciful Redeemer, that he may keep you from a Miscarriage, which cannot be recall'd and redress'd throughout Eternal Ages. The Lord show unto you the *Path of Life*! Attend unto these, as the last words that I may speak before the Prayer, with which I am immediately to take a long *Farewell* of you. You are not just going to be *Confirmed* for ever. If the Great God presently find you under the power of *Prejudice* against any of His Truths and Wayes, or of *Enmity* against what has His blessed Name upon it, you shall be fixed, and settled, & confirmed in it, until the very Heavens be no more. But they are very terrible *Plagues* and *Pains*, which you may be sure will accompany this everlasting Disposition of your Soul. On the other side, if God now find your Soul, under the power of Inclinations to *Love Him*, *Fear Him*, *Serve Him*; & to esteem the Lord Jesus Christ above a thousand Worlds; you shall then be *Confirmed* in the perfection of such a Temper, and of all the *Joy*, that must Accompany it. Which of these is the Condition that I now leave you in.

H.S. *Sir, I hope the latter of them.*

MIN. The Good God make it so; and grant that I may find you at the Right hand of the Lord Jesus, *in the Day of His Appearing*. May this *Ladder* prove as a *Jacobs Ladder* for you, and may you find the *Angels* of the Lord Jesus ready here to convey your departing Soul into the Presence of the Lord.

*After this Discourse; ascending the* Ladder, *he made the following Speech.*

*Young Men and Maids*; observe the Rule of Obedience to your Parents; and Servants to your Masters, according to the will of God, and to do the will of your Masters: you take up wicked ways, you set open a Gate to your *Sins*, to lead in bigger afterwards; thou can'st not do any thing but *God will see thee*, tho' thou thinkest thou shalt not be catched, thou thinkest to hide thy self in Secret, when as God in Heaven can see thee, though thou hast hid it from man. And when thou goest to *Thievery*, thy wickedness is discovered, and thou art found *Guilty*. O Young Woman, that is Married, and Young Man, look on Me here; be sure in that Solemn Engagement, you are obliged one to another; *Marriage* is an Ordinance of God, have a care of breaking that Bond of *Marriage-Union*; if the Husband provoke his Wife, and cause a Difference, he sins against God; and so does she, in such Carriage; for she is bound to be an *Obedient Wife*. O you Parents that give your Children in Marriage, remember what I have to say, you must take notice when you give them in Marriage, you give them freely to the *Lord*, and free them from that Service and Command you ought to have, yet you ought to have a tender regard to them. O thou that takest no care to lead thy life civilly and honestly, and then Committest that Abominable Sin of *Murder*, here is this *Murderer*, look upon him; and see how many are come with their eyes to behold this man, that abhors himself before God; *that* is the Sin that I abhor my self for, and desire you, take Example by *me*; there are here a great many Young People, and O *Lord, that they may be thy Servants*! Have a care, do not sin; I will tell you, that I wish I never had had the opportunity to do such a *Murder*; if you say, when a person has provoked you, *I will Kill him* : 'Tis a thousand to one, but the next time *you will do it*. Now I Commit my self into the Hands of Almighty God.

## His Prayer.

O Lord our Good God; thou art a Merciful God, and a Gracious and Loving Father; Alas, that thou shouldest *Nourish up Children that have Rebelled against Thee*! O Lord, I must confess, thou gavest me opportunity to read thy *Written Word*; Thou art also my Creator and Preserver; but, Lord, I have not done according to the Offers of thy Grace; thou hast not hid from me the opportunities of the Good Things & Liberties of thy *House* and *Ordinances*; but I have waxed wanton under the Enjoyment of them. I have given thee just cause to provoke thee to Anger, and thou hast left me to *Shame*, not only on my self, but on my Relations. O Lord God I do confess that I have sinned against thee, & done all these Iniquities *against Thee*, and before thine eyes. Lord, I have sinned especially against thee; pardon my Sins of Youth; Lord, pardon this bloody Sin I stand here Guilty of. O Lord, hide not thy face from me; I humbly beg it of thee: for there is no man *can Redeem his Brothers Soul*, but only the Blood of Jesus Christ must do it. Let it be sufficient to satisfie for my poor Soul. I have not done any thing that thou shouldest be pleased to shew me thy *Love*, or that I should have any thing from thee, but only *Everlasting Misery*. I am unworthy to come to thee; yet Lord, for thy *Mercies* Sake have pity on me. Now I am coming to *Judgment*, Lord, let the Arms of thy *Mercy* Receive my Soul, and let my sin be Remitted; Good Lord, let not my sins which *Condemn* me here in this world, rise up to *Condemn* me in the World to come; though they have *Condemned* me in this world, shew mercy, Lord, when I come before thy *Judgment Seat*. If my Soul be not humbled, Lord, humble it; let my Petition be acceptable in Heaven thy Holy Mountain. I am unworthy to come into thy *Presence*, yet O let me come into thy *Kingdom*; and deliver my Soul from *Blood Guiltiness*, in the *Blood* of Jesus Christ. O let my *wounded Soul* mourn for my Sin that hath brought me here, *Sin brings* Ruine to the poor Soul; wo is unto me for mine Iniquity. *If I had gone to Prayer in the morning when I committed this Sin, Lord God, thou wouldest have kept back my hands from shedding innocent Blood*. O Gracious God, Remember thou me in *Mercy*; let me be an Object of thy pitty and not of thy wrath; the Lord hear me and pardon my sins. Take care of my poor *Children*: I have scattered them like stragling sheep flying before the Wolf; pitty the poor Children that go like so many Lambs that have lost their Keeper; that they may not come to such a *Death* as I do! Lord, for the sake of Jesus Christ, and the *Righteousness* of thy Son, accept my Soul, and receive me into the Arms of thy mercy; that I may enjoy Everlasting *Rest*. Pardon all my sins; and let the Prayers of all those that have put up their Petitions for me, be accepted for the sake of Jesus Christ. Now I am coming, now I am coming, thou mayest say, *I called to thee, and thou wouldest not come*; I must say, my sin brought me here, O the World, and the corrupt nature of man, that has proved my ruine! O Lord, Good Lord, let me enjoy Rest for my Soul. The desire of my Soul is to be with thee in thy Kingdom, let me have a share in that Kingdom. Now is the time, Lord Jesus; the Grave is opening its mouth; I am now living, though *dead* in *Sin*; let my prayers be heard in heaven thy holy place; thy hands hath *made* me, and I know thou canst *Save* me; hide not thy face from me; and affect the hearts of thy people with this sad Object, that they may labour to serve thee betimes, & may not give themselves up to *Profaneness* and *Wickedness*, especially that Sin of *Drunkenness*, which is an *in-let of all Abominations.*

(*When thou hast thy* head full of Drink, *the Remembrance of God is out of thy heart*; *and thou art unprepared to commit thy self and Family unto God*; *thou art unfit to come into Gods Presence. I have cause to cry out and be ashamed of it, that I am guilty* of it, *because I gave way to that Sin more than any other, and then God did leave me to practice* Wickedness, *& to Murder that dear Woman, whom I should have taken a great deal of contentment in, which, if I had done, I had not been here to suffer this Death.*)

Thou art Holy, Just, and Good, & therefore O Lord have mercy on me, for the sake of thy Son pitty me, now Lord, I am coming. O, that I could do thee better Service.

(*Many of you that behold me, I* [now] *wish you never had seen me here.*)

Lord, receive my Soul into a better place, if it be thy blessed will; 'tis a day of *great Trouble* with me; my Soul is greatly troubled; give me one Glimpse of Comfort in thy *Kingdom*; by and by let me have one dram of thy *Grace*. Accept of me now at this time, 'tis the last time; Good Lord, deny me not, give me, as the Woman of *Samaria*, a *Taste* of that *Living Water*, that my soul may Thirst no more. I beg it for the sake of Jesus Christ. *Amen.*

After this, he was, by the Prayers of a Minister then present, Recommended unto the Divine Mercy. Which being done, the poor man poured out a few broken Ejaculations, in the midst of which he was turned over, into that Eternity which we must leave him in.

The Speech of *Hugh Stone*, in the Prison, the morning before his Execution.

*When Young People are Married, they make use of Prayer in their Families, and when they Pray, they do believe there is Sincerity and Affection in their Prayer*; *but when Difference between a Man and his Wife doth arise, then that doth occasion hindrance of Prayer in their Family*; *and when Prayer is wholly omitted, it let's in all confusion*; *and every evil work*: *He said*, That he used to Pray in his Family, but when he did Pray, it was in a formal manner, but now from the Consideration of Eternity that he was going into, he was made the more Considerate in his Prayers that he made, and did hope that now he had the Spirit of Prayer in his Praying.

## IX

On *June* 8. 1693[.] Two Young Women, (the one *English*, t'other *Negro*) were Executed at *Boston*, for murdering their *Bastard Children*.

The *English* Young Woman, gave to the Minister, who Preach'd that Afternoon, the following Paper of *Confessions*; which he took occasion, in the Sermon, to publish unto the Congregation, where she also was then present before the Lord.

I am a miserable Sinner; and I have justly provoked the Holy God to leave me unto that Folly of my own Heart, for which I am now Condemned to Dy. I cannot but see much of the *Anger* of God against me, in the Circumstances of my woful Death; He hath Fulfilled upon me, that Word of His, *Evil pursueth Sinners*. I therefore desire, Humbly to *Confess* my many Sins before God, and the World: but most particularly my *Blood Guiltiness*. Before the Birth of my *Twin-Infants*, I too much parlyed with the Temptations of the Devil, to smother my Wickedness by Murthering of them: At length, when they were Born I was not unsensible, that at least, *One* of them was alive; but such a Wretch was I, as to use a *Murderous* Carriage towards them, in the place where I lay, on purpose to dispatch them out of the World. I acknowledge that I have been more Hard hearted than the *Sea Monsters*; and yet for the Pardon of these my Sins, I would Fly to the Blood of the Lord Jesus Christ, which is the only *Fountain set open for Sin and Uncleanness*. I know not how better to Glorify God, for giving me such an Opportunity as I have had to make sure of His Mercy, than by advising and entreating the *Rising Generation* here, to take Warning by my Example; and I will therefore tell the *Sins*, that have brought me to my shameful End. I do Warn all People, and especially, *Young People*, against the Sin of *Uncleanness* in particular; 'tis that Sin that hath been my Ruine; well had it been for me, if I had answered all Temptations to that Sin as *Joseph* did, *How shall I do this Wickedness, and Sin against God*? But, I see, *Bad Company* is that, which leads to that, and all other Sins; and I therefore beg all that Love their Souls to be familiar with none but such as fear God. I believe, the chief thing that hath brought me into my present Condition, is my *Disobedience to my Parents*: I despised all their Godly Counsels and Reproofs; and I was always of an Haughty and stubborn Spirit. So that now I am become a dreadful Instance of the Curse of God belonging to

*Disobedient Children*. I must Bewayl this also, that although I was *Baptised*, yet when I grew up, I forgot the *Bonds* that were laid upon me to be the Lords. Had I given my self to God, as soon as I was capable to consider that I had been in *Baptism*, set apart for him, How happy had I been! It was my *Delay* to Repent of my former Sins, that provoked God to leave me unto the Crimes, for which I am now to Dy. Had I seriously Repented of my *Uncleanness* the *First Time* I fell into it, I do suppose, I had not been left unto what followed. Let all take it from me; they little think, what they do, when they put off turning from Sin to God, and Resist the *Strivings* of the Holy Spirit. I fear, 'tis for this, that I have been given up to such *Hardness of Heart*, not only since my long *Imprisonment*, but also since my Just *Condemnation*. I now know not what will become of my Distressed, perishing Soul. But I would humbly Commit it unto the Mercy of God in Jesus Christ; *Amen*.

## X

In the Year, 1694. A miserable *Indian*, called *Zachary*, was Executed for *Murder*.

He understood so very little English, that it put the English Minister, who, after his Condemnation, visited him, unto an Inexpressible deal of trouble, to convey unto him, the *Principles* and the *Directions* of our Holy Religion. But the Lord so succeeded the endeavours used upon the wretched Salvage, that within a little while, he could give a sensible, tho' a Shattered, Account, of the *Fundamentals* in Christianity. And such an Impression, had the Doctrine of *Grace* upon him, that he professed himself, desirous rather to *Dy*, than to *Live* at his Old sinful rate. He seem'd, even to long for his Execution, that so he might be delivered from all disposition to Sin against God. But all his Hopes of Everlasting Salvation, he seem'd very Suitably to place, on the Obedience which the Lord Jesus Christ, had yeelded unto God in the room of Sinners.

Of this poor creature, nothing had been here mentioned, if it had not been to introduce the mention of this one passage.

He said, *That the Thing which undid him was This*: *He had begun to come, and hear the Preaching of the Gospel among the Indians*: *But he minded the Indian-Preacher, how he lived*; *and he saw plainly that the Preacher minded his Bottle, more than his Bible*: *he lov'd Rum too well, and when his Rum was in him, he would quarrel with other people, and with himself Particularly. This* (he said) *Prejuduced him against the Gospel. So he lived as a Pagan still*; *and would be Drunk too*; *and his Drunkenness had brought all this misery upon him.*

## XI

In the Year, 1698. Was Executed at *Springfield*, one *Sarah Smith*.

Her Despising the continual Counsils and Warnings of her Godly Father-in-law laid the Foundation of her Destruction. When she was married, she added unto the Crime of *Adultery*, that of *Stealing*; which latter Crime occasioned her to fly unto *New Jersey*. Afterwards coming to Reside in *Deerfield*, her (second) Husband was carried captive unto *Canada*: But the woman, in Grievous Horrour of mind, for the Breaches of the *Seventh* and *Eighth* Commandment, received many most suitable counsils, from Mr. *Williams*, the worthy Minister of that place. In conformity to his Counsils and Warnings, for a while she led a Reformed life, and seemed much affected with the word of God, in the publick Dispensations of it. But e're it was long, she lost her Seriousness, her Tenderness, her Convictions; and Relapsed into the Sin of *Adultery*. Her first Relapse into that Sin, was attended with a *Conception*, which, tho' she endeavoured for to render it an Abortive, the Holy providence of God would not suffer it to be so. She did, with much Obstinacy, Deny and Conceal her being with *Child*: and when the *Child* was Born, she smothered it: but the Neighbours found it out immediately. She then owned the matter, but made the usual pretence, *That the Child was Dead Born*: and remain'd as poor Sinners undone by the Sins of *unchastity* use to be, under extream Hardness of Heart. Mr. *Williams* rarely visited her, but found her guilty of New *Lyes*; tho' sometimes violent pangs of Horror would come upon her, wherein she detected her own *Lying*, and seem'd greatly to Bewail it. The Honourable Judges, desired Mr. *Williams* to go down unto *Springfield*, (which was the place,) at the *Time* of her Execution; who then found her under an astonishing stupidity of Soul: and yet not pretending to Hopes of Happiness in another world. He found her guilty of *more Lyes*! which afterward she confessed so to be; she *slept* both at the *Prayer* and the *Sermon*: in the publick Assembly on the day of her Execution: and seem'd, the most unconcern'd of any in the Assembly: professing therewithal, *That she could not but wonder at her own unconcernedness*. At her Execution, she said but little, only, *That she desired to give Glory unto God, and to take shame unto her self, and that she would warn all others, to beware of the Sins, that had brought her unto this miserable End; especially, Stealing, Uncleanness, Lying, Neglecting to Read the Scriptures, and Neglecting to Pray unto God*. She had absented her self much from the word of God, on *Lords-Dayes*, and *Lecture Dayes*; and staid at home, till she had fallen into this capital Transgression: *Then*, she would come unto the meetings, with some seeming Devotion. She had Sinn'd away great

Convictions, and Awakenings; and Satan, with *Seven more unclean Spirits*, entred into her; and God, seemed then to withhold from her, the Efficacy of the means of Grace and Good, which His Faithful Servants in the Neighbourhood, used with her.

## XII

On *November* 17. 1698. There was executed in *Boston*, a miserable Young Woman, whose Extraordinary circumstances rung throughout all *New England*. On this Day of her Execution, was Preached the *Sermon*, which we have now placed, at the Beginning of this History, as an *Inscription* upon our, PILLARS OF SALT. Because the last passages of that *Sermon*, gave a summary Narrative, of what it is fit the publick should know concerning that Criminal, I have Transferr'd them, into this place. The *Sermon* Concluded in these words.

Be astonished, O Congregation of God, Stand astonished, at the Horrible *Spectacle*, that is now before You: This *House*, and perhaps this *Land*, never had in it a more Astonishing *Spectacle*.

Behold, a *Young Woman*, but an *Old Sinner*, going this Day to *Dy before her time*, for being *Wicked over-much*! Behold, One just *Nineteen* Years Old, and yet found *Ripe* for the *Vengeance* of a *Capital Execution*. Ah, Miserable Soul, *With what a swift progress of Sin and Folly, hast thou made Hast unto the Congregation of the Dead*! Behold a Person, whose Unchaste Conversation appear'd by one *Base Born* Child many months ago! *God then gave her a Space to Repent, and she repented not*: She Repeted her Whoredomes, and by an Infatuation from God upon her, She so managed the matter of her next *Base Born*, that she is found Guilty of its *Murder*: Thus the God, whose Eyes are like a Flame of Fire, is now casting her into a *Bed* of Burning *Tribulation*: And, ah, Lord, *Where wilt thou cast those that have committed Adultery with her, Except they Repent*! Since her Imprisonment, She hath Declared, That she believes, God hath Left her unto this *Undoing Wickedness*, partly for her staying so profanely at Home sometimes on *Lords-Dayes*, when she should have been Hearing the *Word of Christ*, and much more for her not minding that *Word*, when she heard it. And she has Confessed, That she was much given to *Rash Wishes*, in her *Mad Passions*, particularly using often that Ill Form of speaking, *I'll be Hang'd*, if a thing be not thus or so, and, *I'll be Hanged*, if I do not this or that; which Evil now, to see it, coming upon her, it amazes her! But the *chief Sin*, of which this *Chief of Sinners*, now cries out, is, *Her Undutiful Carriage towards her Parents*. Her *Language* and her *Carriage* towards her *Parents*, was indeed such that they hardly *Durst* speak to her; but when they *Durst*, they often told her, *It would come to This. They* indeed, with Bleeding Hearts, have now *Forgiven* thy Rebellions; Ah, *Sarah*, mayst thou Cry unto the God of Heaven to *Forgive* Thee! But under all the doleful circumstances of her *Imprisonment*, and her *Impiety*, she has been *given over*, to be a prodigy of still more *Impenitent Impiety*. A little before her *Condemnation*, she Renewed the Crimes of her *Unchastity*; she gave her self up to the *Filthy Debauches*, of a Villain, that was her Fellow-Prisoner; and after her *Condemnation*, her *Falsehoods*, and her *Furies* have been such, as to proclaim, That *under Condemnation she has not Feared God*. Was there ever seen such an *Heighth of Wickedness*! God seems to have Hanged her up in Chains, for all the *Young People* in the Countrey, to see, what prodigies of *Sin* and *Wrath* it may render them, if once they *Sell themselves* thereunto. Behold, O *Young People*, what it is to *Vex* the *Holy Spirit* of God, by *Rebelling* against Him. *This*, This 'tis to be *Given over of God*! And yet after all this *Hard-hearted Wickedness*, is it not possible for the *Grace* of Heaven to be Triumphantly Victorious, in Converting and Pardoning so *Unparallel'd* a *Criminal*? Be astonished, Miserable *Sarah*, and Let it now break that *Stony heart* of thine, to *Hear* it; *It is possible*! *It is possible*! But, O *thou Almighty Spirit of Grace, do thou graciously Touch, and Melt this Obstinate Soul, and once at last, mould her Heart into the Form of thy Glorious Gospel.* The *Glorious Gospel of God*, now utters unto thee, Undone *Sarah*, that Invitation, *Tho' thou hast horribly gone a Whoring, yet Return unto me, saith the Lord, and I will not cause my Anger to fall upon thee.* The *Lessons* of this *Gospel* have been both privately and publickly set before thee, with a vast variety of Inculcation. If all the Extraordinary pains that have been taken for the softening of thy *Stony Heart*, be Lost, God will dispense the more terrible Rebukes unto thee, when He anon breaks thee between the *Millstones* of His Wrath.

Oh, Give now a great Attention, to some of the *Last Words*, that can be spoken to thee, before thy passing into an astonishing Eternity.

The Blessed Lord JESUS CHRIST hath been made a *Curse* for Us; there has been a most Acceptable *Offering* and *Sacrifice*, presented by the Lord Jesus Christ unto God, for all His Chosen: there is a *Fountain set open for Sin and for Uncleanness*: and thou, O *Bloody* Sinner, art Invited unto that *Open Fountain*. Such is the Infinite *Grace* of God, that thou mayest come as freely to the *Blood* of the Lord Jesus Christ, for the Forgiveness of thy Sins, as they that never Sinn'd with a Thousandth part of so much Aggravation; *Come, and Welcome*, says the Lord, who *Receiveth Sinners*. If God Enable thee Now, to *Lay Hold* on the *Righteousness* of the Lord Jesus Christ, tho' thy Faults are Infinite, thou wilt yet before Sun-set *Stand without Fault before the Throne of God*. Thy Soul is just sinking down, into the Fiery Ocean of the Wrath of God, but the *Righteousness* of the Lord Jesus Christ, is cast forth unto thee, once more, for thee, to *Lay Hold* upon. Oh! *Lay Hold* upon it, and *Live*! If God help thee, to do so, *Then*, as it was said, *The* Mary *whose Sins are many, has them Forgiven her*, So it shall be said, *The* Sarah, *whose Sins are many, has them Forgiven her*! *Then*, as it was said, Rahab *the Harlot perished not*, so it shall be said, Sarah *the Harlot, perished not*! Tho' the *Blood* of thy murdered Infant, with all thy other Bloody Crimes, horribly Cry to God against thee, yet a louder and better Cry from the *Blood* of thy Saviour, shall drown that formidable Cry. Yea, *then*, There will be *Joy in Heaven* this Afternoon *among the Angels of God*; the *Angels* of Heaven will stand amazed, and say, *O the Infinite Grace, that can bring such a Sinner unto Glory*! But if ever the *Blood* of the Lord Jesus Christ, be applied unto *thy Heart,* it will immediately *Dissolve* that Heart of thine; it will cause thee to *Mourn* for every Sin, to *Turn* from every Sin, to give thy self entirely unto *God.* It will be impossible for thee, to Go on in any *Known Sin*, or to *Dy* with a *Ly* in thy mouth, no, thou wilt rather *Dy* than commit any *Known Sin* in the World. If this *Disposition*, be not *produced* in thee, before Three or Four short Hours more are Expired, thy Immortal *Spirit,* will anon pass into Eternal *Torment*: thou wilt before To morrow morning be a Companion of the *Devils* and the *Damned*; the Everlasting *Chains of Darkness* will hold thee, for the *Worm that never dies, & the Fire that never shall be Quenched*: thou shalt fall into the *Hands of the Living God*, and become as a glowing Iron, possessed by his Burning Vengeance, throughout Eternal Ages; the God that *made thee, will not have mercy on thee, and He that formed thee will show thee no Favour.* But for his Mercy, and Favour, while there is yet hope, we will yet Cry unto Him.

Advertisements.

There is now in the Press, and will speedily be Published, A Book, Entitled, *The Folly of Sinning.* Opened and Applied in two Sermons, Occasioned by the Condemnation of One that was Executed at *Boston* in *New England,* on *November* 17. 1698. By the Reverend Mr. *Increase Mather,* Præsident of *Harvard Colledge* in *Cambridge,* and Preacher of the Gospel at Boston in New England.

Sold by *Michael Perry,* at his Shop over against the *Town House,* in *Boston.*

There will also be Published, A Book, Entitled, *Decennium Luctuosum.* Or, An History of *Remarkable Occurrences,* in the *Long* WAR, which *New England* hath had with the *Indian Salvages,* from the year 1688. to the year 1698. (with some other Memorables) Faithfully Collected and Improved.

Sold by *Samuel Philips* at the Brick Shop near the *Town House* in *Boston.*

## Source Notes

Cotton Mather's *Pillars of Salt* (Boston, 1699) originally was printed by B. Green and J. Allen for Samuel Phillips. Three years later Mather included it in *Magnalia Christi Americana* (London, 1702) as "An Appendix" of "The Sixth Book." The copy text used for the anthology is taken from Mather's original 1699 publication.

Of the dozen examples that make up *Pillars*, six had been previously published. In section "V" of *Pillars*, the account of Nicholas Feavor and Robert Driver, two servants who were executed for murdering their master, Mather acknowledged his use of his father's *The Wicked mans Portion* (1675), which included the confessions of both Feavor and Driver. The information in section "VII," concerning James Morgan, was previously developed in several publications. Shortly after Morgan's execution in 1686, Increase Mather published his execution sermon "to gratifie some who have perhaps been too importunately desirous to have it so." Published as *A Sermon Occasioned by the Execution of a Man Found Guilty of Murder*, Mather's text (perhaps to gratify certain importunate booksellers) included an account of Morgan's crime and his final confession. This text was republished in Boston later in that year and then republished a third time in London in 1691. Following his father's example, Cotton Mather soon saw his first publication, *Call of the Gospel* (1686), published, which included both the sermon he preached to Morgan and Joshua Moody's "An Exhortation to a condemned malefactor." One year later (1687) all three sermons and all supplemental material concerning Morgan, including the dialogue later used in *Pillars*, were republished in one volume under Increase Mather's original title. Morgan's execution was described in a letter written by John Dunton, a London bookseller who then was visiting Boston. Struck by the solemnity of the ritual, Dunton later importuned the Mathers and Moodey to publish their sermons, and it was he who later published Increase Mather's sermon in London. For the text of Dunton's letter, see Miller and Johnson, 413–20. The material included in section "VIII," concerning Hugh Stone, was taken from Mather's original publication, *Speedy Repentance urged* (Boston, 1690). This text not only offered "some Account concerning the Character, Carriage, and Execution of that Unhappy Malefactor" but also "certain Memorable Providences Relating to some other Murders." Section "IX," concerning two women executed for infanticide, was based on Mather's previous publication, *Warnings from the Dead* (Boston, 1693). In addition to the two execution sermons he delivered, Mather added the "Last Confession" of one of the women (Elizabeth Emerson), which he then used in *Pillars*. Sarah Smith, whose execution for infanticide is discussed in section "XI," was the target of *Warnings to the Unclean* (Boston, 1699), a particularly severe execution sermon delivered by John Williams. Finally, Sarah Threeneedles, the most recalcitrant of all of Mather's anti-apostles, aroused the indignant pens of three ministers. Samuel Willard published the two sermons he preached to Threeneedles as *Impenitent Sinners Warned of their Misery* (Boston, 1698), "to which are subjoyned the Solemn Words spoken to her." Increase Mather also published two sermons

"Occasioned by the Condemnation" of Threeneedles: *The Folly of Sinning, Opened & Applyed* (Boston, 1699). After delivering his sermon to Threeneedles, Cotton Mather used it as the basis for the original *Pillars of Salt*. Although the title page advertised it as "An History of Some Criminals Executed in this Land," *Pillars* began with Mather's address to the condemned woman.

The journals of John Winthrop and the diaries of both Cotton Mather and Samuel Sewall offer information on several criminals mentioned in *Pillars*. For an interesting account of Mary Martin (section "I"), see Winthrop's journals, 302–03. For information concerning Feavor and Driver (section "V"), see Sewall's *Diary*, I, 8. For additional information concerning Morgan (section "VII"), see Mather's *Diary*, 122, and Sewall's *Diary*, I, 123–26. For information concerning Elizabeth Emerson (section "IX"), see Mather's *Diary*, 165, and Sewall's *Diary*, I, 379. For information concerning Sarah Smith (section "XII"), see Sewall's *Diary*, I, 483. Finally, for information concerning Sarah Threeneedles (section "XII"), see Mather's *Diary*, 276–80, and Sewall's *Diary*, I, 486. According to Mather, the crowds who gathered to hear him preach to Threeneedles was exceptional: "the greatest Assembly, ever in this Country preach'd unto was now come together; I could not gett unto the Pulpit, but by climbing over Pues and Heads . . ." (279).

**Death**

The certain *Wages of Sin* to the Impenitent:

**Life**

The ſure *Reward of Grace* to the Penitent:

Together with the only *Way* for

# YOUTH

To avoid the former, and attain the latter.

Deliver'd in three **Lecture Sermons**; Occaſioned by the *Impriſonment, Condemnation* and *Execution*, of a Young Woman, who was guilty of Murdering her Infant begotten in Whoredom.

To which is added, An *Account* of her manner of Life & Death, in which the Glory of free Grace is diſplayed.

By Mr. **John Rogers**, Paſtor of the Church of *Ipſwich*.

1 Tim. 1. 16

*Boſton*: Printed by *B Green*, and *J. Allen*, for *Samuel Phillips* at the Brick Shop. 1701.

[ ESTHER RODGERS ]

# *The Declaration & Confession of Esther Rodgers*

[ 1701 ]

Reader;

*This Serves only to draw the Curtain, that thou mayst behold a Tragick Scene, strangly changed into a* Theater *of* Mercy, *a* Pillar of Salt *Transformed into a Monument of Free Grace; a poor Wretch, entring into Prison a Bloody Malefactor, her Conscience laden with Sins of a Scarlet Die, but there by the Gracious and Powerful, but various workings: first of the Spirit of Bondage, then of Adoption; the space of Eight Months she came forth, Sprinkled, Cleansed, Comforted, a Candidate of Heaven.*

*Whilst she was under Confinement, after she had conceived in her self good Hope of finding Mercy with God, through Christ, she was ready to give a reason of her hope, to such as were Serious and Pious, with Meekness, and much affection. And truly the Reasons and Grounds she went upon were Scriptural, and so able to bear the weight she put upon them; (which Hope the result of her Faith) kept her Company to the last, and failed her not, when she had most need of it. When she walked the dolorous way to the place of her Execution, and approaching near to it, after a little Reluctancy of the Flesh, as soon as she ascended to behold the fatal Tree, her Faith, and courage revived, and she lift up her Feet, and Marched on with an Erected, and Radiant Countenance, as unconcerned with the business of Death, at once out doing all the old* Roman Masculine *bravery, and shewing what Grace can do, in, and for the Weaker* Sex; *and this in Presence of a Multitude of Spectators, of whom this Relator was One, and an Admiring Observer: All which is to be Ascribed, Firstly, To the Infinitely Rich, and Free Grace of God; but Ministerially, and Instrumentally to the Labours, Prayers and Endeavours of the Reverend Elders of the Church of* Ipswich, *and many other good Christians there; after her Apprehension in* Newbury *where the Fact was Committed.*

*She was Conveyed, (and it was happy for her) that she was Conveyed to the Prison in* Ipswich; *where are to be found,* (A Nation) *Pardon the Expression, Of Sound, Serious and Praying Christians, who made Incessant Prayers to Heaven in her behalf, Praying not only for her, but with her, in their own Houses, joyning & turning their Private Meetings into whole days of* Fasting and Prayer; *and continuing till the Stars appearing: Yea, by Turns in the Prison also. So turning a* Den of Theives, *(to use Dr.* Wilds *words) into a House of Prayer; and had there been some Thief there, (for I know not who was there) he might Perhaps, with her, been sharer of the benefit. Their Worthy Pastor also, took constant & unwearied pains, Plying the Oar, To waft over her Soul to Heaven; and saw the fruit of all his Labours, and Travels with her, through the Blessing of God, Namely a great & gracious change wrought in her, which she Humbly, Affectionately, and Thankfully acknowledged.*

*And now, Let the Great God of Heaven, have all the Praise & Glory of this Action: And let that unhappy Tree; indeed happy in this, that the first that Suffered on it, was (we trust) Fruit Consecrated: But if it be the Will of God, that there may never be Occasion again to make use of it to such Fatal purposes, but only stand as a Buoy, or Seamark, to point out the Rocks and Shelves, where she Shipwrackt her honour; and that all others may* HEAR & FEAR, &c. *Which is the Desire and Prayer of,*

Your Servant in the Lord,
SAMUEL BELCHER.

## The Declaration & Confession of Esther Rodgers, *Of* Kittery *in the Province of* Main, *in* New England, *Single woman.*

I was born at *Kittery* sometime in May, 1680. At the Age of Thirteen came to live as an Apprentice to Mr. *Joseph Woodbridge* of *Newbury.* Had little or no thoughts of God or Religion, though Living in a Religious Family; was taught to Read, Learned Mr. *Cottons* Catechism, and had frequent opportunities of going to Publick Meetings; but was a careless Observer of Sabbaths, and Hearer of Sermons; no Word that ever I heard or read making any Impression upon my Heart, (as I Remember) Neither did I at all give my self to Secret Prayer, or any other Duty that concerned the Salvation of my Soul. And because I thus neglected God, refused his Counsil, and would not walk in his Ways, therefore he justly gave me up to my own hearts Lusts, and ways of Wickedness.

About the Age of Seventeen, I was left to fall into that foul Sin of Uncleanness, suffering my self to be defiled by a *Negro* Lad living in the same House. After I perceived that I was with Child, I meditated how to prevent coming to Publick Shame; Satan presently setting in with his Temptation, I soon complyed and resolved to Murder the Child, if ever I should have one born alive: and continued in my wicked purpose all along, till I had the fatal Opportunity of putting it into Execution. Being delivered of a Living Child, I used means presently to stop the breath of it, and kept it hid in an upper Room, till the Darkness of the Night following, gave advantage for a Private Burial in the Garden.

All this was done in Secret, no person living whatsoever, no not so much as the Father of the child himself was privy to my disposal of it, or knew that I ever had such a Child.

Afterwards reflecting on what I had done, was followed with some Awakening, Frights and Convictions during my abode at Mr. *Woodbridges*, which was about half a year. Yet, never making any serious Address to God for pardon of these my great and hainous Sins. But thence I went to *Piscatequa*, where I lived in a publick House, and soon got over and rid of all my Fears, and even all thoughts thereof, giving my self up to other wicked Company and ways of Evil.

About a year after, I returned to *Newbury* to Mr. *Joseph Woodbridges* again, where my former Sins came fresh to Remembrance, and troubled me a while; which together with other reasons, occasioned my Removal to another place in the Town. But there also I took all Opportunities to follow my old Trade of running out a Nights, or entertaining my Sinful Companions in a back part of the House. And there I fell into the like horrible Pit (as before) *viz.* of Carnal Pollution with the *Negro* man belonging to that House. And being with Child again, I was in as great concern to know how to hide this as the former. Yet did not so soon resolve the Murdering of it, but was continually hurried in my thoughts, and undetermined till the last hour. I went forth to be delivered in the Field, and dropping my Child by the side of a little Pond, (whether alive, or still Born I cannot tell) I covered it over with Dirt and Snow, and speedily returned home again. But being Suspected and Examined, about having had a Child since my going out, made little or no answer (that I remember) till the next Morning. The Child being found by some Neighbours was brought in, & laid before my Face, to my horrible Shame & Terror; under which Confusion I remained during my Confinement at *Newbury*, being about one Month, Thinking only of the punishment I was like to suffer, without any true concernedness as to my Sins against God, or the State of my Immortal Soul; till some time after I came into *Ipswich* Prison; when and where it pleased the Great and

Gracious God to work upon my heart, as in the following Relation I have given account of.

*A Relation of her Experience, both of some Conviction and Comfort received in the Prison: Communicated to a certain Gentlewoman of the Town, with whom she was very free, before and afterwards.*

## Taken word for word from her own Mouth.

The first time Mr. *Rogers* came to see me; after much other Discourse, he told me of the odiousness of Sin; and that if ever I came to be sensible of it, I should loath it, and not because of my own punishment procured thereby, but because of the Dishonour done to God. Then after he was gone, I began to think that I never loathed Sin so as yet, and was in a dreadful Case indeed; to think what a wretched Condition I had brought my self into, and had dishonoured God: insomuch that I could not Rest, I was so dreadfully hurried; and Satan made me believe that it was impossible such a Sinner, should be Saved. And I could not Read, nor Sleep, nor have any Rest night nor day. After a while God made me to think that it was Satans Temptation to keep me from Repentance: But if I could Repent and Believe in the Lord Jesus Christ, I might find mercy, although I was such a Sinner. And although I am such a vile Sinner, I hope God has made me sensible of my sins, he has made me to loath my self, and truly to Repent for Sin. God has made me to see that there is nothing that I can do can save me, but that there is a sufficiency in the Lord Jesus Christ. And I do throw my self at his Feet for mercy, and have hope from his promises. *Let the wicked forsake his way, and the unrighteous man his thoughts, and let him Return to the Lord, for he will have mercy on him: and to our God, for he will abundantly pardon.* And I do so far as I know my self, Repent of my so great sins against so good a God; for that which has been the delight of my Soul, I do now abominably hate! And again 'tis said, *He that confesseth and forsaketh his sin, shall find mercy.* I can truly say, I have confessed my Sins before God and man, and do desire truly to Repent for them. Isa. I. 18. *Come now let us reason together saith the Lord, though your sins be as scarlet, they shall be white as snow, though they be red like crimson, they shall be as wool.* I hope I have hated the evil of my ways; and do hope to have my Soul washed and cleansed in the Blood of Jesus Christ.

During her Imprisonment (which was more than eight months) she was frequently visited by Ministers, and other Christians of the Town and

Neighbourhood, to whom she gave little Encouragement for a considerable time, being very much reserved, partly thro' natural temper, partly by power of Temptation as was judged; that she could not open her mind or condition at all; nor make any other answer to Questions propounded, than yea or no: till after a while she obtained more freedom of spirit, and liberty of speech. Then would she speak of her sins with aggravation, and express sorrow for them with great affection: related the distressing, and almost despairing thoughts of her mind in the time that she kept silence; as that God who had left her to fall so dreadfully into sin, would now leave her to an hard and impenitent heart, that she should be damned; found a great averseness at first, against going to the Publick Assembly on Sabbath and Lecture Dayes, (for which she had liberty twice every week) lest her heart should be more hardned, and her Condemnation more heightned thereby. But it was not long before she found a better fruit and effect of her attendance thereupon: She felt the power of the Word preached, inlightning, convincing, humbling and softning of her heart. Also that the words spoken to her in private made deep and lasting impressions on her Soul: that she began to delight in hearing the Word publick or private; and set her self to search the Scriptures diligently, out of which she collected many Texts, that encouraged her to hope for mercy and pardon, as particularly these, *Prov.* 28, 13. *Isa.* 5.5[,] I.7.[,] *Mat.* II. 28, and *Isa.* I. 18. on these was her Meditation day & night; and though she professed not to rest on these promises, yet was by them encouraged and drawn to come unto God through Jesus Christ, and to hope in him according to his Word. And having once laid hold on that Hope set before her in the Gospel; she did not, would not, ever after let it go; and tho' she could not so well express the reasons and grounds of her hope, as was desired, yet would not by any means be beaten off from it: and tho' sometimes she felt a sinking fear come upon her, yet that did not long abide. But still said she, my Hopes prevail against my fears; at length all fear was in a manner cast out, and she was even filled with hope, comfort, and joy in believing: Spake very sensibly of the Nature of Faith, which said she, I never understood before, but now I feel the power of it; 'tis quite another thing than most people take it to be, or then I my self did conceive of it. I should at any time before have answered yes to such a Question, *Believest thou to be Saved by Christ?* whereas now I know, that I neither did believe, nor knew I what it was to believe. O Believing is a great and difficult work, 'tis the mighty work of God himself, that any do believe. This was after she had heard a publick Discourse on the Apostles words to the Jaylor, *Acts* 16.31. Having before heard those words of our Saviour, *Mat.* 18.3. spoken to; and being afterwards asked what she thought or experienced about Conversion, said, I am sure there is a great Change, I think a thorow Change wrought in my whole nature: I now see all things otherwise then I did before; Sin is become very odious, and Christ very precious to me; I see the folly and filthiness of the ways of sin, and in some measure am made to discern the Excellency of Gods ways, and do find more delight and pleasure therein, then ever I did in my former courses. Oh! I can truly say, I loath myself for my sins, I abhor my self; and if I were to live a thousand years in this world, it should be in the hatred of all Evil. Again she said, I would not for all the world be among my sinful Companions, and in the state I then was: I find a thousand times more comfort and delight in the Prison alone, than ever I did with them. When News was carried to her, that her Life was likely to be prolonged near two months by the Courts Adjournment, it rais'd no sudden joy in her, as was expected: and though she could not but wonder at it her self, yet gave this reason for it: I find (said she) a willingness in me to accept the punishment of my sins, and a readiness to glorify the Justice of God by suffering that Death I have deserved, in hope of receiving his mercy to Eternal Life; but I submit to his pleasure. In the time of this Reprieval, she had many opportunities of going to the private Meetings of Christians in the Town, who spent whole days in Prayer with Fasting on her account; and though she joyned not in any Conference with them, yet profest her delight in hearing them, that she found much sweetness in their society, and desired to be gathered with such at Death.

When the time of her Trial came, tho' she would have acknowledged plain matter of Fact, yet could not plead Guilty according to the Form of her Indictment; but being brought in Guilty according to Law and Evidence, of Wilful Murder committed by her, & thereupon being Condemned to Dy, was not at all surprised; but as she before expected, so afterwards approved the Verdict and Sentence, that they were just and right. After Condemnation she was much more free and enlarged in discourse than before: and being often asked, how her Faith and Hope in God and Christ held out; she would answer, without Doubting and Wavering; being askt whether she was never assaulted with Temptations to Unbelief or Fear, since her beginning to hope: Answers, yes at the first, but not lately; neither have I been troubled with terrifying Dreams or Fancies, as formerly I was: nor can I possess my self with fearfulness when I endeavour it by thinking on the most awful circumstances of my Condition and manner of Death which I am to suffer; but in the midst of those thoughts, *Gods comforts delight my Soul*, and I think, that at such times I feel the greatest incomes of joy and sweetness.

On the last Sabbath of her Life on Earth, she presented this Bill to be Read in the Congregation, which was wholly Dictated by her own Mouth, though Written by another hand.

Esther Rodgers *having received a Sentence of Death, which ere long is to be Executed on her Body, being sensible of the just Hand of God for her Great and Crying Sins and Crimes, that she is found guilty of before God; Humbly begs the Prayers of all Gods People in this Congregation for her: being made in some measure sensible of her sad and deplorable Condition, she earnestly begs, that the Lord would still look down in Mercy upon her, to give her Assurance of the Pardon of all her Sins, and to Wash and Cleanse her from,* THAT SIN *of* BLOODGUILTINESS, *in the Blood of the Lord* JESUS CHRIST; *that her Faith and Hope may be only upon the Mercy of God in Christ, for* SALVATION: *and that the Lord would Strengthen and Uphold her, and carry her through that hard and difficult Work when called thereunto, that she may not be dismayed at the Sight and Fear of* DEATH: *but that her Mouth may be Opened, and her heart enlarged to declare to Others, what the Lord has done for her Soul, and also to Warn them that are Beholders to take heed by her Example, least they fall into the like Condemnation.*

The Lord was pleased to make this a good Day unto her, and she was much strengthned and refreshed by what she heard from those words, *Act.* 16. 31. *Believe in the Lord Jesus Christ, and thou shalt be Saved.* In which discourse, the *Subject, Object*, and *Principal* Act of true Justifying and Saving Faith, were touched upon: And in the close of all, the extent of the Promise being considered, it was particularly applyed unto *her* upon *Believing*. The Apostle there did not speak to the Jaylour only, but the Charge and Promise both are Universal. "*Let every one believe on the Lord Jesus Christ, and Whosoever believeth shall be Saved.* This was often repeated by our Saviour, particularly unto *Martha*, Joh. 11. 26. *Whosoever liveth and believeth in me shall never Dy.* Nay further to manifest the Riches of Grace and Power of Faith: He saith, *I am the Resurrection and the Life, He that believeth in me, though he were Dead, yet shall he live.*"

"Here is One in the Congregation at this time, of whom it may be thus spoken, That she is a Dead Woman; not only that she was dead in Trespasses & Sins, but is Dead in Law, and by a Sentence of Condemnation must be put to Death before another Sabbath come about: And yet there is more than a possibility through Grace, that she may Live again; though not in this World, yet for ever in a better, where she shall neither sin nor sorrow more. Who hath begotten thee to such a lively hope, or hope of Eternal life, O thou Dying Malefactor? Has the Spririt of the Lord Jesus wrought this in thee by his Word or no? O Examine (whilst there is Opportunity) thy Hope by thy Faith, and see if that be well grounded on Christ Himself, according to the Word. Not on thine own Prayers, Tears, Humiliations, Sorrows or Repentance, but on the Free Mercy of God, and Merits of Christ alone. If so, it can never rise too high, or will make ashamed by its fall. Yet must thou continue instant and constant in thy Looking unto this JESUS, who is not only the *Object*, but *Author* and *Finisher* of thy Faith, to establish, strengthen and enable thee to persevere in Faith & Hope to the End; that thou mayst not be found to be one of those who draw back to perdition, but of those that hold out to the Saving of their Souls. Be sensible, that the same Almighty Power which at first enabled thee to believe, is necessary to keep and carry thee through Faith to Salvation. Beg of God to strengthen thee against new Fears, or any Temptations to Unbelief: Say with him, *At what time I am afraid, I will trust in thee*. And God of his Infinite Grace grant this good Evidence of true Partnership in Jesus Christ both to *thee* and *Us*, *viz*. That we may hold the beginning of our Confidence stedfast unto the End. *Amen.*" *Heb.* 3. 14.

The Night before her Execution, she said to many coming in at once to visit her: Oh! I have had the joyfullest day to day that ever I had in my whole life. I bless God that ever I came into this Prison. When one of the Company asked her, what she thought of the poor murdered Infants, whom she was instrumental to bring into the world, and then perhaps of sending them to Hell. She answers, I have greatly mourned for my cruelty and wrong to them, as well as Sin against God in all that I have done. Question again; *But how do you think to answer the Cry of their Blood? Answ.* I trust I have an Advocate, and many like things.

The next Day (which was appointed for her Execution) being Lecture Day, *July* 31, 1701. This other Bill was presented by one that took it from her own mouth.

Esther Rodgers *a poor Prisoner of Hope, under Sentence of Death, which is in a few hours to take place upon her, being through Gods Grace made sensible of the just hand of God upon her, for her great and crying sins she was found guilty of before God and man: Considering she is upon the Brink of Eternity, which she hopes will be a Blessed Eternity to her; and having a comfortable assurance thereof, thro' Gods infinite mercy in Christ vouchsafed to her so great a Sinner, she humbly begs the Prayers of all Gods People for her, as being the last time she shall enjoy such a benefit here in this world; that the Lord will be pleased to stand by her, and strengthen her, that her Faith and Hope in Christ may hold out to the end; & that her heart may be opened & enlarged to declare to others what God has done for her Soul; and to give warning to those that are Standers by, to take heed of falling unto any such ways and courses, as she has been left unto.*

Some time before the Publick Lecture began, the Reverend Mr. *Wise* went in to visit the Prisoner, and began to quaery with her, about her

Spiritual Condition, *viz*. In what preparation she was for Death, that was now approaching?

Her answer was in expression of much comfort and assurance of her future well being.

In the interim of time came in a Gentlewoman that was her peculiar Visitant, and asked her how she found her self this morning? She answered, her hopes and comfort continued.

Quest. *Whether, when her Coffin was brought in, it did not daunt her?*

*Answ.* No, but it rather ministred matter of comfort to me. Then Mr. *Wise* replied to what he heard from her, that if this were real, the effect of a Saving Change upon her heart, she of a poor miserable Malefactor was become one of the greatest Favourites to the King of Heaven. Why *Esther* can you entertain Death, and such terrible Forerunners of it in such Triumph? Then you are very happy: But are you not mistaken? Will you give me leave to make a more exact scrutiny into the State of your Soul? Then pray, be free and plain hearted, that I may have a particular account of your Spiritual State[.] For this she desired Privacy: whereupon the whole Company withdrew: And Mr. *Wise* proceeded in discourse with her after this manner.

*Esther*, The Godly after Grace is implanted, God is want to order that they pass variety of trials for the proof of the soundness of their State, that Divine Grace in them may grow into greater assurance: So that to put you upon an Examination of this nature, will be no disadvantage to you. Therefore let me have liberty more critically to enquire into the ground of your fore mentioned hopes: I would not at such a time molest your Spiritual quiet, yet you are now within a few hours to appear before a Jealous and Omniscient Judge; you cannot be too curious in setling all things right between Him and your Soul, under the benefit of means. There is no room to err twice in this Adventure. If there be any essential error in your State, and it continues, you are undone for ever. Therefore take my freedom in good part.

Quest. *Where are your hopes placed?*

*Answ.* In the Mercy of God, and Merits of Christ.

Quest. *You have been a very great Criminal, What sense have you had of Sin? have you seen it exceeding sinful?*

*Answ.* Yes, It has been a greater grief to me that I have offended God, than for what I have, or shall yet endure for my Sin. The time hastens, give me a distinct account of the work of Gods Spirit upon your heart.

*This Relation she makes agreeable to the former.*

*Says she,* When I came first into Prison, I was altogether careless, unaffected and unconcerned about my condition. Mr. *Rogers* came to visit me, and in discourse with me, did so open and lay out my condition before me, in the terrible circumstances and aggrevations of it, that I was smitten in my heart, and filled with terrible thoughts about it. He told me also I must seek to God to doe all for me that I needed to have done. That I could not mend my heart no more than make it, *&c.* The trouble of my mind continued upon me, and All the Sins of my Life came to my Remembrance: I fell into great horrours, and was in great distress & perplexity about my condition: I saw my self in a very miserable State by reason of Sin, and the Justice of God. I had very great and sore Conflicts in my Spirit, and many great Temptations. But it pleased God after some time to come in with much Comfort into my Soul, by many precious Promises, as that in *Ezek.* 18. 32. *I have no pleasure in the Death of him that Dyeth, saith the Lord God, wherefore Turn your selves and live ye*; and others that have been already mentioned. The Peace and Comfort of my mind, (*said she*) is great and continued: When I think of my Sins they disappear, and fly from me, I many times have endeavoured to terrify my self with the thoughts of Death, and my Execution, it seems rather a matter of comfort than terror to me. At times my spirit has been somewhat damped, but my comfort and peace return. Mr. *Wise* further quaeried with her about the sense she had of indwelling sin: And by her answers she did discover a considerable knowledge of the Mystery in Christianity; that though she was well confirmed (by the beams of Divine Favour) of the compleatness of her Justification, yet did discern that her Sanctification was incompleat from the sense of heart Evils, Darkness, Wandrings, under sacred means, and vain imaginations *&c.*

To make some Tryal of the Firmness and manner of her Faith, 'Twas queried,

*Whether she found it hard to believe*?

*Answ.* Yes, But yet she desired to roul [sic] her self upon the Mercy of God, for He had said, *Come unto me all ye that are weary and heavy laden, and I will give you Rest.*

Hereupon, the Minister gives her his charitable Opinion of her good Estate, of which he had a peculiar esteem from the Account she had given him, that the special instrumental cause of her Awakening and Comfort, was an Ambassador of Jesus Christ. So having Recommended her condition to the God of all Grace and Consolation by Prayer, repaired to the Publick Lecture.

After Lecture, the High Sheriff prepares a Cart to carry her from the Goal, to the place of Execution: But she earnestly desiring of him the liberty to walk on Foot; it was granted to her, and two or three of the Neighbouring Ministers did her the Favour to Walk with her, who did by turns endeavour to fill up the time with such Divine Passages of discourse as might best suit her condition; mixing with words of Consolation, something of Terrour and Caution. Her Behaviour was very grave and Christian from first to last. She retained an invincible Courage, and yet manifested nothing that had the least Tincture of a vain glorious Confidence. One of the Ministers thus glossed on her present circumstances for Terrification.

*O Esther*, How can your heart abide! Dont you here behold terrible displayes of Justice: you are surrounded with Armed men, which signifies that God and man has determined to rid the World of you ; and you are thus beset, that you may no ways escape. The terrible place and Engines of Destruction, are but a little before us, where you must in a few Minutes Expire; and there lyes your *Coffin*, that must receive your perishing Body: How can you bear the sight of all these things? She turns about, and looking him in the face with a very smiling countenance, sayes, I know I am going to the Lord Jesus Christ. The manner, the Christian Bravery, the Chearfulness, and suddenness, with the profound matter of her Reply was suprizing and astonishing; Yet not to clip or over load the Wings of her Soaring Faith; they told her, that God did put much honour upon, and signalize his Grace to her, in that she had been the Subject of Prayers generally through the Neighbourhood. And now in that Christian and Civil Attendance that was given her in her last Journey; and from the interest she had obtained in the hearts of that Sacred Order of men, intrusted with the Keys of the Kingdom. So that they might in a humble confidence and hope, pronounce an Absolution, though not from the Temporal Punishment, yet from the Condemning Guilt of all her great Abomination; (upon a presumption of her gracious state) founded on those words *Mat.* 16.19: *Whatsoever thou shalt loose on Earth, shall be loosed in Heaven.* The Discourse seem'd very delightful to her, making suitable, though short Replies to all.

Having walked above a mile, she seem'd a little to flag and faulter in her pace; which together with a sudden paleness of countenance occasioned, one of the Ministers observing it, to ask her, How she did now? whether she felt any alteration? To which she replyed, thus; some sudden qualm of faintness and fear came upon me, but it is over, and I am very well; so presses forward again with her usual vigour. Being come in sight of the Gallows, was askt, whether her heart did not now fail her: She answers, No, but the nearer I approach, the more I feel my strength and joy to increase. When come to the Foot of the Ladder she seem'd no ways altered by any distress invading from the terrible Spectacles then in view. Mr. Sheriff having settled his Guard, and Read the Death Warrant, asked, what she did desire further before Execution? She turning to the Ministers, desires one of them to pray with her. Prayer being ended, Mr. Sheriff bids her go up the Ladder, she readily obeys; But first with very affecting Gestures, takes her leave of the Ministers, giving them many thanks for all their kindness to her; and this she does with a mixture of Tears, and a show of moderated sorrow, and so without stop or trembling went up the Ladder; and turning her self about, made the following Discourse to the People, and Prayer to God.

*The last Dying Words and Prayer of* Esther Rodgers, *upon the Ladder, just before her Execution, taken in Short-hand by some there present,* July 31, 1701.

Here I am come to Dy a Shameful Death, and I justly deserve it: Young People take Warning, O let all take Warning by me; I beg of all to have a Care. Be Obedient to your Parents and Masters; Run not out a Nights, especially on Sabbath Nights, Refrain bad Company for the Lords Sake. Here me poor Souls, Keep Gods Sabbaths, mind the Word of God, and let good People be your Company, Mind it for the Lords Sake: Do it if you love your Lives: for Gods Sake mind your own Souls. O Run not abroad with wicked Company, or on Sabbath day Nights, and so forget what you have heard. Improve time, you do not know what Comfort is to be had and found in Gods Ways; If you do not love God, he will not love you; If you go on in Sin, you will provoke God. O let me beg of you all to hear me! for the Lords Sake Remember me! O let every one Remember me! Let me beg of all Young Ones, be not Disobedient, go not with bad Company, O my dear Friends—Take Warning by me. Here I come to Dy, and if God be not Merciful to my Soul, I shall be undone to all Eternity—If I do not turn by Repentance. I Bless God, I have found more Comfort in Prison, than ever before. O Turn to God now. O how hard it is to Repent; If you go on in Sin, God may give you up to a hard Heart. Oh! Turn whilst the Day of Grace lasts.

## Her Prayer.

O LORD JESUS, *I humbly beg of thee, Look upon me in Mercy, God for Christ Jesus Sake have mercy upon me. It is nothing that I can do for a Pardon—All my Prayers and Tears cannot Save me—But it is through the free Grace, and Mercy of God in the Blood of Jesus Christ. O Lord, Sprinkle that Blood upon my Soul, that will wash away all my bloody Sins. I beg pardon through him of all those sins I am guilty of. O Lord Jesus have Compassion upon me, and say to me, as thou did to the Penitent Thief:* This day shalt thou be with me in Paradise. *Oh Lord, I come, Receive my Soul. Thou hast said,* Come unto me all you that are weary and heavy laden. And they that are a thirst, thou wilt give the Water of Life to. *Lord, I thirst, have mercy upon me, for the Lord Jesus Christ's sake, O Receive my Soul, Dear Lord Jesus, I beg of thee: Have Compassion upon me, have mercy upon me, O Lord, for Christ's sake. O pity me, and have Compassion upon me. Lord Jesus be with me, and carry me through—Thou hast said,* Whosoever comes unto thee, thou wilt in no wise cast them out. *O Lord I come to thee, O Lord cast me not out. Though I have deserved Death and Damnation—my sins have deserved Hell—a thousand Hells; yet Lord pity me, and pardon all my Sins, and give me an interest in Jesus Christ. Lord Jesus, thou hast said,* Whosoever believeth on thee, shall never dye. *O Lord I believe, help thou mine unbelief. O Blessed Jesus, Receive my Soul, Blessed Lord Jesus, I come to thee, fit and and prepare me for thy self. If my heart be not humbled, humble me to the Dust. O Lord Jesus, I have been guilty of Blood enough to Damn me to all Eternity. O Lord have mercy on me, hear me, pity and pardon me. Lord I bless thee, that thou givest me any hope*; thou deliverest from the Grave, and out of Hell: *I might have been before this time in the Grave with the Dead, and in Hell with the Damned. Lord Jesus, thou canst give me a heart to Repent, I do Repent that ever I have sinned against so good and so gracious a God. O Lord, pity me, and send thy Holy Angels to guard my Soul into the Heavenly Kingdom, as thou didst for* Lazarus. *O pity me, for Jesus Christ's Sake*: To whom with thee, O Father, and the Holy Spirit, be ascribed all Honour and Glory for ever *Amen.*

Then Mr. *Parson* said to her, *The Lord is the Hearer of Prayers, and will hear thee—*

Mr. *Belcher* said, *He that has helped thee to make this Prayer will also hear thee—*

She then said, *O Lord Jesus Look down upon me, and Save my Soul; I trust thou wilt Receive my Soul. O Lord I commit my Soul into Thy Hands. O Father of Mercies have Mercy on me. O now Lord Jesus is the Time:—I am upon the Brink of Eternity, O Lord have Mercy upon me. O Thou Father of our Lord Jesus Christ, into thy Hands I commit my Spirit. O Receive thou it. Have Mercy upon me, and Pity me for Jesus Christ's Sake.*

Then the Officer binds an Handkerchief upon her Face—which she cheerfully receives, with Eyes and Hands lift up to Heaven.

Mr. *Wise* said, Now is the great Crisis of Time. Does your Faith hold in God and Christ still—

She answers, *God be thanked it does, God be thanked.*—

Then being bid to lean her Head back upon the Ladder, to receive the

Halter, She readily does it ; and Cryes, *O Lord Jesus, Now Lord Jesus, I am a Coming: O Come Lord Jesus by Thy Pardoning Mercy, to Save me Now, or I Perish for ever. My Blessed Jesus,—O Lord Jesus, have Pity upon me, O Good Lord.*—And thus she remains lifting up her Hands to Heaven, till Mr. *Wise* said again; We have Recommended you to God, and done all we can for you, and must now leave you.—

If your Hopes can lay hold upon the irresistible Grace and Mercy of God in Christ, and you can cast your self into His Armes, you are Happy for Ever.—And so we must bid you *Fare-Well.*

THE manner of her Entertaining DEATH, was even astonishing to a Multitude of Spectators, (being as was judged Four or Five Thousand People at least) with that Composure of Spirit, Cheerfulness of Countenance, pleasantness of Speech, and a sort of Complaisantness in Carriage towards the Ministers who were assistant to her, with their Prayers and Counsils, that even melted the hearts of all that were within seeing or hearing, into Tears of affection, with greatest wonder and admiration. Her undaunted Courage and unshaken Confidence she modestly enough expressed, yet stedfastly held unto the end. So that he must needs want Faith for himself, that wants Charity for such an one.

*Finis.*

## Source Notes

"The Declaration and Confession of Esther Rodgers" was published as part of *Death The certain Wages of Sin to the Impenitent* (Boston, 1701), a collection of the three execution sermons delivered by John Rogers, Jr. (1666–1745). The oldest son of the former Harvard president, Rogers was born and raised in Ipswich and, after finishing his education at Harvard (1684), he returned there and assisted his uncle, William Hubbard, who was minister to the First Congregational Church. Rogers was ordained in 1692, and when Hubbard's health began to fail in 1702, he assumed responsibility for the Ipswich ministry. By the time he encountered Esther Rodgers, he already had established a reputation for evangelicalism. In his *Diary,* Sewall frequently mentioned both his friendship with Rogers, with whom he often stayed with when visiting Ipswich, and the minister's emphasis on evangelical preparation. For such references, see II, 14, 31. Rogers remained in Ipswich his entire life. Not a prolific writer, *Death The certain Wages of Sin* was only one of four publications: an election sermon (1706), a funeral sermon (1739), and a short "Attestation in favor of the revival measures of Whitfield and Tennent"

(Sibley, 3, 276). By far the most ambitious of his publications, *Death The certain Wages of Sin* was endorsed by four other ministers. In addition to his uncle and colleague, William Hubbard, who wrote the first preface, Nicholas Noyes and Joseph Gerrish contributed a second preface, while Samuel Belcher added an introduction to "The Declaration and Confession of Esther Rodgers." For a brief biographical sketch of Rogers, see *Sibley's Harvard Graduates*, III, 273–76.

Sewall also was one of the judges when Esther Rodgers was tried and convicted. Concerning the trial, Sewall commented in his *Diary*: "To Ipswich; Try Esther Rogers. Jury next morn ask'd advice, then after, brought her in Guilty of murdering her Bastard daughter. July, 17. Mr. Cooke pronounc'd the sentence. She hardly said a word. I told her God had put two children for her to nurse: Her mother did not serve her so. Esther [in the Bible] was a great saviour; she, a great destroyer. Said did not do this to insult over her, but to make her sensible" (II, 39). For a discussion of the Rodgers texts, see Williams, "Behold a Tragic Scene."

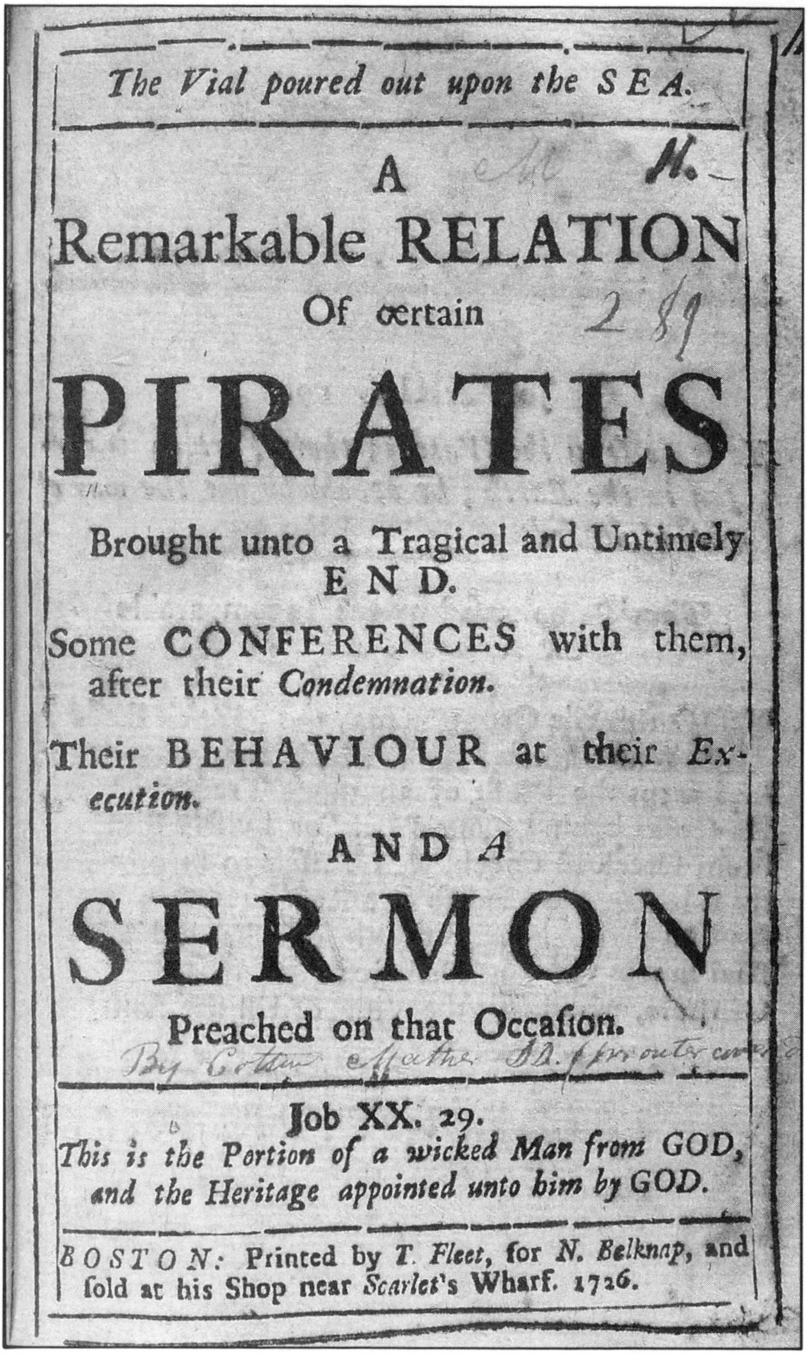

*The Vial poured out upon the* SEA.

A

Remarkable RELATION

Of certain

PIRATES

Brought unto a Tragical and Untimely
END.

Some CONFERENCES with them, after their *Condemnation.*

Their BEHAVIOUR at their *Execution.*

AND *A*

SERMON

Preached on that Occasion.

Job XX. 29.

*This is the Portion of a wicked Man from* GOD, *and the Heritage appointed unto him by* GOD.

*BOSTON:* Printed by *T. Fleet,* for *N. Belknap,* and sold at his Shop near *Scarlet's* Wharf. 1726.

[ WILLIAM FLY ]

# *The Vial Poured Out upon the Sea*

[ 1726 ]

JOB XXIV. 19.

*He is swift as the Waters; their Portion is cursed in the Earth*; he beholdeth not the way of the Vineyards.

Thus Paraphrased by the Incomparable Sir *Richard Blackmore.*

To this vile Crue you may the PIRATE add
Who puts to Sea the Merchant to invade,
And reaps the Profit of another's Trade.
He sculks behind some Rock, or swiftly flies
From Creek to Creek, rich Vessels to surprize.
By this ungodly Course the Robber gains,
And lays up so much Wealth, that he disdains
And mocks the poor, unprofitable Toil,
Of those, who plant the Vine, or till the Soil.

## A Remarkable RELATION of a *Cockatrice* crush'd in the Egg.

A Vessel of that sort which they call, a *Snoe*, belonging to certain Merchants in *Bristol*, and commanded by *John Green*, of that City, sailed from *Jamaica*, some time in *April*, 1726, bound for *Guinea*. The Boatswain, *William Fly*, having before concerted with some aboard, (in a way of

Revenge, they said, for *Bad Usage*) the Destruction of the *Master* and the *Mate*, and the proper *Consequences*, on May 27, about One a Clock in the Morning, he, with one *Alexander Mitchel*, went into the Cabin, and siezing on the Master, held his Hands, while *Mitchel* wounded him. Then they hawled him up; who perceiving their Intention to throw him overboard, beg'd, *For the Lord's Sake, don't throw me overboard*; *For if you do, you throw me into Hell immediately*. But *Fly* bid him say, *Lord, Have Mercy on my Soul*! And when he siezed the Mainsheets with his Hand, to prolong his Time, the merciless Monsters, with a Cooper's Broad-axe, cut off his Hand, and threw him over-board. While this was a doing, one *Samuel Cole*, presently assisted with *Mitchel* and one *Winthrop*, secured the Mate, whose Name was *Thomas Jenkins*, and brought him upon Deck, telling him, *that he should go after the Master*. Accordingly, having first cut him down the Shoulder with a Broad-axe, they threw him over, just before the Main Shrouds. After he was thrown over, he cried out unto the Doctor, *For the Lord's Sake, to fling him a Rope*. But *Fly* soon secured the Doctor, and put him in Irons; and confined the Gunner also and the Carpenter, who were not for their Turn.

Two Days after this, they met one of the Ships, that came out in Company with *Green*, and hailing them, ask'd, How Captain *Green* did. They answered, *Very well! At your Service*! But upon consulting, whether they had best attack that Ship, they left her, in Consideration, That they had not Hands enough to Man her. So, they bore away for *North-Carolina*; Where, off Cape *Hattaras* Bar, on June 3. there lay a Sloop at Anchor, whereof the Commander was one whose Name is *Fulker*. Some of the Sloop's Hands went aboard *Fly*, who was now become the Captain of the *Snoe*, supposing them to want a Pilot. *Fly* commanded *Fulker* aboard, and informed him, *They were Gentlemen of Fortune*; and let him know, that they must have the *Sloop*, if it sailed better than the *Snoe*. The contrary Winds rendring the *Sloop* unable to be brought off, our New Captain fell into a great Passion, and swore he would burn her, and bringing *Fulker* to the Geers, (who it seems, unadvisedly provoked them) inflicted a severe Scourging upon him. The Boats Crue, could not bring the *Sloop* any further than the Bar, but there she bilg'd and sank; and the Pirates endeavoured then to set her on Fire, but could not make the Fire to take. *Fulker* and his Men, and his Passengers, were detained Prisoners by *Fly*; But on June 5. they sailed from thence; and on the Day following they saw a Ship commanded by one whose Name is *Gale*, bound from *Barbados* to *Virginia*. They could not come up with *Gale* till the next Morning; when they hoisted their *Black Flag*, and fired several Guns at the Ship; and there being little Wind, *Gale* struck; and *Fly* made the Men his Prisoners; but robbed the Ship only of several Sails, and some Cloaths and small Arms; and after a Captivity of

Two Days released them; at the same time giving *Fulker*, and one of his Passengers, and a Servant, and *Green's* Doctor, their Liberty. However they forceably detained one *William Atkinson*, who had been Commander of a Brigantine, but left her for a Passage home in *Fulker*, bound then for *Boston*; And who had often declared, That if the *Pirates* ever took him, he would humour them, till he could see his first Opportunity to rise upon them. They wanted him to be their *Pilot*, for the Coast of *New-England*; which they told him, he should be, or, *They would blow his Brains out.* It seems, they forgot, how bad a Coast *New-England* has been for *Pirates* to come upon! Off of *Delaware Bay*, they met a Sloop commanded by one *Harris*, bound from *New-York* to *Pensilvania*, having about Fifty Scotch-Irish Passengers aboard; which upon their hoisting of their *Black Flag* Surrendred unto them. After they had a little ransack'd the Vessel, and kept her twenty four Hours, they forced a Lusty Blade, one *James Benbrook*, from her, and so dismiss'd her. *Fly* bore away for *Martha's Vineyard*, pretending to Water there, and so away for *Guinea*; But the *Pilot* purposely miss'd the port, (whereat *Fly* was very angry,) and on June 23. bearing Eastward, they mett with a *Fishing Schooner*, on *Browns* Bank; from which upon *Fly's* hoisting his *Black Flag*, and threatning to sink her, the Master came aboard them, & *Fly* told him, he must have the *Schooner*, unless he could inform him, where to get a better Sailor. About Noon, they saw some other *Schooners*; and *Fly* sent that *Schooner* with seven hands after them. *Fly* (who had now entirely sold himself to the God of *Ekron*,) and Three other Pirates, whereof one (*Samuel Cole* aforesaid) was in Irons upon Suspicion of Mutiny, remained aboard the *Snoe;* and fifteen others that had been taken by him; namely, *Fulker's* Mate, a couple of his Boys, *Green's* Gunner and Carpenter, five of *Gale's* Men, *Benbrook*, Three Fishermen belonging to the *Schooner*, and our *Atkinson*. While the *Pirates* were gone upon their chase, there appeared in Sight several other Fishing-Vessels; and *Atkinson* by telling *Fly* what he saw, drew him forward, from his two Loaden *Guns*, and *Sword*, which he had with him; and while *Fly* satt on the *Windlace* with his Prospective-Glass, *Benbrook* and *Walker*, (who had been *Fulker's* Mate) upon the Direction from *Atkinson*, secured *Fly*, and put him in Irons; and *Atkinson* struck another of the *Pirates*; and with the Help of the Carpenter, soon confined the other Two. Thus they made themselves Masters of the *Snoe*; the rest of the Prisoners all the while standing unactive, not being made acquainted with the Design, which was now managing for their Deliverance.

On June 26. the Happy *Captors* brought in their *New Captives*; having *taken them Captives, whose Captives they were.* So, *The Triumphing of the wicked*, was *but for a moment.*

And, the *Special Court of Admiralty* which the *Act of Parliament* has ordered for the Trial of *Pirates*, (Whereof the chief Judge, was the Honourable WILLIAM DUMMER Esqr. the Lieutenant Governour, and Commander in Chief, of the *Massachuset-Province*,) quickly tried these *Four Pyrates*, and after plain and full Conviction, on July 3. pass'd the just *Sentence of Death* upon them; namely, upon *William Fly*, the upstart Captain, who was a Young man, about Seven and twenty years of old; *Henry Greenville*, a married Man about forty seven years of Age; *Samuel Cole*, about Thirty seven years of Age, having a Wife and seven Children; And, *George Condick*, a Youth of Twenty, or thereabouts.

They were now cast into a place, Where, besides the *prayers*, which abundance of Godly Christians made for them, That in *the Destruction of the Flesh* their *Spirit* might be *Saved*, great pains were taken, by the Ministers of City, to dispose them for a Return unto God.

## The Execution.

And now, *speedily*, that is to say, On *Tuesday*, the *Sentence against the Evil Works* of these Men, must be executed. One of the Four, namely, *Condick*, was Reprieved. As for *Fly*, he had been all along, a most uncommon and amazing Instance of Impenitency and Stupidity, and what *Spectacles of Obduration* the Wicked will be, when they have by a course of Wickedness under and against Warnings, provoked the GOD of Heaven to withold His Influences from them. The Sullen and Raging Mood, into which he fell, upon his being first *Imprison'd*, caused him to break forth into furious Execrations, and Blasphemies too hideous to be mention'd; and not eat one morsel of any thing, but subsist only upon a little Drinking, for almost all the remaining part of his Life. He declined appearing in the Public Assemblies, on the *Lords-day*, with the other Prisoners, to be under the appointed means of Grace, because, forsooth, *he would not have the Mob to gaze upon him*. He seem'd all along ambitious to have it said, *That he died a brave fellow*! He pass'd along to the place of Execution, with a *Nosegay* in his hand, and making his *Complements*, where he *thought he saw occasion*. Arriving there, he nimbly mounted the Stage, and would fain have put on a Smiling Aspect. He reproached the Hangman, for not understanding his Trade, and with his own Hands rectified matters, to render all things more Convenient and Effectual.

When he was called upon, to *Speak* what he should judge proper to be spoken on that sad occasion, at least for the Warning of Survivers, he only said, That *he would advise the Masters of Vessels to carry it well to their Men, lest they should be put upon doing as he had done.*

At the same time, he declared his obstinate Refusal, to *Forgive* the Person that had been the Instrument of bringing him to Justice. When the Necessity of that *Charity* was urgently press'd upon him; and advantage taken from a Recital of the *Lords-Prayer* used among the Devotions of the Criminals on the present Occasion, to urge it; he still persisted in his *Unrelenting Frame*; and an Expression of that Importance was in the last words, he Expired withal. But it was observed and is affirm'd, by some Spectators, that in the Midst of all his affected *Bravery*, a very sensible *Trembling* attended him; His hands and his *Knees* were plainly seen to *Tremble*.—And so we must leave him for the *Judgment to come*.

The other Two, *Cole* and *Greenville*, had much greater Signs of *Repentance* upon them. They made their *Prayers*, and seem'd continually *praying*, and much affected. They desired the Spectators to take *Warning* by them. And they mentioned Profane *Swearing* and *Cursing*, with *Drunkenness* and *Sabbath-breaking*, as Crimes which were now particularly grievous to them. They also justified the *Court*, as well as acknowledged the *Justice* of the Glorious GOD, in the Punishment they were now brought unto.

A Minister present having made a Pertinent and Pathetic *Prayer*, the Officer, willing that all that was possible might be done for their good, after some time, ask'd them, whether they would have another *Prayer*. *Fly* did not accept the offer, but said, *If the other Two be Ready, I am*! However, the *other Two* desiring it, another such *prayer* was made by another Minister; and after *that*, another by a Third; with which they joined attentively. (while *Fly* look'd about him unconcerned.)

Then the Execution was finished; And *Fly's* Carcase hanged in Chains, on an Island, at the Entrance into *Boston*-Harbour.

*Cole*, being one that could use his Pen, did on the Morning before his Execution, give out a Paper, in which "he Lamented his early accustoming of himself to Profane *Swearing*; and Blasphemous *Language*; and Excessive *Drinking*; and his frequent *stealing of Liquors* from his Master, for the Satisfaction of them who hired him to do it. He added his bitter Lamentations, that when he came to *Man's Estate*, he abandoned himself to criminal Pleasures, to *Drinking*, *Dancing*, *Whoring*, and the rest. He begg'd all *Sea faring-Men* to take Warning by his Ignominious and Miserable Death; to which he was now brought, by the Enticements of the Wicked. He confess'd himself to be justly Condemned; and gave abundance of Thanks, for the Assistance of Good Ministers, and the wholesome Instructions and holy Directions they had given him, and express'd his Hope of entring into

Heaven, by the Blood of His Glorious Redeemer. And he earnestly desired, that this Paper might be published to the World.["]

The poor Man, in the Prison, had owned unto a Minister, That from the Moment of the *Murders* on Board, he never had a minutes Quiet in his Mind, but was continually Meditating how to run away from the *whole World*, and if it were possible run away from *himself.* The Apprehension of his having some Intention to knock the *Vessel* on the Head, and perhaps the *Captain*, caused them, for some Days before Mr. *Atkinson's* happy Revolution, to lay him in *Irons*, and every Day cruelly to bestow more than an Hundred Lashes upon him; whereof he continued Sore to his Death. He now saw the Glorious GOD, beginning to Execute on him *His* Vengeance, by the Hands of his *own* Bloody Companions: And he endured such *Miseries*, as made him look upon his forlorn Circumstances in the *Boston*-Gaol, as a sort of a Deliverance. It was *there* endeavoured, that this *Construction* of his *Miseries* might be set home upon him. However, it was admirable to see, how the Vengeance of GOD, sometimes makes *Accomplices* in Sin, horrible *Scourges* to one another!

It was a Saying of the *Orientals, Happy is he, who corrects his Faults by the Faults of others.* And now, *Happy* would our *Sea-faring* People particularly be, if the *Crimes* and the *Ends* of some whom they have seen *Drowned in Perdition*, might effectually cause them to beware of the *Faults*, with which they may any of them charge themselves.

Upon those words used unto *Achan* just before his Execution, *The Lord shall trouble thee* THIS DAY; the Jews have a Charitable Fancy, That on THAT DAY, he saw an end of all his *Trouble*; and that in the world to come he shall have no further *Trouble*, but be found among the Penitent and the Pardoned. With the *Malefactors*, who dy Penitent and Pardoned, it will be so; But the Infallible Judgment of who are so, is what none but GOD *the Judge of all, can determine* .

*Finis.*

## Source Notes

Cotton Mather's account of William Fly and his fellow conspirators was published as the introductory section of *The Vial poured out upon the Sea* (Boston, 1726). Mather's title for his pirate account was "A Remarkable Relation Of A *Cockatrice* crush'd in the Egg." Since a cockatrice (also known as a basilisk) was one of the deadliest of fabulous serpents (whose merest glance could kill), Mather's title provided readers with an obvious perspective from which to read the text. Following the "Remarkable Relation," he included two long dialogues between himself and Fly. In these exchanges the minister attempted to accomplish in print what he failed to do in person. Fly was one of the most stubborn and defiant pirates ever executed in Boston, not only refusing to cooperate with the authorities but also to express any of the expected signs of penitence. Rather than have the public perceive the recalcitrant pirate as bold, Mather set out in print to render him more foolish than courageous, more damned than defiant. In the dialogues (presented as the conferences he held with the pirates in jail), the minister demonstrated Fly's depravity. Despite the imminence of his execution, the pirate refused to either confess or to forgive. When asked to confess, he responded: "*I can't charge my self with Murder. I did not strike and wound the Master or Mate!*" (8) When asked to forgive, he replied: "*Tis a Vain Thing to dissemble. No; I can't. There are those, that I can't forgive*" (19). Fly even went so far as to justify the mutiny and murders: "*I shan't own myself Guilty of any Murder.—Our Captain and his Mate used us Barbarously. We poor Men can't have Justice done us. There is nothing said to our Commanders, let them ever so much abuse us, and use us like Dogs*" (21). In Mather's account, then, Fly revealed himself to be blindly and stupidly wicked. In concluding his dialogue, the minister surrendered his struggle to save the pirate's soul: "We can do no more, but with *Tears* (which, alas, you have not for yourself!) Lament the unaccountable and unparallel'd *Obduration* that you are given up unto" (21). After his dialogues, the minister inserted his execution sermon, which appropriately took its text from Job 4: 21: "*They Dy even without Wisdom.*" Following this sermon Mather added his execution account, thus using the beginning and the end of Fly's story as a frame narrative for his sacred lessons.

Although his career as a pirate captain lasted barely a month, Fly attracted considerable attention. In addition to the accounts included in *The Boston News-Letter* and *The Boston Gazette* (from June to July 1726), three narratives were published in Boston shortly after the executions: Mather's *Vial*, Benjamin Colman's *It is a Fearful Thing to Fall into the Hands of the Living God*, and Joseph Edwards' *The Tryals of Sixteen Persons for Piracy*. Fly even caused enough of a stir to receive his own chapter in the second volume of Daniel Defoe's *A General History of the Pyrates* (London, 1728). For more recent accounts of Fly, see Dow and Edmonds, Snow, Rankin, and Williams, "Puritans and Pirates." For the best recent discussions of piracy, see Rediker, "Under the Banner" and *Between the Devil and the Deep Blue* and Ritchie.

# Faithful Narrative

OF THE

# Wicked Life

AND

# Remarkable Conversion

OF

## *Patience Boston* alias *Samson*;

Who was Executed at *York*, in the County of *York*, *July* 24*th*. 1735. for the Murder of BENJAMIN TROT of *Falmouth* in *Casco Bay*, a Child of about Eight Years of Age, whom she Drowned in a Well.

---

With a PREFACE by the Reverend Messi. *SAMUEL* & *JOSEPH MOODY*, Pastors of the Churches in said Town.

---

Jer. 31. 19 —— *I was ashamed, yea, even confounded, because I did bear the Reproach of my Youth.*

Isai. 1. 18. —— *Though your Sins be as Scarlet, they shall be as white as Snow; tho' they be red like Crimson, they shall be as Wooll.*

1 Cor. 6. 11. *Such were some of you; but ye are washed &c.*

---

*BOSTON*: Printed and Sold by *S. Kneeland* and *T. Green*, in Queen-Street over against the Prison, 1738.

[ PATIENCE BOSTON ]

# *A Faithful Narrative of the Wicked Life and Remarkable Conversion of Patience Boston*

[ 1738 ]

## To the Candid READER.

*This astonishing Relation of a bloody Malefactor's Conversion, was taken from her Mouth while she was in Prison, and being publickly read to her on the Lecture a few Hours before her Execution, she did unconstrainedly own it, as what she had in very Deed experienced.*

*It must be confessed, that it could not be exactly taken in her own Way of expressing her self; However we are perswaded, that if our Readers could have been Eye and Ear Witnesses of the Emphaticalness of Pronounciation, and of the Spirit with which she uttered Things in themselves infinitely momentous, it must needs have been vastly advantageous to her Character, as a singular Instance of a distinct and thorough, as well as marvellous Work of sovereign and superabundant Grace. Let* GOD *have all the Glory!*

*Here is nothing false or feigned. We are ready to think that more Care could scarce have been taken in offering to the Publick what may be depended on—The Account was not drawn up in haste, but Things were written down at twenty several Times—One Day Week and Month after another.*

*And we trust here is nothing but what may be to the Use of Edifying, by the divine Blessing, to which we recommend the whole;—Concluding with a brief and honest Account how the following Relation comes into thy Hands: It is even thus; A judicious Gentleman of good Learning, and of universal Esteem for Piety and a* PUBLICK SPIRIT, *having Business at our Court, saw a Copy of the Narrative, and being affected to Admiration with the Contents of it, Enquired why it was not printed? and understanding that one Reason of Delay was want of Subscriptions, he was generously moved to be at the whole Expence necessary unto this Publication.*

Samuel Moody
Joseph Moody.

*York, April 24th.*
1738.

## The Relation of *Patience Boston* alias *Samson*, in her 23d Year. Taken from her Mouth.

I Was born at *Menomey* on *Cape Cod* Dec. 26. 1711. My Father's Name was *John Samson*, my Mother's Maiden Name was *Sarah Jethro.* I suppose I was Baptized in my Infancy, my Mother being in full Communion with an Indian Church at *Nosset*, as I have been informed; for my Mother died when I was but about three Years old: Soon after which my Father bound me out to Mr. *Paul Crow*, a Religious Family in which I was taught to Read, and learned the *Assembly's Catechism* thro'. I had seasonable and frequent Warnings against sinful Courses, and was put on secret Prayer. But I was very Wicked, and took little notice of what was said to me. I used to play on the Sabbath, tell Lies, and do other Wickedness. And three Times I set Fire to the House, when I was about twelve Years old. My Mistress would tell me that if I did not repent and turn to God, he might justly leave me to greater Sins. She was greatly concerned for me, and told me she was much afraid I should come to the *Gallows*; and though she might not live to see it, she expected no other but that I should come to some untimely End, if I did not speedily reform. Sometimes she would tell me about *Christ's* Dying for poor miserable Sinners; and I read in my Testament how cruelly *Christ* was buffetted scourged and spit upon, which sometimes affected me, and I asked my Mistress who Christ was? She told me He was the Son of God, and that his Father gave Him to die for Sinners. And told me of the Prophecies concerning Christ, particularly, I remember she mention'd that of his being *a Man of Sorrows, and acquainted with Grief.* Now my Mistress observing as I suppose, that I was something affected, and hoping I might be under some Convictions, she pressed me to repent of my many and heinous Sins, and mention'd Christ's Word to me about the *Joy* that would be in *Heaven* over a *repenting Sinner* —Thus she followed me continually with Reproofs, Instructions, Counsels and Warnings; and moderate seasonable Corrections, as long as she lived, which was till I was about fifteen Years old; and on her Death-Bed she charged me to mind the Counsel she had given me, and to refrain from evil Words and shun bad Company, and keep the Sabbath strictly, and never tell any more Lies, and to keep my self from the Sin of Uncleanness, and to pray to God for Grace. These Things considerably moved me for a Time, and I think I could not have mourned more, if my own Mother had died then. I am sure now, since my Eyes have been opened, I see that she was a Mother to me, though I was a wicked mischievous and rebellious Servant. One Thing among other shews that I was not only Profane, but set on Mischief. My Master had an Uncle, an old Man that lived in the House, whom I used to mock and study to vex, particularly by turning the Cattle into the Corn when the Folks were gone to Meeting, and then calling on him to drive them out, making him believe they broke into the Field. Now my Mistress being dead, my Master would often put me in Mind of her good Counsel &c; but I had soon worn off that little Sense I had of Religion. My Convictions were too weak for my strong and violent Corruptions. I went out a Nights, and kept bad Company, and followed lewd Practices, till I was freed from my Master, after which I thought my self happy that I had no Body to Command me. I might do as I pleased, and I grew worse and worse, and fell into the Sin of Stealing, and all with little or no Remorse of Conscience. In about a Year, I was Married to a Negro Servant; and because his Master would have it so, I bound my self a Servant with him during his Life Time, or as long as we both should live.

After this I was drawn in to the Love of strong Drink, by some Indians, & used to Abuse my Husband in Words and Actions, being mad and furious in my Drink, speaking dreadful Words, and wishing bad Wishes to my self and others. After I found I was with Child, I had tho'ts of murdering it, and whilst I was big I ran away from my Master, my Husband being Absent on a Whaling Voyage; and I drank hard, and broke the Marriage Covenant, being wicked above Measure. After I got Home, I was delivered of a Child, which I had hurt in my Rambling, so that both its Arms were broken, as was found in Dressing the Child; and it died in a few Weeks, so that I now think I am Guilty of its Death. But my Conscience then was in a dead Sleep. I went on in Drinking, Lying, Swearing, and Quarelling with my Husband, who gave me little or no Occasion, unless by his continual good Counsel. But after I found my self to be with Child again, I was brought under some Conviction; so that I refrain'd from my wicked Courses, and loved to hear my Husband read, and would sit up to read my self after the Folks were in Bed, and loved to hear the Word Preached, and began to pray in Secret, according to my first Mistress's Counsel, though I have never practiced this great Duty before. I went also to speak with the Minister, about my Spiritual State and present Troubles, who gladly received me, and both Counselled and Encouraged me; gave me a Catechism and turned me to several Answers which he judg'd suitable for me, advising me to think much of them. He gave me also an excellent little Book, and came to me with farther good Instructions. My Convictions continued several Months, and good People hoped I was becoming a new Creature. But I left God, and he left me; which made me think of my first Mistress's Words to me, '*That Sinning would make me leave Praying or Praying would me leave Sinning.*' I left off Prayer, and soon returned to wicked Courses, drowning all good Tho'ts, Desires, Purposes and Beginnings of Reformation, in strong Drink; growing worse than ever before, till I grew near my Time, when I was something startled at the Tho'ts of Death, concluding I must certainly go to Hell, if I died then. For besides all my other heinous Abominations, I had *Murder* in my *Heart* towards my Second, as well as my first Child; and so I had after my Child was born, attempting something that way when I perceived it's Crying, and it's taken up my Time to tend it, caused some Uneasiness in the Family. And when at the end of two Months, it pleased God to take away the Child by sudden Death in the Bed by us, which terrified me not a little; yet in less than a Month, getting mad with strong Drink, I quarrelled with my Husband, and to vex him, told him that I had Murdered our last Child, and stood to it, appealing to God as a Witness that I had killed it; so that my Husband said, he must go to the Justice, and inform against me. I told him, I would go with him, and accuse my self before the Justice, which I did. He perceiving that I was in Drink, put me off till the next Morning: But I got more Drink on purpose to harden me in the Lies I had framed against my self; and being sent for, I still affirmed that I had killed my Child. But the Justice not finding me sober, put off a full Examination to the Afternoon. Accordingly, towards Night he came to my Master's, and hearing his Voice, I presently ran to my Bottle, and drank more Rum; and a third Time affirmed my self to be guilty of murdering the Child, and was sent to Prison. After I came to be confined, I was in a distressed Condition, not so much for my wicked Heart or wicked Life; for I saw little of either: as for fear of Death and Hell, not being fit to go into another World. But I was resolved and fixed in my Mind, not to tell any more Lies; for I knew that if I went out of the World with a Lie in my Mouth, my Punishment from the Hand of God would be the greater; and I had little or no Hope of escaping Punishment from the Hand of Man. For as I said, I had three Times accused my self before the single Justice who sent me to Prison, and afterwards before three Justices together, all which witnessing against me on my Trial; I expected no other, but to be Condemned and Executed. So I prayed to God three Times a Day for the Pardon of all my Sins, especially that of Lying so often against my Conscience, and thereby destroying my own Life. This I thought was a greater Sin, than if I had indeed Murdered my Child.

But when I came on my Trial; pleading Not Guilty, I was acquitted, and my Heart rejoyced. I was sent back again to Prison, till Security should be given for the Charges; but I chose rather to be Bound to a new Master for two Years, than to go back to my last Master; and my Husband consenting, I was Bound to Capt *Dimmick*, who after about a Year sold me, at my desire, to Mr. *Joseph Bailey* of *Casco Bay*, I being enticed by an Indian Woman who was sold in those Parts; and the great Thing that moved me to desire to go into the Eastern Parts was the Hope I had of more Opportunity to follow my wicked Courses. And I have ever since, lived in Drunkenness, and Swearing; and once again accused my self of Murdering a Child, which I affirmed I had had there, which appeared to every Bodies Satisfaction, to be a meer Falshood; for nothing was to be found where I said I had buried the Child, and a Number of Women on Examination declared I had not then been delivered of a Child.

I am thus free and full in confessing my heinous Trangressions, with the dreadful Aggrevations of them, that I may justify God, and be a Warning to Sinners, especially young People, not to give Way to the beginnings of Sin; but to resist Temptations, and avoid the Occasions of Evil: As also that the sparing Mercy, Long Suffering Patience and pardoning Grace of God may be magnified, and many may be excited to praise and glorify the Name of the Lord, and that despairing Sinners may come to hope in God's Mercy, if it may appear that such a Monster of Wickedness is plucked as a Firebrand out of everlasting Burnings, and received into Gods Favour through Christ.

But to speak of that horrid wilful Murder, of which I have indeed been guilty. From some groundless Prejudice which I had taken against my Master, to whom I was sold by Mr. *Bailey*, I did last Fall bind my self by a wicked Oath that I would kill that Child, though I seem'd to love him, and he me; which is an Aggravation of my bloody Cruelty to him. Having solemnly sworn that I would be the Death of the Child, I was so far from repenting of it, that I thought I was obliged to fulfil it. And I often renewed my Resolution when I had been in Drink, and made my Master angry, that to be revenged on him, I might Murder his Grand-Child, of which I thought he was very fond, having bro't him up from his Infancy. I would have killed my Master himself, if I could have done it; and had Thoughts of putting Poison into his Victuals, if I could have got any. But when the Time came for me to be left under the prevailing Power of Satan's Temptations; I took the Opportunity of my Master and Mistress being from Home, and both his Sons also abroad; that the Child and I were left alone. The

Evening before I had been contriving to burn the Barn, but was prevented: I had also once before drawn the Child into the Woods with me, designing to knock him on the Head, and got a great Stick for the same Purpose; but as I was going to lift it up, I fell a trembling, from a sense of God's Eye upon me; so that I had not Power to strike.—But now, as I was going to say, when the Time was come to fill up the Measure of my Iniquity; I went to the Well and threw the Pole in, that I might have an Excuse to draw the Boy to the Well, which having done, I asked his Help to get up the Pole, that I might push him in, which having done, I took a longer Pole, and thrust him down under the Water, till he was drowned. When I saw he was dead, I lifted up my Hands with my Eyes towards Heaven, speaking after this Manner, Now am I guilty of Murder indeed; though formerly I accused my self falsly, yet now has God left me &c. And it seemed as if the Ground where I went was cursed for my sake, and I thought God would not suffer me to escape his righteous Vengeance. I went forthwith, and informed the Authority, and when the Jury sat on the Body, I was ordered to touch it: This terrified me, lest the Blood should come forth, to be a Witness against me; and I then resolved in my Heart, that I would be a Witness against my self, and never deny my Guilt; so I tho't God would not suffer the Child to bleed; then I laid my Hand on it's Face, but no Blood appeared. Yet after this, I would fain have covered my Sin in Part, as if the Child had of himself fallen into the Well, and I was tempted to thrust him down under the Water. After the *Jury* had bro't in wilful Murder, I was sent to Prison, but got Drunk by the Way, having little Sense of my dreadful Case; yet my Temptation in Part was to drink that I might forget my Sorrow. After I was shut up, I encouraged my self that I should have a long Space to repent, and have nothing else to do for most Part of a Year; and I set on Praying and Reading, Day and Night. While I was awake, my Thoughts were upon my former wicked Life, and present woful Condition that I had bro't my self into, by Murdering a poor innocent Child, that never did me Hurt. And I wholly refrained from strong Drink, and desired I might have good Books to read, and seemed glad when any came to Visit me; but did not at first desire Visits from Ministers, till I found how desirous they were to help me, and that I might speak freely to them, and that I needed their Direction. The first Minister that visited me, was the Minister of a neighbouring Congregation, (the Minister of the Town being from Home,) He endeavoured to shew me my utter Inability to Help my self: I might as well, he said, reach the Heavens with my Arm, as turn from Sin to God; leading me in his Discourse to Christ, and Faith in him, with a diligent Use of all Means, in order to a thorough Conversion; telling me I must spend *all* my Time in Prayer Reading and Meditation, as being liable every Day to a natural Death, as well as others. So he pressed on me a speedy Repentance without the least Delay. Those Words seemed to sink down into my Heart, and had an abiding Influence. Thus by variety of Helps, I was lead something into the Knowledge of my Self, how unable I was to repent & believe, and how necessary Faith was. I saw it to be really so by plain Scripture, especially by several Places in John, particularly, John 3. 16. *God so loved the World, that he gave his only begotten Son, that whosoever believeth in him, should not perish, but have everlasting Life.* So my Mind ran much on Believing in Christ. But I thought I must repent too, and that of all my Sins. And in Reading, Praying, Hearing the Word preached, and discourse with such as visited me; I thought I had got some Sense of Sin, in many Ways wherein I had practised it from my Childhood. But it troubled me, that I could not see the Sin of Murder, as I concluded I must see it, before God would pardon me. And I had an earnest desire that the Congregation would pray for me, that I might have a further Discovery of the Evil of Sin, of all my Sins, and especially *Murder.* Then a Note was written for me, and my Desires were offered up to God. I found no great Alteration all that Week, though I held on in the Use of Means, thinking I would not, I must not despair. If I despaired, I thought I should be as *Cain.* But the next Week after, (the People of God still spreading my Case before the Lord) I had such strong Convictions and killing Terrors as amazed me: My Sins were set in Order before me, especially the Sin of Murder; So that though I had desired to see my Sins, yet I could not bear the Sight of them; for the Sense I had of the Wrath of God against me for Sin, was intollerable; my Conscience seem'd all on a Flame. I sent to desire that the Minister would come to me; but he not being at Home, the School Master came, and talked and prayed with me, and I had some Relief for the Present. But my Distress returned, continued, increased. My Sins appeared too great to be Pardoned. God, I thought, had utterly forsaken me. I could not Pray for five Days together, whereas I used to pray six Times a Day.—Now I did not dare to take the Name of such a holy and glorious God into my Mouth, in this Way. The Prayers of such a Monster of Wickedness, I thought, would be an Abomination to the Lord. I had indeed some encouraging Places of Scripture brought to my Mind, such as *Isai. 55[.] 6. 7.* &c. yet I could not believe any Word of Comfort or Encouragement belonged to me. And the Destroyer of my Soul hurried me, hurried me from Day to Day, to murder my self; and if I could have found a Way to put an End to my Life, I should surely have done it. I wished for a Knife, or a String, my Garters and Coat-String being taken from me. I wished I could have gone to the Water, which I saw through the Grates, to have Drowned my self. I wrung my Hands, and beat my Breast, and could have torn into my Vitals, if I had strength to do it. All the while, laying the whole Blame on my self. I had been convinced indeed that my Heart was as full of Enmity against God, as any Serpent against Man; but my Enmity in these Agonies of Soul, did not appear to be working. I thought I had so dishonoured God beyond all Example, that he could not bear the Sight of me among the Living on Earth; I had as good go to Hell, I thought, first as last, having not the least Glimpse of Hope, ever to escape that Place of Torment. I knew Hell would be worse still, though all the Pains of Travail and Sickness, with all the Anguish I ever felt before, was nothing to this; but I saw plainly that I deserved eternal Misery, and Hell was the only fit Place for me. I was angry with the Prison Keeper for restraining me from my self-murdering Desires. The Ministers and others visited me in this Condition, and would encourage me to hope in the infinite Mercy of God and Merits of Christ, mentioning many Promises and Examples of pardoning Mercy, out of the Scriptures; but nothing reached me. I could take hold of nothing till the Time of Mercy and Love was come, I could not be perswaded to believe, that ever such a Sinner as I had been, was pardoned. I thought of *David*; but then I considered that he committed only two great Sins, whereas I had committed all Kinds of Sins, I thought, and had committed Adultery and Fornication often, and often committed Murder in my Heart; but *David* only once fell into those Sins, and I thought he did not Sin with such an Heart as I did; for he was a Man after God's own Heart. So that after all that I had read, or heard, or could think; my Case seemed desperate, till I seemed to have some Glimmering of Hope, and a Day or two after such Light and Joy, so sweet and good, that I can no more express it, than I can make known the desperate Sorrow and Anguish that went before, in the Extremity of it. It came after the following Manner; I went to Bed one Night, full of Trouble; but not in utter Despair. It was long before I could get any Sleep, as I had before lien whole Nights waking, whilst I meditated on nothing but Terror. But falling asleep at length, I slept I suppose till after Midnight, then awaked in a more calm and easy Frame than I had been for a Week before, when I used sometime to cry out at my first Waking, that I was going to Hell! But now I could think about Believing in Christ. All my Thoughts seemed to run upon Believing, Believing; and I could pray that God would enable me to believe, and give me converting Grace. And it was plain to me that it must be the Almighty Power of God, to make me believe. And I began to hope he would do it for Christ's Sake, being perswaded that he was able to do it for me, having read two Sermons of Dr. *Increase Mather's* on Isai. 63. 1.—*Mighty to save*; Wherein he shews that Jesus Christ is a mighty Savour. For though I had read several Books, yet none of them seemed so plainly to lead me to Christ, as that Book. I had indeed in my Extremity forgotten this, and all Grounds of Encouragement; but now it was a great Help to me, that by Books and Ministers and good Christians, both Men and Women, I have been so abundantly directed to Christ, and encouraged to trust in him. And as I lay waking and musing about this mighty Saviour and about believing in Christ for Salvation; these Words came fresh into my Heart. *Weeping may endure for a Night, but Joy cometh in the Morning.* I did not remember that ever I had read such Words in the Bible; yet I thought it was God spoke it to my Heart. It was not like Man's speaking. Yet after this I was ready to give Way to some unbelieving Thoughts, that would be rising in my Mind, or were cast into me; till I had another Scripture, which though at first I did not know to be any Part of God's written Word, yet afterwards I found to be Christ's Words to unbelieving *Thomas* , John 20. 27. *Be not faithless, but believing;* and it is added, v. 29. *Blessed are they which have not seen, and yet have believed;* which is further Matter of Comfort to me. I had not seen Christ, with my bodily Eyes; but I think he has spoken to my Heart, by his Spirit; and that I have seen him by the Eye of Faith. Now I was carried out in more free Confession of my Sins, so many and great, and especially the Sin of Murder; and more earnest in my Prayers that God would blot out my Transgressions, and cast my Sins behind his Back, than ever in my Life before. When the Morning came, I looked out, and all Things seemed pleasant and smiling. I thought if I was to be Executed that Day, Death would seem pleasant to me. God seemed now to accept my Prayers and Praises, which could never enter into my Heart to believe, in the Time of my Distress. But I soon found some jealous Thoughts arising in my Mind, least I might flatter and deceive my self; That such a one as I should ever obtain pardoning Mercy, seemed too good News to be true, and I was suspicious of a false Spirit, and the joy of a Hypocrite. But examining my Heart, I could not find that I depended on any Thing in my self. I had I thought been emptied of *self Righteousness,* and seen all to be but as *filthy Raggs;* and I could not but believe in Christ, though it was with a Mixture of Unbelief. Now Sin seemed to be the most hateful Thing in the World to me, and I loathed my self for Sin, because God had been so dishonoured. I had a comfortable Day, beyond all the Joys that the World could afford, above all the Pleasures of Sin. Several comfortable Scriptures were brought to my Mind. John 3. 16. Rev. 22. 17.—*Whosoever will, let him take the Waters of Life freely.* I wished I could glorify God, my Heart seemed to be set on Glorifying of God. I wanted to have some good People come, and help me to praise God. I desired also to know from some that had Knowledge in the Scriptures, and were acquainted with the Way of God's Spirit; what the Meaning of this strange Alteration in my Condition was, and how it used to be with such as were Converted, and what used to follow on Believing in Christ, and whether a false Spirit might not cause Light and Joy. I had none to open my Mind to all that Day; but in the Evening I acquainted the Woman of the House something with my new Condition, and she asked me whether I would speak with the Minister? at which I was glad, and the Minister was called, and I related to him, as well as I could, what I had experienced of Light and Comfort, and what my Desires were, having made known to him my Trouble and Distress before. He gave me Counsel and Caution, and encouraged me to hold on seeking and waiting for further Discoveries. I passed the Night following in a joyful, yet mournful Frame; seeing now what a glorious and holy and gracious God I had sinned against. My Heart seemed to be melted within me, and Sin appeared worse than Hell. I hated Sin, because God hated it; and I loathed my self for Sin, and for my dishonouring God, more than ever I loathed a Toad, or a Rattle Snake. But still rejoycing in my Saviour, and weeping for Joy, praying that God would not take his Holy Spirit from me, and that I might have a Heart to love and praise the Lord, so long as I lived. I was greatly strained to know how I should behave my self, and what I should do to glorify God. I thought I would while I lived, and especially when I came to die, give Warning to all, and especially to *Young People*, of the Evil and Danger of Forsaking the Lord and running into Temptation, and following sinful Courses, to provoke God further to leave them. The shameful Death I was to die, had now no Terror in it, so long as I thought Christ, by being made a Curse, redeemed Sinners from the Curse of the Law. I cannot easily express how willing I was to die for my Sin by the Hand of Justice, that the Guilt of Blood might not lie upon the Land. I thought I would not be released, if I might. Now I saw it was easy to believe, when in the Light; though it seemed so hard, and sometimes impossible, while in the darkness of my natural Estate. But I was told, I must expect to meet with Darkness still as well as Light, and that I must endeavour to believe in the Dark: so I thought I would; but then I tho't also that I should believe when God helped me to believe, and that if he should leave me, I was gone. My Comfort continued, without any considerable Darkness, for several Days and Nights; after which I had a short Time of Trouble, an Hour of Darkness. It brought me into a trembling Condition, yet I was enabled to believe still, and to rejoyce, though with trembling. This was not like the Darkness and Terror I had been in before. I tho't now God was only chastening me, to do me Good, and make me more watchful and humble and thankful, and with the returning Light and Comfort, I took great Delight in reading good Books, especially the *Bible*. I have seen more in a Verse, than formerly I could do in all the Bible. Good People, that I used to despise and hate in Time past, seem the most excellent in the World.

After this was the *Friday Lecture*, for two Sabbaths before which, I was not out; the first of them, I was not well; and on the other, I was in such Distress of Soul, and so hopeless of getting any Good, that I had no Heart to go to Meeting; but being in so comfortable a Frame the most of that

Week I attended the Lecture with Joy and Delight of Soul, beyond what I ever had at any merry Meeting for Drinking, or lewd Practices. The Text was Jer. 10. 16. *The Portion of Jacob is not like them.* Doct. *No People in the World have such a Portion as the People of God.* I thought I could have sat all Day and all Night, under Christ's Shadow, his Fruit was so sweet to my Taste, sweeter than Honey to my Mouth. I returned to my *beloved Prison*, which seemed a most *pleasant Place* to me, since I *met with Christ here*, and have had Communion with God in holy Duties. Prayer is my Delight. I am sometimes so carried out that I can't break off, till I am spent. I am ready to sink down; but at other Times, I am so troubled that I cannot speak in Prayer, God seems to shut the Door against me; and not to welcome me into his Presence. Especially once that after Morning Prayer, I had neglected Reading and Praying, (having some Work to do) till towards Night; though my Conscience, I can't tell how many Times in the Day, checked me for it. Yea I thought afterwards, it was the Spirit of God by my Conscience, that moved me to holy Duties. I found when I came to Pray that God was withdrawn from me; that I could scarce speak a Word. The Thoughts of my having quenched the Spirit, in not readily complying with his Motions, quite overcame me; so that I was fain to go from my Knees to my Bed; where I lay sadly bemoaning my self, that I had grieved away the good Spirit of God; and when he would return to me I could not tell. Then I saw what a poor weak Creature I was, and how impossible it was for me to perform any Duty, except the Lord was with me, enabling me by his Grace. Nor could I make one Prayer more till Help was called in, and I had the Meaning of God's Dealing with me opened to me, and had divers Examples of poor Indians converted, and how they lived, and how they died, read to me; by which I was refreshed and revived, and could pray with usual Liberty and Enlargement. And in the Night following, I had sweet Scriptures brought to my Mind out of the Psalms and Gospels, particularly that in the fourth Psalm, *Thou has put Gladness into my Heart, more than in the Time when their Corn and Wine increased.* As Dr. *Mather's* Sermons in general on Christ the mighty Saviour, have been exceeding helpful to me; so I would mention one Passage in particular, which was as Life from the Dead to my Soul. It is near the End of the first Sermon in these Words—"Believing Sinners are they unto whom this Saviour will be the Author of their eternal Salvation. Their Salvation is begun, as soon as they believe. He that believes, *hath* everlasting Life. It is not only true, that he shall have everlasting Life; but he *hath* it already, in the beginning of it; and is in Respect of the Promise of God, as sure of Heaven, as if he were there already. John 3. 16. *God so loved the World, that he gave his only begotten Son, that whosoever believes in him, should not perish but have everlasting Life.*" It was not long after this before the Lord did as it were tell me, he would more thoroughly break my Heart for Sin, and then bind it up, and heal it. Accordingly, I found renewed inward Mourning and Grieving for Sin, as against a glorious holy good and gracious God. I was pained at my very Heart; I felt it as plain as I could do a Sore breeding in my Flesh. I had a more steady and continued Sorrow for my Sins; I thought I would have given a World had I a World to give, that I had never sinned as I had done. My Sin was ever before me, and it seemed to make me Heart sick, to look back on any, and on all my wicked Ways. I loathed and abhorred my self. It was my fixed Perswasion that there was not one in all this Country, who had been so bad as I. I thought of many Malefactors that I had read or heard of, and many Examples that were read to me, out of Dr. *Cotton Mather's* Church History; but I saw my self worse than any of them. So I hoped God was humbling me yet more, and killing Sin in my Heart. It seemed better to have humbling Considerations set before me, than any Thing that might have a tendency to lift me up. I dealt plainly with my self, and it seemed hateful to me to be flattered; I could not abide any Thing which looked that Way. My Affections to earthly Things seemed to be more deadned; and my Love, I hope, was fixed on that which is Good. How sweet was reading and praying and musing and hearing and speaking of Christ! Good Books were precious to me, but the *Bible* seemed more *delightsome* than any Book; and *Christ* was more *precious*. I hope I have a Treasure in Heaven, because my Heart is there.—The Rev. Mr. *S.* of *Falmouth* came to visit me, and dealt plainly with me; and I thought I had cause to bless God, not only for the great Encouragement he gave me, but for laying open my Sins before me in such a Manner as he did. He visited me a second Time, and assured me, that his plain Dealing with me, was in Faithfulness to the Lord, and in Love to my Soul; affectionately renewing the Encouragement he had given me; and among other precious Scriptures mentioned that in I. Tim. 1. 15. *This is a faithful saying, and worthy of all Acceptation, that Jesus Christ came into the World to save Sinners; of whom I am chief.* I was comfortable for several Days; but then as the *Sabbath* came on, I was strangely hurried with new Temptations; and falling under Fears again that my Heart was not right, I grew more and more discouraged about my eternal State; and it was strongly suggested to me that if God would convert me, he would do it of his own Mind; and not for my Prayers, or the Prayers of any for me. So I thought to wait, and see what God would do for me; and not to use any Means. The Temptation prevailed so far upon me on Saturday Evening, that I thought I should not go to Meeting, the Mind I was then in: but it was a wicked Mind, and I was soon made to see it; for my Sins were again set in order before me, especially the most heinous of them; and I had *Blasphemous Thoughts* cast into me, such as are not fit to be mentioned. My Terror increased, and I feared God might by a

Thunder Bolt or some other Way, strike me dead; but I strove against such abominable Thoughts. I think I can say, my Soul did, and does hate them. I cried to the Lord, and Help was unexpectedly sent in, after it was Night. I had seasonable Relief, and could take my natural Rest; yet not without getting up more than once, in the silent Night, to pray. And in the Morning I could joyfully attend the publick Worship, and in the Afternoon Exercise I was so delighted, that I wished the Meeting might not be done so soon as usual; I thought I could have sat and heard the Word, many Hours. I returned to Prison in my Chains of Iron; but more comfortable than I could have been with a Chain of Gold, in my former imprisoned State of Soul. The Prison-Keeper came to me, counselled and comforted me; and what he said to me, seemed to take hold of me. I have reason to bless God for putting me into the Hands of such as are so kind to me and tenderly concerned for me, both as to my Soul and Body; I hope God will reward them. I now see the Kindness of the Lord, in all the Kindness that good People in this Place are continually shewing me. I believe it is for Christ's sake; and whatsoever becomes of me, God will reward them. I find the Lord is discovering to me more and more of the Hardness of my Heart, which I never was sensible of before this Time of my Imprisonment. When I was in Prison before, if any Body had told me what an Heart I had, I could not have believed it. This makes me justify God, and wonder I am out of Hell; and I think I should desire to serve God, and do something for his Glory and the Good of Souls whilst I live, though he should turn me into Hell at last. I was much affected with the Case of the Prisoners at *Boston*, especially when the Day came for their Execution, having heard that they were too little sensible of their own Condition: I prayed for them as well as I could; and it seemed to me, in the Hope I then had that God had begun good Work in my Soul, that I would have been willing to take the Place of one of them; if an Exchange might have been made, and he might take my Place, to have more Time to prepare for Death. But I had need improve all the Time I may have, if it were much more, in Mourning for my wicked Heart and Life; by which I have dishonoured God, and destroyed my own Soul. Soon after this, I had a further and deeper Sense than ever, of the Hardness of my Heart. The whole Night after the three Malefacters were Executed at *Boston*, and all the next Day, and the Night following, till almost Break of Day; I was distressed, not only on the Account of my horrid Guilt, and Liableness to eternal Wrath, for my wicked Life, and bloody actual Sins; but for the Wickedness of my Heart. I could not read, I could not pray, and when the Minister and others came to talk with me, I could not speak, or if my Mouth was opened sometimes, it was only in Way of self Condemning. My Conscience was continually accusing of me, God seemed to frown upon me; and Satan ready to devour me. I could take

Comfort in nothing: I had sweet consolation in Scriptures before; but I could find no Relief on looking back on any of them. One Word was mentioned to me that seemed to relieve me, for about a Quarter of an Hour; It was John 10. 28. &c. *I give unto them eternal Life, and they shall never perish, neither shall any pluck them out of my Hand* &c. Then I was utterly benighted again, and feared that God had given me up. Rom. 9. 18. was a dreadful Word to me, and would be running in my Mind, all Day and all Night; for I could sleep but very little, for two whole Nights. Now I tho't I understood what I had heard about *Pharaoh*; That his Hardness of Heart was a worse Judgment than all the ten Plagues that were upon him, and upon his People. I was ready to wish I had never been born, and I had a more wicked Thought than that in my Heart; for I wondred that God would make me, when he knew that I should so Sin against him. Before my Heart was changed, I had had Thoughts more Blasphemous, and then I harboured them more than I could do now; for now I desired to justify God, and though I could not so fully as I would; yet I was greatly troubled and vexed at my self, that I could not love the Lord as I had done before. All the outward Crosses I had met with seemed nothing to this Plague of an hard Heart. I think, if my Distress had continued to that Degree a few Days, it would have distracted me. The Door of Mercy seemed to be shut against me; and to miss of the Favour of God, after I had had such Hopes, seemed worse to me than if I had never been brought out of my first Darkness into such marvellous Light. I hope this inexpressible Distress I was in humbled me; And the return of Light and Comfort again was the more sweet to me. And that Word came unto me with Power, *Be of good cheer, thy Sins be forgiven thee.* Then I thought of a Passage in Dr. *Mather*, which I mention'd before, as Life from the Dead to me, and I could reason about what God had done for me; That having spoken Peace to my Soul, and changed my Heart, I should never quite fall away.

I thought my Salvation was begun when I first believed, and God would finish his own Work; and I thought it was not for any to direct God how he should do it, or when. When I came to see the Light of another Morning, to find that I was not only out of Hell, but to have fresh and lively Hopes of getting to Heaven; how thankful, as well as joyful, did I seem to be! I never was so thankful before; and my Peace and Joy continued to and through the Sabbath, excepting once in the Forenoon, when Rev. 21. 8. was mentioned, that *Whoremongers, Adulterers, Thieves, and all Liars should have their Part in the Lake that burns with Fire and Brimstone;* this struck a Damp to me, knowing that I had been a Fornicator, Adulterer, Thief and Liar, besides my Blood Guiltiness; it filled my Heart with Grief, and my Eyes with Tears. But after, in the Sermon, the Example of the Woman who washed Christ's Feet with her Tears &c. was mentioned out of *Luke 7.* and what Christ said about the Creditor's frankly forgiving the greater as well as lesser Debtor, though he owed ten Times as much as the other; my Spirit revived, and I thought none in the World had more cause to love Christ than I; who had so much forgiven me. The Example also of *Manasseh* was mentioned, and how he was humbled and pardoned, though he had filled *Jerusalem* with innocent Blood, from one End to the other. So in the Way of Believing I had Joy and Peace; which continued without prevailing Darkness and Distress for several Days.

The Rev. Mr. *W.* of *Berwick* preached a Sermon at *York*. In Sermon Time, especially towards the Close, I hope I had real Communion with God, under a believing sense of his gracious Presence with his People in his House. And in Prayer after Sermon, my Soul seemed to be so much in Heaven where God is most gloriously present; that I had for a little while forgot as it were that I was yet upon Earth. I can't remember that ever I had that Degree of Comfort before or since, though in its Strength it lasted not long.—It was some Time before that, I heard a Sermon from Rom. 9. 18. *Therefore he has Mercy on whom he will have Mercy, and whom he will be hardneth.* I had often read the whole Chapter, being directed to it by the Minister; but was never so sensibly convinc'd how necessary and how reasonable a Thing it was to submit to God's Sovereign Will in all Things. It was shown in one of the Sermons, how that there were many that did grudge the Grace of God to others, especially such as had been black and bloody Sinners.

I thought if God should have no Mercy on me, but harden me to my eternal Ruin, he was just; he might do what he would with his own. I thought if I were damned, I desired others might be saved.

This was before we heard of the Court's Ajournment. The Minister applied himself to me, and told me, he hoped I would no more behave my self proudly before God and Man. I must confess I had dreadful risings of Heart against God's Decrees concerning the Children of Men, and his Disposing of them, according to his mere Will and Pleasure; but I hoped I should never more be found fighting against God. Yet I have found since that there was much Ignorance and Rebellion remaining. I was sometimes sorely Tempted to deny my Guilt on my Trial; and while this Temptation lasted, I had no inward Comfort. The vain Hope I had of escaping the Gallows, and enjoying my Child, and going back to my Relations and Acquaintance, afforded me many pleasing Tho'ts; but it was not like the Joy of the Lord I had before, and have had since. When the Minister ask'd me after my Recovery from the Temptation, which was best, carnal Joy, and worldly Comfort; or the Joy of the Holy Ghost? I could not but say that spiritual Comfort was a Thousand Times, a Million Times the best.

That wicked Frame continued a Week or Ten Days. I was tempted on

Saturday, not to go to Meeting the next Day, having been in a dark Frame the Sabbath before. I did not find those Longings for the Sabbath, and Rejoycings at the near Approach of it; as I had sometimes found. Besides I had so grieved such as used to visit me, and now knew of my evil Frame; that I was ashamed to be seen by them. I thought I would go to Meeting no more till my Trial was over: But one that heard me speak my Mind, told me God would change it: and entreated me, if I had any love to God, or my own Soul; that I would not stay away from Meeting. This put me on thinking how few Sabbaths I had to live; for my solemn Vow came to Mind, and indeed was almost always in my Mind; and though in that bad Frame I began to wish I had not made it: yet having made it, I began to think again I must fulfil it; and there was but two Sabbaths and a Lecture before the sitting of the Court; and how shall I answer it (thought I,) if I should neglect them. Thus I was enabled to take up a Resolution that I would attend the publick Worship, and nothing should hinder me.

But that very Night my poor Child was taken with a Fever, so that I could not carry it out; and was justly deprived of the Opportunity. My Child was dangerously ill. I examined my self, whether I was willing to part with it; and hoping God would take it to himself, I think I was willing. (And before this I had been brought I trust to justify God, though he should cast it into Hell.) I thought also that my own Death would be easier, if my Child was gone before; so I was willing God should do as he pleased. I desired the Prayers of the Congregation for it; and when God was pleased to restore it, I desired to be a truly thankful, and thought God might graciously continue it to me as a Comfort in my lonely Condition.

For many Days before my Trial I was fixed in my Resolution, as I had been for the most Part from the Time I made the Promise; to Plead Guilty. And I was so pressed in my Conscience to take the Guilt of Blood from the Land, on my self; that nothing could prevail with me to deny the Fact; Yea when I had Liberty to plead again after I had once pleaded Guilty; my Conscience constrained me to do it a second Time.

One of the Judges asked me why I did not plead *not Guilty* now, as I did on my Trial at *Barnstable*; I answered, because then I was not guilty, but now I was. I was further asked, whether I had not been over perswaded by any Body to plead as I did? I answered no; but I did it to please God. Some before my Trial, that were jealous lest I should be awed by Men to plead guilty, examined me pretty strictly about the Matter; I could not but speak with some Earnestness, and say to this Purpose; You and I shall appear before the Judgment Seat of Christ, and then you'l know that I own my Guilt because I dare not dishonour God, and wrong my Conscience. After my Trial I had Peace in my own Mind, and desired to be humbly thankful to God that he had helped me in a Time of so great Temptation. I desired still to trust in God, and not in my self; and notwithstanding new Exercises that I had before my Condemnation, I was carried through all, and was enabled to receive my Sentence with Silence in my Heart as well as Lips; Yea I hope I received it with thankfulness, and it was in my Mind to thank the Judges, and desire their Prayers; but I had not the Confidence to do it: However they gave me good Counsel, and encouraged me out of the Scriptures, and let me know that I should not be forgotten of them. I could not forbare to send from the Prison to thank the Judges for their Tenderness as well as Faithfulness, and to desire their Prayers. Since my Condemnation I have been more settled in my Mind, than before. I have been desirous to improve my Time in nothing but religious Exercises; I find the more I read and pray, the more delightsome it is to me; and I can hardly allow my self Time for necessary Sleep. I have still new Discoveries of the hardness of my Heart, and that my Strength is but Weakness. And by these and many other humbling Considerations, am I brought to put my Mouth in the Dust, if so be there may be Hope. And I have Hope through Grace, that such a Monster of Wickedness as I, may be saved. My Surety, I trust, has paid my whole Debt; and I know he is able to sanctify me by his *Spirit*, as well as justify me by his *Righteousness*.

The *Catechism* I learnt in my Youth, is often brought to my Mind, and many precious Words that I had heard and read for my seasonable Rilief and Comfort. My Soul is carried out in Love to good experienc'd Christians that come to see me. Methinks now I can understand their Language, and sweetly relish it, which in Years past I had no Savour of; because I did not know the Meaning of it. Spiritual Things are sweeter to me than Meat, Drink or Sleep. Sometimes it seems to me I could speak and hear of the Things of Christ Day and Night without Weariness. But I am not always in such a Frame. Death, Judgment and Eternity appear awful to me. I have many Jealousies, lest my Faith should not be right: I know, if I have true Faith though weak, Christ has prayed for me that my Faith fail not. Now whilst I am speaking of these Things, I am enabled so to trust in Christ that I could be willing to die this Day, if it were the Will of God. I could just now, depending on the Promises of God, venture into another World—I have been lately helped by those Words 2. Tim. 2. 3. *Thou therefore endure Hardness, as a good Soldier of Jesus Christ.* And by the 19th v. of the same Chapter, *Nevertheless the Foundation of God standeth sure, having this Seal, The Lord knoweth them that are his.*—Thus I was fortified before my Trial, and have been more established since.

I was told this Morning (*June* 30) by one that looked in through the Grates (after he was denied coming into my Room) that by pleading Guilty, I hanged my self; but it did not move me, as such Temptations used to do, before my Trial. Yet I dare not trust my self, or depend on Grace received. I would depend on Christ alone (whatever Trials I may yet have) to uphold, strengthen and carry me through.

I have been much concerned for my Child. I once thought that all Children went to Heaven, and did not see so clearly the Justice of God, if it should be otherwise; but one Night, as I was sitting with my Child in my Lap, and looking on it, I think it was made plain to me that my Child had the same sinful Nature that I had, and stood in as much need of a Saviour; and that it would be just with God to damn it. And I hope I have been enabled to believe for my Child, as well as for my self.—Afterwards, when I was told I need not be distressed for my Child, either as to its Soul or Body; because it was disposed of into a Family where much Care would be taken for the Welfare of both; I presently thought and said, I had found by woful Experience how little a religious Education would signify without the sanctifying Work of God's Spirit on the Heart. I knew that if Christ would give Grace to my Child it would have Grace, else no Means would avail any Thing—And yet I desire to bless God for a religious Education. If I had not learned to read, and been taught my Catechism, it would have been harder for me to come to the Knowledge of God & Christ.—How are we condemned by the Covenant of Works, and relieved by the Covenant of Grace.

*THE Reader will excuse it that the Narrative breaks off so abruptly, and will give us leave to supply the Deficiency with the following Extract from the Diary of a Person that was much Conversant with the Deceased, during her Confinement.*

I Being providentially at the House of the Rev. Mr. *Moody* Nov. 21. 1734. The Prison-Keeper's Wife came down in haste, and said she was afraid the Prisoner would be distracted, she was in such Distress. We went up, and found her crying out in a most terrible Manner, such as I never heard the like. She smote her Hands together often, and kept continually lamenting and roaring and shrieking, for I think Hours together, with little Intermission. Some of her Expressions, which she repeated with utmost Vehemency, ten or twenty Times together, were such as follow—O I have offended a merciful God! a merciful God! I have offended the God and Father of our Lord Jesus Christ. O Sin, Sin, Sin! &c. O now I find it is an evil and bitter Thing to depart from the Living God! O the Sin of Murther! Murther! Murther!—O the Sin of Lying.—O I used to play a Sabbath Days!—O my putting off my returning to God!—O to die Christless! to die Christless, to die without an Interest in Christ! O to part from Christ! To part from Christ! O the Door of Heaven is shut against me!—O my God, my God, my God! why hast thou forsaken me!—O *Patience! Patience!*

you wicked Wretch, you first forsook God, and then he forsook you! O he is a good God! He is a good God! He is a God of Truth, He will be as good as his Word! He will be as good as his Word!—O God's Anger! God's Anger! God's Anger!—O the Wrath of God! the Wrath of God!—O my dear Soul! my dear Soul! God's Anger is burning in my Soul! O that Fire there is cool, to what I feel in my Soul!—O my Soul is in Hell; my Soul is in Hell!—She had some Intermissions, in which she was more comfortable, and uttered such Expressions as these, I will Pray, I will Pray—I *do* believe what Christ has said in John, *All that the Faith giveth me, shall come to me; and him that cometh to me, I will in no wise cast out.* —I do love God, I have loved him ever since I have known him.* In the Afternoon and at Night she was I think quite distracted, and through Horror and Amazement of Soul, spake she knew not what her self; such Expressions as I never heard, nor read of. Two Persons sat up with her all that Night, in which she rested but little; tho' the extremity of her Distress and Destraction was only by Fits.

*Nov.* 25. Being sent for I visited the Prisoner, and found her in great Distress, crying out as before; but left her in a very humble, calm, comfortable Frame of Spirit.

*June* 20. 1735. I found the Prisoner Melancholly at Noon; but at Night she was very chearful, and was well satisfied in what she had done in Pleading Guilty Yesterday; and thinks she should not be surprized if she were to be executed to Morrow, and rejoyces that she is out of the Reach of Temptation to deny the Fact, and hopes she own'd it out of true Love to Christ.

*July* 16. *Patience* I think is in an excellent Frame; free and chearful, and above the Fact of Death. In reading a Book of the Rev. Mr. *Stoddard's* to Day, she thought she was as sure of going to Heaven as she could desire to be. Nor should she be afraid to say to Christ if bodily present, as *Peter* did, *Thou knowest that I love thee.* And is more sure that she loves Christ, than that she loves her Child at her Breast, or any Creature in the World. When she was in such Anguish of Spirit, after her first Comfort; she says the Thought of having sinned against an Holy God, and of being separated for ever from Christ, was most of all distressing to her (which as I remember is agreeable to the Expressions she uttered at that Time.) She hopes she shall speak more freely on the Gallows, of what God has done for her Soul; because then there will be no Danger of her bringing a Scandal on Religion, by her after Conversation.

She is unwilling the common Whipper should Execute her, because he

*This was some Time after she had received the Light and Comfort mentioned in the foregoing Relation.

is an idle Man, and will mispend the Money he gets: and that *Sambo* a Negro should not do it, because it would be a dishonour to the Church of which he is a Member.

A Young Man brought her a Bottle of Rum t'other Day, and offered her a Dram; She took about a Jill in a Mugg, with which she made some Punch for her Child, not well; but never tasted a Drop her self. Such a victory has she got, by the Grace of God, over the Sin that did so easily beset her; and in which she has been overtaken even since her Imprisonment.—She *is* comfortable she says, and can't be otherwise; because the Spirit of God comforts her; and if it were not for that, she thinks she should be destracted again with Fears and Terrors.

*July* 23. Being called by the Prison Keeper's Wife, I went up to see the Prisoner. I found her very sorrowful, and she began to utter some despairing Words, as if there was no Hope for her; but I told her it was sinful for her to speak so, and asked her whether she had not seen Sin to be worse than Hell, &c. After some Discourse she was more still, and soon came into a calm and comfortable Frame, and so continued (blessed be God!) most of the Day.

The Rev. Mr. *A.* of *Oyster River* came to see her. She spake freely to him, and among other Things told him, she was not afraid to speak as a Dying Person, that she had truly believed on the Lord Jesus Christ. He talk'd excellently to her, and after expounding Part of *John* 14. Prayed with her. At Night standing by the Window, I heard her reading the 3d Chapter of *John*. When she came to those Words v. 15. She stop'd and said, O dear, sweet! *That whosoever believes in him, should not perish, but have eternal Life.*

*Thursday July* 24. I understand the Prisoner slept most of the Time from two or three o'Clock this Morning, till near eight. She tells Mr. *P.* of *Somersworth,* that she had this Morning a more realizing Sense of Death, and some Fears; but her Hopes were above her Fears. He prayed affectionately and particularly with her. After the Lecture preached by Mr. *Moody* from 2. *Chron.* 33. 9.—I went up with the Prisoner; She finds it hard to part with her Child. Mr. *Moody* read to her the Passage of *Abraham's* offering up his Son.

When the *Sheriff* came, she desired to be alone a few Minutes, and then came out, and with a composed Countenance said, I am ready. She walked to the Place of Execution in the same calm Temper. When she came there she behaved her self very decently. Mr. *A.* made a Speech from a Text of Scripture, and prayed. Then she prayed her self with a distinct and audible Voice and pertinent Expressions, as near as I can remember to this Purpose,—"She adored God as infinite and unchangeble; She confessed her Sins, naming several, and prayed that she might be cleansed in the Blood of Christ. She over and over committed her precious Soul to God, begging Mercy for Christ's sake, acknowledging that God out of Christ is a consuming Fire. She acknowledged the Justice of God in what was befallen her, for that she was guilty of Murder, and blessed God for bringing her thither, and granting her that Opportunity, and for giving her Comfort; admiring at it that such a one as she should have Comfort. She prayed for true Faith in Jesus Christ, Lord (said she) I believe, help thou mine Unbelief! She prayed for her Child, that it might be brought up in the Fear of an infinite God, and gave it up to Him. Lord, said she; it is not my Child, but thine. The Lord hath given, and the Lord hath taken away, blessed be the Name of the Lord. She pray'd for the innumerable Spectators (as she expressed it) That they might all take Warning by her, and beware of the Sins of Drunkenness, Lying &c. and that God would awaken secure Sinners. She pray'd for the Ministers that had been helpful to her, that God would reward all their Kindness. And for the Man that was to execute her, that he might be sensible of all his evil Ways, and that this Providence might be sanctified to him. And finally, that God would be with her the few Moments she had to live, and carry her thro' that last Trouble."—Then she asked, whether there was any Time left? And being told there was, she began to warn all, especially Young People, against the Sins of Drunkenness, Lying & c; but seemed to be faint, and a little confused, and so she was bid to sit down. Then a Paper, at her desire, taken from her Mouth was read, during which she sat down on a Board that lay across the Cart, and read in the Bible, with such composure and calmness a Mind, it was truly admirable.—After this Mr. *Moody* made a short Speech, to this Purpose—That he had suffered Reproach already on the Account of the dear Child of Christ standing there, and expected to suffer more for what he was now going to say; and then told the Multitude, he had two Things to say to them, 1st. That he verily believed that Hundreds there present if they did not begin to seek God in earnest that Night, would perish for ever. And 2d. That if they would begin now in earnest, and hold out but a Fortnight, he hoped many of them would secure their eternal Salvation. This I well remember was the Substance, and true Import of what was then spoken; though it has been represented much otherwise. Before this, when the Prisoner first went up into the Cart, Mr. *Moody* declared to her, that if she had told him the Truth, as he believed she had, her Sins were all forgiven, and she had a saving Interest in Christ; and this he had Authority to say to her as a Minister of Christ. She was asked several Times, whether her Faith held out, and she professed it did. After the Rope was about her Neck, I asked her whether she did not believe that Christ, who had helped her along so near her End, could help her along the few Steps that yet remained? She (evidently with a Smile, which several others besides my self took notice of) answered, Yes. After her Face was covered, Mr. *Moody* asked her, whether she remembered what she designed to say? She said, Yes, and added, *Lord Jesus receive my Spirit.* Soon after which the Executioner did his Office, and the dear Saint I doubt not quietly slept in Jesus. I believe there never was a justly condemned Malefactor, that had a greater Interest in the Hearts and Affections of the Children of God, than the Deceased.

*Finis.*

## Source Notes

*A Faithful Narrative of the Wicked Life and Remarkable Conversion of Patience Boston* originally was published and sold in 1738 by the Boston printers, Kneeland and Green. According to the title page, Boston ("alias Samson") was executed in York, Maine, on July 24, 1735, roughly three years before the narrative appeared. In addition to Boston's account of her sinful life and saintly conversion, the text included a preface written by the ministers Samuel and Joseph Moody and dated April 24, 1738. In their preface, the ministers stated that the narrative "*was taken from her Mouth while she was in Prison, and being publickly read to her . . . she did unconstrainedly own it*" (119). The Moodys, however, revealed that, since "*it could not be exactly taken in her own Ways of expressing her self,*" they provided Boston with rhetorical as well as spiritual expertise (119). While stressing that "*nothing false or feigned*" was in the text, they further revealed the time and effort they put into the project: "*We are ready to think that more Care could scarce have been taken in offering to the Publick what may be depended on—The Account was not drawn up in haste, but Things were written down at twenty several Times—One Day Week and Month after another*" (119). Rather than acting in the capacity of a mere amanuensis, the Moodys directed both Boston's performances in print and in public. Since the text abruptly switches from a first person to a third person narrative towards the end, it is obvious that the Moodys offered Boston both words and comfort.

Shortly after Boston's execution, Kneeland and Green published a brief eight-page narrative of Boston's life, *The Confession, Declaration, Dying Warning and Advice of Patience Samson* (Boston, 1735), but no copy of this text has been found. What little notice the newspapers took of Boston was confused. *The Boston Weekly News-Letter* of June 26, 1735, stated: "We hear that from *York*, That at Superior Court held there last Week an Indian Woman received sentence of Death for the Murder of her Bastard Child." Similarly, *The Boston Gazette* (June 30, 1735) reported: "We hear from York, that the Indian Woman under Sentence of Death for the Murder of her Bastard Child, is to be Executed. . . ." Both papers later noted that Boston's crime was murder rather than infanticide. The *News-Letter* (July 31) announced that "Last Thursday was executed at the Town of *York*, in the County of *York*, the Indian Woman condemned at the last Assizes for the Murder of her Master's Son." And the *Gazette* reported: "We hear from *York*, that on Thursday last the Indian Woman was Executed there for the Murder of her Master's Child. . . ." For a recent discussion of the *Faithful Narrative*, comparing it to "The Declaration and Confession of Esther Rodgers," see Williams, "Behold a Tragic Scene."

For information concerning the Moodys, see *Sibley's Harvard Graduates*, IV, 356-65 (Samuel), and VI, 259–62 (Joseph); see also Frederick Lewis Weis's *The Colonial Clergy and the Colonial Churches of New England*, 144 (Samuel) and 143 (Joseph). In addition to helping his father in print and in the pulpit, Joseph Moody became famous for his highly eccentric behavior. Known as "Handkerchief Moody," he suddenly began wearing a handkerchief over his face in 1738, "which he never raised unless his face was turned to the wall or his eyes screwed tight shut" (*Sibley's* 260). Hawthorne, in "The Minister's Black Veil," modeled his Parson Hooper on "Handkerchief Moody," which the author acknowledged in a well known footnote. According to the legend surrounding Moody, the veil was worn to symbolize the minister's sorrow over the accidental death of a childhood playmate and the more recent death of his wife (see *Sibley's* 261). Regardless of the causes, it is interesting to note that "Moody's mind cracked" at about the same time he and his father were ministering to Boston, as the preface they wrote for the narrative was dated "*April* 24th. 1738" (ii). Both infanticide and Boston are treated briefly in Laurel Thatcher Ulrich's *Good Wives.*

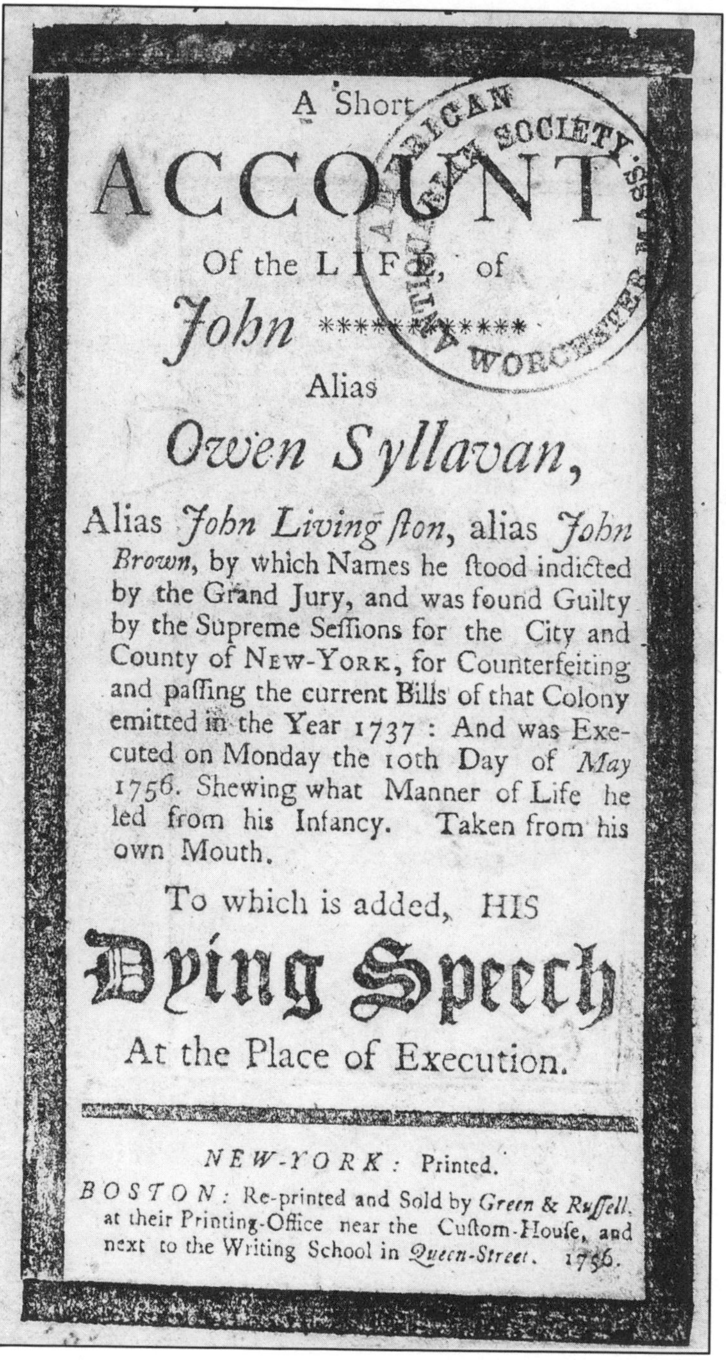

A Short

ACCOUNT

Of the LIFE, of

*John* **************

Alias

*Owen Syllavan,*

Alias *John Livingſton*, alias *John Brown*, by which Names he ſtood indicted by the Grand Jury, and was found Guilty by the Supreme Seſſions for the City and County of NEW-YORK, for Counterfeiting and paſſing the current Bills of that Colony emitted in the Year 1737: And was Executed on Monday the 10th Day of *May* 1756. Shewing what Manner of Life he led from his Infancy. Taken from his own Mouth.

To which is added, HIS

Dying Speech

At the Place of Execution.

*NEW-YORK:* Printed.

*BOSTON:* Re-printed and Sold by *Green & Ruſſell*, at their Printing-Office near the Cuſtom-Houſe, and next to the Writing School in *Queen-Street*. 1756.

[ OWEN SYLLAVAN ]

# *A Short Account of the Life of John ******* Alias Owen Syllavan*

[ 1756 ]

I was bred and born in the County of *Waxford* in *Ireland*, of English Parents near the Town of *Fedard*, and from my youth I was always in all kind of Mischief; so that I never minded Father nor Mother, Sister nor Brother; but went on in all Manner of Vice, till I came to the Age of eleven Years, or there-abouts; I was confined by my Parents in a Room, and fed upon Bread and Water for a considerable Time, and then I seemed to humble myself; till I again obtained my Liberty, and after that I was ten Times, worse than I was before; so that my Parents was obliged to send me to another Place, some Distance from home to a School-Master, who my Parents gave strict charge to keep me from Vice, and keep to my Learning.

And the first Night that I lodged there, I was called by an evil Spirit by my Christian Name; *John, John, John, John,* and that for several Minutes together, to the Surprise of myself, and all the Family: and so continued for three or four Nights together, before there was any Notice taken of it; but the fourth Night my Master set up, and Read by me till Eleven o'Clock; and then the Spirit began to call again, *John, John, John,* and that every Minute, for sixty Times together by my Master's Watch; and that lasted so for three Months together. The Ministers from sundry Parishes came to set with me; as also sundry Persons, who always pray'd by me, and giving me all good Advice in their Power, begging and praying of me, to Repent. Then I began to fear GOD; and finding so many Hundreds of People that came to see me from far and near, who took pitty upon me. At last some of them concluded to take me to one of their Houses, which they did; as soon as it was eleven o'Clock, the Spirit began to call again, *why John! why John! why John!* it called so loud that the Windows shook, and every one in the House trembled for Fear, except myself. I was taken Sick about five or six Days, before the Spirit had done calling, and during my Sickness it called louder then before; and as I laid in Bed, there was something that seem'd to press me between my Shoulders with a Hand, but saw nothing.

So this continued till I was Removed to my Parents, who then took Compassion upon me; and to the best of my Knowledge I lay Sick, for about the same Time as the Spirit had called to me before, but not troubled with any more of that evil Spirit. So it pleased GOD to restore me to my former Health, and I went to School again; but fell from Good to Evil, by provoking my Parents and giving ill Advice to others, such as my Playmates, &c. And when my Parents chastised me for my Faults, I look'd upon it as Tyranny, and told them several Times to exercise their Tyranny upon me. And when I was about thirteen Years of Age I deserted from my Parents, and stroll'd away to a Place called *Bellaback*, near the Passage of *Waterford*, so coming down to the Water Side, there was a small Boat ready to push off, and I desired of them to take me aboard, which they refused and told me they was not going over the Ferry; but told me they was going to *Waterford*, I asked of them to give me a Passage there, for I wanted to see my Aunt; so they asked my Name, and I told my Name was *Owen Syllavan* which was a Lye, for it was there I changed my Name, and so they gave me my Passage to *Waterford*, and I strol'd from Place to Place, till I came to the County of *Limerick*. There was a Gentleman Riding along, asked me whose Son I was, I made answer I was born in *Dublin* and of poor Parentage, and that they were Dead, and I told him I was going to *Cork*, expecting to find some Relations, and told him my Name was *Owen Syllavan*.

The Gentleman told me if I would go and live with him, he would be my Friend and Relation too, with that I consented and went with him to his Country-Seat, his Lady looking out of the Window, he with a smiling Countenance said, I have brought you a pretty Boy to wait upon you, the Lady seemed to like me very well, and I gave them an Indenture to serve for seven Years, and so become my Lady's running Foot-Page. And was train'd up to running, and served them almost six Years, which pleased me better than Schooling; and in the sixth Year of my Servitude, I seemed to be home sick; and set a Resolution if I should be sent of an Errand that way, I would make the best of my Way Home, which was about 100 Miles: And soon after my Master wanted me to carry a Letter to a Gentleman, about twenty Miles distance. I embrac'd that Opportunity, delivered my Letter, but did not wait for any Answer; but went direct for *Waterford*, where I arrived the same Day, about four o'Clock in the Afternoon, which was seventy Miles. When I came to *Waterford*, I drank a Tumbler full of Wine, and being very Hot, I was taken with a Pluratick Pain, and lay Sick there for some Time; although I was then about thirty Miles from my Father's House, I would not let myself be known; but told the People, that my Errand was as far as

*Waxford* Town. After I got well I went down to the Wharf, where I saw several Passengers going on Board of a Vessel bound for *Boston*, in *New-England*; so I goes up to the Captain, and agrees with him for my Passage; and Bound my self for four Years, and in a few Days set Sail for *Boston*; where we arrived in about nine Weeks: but having many Souls on Board, we was very Scant of Provision. I agreed with the Captain to serve him three Years more, for as many Biscuit as I could Eat, during the running of three Glasses, which caused the Captain to burst into a Laughter, and so consented to it: but I was to have no Water during the Time. After our Arrival at *Boston*, I told the Captain I had as soon be Sold for seven Years, as for a Day; since I must be Sold, and to get for me as much as he could. And he Sold me to one Captain *Gillmore*, living about twenty-four Hours Sail to the Eastward of *Boston*, to a Place called St. *George's-River*. I served that Gentleman two Years and an half, in chopping of Wood and clearing of Land; and hearing of a *French* War, my Master and all the Family Removed to *Boston*, except my self; my Master Sold the Remainder of my Time to Captain *Bradbery*, who I served two Years, as a Soldier, and proved faithful to my King and Country.

And after that, contrary to my Master's Will, I listed under Captain *Waldo*, in General *Shirley's* Regiment of Foot, for *Cape-Breton*, and after that, I was Drafted into Captain *Gordon's* Company of Grenadiers, and took great Delight in the Discipline, which pleased my Officers exceedingly, and they was pleased to put me chief Armourer of the Regiment; and some Time after, they thought proper that I should Number and Engrave the Arms of the Regiment belonging to Governor *Shirley*, as also Sir *William Pepperrell's* Regiment's Arms, and so continued as Armourer for two Years; then I unhappily Married a Wife, which proved a Torment to me, and made my Life uncomfortable; and she was given to take a Cup too much, and I for my Part took to the same; and through her aggravating Tongue, neglecting my Business, I was turned out, and was obliged to do private duty again as a common Soldier. And after I was off Duty, I took and set myself up as a Silversmith, and followed Engraving and Seal-Cutting; and as I was Moulding, I cast a *Spanish* Dollar amongst the rest of my Work and laid it down on the Work-Bench, so that I did not care who saw it; and by an ill-minded Man who made it his Business to inform against me, I was taken up for the same and Try'd by a General Court-Marshal; I pleaded Guilty, and by the Dollar's being good Silver was acquitted, and some Time after, I quarrel'd with a brother Soldier, and he complain'd to his Officer about it, and for that Crime I receiv'd Fifty Stripes; and in a short Time after the Regiment was broke, I came to *Boston*, and sat up to Engraving; and in that Time there came two Men who perswaded me to Engrave them a Plate for *New-Hampshire* Money, which I did, and they Rewarded me well for it. I thought it was an easy Way of getting Money, so I Counterfeited the *Boston* Bills of Credit; but never made none above *Forty Shillings*. Soon after, my Wife and I having differed together, she cry'd out Hey, you Forty Thousand Money-Maker, which was heard by some of the Neighbours, who made a complaint against me; for which I was Apprehended, and stood Tryal, and was acquitted, by Reason they had no Law for that Money: The Attorney-General desired that I should be continued in Custody till next Court, or give Bail for my Appearance; the next Sessions they found a Bill against me for Forgery, and was found Guilty, for which I stood two Hours in the Pillory and received Twenty Lashes at the public Whipping-Post; during my Confinement, I engraved three sorts of Plates, two of *New-Hampshire* Money, and one for *Boston* Currency, and for want of a Rolling Press, struck it off by Hand, sign'd it in Goal and gave it out by Quantities to my Accomplices, and some Time afterwards, being in low Circumstances, two Gentlemen came and paid my Bill of Costs, and took me out of Goal; soon after I came out of Confinement, the *New-Hampshire* Money was found out to be false, (that is the first Money that I Engraved for the Gentlemen,) one of them turned King's Evidence and swore against me for engraving the Plate, and against his Confederate; but both got clear by Swearing it upon me; for my Part I made my Escape and got into *Rhode-Island* Government, where I met with a Man who I had known in *Cape-Breton*, where I laid concealed for some Time; he and sundry more came to me, and desired of me, and intreated of me to cut them a Plate, which I did and struck off *Twelve Thousand Pounds*, and divided the Money amongst them, as I thought proper; and in one Day I changed and past about *Sixteen Hundred Pounds*, and got good Money for it; and coming through the Town of *Providence* one of my Accomplices Wives was taken up for Counterfeiting Money. I told her before she should Swear, that she might say she had the Money from me; and she would never have been taken up, if she had not taken a Bill clandestinely and Sign'd it herself.

My Partner *Nicholas Stephens* and I, rid about three Miles out of Town, and divided the good Money we had by us, and then parted; he Rid in Town and there gave himself up as an Evidence, in behalf of King and Country, and they confin'd him to Goal; and he brought in seven or eight more, who all pleaded not Guilty and swore they had the Money of me, and received it for good Money in Trading; and in about a Week after, I was taken and confin'd to Goal: I was brought to Examination and pleaded Guilty, and said that those People that was in Goal I had Cheated in Trading. I had hid about *Four Thousand Pounds*, which the Authority demanded of me; I told them that I would not deliver the Money till they would deliver, and Discharge the Innocent now Confin'd; and after they were Discharged, I was brought out under a Guard and delivered up the Money; soon after that, I was brought to Tryal and found Guilty; and was Branded in both Cheeks with the Letter R. and Cropt in both my Ears, so I was returned to Custody again. I broke out of Goal and saw *Nicholas Stephens* Cropt and Branded, the High Sheriff of *Providence* came to me, and desired of me to return to Prison, for he said he should loose his Place; with that I went very quietly, and soon after, on a Monday I broke out of Goal and went to a Husking Frolick about three Miles out of Town, and differ'd with the Company, and got almost Kill'd, and the next Morning returned to my old Prison again, then I was put in strong Irons and confined very close; but I soon found Means to break out again; although they pursu'd me very close, sent Post haste after me, and did all they could to Apprehend me; but all in vain, till I came to *Dutchess* County, in the Province of *New-York*; and going from House to House, there was a Person that knew me, and asked if my Name was not *Syllavan*? No, said I, you are mistaken in the Person my Friend; and so I went off for fear he would betray me; which he did, by describing my Visage and Apparel, and said, he was sure it was *Syllavan* the Money-Maker.

Then I provided my self with a secret retreating Place, at the Side of a Swamp; in a large unfrequented Wood: but hearing that some of my Accomplices were taken, and expecting they would betray me, or discover my Habitation. I therefore abandoned it, and fled to the Mountains, where I concealed my self seven Days; till being compel'd by Hunger, I ventured to a House of my Acquaintance, hoping they would favour my Concealment; and having cut a Plank in the Floor of the House, I dig'd a Cavity under the Hearth, and had a Fire-place, the Smoke of which issu'd by a Vent into the Chimney above; I had not been long conceal'd there, before the House was surrounded by several Men: so I suffer'd myself to be taken, and surrender'd to them. First I was carried to *New-Haven* Goal, and afterwards removed to *New-York*.

During my stay in *Dutchess* County, I made large Sums of *Rhode-Island* Money, of six Assortments, and of the *New-Hampshire* Currency *ten or twelve Thousand Pounds*, and left the Plates with my Accomplices; of *Connecticut* Money, I made three Sorts, and printed off about *three Thousand Pounds*, and lef[t] the Plates with my Accomplices; of *New York* Currency four Sorts, and had four different Sett of Accomplices; and there was four Sorts Counterfeited by my Accomplices, which I had no Hand in at all; and all of the new Currency, with the following Signers Names to it, viz. *De Lancey, Depuyster*, and *Livingston*. All my Accomplices deserv'd the Gallows, as well as myself; but I will not betray them, or be guilty of shedding their Blood.

And then turning to the Spectators, said, well Gentlemen, *You may all take Warning by me, and look out for the King of Terrors; and told the Sheriff that he must needs confess, that he was not willing to die. Then looking about him, said, I see none of my Accomplices here; but I hope they will burn and destroy all the Money, Plates and Accoutrements, that they have by them, and that they may not die on a Tree as I do. Then call'd to the Executioner and said, don't pull the Rope so tight, it is hard for a Man to die in cold Blood: after which he cried out* O good GOD! O good GOD! *have Mercy on my Soul! then said the Lord's Prayer. Just as he was turn'd off the Cart, he cry'd,* LORD have Mercy on my Soul.

*Finis.*

## Source Notes

According to information supplied on the title page, *A Short Account of the Life, of John ***** Alias Owen Syllavan* originally was published in New York and then soon "re-printed and Sold by Green & Russell" in Boston during the latter half of 1756. Since the New York edition has not been located, the Boston edition text has been used for this anthology.

Owen Syllavan (also spelled Syllivan) was one of the most notorious and most productive of all early American counterfeiters. In his *Counterfeiting in Colonial America*, Kenneth Scott devoted an entire chapter to Syllavan ("Chapter Five"), which traces the counterfeiter's movements throughout Canada and New England. According to Scott, Syllavan, although "drunken, quarrelsome, and exacting," was an excellent self-taught engraver who cut plates for a variety of currencies and who employed an extensive network of accomplices to pass his spurious bills (122). According to several newspaper accounts, he went to his death as defiant as his narrative depicted him to be. Both *The Boston Gazette* (May 24, 1756) and *The Boston Weekly News-Letter* (May 27, 1756) reported:

> *Owen Syllavan*, before he was turn'd off on Monday last, declared, That some Years ago he struck off near Twelve Thousand Pounds of Rhode-Island Money, and passed above sixteen Hundred of it in one Day:—That of New-Hampshire Currency he made Ten or Twelve Thousand Pounds:—Of Connecticut Cash he struck off about Three Thousand Pounds:—And of New-York Currency he printed large sums of 4 different Emissions; the last of which was the Bills signed Oliver DeLancey, John Livingston, and Isaac DePeyster, and dated so late as March 25, 1755; to do which he had four Setts of Accomplices, who, he said, printed and passed other large Sums at Times unknown to him: And that he left several different Plates and Stamps with his Confederates, all of whom he allowed deserved the Gallows as well as himself; but would not betray

> them one of them, or be guilty (he term'd it) of shedding their Blood:— Soon after which he took a large Cud of Tobacco, and turning round to the People said, *I cannot help smiling, as 'tis the Nature of the Beast*. And being ask'd, for the Benefit of the Publick, of what Denomination the Bills were which he printed of the New-York Money, answered, *You must find out that by your Learning*; and so died obstinate.

The execution, however, did not take place without incident and delay. On May 20 *The Boston Weekly News-Letter* printed a curious report from New York: "Owen Syllavan, alias John Livingston, alias John Brown, the forty thousand Pound Money-Maker, who was to be executed on Friday last pursuant to his Sentence, for the Want of a Hangman was respited until Saturday; but the Gallows being cut down on Friday Night by Persons unknown, and Jack Ketch, Esq; being still wanting, his Time was farther prolong'd to this Day, when he is certainly to make his exit."

A
BRIEF ACCOUNT
OF THE
L I F E,
AND ABOMINABLE
T H E F T S,
OF THE NOTORIOUS
Iſaac Fraſier,
Who was executed at Fairfield, Sept. 7th, 1768, penned from his own Mouth, and ſigned by him, a ſew Days before his Execution.

Printed & ſold by T. & S. Green, in New-Haven.

# *A Brief Account of the Life and Abominable Thefts of the Notorious Isaac Frasier*

[ 1768 ]

Fairfield, September 7, 1768.

This Day was executed here, pursuant to his Sentence, Isaac Frasier, for Burglary.—He behaved with a good Deal of seeming Unconcernedness, 'til a little while before he was turn'd off—and it is generally thought that he had a secret Hope of escaping his Punishment. The Execution was attended by a very great Concourse of People. He made no public Speech, but when he found his Fate was determined, and there was no Hope of his being cleared, he appeared to be in the utmost Anxiety.

At the Criminal's Desire, the Rev. Mr. Hobart, of this Place preach'd a Sermon to him, before he was carried to the Place of Execution—and Rev. Messrs. Ross and Beebe, attended him at the Place of Execution, praying with, and admonishing him in his last Moments.

## *A brief Account of the notorious* Frasier.

I Isaac Frasier, being condemned to die, and expecting soon to leave this world, am desirous to inform my fellow men of my execrable wickedness, in house-breaking, and stealing, hoping my example and untimely end, may be a means to deter others from the like heinous iniquities. I was born at North-Kingston, in the colony of Rhode-Island, in New-England, Feb. 9th, 1740. My parents were John and Martha Frasier, persons in low circumstances. My father died in the expedition to Louisbourg, in 1745; my mother is still living in Rhode-Island, or lately dead. My mother being left in such low circumstances that she was unable to give me any education, I was learned no more than just to know my letters and write my name, which I have since intirely forgot. My mother tho' poor yet always had the character of an honest person among her Neighbours, and she took pains to inculcate a principle of honesty into me, in my tender years: and once when she sent me to pick some ears of corn, upon bringing them to her I told her I had taken them from a field belonging to a neighbour, upon which, she chastized me severely, and went with me to return the corn. At the age of eight years, I was bound an apprentice to one Sherman, a shoe-maker, with whom I lived eight years, in the most abject condition, my allowance of food being so small that I was often induced by hunger to take provision to satisfy the cravings of nature.

My mistress, whose duty it was to have set me a good example, was in some measure the means of eradicating from my mind, the few principles of honesty which had been implanted by my mother's wholesome instruction; for she frequently gave me her snuff-box, to fill from a Snuff-Mill in the neighbourhood; sundry other trifling articles I pilfer'd, which she seem'd to countenance. At the age of 16, (my master failing in business) I inlisted in the service of Rhode-Island, under one Capt. Hammond, for the campaign in 1756. At the end of this campaign, I returned to my old master Sherman, with whom I spent the winter. In the spring, I inlisted again, under one Capt. Green, upon my return from this second Campaign, my master sold the remaining part of my apprenticeship to Capt. John Whiting of Newport, with whom I went into the war the two next campaigns; after this, return'd to Newport, where I lived till Feb. 1760, when I stole from one Mr. Gent of that town, a watch and money, to the amount of six or seven hundred pounds old tenor; for this I was taken up, confessed the fact, and was sentenced to be whipt at the cart's tail, which punishment was inflicted. The money was chiefly returned; for the charges I was sold at public vendue, and purchased by Capt. Whiting, who sent me one cruize on the privateering account, with Capt. Mitcherman; after the taking one prize, we returned to port, when I was committed to Newport gaol to secure me for another cruize, but growing sickly, got the liberty of the gaoler's house; from whence I soon made my escape, and went into Boston government. It being a time when they were inlisting soldiers, I inlisted under Capt. Gamaliel Bradford, for the campaign in 1760. On my return from the camp, I had the small-pox, at Norton, in the Massachusetts. I made Norton, the place of my abode till the next spring, when I inlisted under Capt. Williams of Taunton, but very soon left him, and went to Farmington, in Connecticut, where I inlisted under Capt. King, but at the marching of the company, being out of health, was left behind. Upon my recovery, I went to Newtown, in Connecticut, where I wrought as a labourer (with one Hezekiah Booth) about 5 months; in this town, I resided two years, hiring myself out to work at husbandry; while here, I stole from the inhabitants of the town, (with whom I was in good credit) several things; particularly from the widow Grant, £. 9. lawful money, which has never been discovered to this day; also some trifles, from Jonathan Booth, was detected and settled the affair, in private. Was also accused of taking from one Amos Northrup, of the same place, £. 3. l. m. to secrete which suspicion and accusation I paid £. 2.10.—But as I am now launching into the eternal world, and expect soon to stand before the awful bar of GOD, to answer for my many and great offences, I protest my innocence in that affair; tho' I acknowledge myself guilty of taking from him, at divers times, trifles to the amount of a few shillings. While at this place, after my true character was known, I was suspected and accused of divers thefts, particularly from Jabez and Abel Hurd, of all which I protest my self to be innocent. At a parish in New-Milford, (about the time I left Newtown) I stole a shirt, but settled the affair without punishment.

From Newtown, after my character was entirely lost, I removed to Goshen in Connecticut, where I made but a short tarry. While at Goshen I procured some shews, and employed myself in carrying them about the country. From hence I removed to Canaan, where I lived about a year. When I came to this place, I resolved to renounce my former evil course & to live by honest industry: In this place I was reputed an honest industrious young man; was noticed by the best families in the town, and received many favours from them. I intended to have settled in a place called New-Canaan, where I bought some land for that end; but at old Canaan, I became acquainted with a young woman for whom I had a very great regard, and had reason to think she was not indifferent towards me.[1] Some time after our acquaintance, we agreed to marry, and our intention was published; our attention was then employed in procuring necessary articles for house-keeping. Now my resolution taken at my first coming to this place failed me, and satan overpowered my feeble fortitude; an avaricious temper hurried me down to Woodbury, where, upon the 14th of July, 1765, I broke open and robbed the shop of one Trueman Hinman, of goods to the value of £. 70, or 80 l. m. but being detected, I settled the affair with the owner, without punishment. But the account of it coming to the ears of the grand-jurors, I was complained of and apprehended in the king's name, but made my escape from the officer; when, returning to my intended wife for protection, she utterly refused any further connection with me—which disappointment threw me almost into dispair; now being destitute of the friends I had lately made, I abandoned myself to my former course of wickedness, & having no restraints of character, I gave a rein to my covetous disposition, being extremely desirous to be rich; I now resolved upon it, at all adventures. From Canaan, I went to Goshen in New-York Government, where I stole about £. 15,—was detected, apprehended and

[1] She is said to have been a person of good character, and some fortune.

committed to Sopus goal, from whence I made my escape in a few days, and returned to Sharon in Connecticut, where liv'd a man against whom I harbour'd a grudge, from this person I took a piece of linnen, and threw it away, to gratify a revenge, purely diabolical, for which, and the breaking Hinman's store I was apprehended and committed to Litchfield goal, out of which I escaped in about three weeks; from whence I returned to Mrs. Grant's at New Town (the place from which I took the £. 9,—above mentioned,) from whom I took 218 dollars; was taken up the next day (with the money on me) and sent to Fairfield goal, from whence I broke in eight days. Now being at liberty to pursue my thievish calling, I was not long out of employ for I repair'd to Woodbury where I broke the shop of one Mr. Tomlinson, and took from thence in cash and goods to the amount of £. 20—this booty being too small to satisfy a thirst like mine I went the next night to Waterbury, where I broke the shop of Joseph Hopkins Esq; goldsmith, and took from him in silver and gold to the amount of £.140,—according to his appraisement; I now intended to leave my Connecticut acquaintance for a while, for that end I made the best of my way to Rhode-Island, whither I was pursued and taken, the good of Messrs. Tomlinson & Hopkins being found with me were a sufficient reason for my removal; I came back to Connecticut escorted by attendance suitable to my character and was committed to my present place of residence in New-Haven. Here I made a short tarry till the sitting of the Superior Court, when I was tried, convicted and sentenced to be whipt, cropt and branded as punishment for the first offence of Housebreaking. I was now sold to Mr. Hopkins to defray cost and damages. I tarried with him but a week and then went to Somers, where I robbed the shop of one Kibby of goods and money to the amount of £. 10, or 12—and set out for the Massachusetts Bay; on my road I stole at Pomphret, a coat and vest. My next feat worthy of notice was at Little Cambridge, where I broke the shop of one Fanuiel, out of which I took a number of silk handkerchiefs: in the same place also a taylor's shop from whence I took a suit of old cloaths. I went from this place to Brookline, where I was apprehended and sent to Cambridge goal, had my trial at Charlestown and was sentenced to be whipped, which punishment I receiv'd, and was returned to Cambridge goal; where Kibby hearing of me, came & took me out, and I returned him part of his goods, the remainder, together with the costs I agreed to pay in labour, stayed with him only a fortnight and made my escape to Glasgow in the Massachusetts government, where I took some trifles.—From thence I went to Great Barrington, where I stole from Doctor Whiting of that place, a coat, vest, a pair of knee-buckles & a pair of stockings; after this I hired myself to labor for a few months, after which I went to the Fish-Kills where I stole a horse, was pursued and overtaken at Glasgow, and very narrowly escaped being taken; being obliged to flee out of the tavern leaving my horse and hat behind; from here I went to Providence, where I stole a hat, was taken for it, but settled the affair without trial.

I now took my way to Boston, without any thing material occurring on the road, till I arrived on Boston neck, where I broke the shop of one Davis, and took from thence £. 10 or 12, in goods, with which I went off to Worcester, where going to a hatter's shop, to furnish myself with a hat, (having been bare-headed ever since my Glasgow surprize) I was discovered before I had accomplished my design, and was taken for stealing a shirt in the neighbourhood, (which was found on me) and whip'd; then committed to Worcester gaol, where I with three others broke out. I then returned to Waterbury, and on finding a key in the door of the same shop mentioned above, belonging to J. Hopkins, Esq; went in and robbed it of 3 silver spoons, one or two pair of buckles, and other articles I have forgot. From hence I went to the widow Grant's, at Newtown, broke open her shop again, but being disappointed as to cash, which I much wanted, there being none to be found in the shop at that time, I took a few trifling articles only. My conscience was now so fully seared and all sense of honesty so entirely lost, together with the small share of benevolence to my fellow-men, which I once possessed, that I committed these last robberies without the least remorse, tho' the one was the second, the other the third, against the same persons. The same night I broke the shop of one Booth, in the same town, out of which I took about £. 20 worth of goods, this was about the 20th of August 1766—Being taken soon after, was committed to my old quarters at Fairfield, where I lay till the sitting of the superior court, when I was sentenced to suffer a repetition of the punishment inflicted at New-Haven, which punishment I received; was recommitted, but broke out & escaped the first of October. The next course I steered was for Boston, on my road, I stole a coat and a pair of shoes at Plainfield. I broke again the shop of Mr. Davis, on Boston Neck, and took from thence some small money only; the same night, I broke into a taylor's shop at Roxbury, and took from thence an old suit of cloaths, and a little out of the town, I broke a hatter's shop, and robbed it of three beaver hatts, and got off with my booty. But being advertised for breaking Worcester gaol, was taken up, but having hid my booty before, was released from punishment (upon delivering up my goods) for these last crimes; but carried to Cambridge goal, by virtue of the Worcester advertisement, from whence I escaped soon after and went back to Worcester, where I stole from one Captain Golden's store, a pair of shoes and a gun; and from the same hatter's shop, I attempted before to rob, two beaver hatts and some furr; and from a taylor's shop, three deer-skins, all the same night, and got off undiscovered; but finding my booty too heavy, I stole a horse at Leicester, which I rode to Brookfield, and there turn'd him out, and betook myself to the woods and concealed myself till night, when going to a tavern I was taken up, and committed to

Worcester goal, December 1766, where I lay till the next spring, when I with two others broke goal and escaped. I then went to Boston, stealing at several places on the road. From Boston, I returned to Middletown, in Connecticut, where I committed four burglaries in one night, *viz.* Widow Wetmore's house, of £. 3 or 4 cash, a merchant's shop of 2 or 3 dozen handkerchiefs, a watch, a gun, and several other articles. A taylor's shop of a new coat. A shoe-maker's of 3 pair of shoes and a calf-skin, and went off undiscovered, and sold the effects. I now went to the government of New-York, up Hudson's River, where I wrought till about September, without committing any robberies.[2] My next theft, was about September at Norwalk, where I broke Mr. Gould Hoit's store, and robbed it of 2 pieces of velvet, 2 pieces chintz, some silk handkerchiefs and sundry other articles, to the amount of £. 50 and was not detected.[3]

About the 28th of March 1768, I broke into the shop of Samuel Bradley, Esq; of Fairfield, and robbed it of a quantity of goods, to the value of £. 100 and went off with an intention to go to New-York; the next night at Norwalk, I took a horse from a pasture, broke open a shoe-maker's shop, and took from thence a pair of shoes and part of a side of leather, which I intended to make use of instead of a saddle, but my leather not answering my purpose, I resolv'd upon having a saddle, and a few miles distant, as I was looking round a house for one, I was discovered by a woman who happened not to be in bed; she alarmed the family who took me up, and Mr. Bradley's goods being found about me, I was committed to Fairfield prison, where four days after my commitment, I did the greatest piece of mischief I was ever guilty of at one time. There was one Hoit, a prisoner for debt in goal, with whom I was confin'd in the same room, a day or two, who proposed a scheme to me of burning out of goal, (as there appeared no other prospect of getting out) and when Hoit, was removed to another apartment, he prepared a quantity of tinder, which he conveyed to me (with a spark of fire as I had none allowed me) under the door that parted us; which I kept burning, till eleven or twelve at night, when I set fire to the side of the gaol, but the fire getting the mastery of me, I was in eminent danger of being consumed in the flames, together with Hoit: but my bitter cries with his (we being the only persons in goal) reaching the ears of some of the goaler's family who were up, we were taken out just soon enough to save our lives, but the gaol, court house and gaoler's apartment, which were

[2] He very probably here became acquainted with the woman he afterwards married.

[3] He does not confess where he went to from this place, but says he was married in December, but where, and to whom, he thinks best to conceal; which circumstance undoubtedly conceals considerable mischief committed about that time; which would discover his fate to his wife and her friends were it inserted, which he is desirous they should not be acquainted with. He says she will not know by the name he goes by now, (which is his true name) as he called himself by another to her.

under the same roof were all consumed, together with most of the gaoler's houshold furniture. I was the next day removed to the gaol in New-Haven. On the 27th day of April, I was tried by a special court called for that purpose at Fairfield, found guilty, and condemned to be hanged: but the time of execution not being fixed, I was returned to New-Haven. I still entertain'd some hopes of escaping, which prevented the solemn exhortations of the neighbouring ministers from having their due influence upon my mind; which I now greatly lament, I still remain'd as hardened as ever, and having procured a small saw, a gimblet and a knife, from a person whose name I am under solemn obligations to conceal; by the help of these, I found means to get off my irons, and escaped the night of the 28th of July. I had made several attempts before to get out, but was discovered. I arrived at Durham the next night, where I stole part of a cheese out of a press, a shirt, and several pair of stockings at different places in that town. The next night I went to Middletown, where I broke up three shops, *viz.* The shop of Capt. George Phillips, merchant, out of which, I took 6 dozen silk handkerchiefs, 2 packs of combs, 4 pieces ribbon, some trifles, and about £. 12 cash; likewise a taylor's shop, from whence I took a coat, vest, two breeches patterns, and a deer-skin. Also a Shoe-maker's, from which I took one pair of shoes. Upon committing these last thefts, I found what I had never experienced in all my scene of villainy before, which was, the working of a guilty conscience, whose power was so great that it forced me to recede from my wicked designs several times, but at last, being overcome by the suggestions of the devil, and the temptations of an evil heart, I proved deaf to its loudest calls, and wickedly resisted the strugglings of that faithful monitor.[4] With my booty I crossed Connecticut-river and made the best of my way to Boston, thro' Windham, and Providence. On Friday the 5th of August, I overtook an Irish girl, who was a suitable companion for one of my character, with her I travelled the best part of the day, and at night coming to a tavern, we put up together: where she found means to get my money from me, and being protected by the landlord, and a number of ruffians in the house, I could get by my utmost expostulations and prayers, no more than 19 dollars from her, out of about 40.[5]

From here I went to Charlestown, where I took lodgings in a tavern, the next night, and intended to have staid there till the next week, but a house being robbed in the town about that time, I was taken up on sus-

[4] He declares that he had no accomplice in this affair, notwithstanding his former declaration to the contrary. If he had any other reluctance to the perpetration of these last felonies than the fear of punishment, 'tis probable his awakenings of conscience must arise from the influence the solemn warnings and exhortations given by the ministers, (after his condemnation) had upon him.

[5] This tavern is near Roxbury. He says, he was afraid they would murder him. Likewise that he had no unlawful commerce with this girl.

picion of committing the robbery, and being brought before a justice of the peace, I left him a parcel of my stolen goods, as security for my appearance on the next monday, pretending to go for a certificate of my good character to another place, but being too well known in Charlestown, and not for any virtuous actions, I tho't it unsafe to hazard a return, so left my goods in the Justice's hands. From this place I went to Salem, where I very narrowly escaped being taken by virtue of the advertisement from New-Haven. From thence to Shrewsbury, where I put up at one Beeman's Tavern, where I tarried part of two days and left it in the night, carrying off a waistcoat, a watch, a silver cup and £. 14 in cash. I now took the road to Worcester, where I stole 3 shirts, and proceeded in the road to Springfield; but finding myself pursued, I took to the woods and went to Palmer; from thence to Hadley, where I arrived on the 14th of August, on the night of which, I found the ferries were stopped, but a shower of rain falling the next morning, the ferry-men left their stations, which (as I lay by) I discovered, seiz'd this opportunity, and crossed the ferry to Hatfield. Upon my landing on the other side, my escape was discovered, by the falling of an oar in the boat, and was immediately pursued and taken between Hatfield and North-Hampton, and carried back to Worcester gaol, for stealing the goods and money from Beeman, which affair I settled without punishment; but received ten stripes for stealing one of the last mentioned shirts, which was found on me. The account of my breaking the gaol in New-Haven, reaching Worcester, while I was in custody, I was bro't back to New-Haven gaol, where I am now confin'd, from whence I expect soon to go to the place of execution, where I shall justly die for my villainous crimes. I acknowledge myself to have been guilty of almost an innumerable number of other thefts, but have forgot the order of time in which they were committed. One of which was at Woodstock, about four years since, where I robbed a store of about £. 20 value in goods, but settled the affair with the owner. The rest were smaller.[6]

As I am now upon the verge of eternity, a word of advice to those into whose hands this narrative may come, perhaps will not be amiss.—The beginning of my evil course being early in life, when education would have been most powerful to restrain from vice, and perhaps (by the blessing of God) if means had been used in season, I might have been reclaimed, as I date my ruin from the time I was bound an apprentice: I would therefore beseech parents to be careful in the education of their children, (as they must answer it to a holy God, whose eyes cannot behold sin but with the

[6] The articles taken from each store, are particularly mentioned at his desire, that the owners may know the articles taken by him, in order to exculpate others.

greatest abhorrence) to inculcate those principles into them in the beginning of life, which will make for their eternal welfare, to exhort and warn against the appearance of evil, whose beginning tho' comparatively small, yet often ends in the most gross acts of wickedness; likewise to be careful to whom they commit the charge of their education. I would also exhort masters, (who put themselves in the stead of parents) to instill the principles of virtue and religion, into the minds of their servants and apprentices while young, not forgetting, that for all these things God will bring them to an account.

Young people, may this my violent death be a solemn warning to you, to shun the paths of wickedness I have trod, not to put your trust in uncertain riches, but to remember your Creator in the days of your youth, and to put your trust in the living God; promise not yourselves happiness in an abundance of the wealth of this world; suffer not a love for earthly goods, to divert your attention from pursuing after a treasure in Heaven, where will be no more fighting or sorrow; the love of money, the ruling principle of my mind, has brought me to the grave in the flower of life, when my sun is scarce risen; at the age of 28, I am going down to the house of silence, to be numbered with the dead; I have mocked at sin, and despised correction; but am now reaping with sorrow from the hand of man, the just fruits of my horrid crimes against God and man: yet after death, there is another tribunal—Who can dwell with everlasting burnings! I would warn you against the prophanation of God's holy sabbath, which I have been guilty of from my youth up, lest Satan get an advantage against you, and you fall, while you seem to yourselves to stand.

I acknowledge the lenity of my Judges in allowing me so long a space after condemnation, and the kindness of the ministers of Christ in this, and the neighbouring towns, in the pains they have taken to enlighten my mind, and in praying with and for me. Would return thanks to God, that he has been pleas'd to grant me any space for repentance; and beg that God of his infinite mercy in Christ Jesus, would pardon and forgive my aggravated sins of stealing, wilfull lying, prophaning his holy day,[7] and all that his pure eyes have seen amiss in me, and pray that he who saved the thief upon the cross, would magnify his grace in my eternal salvation.

his
*Isaac* ✠ *Frasier*
mark

*New-Haven Prison. September 5th,* 1768.

[7] He says that he was never addicted to drunkenness or profane swearing, and never guilty of murder.

## Source Notes

According to Wilfred J. Ritz, the first Frasier narrative was the *Account of the Life and abominable Thefts of Isaac Frazier, under sentence of death for burglary*, published by the printer, Samuel Green (New Haven: 1768). Apparently when compiling its Early American Imprint series Readex missed this scarce text, reproducing in its place what seems to be the fourth edition, *A Brief Account of the Life, and Abominable Thefts, of the notorious Isaac Frasier, Who was Executed at Fairfield, Sept. 7th, 1768* (New London: Timothy Green, 1768). The second edition, *A Brife* [sic] *Account of the Life, and Abominable Thefts, of the Notorious Isaac Frasier, (Under Sentence of Death for Burglary)*, was published in New Haven by Thomas and Samuel Green in 1768. The third edition (the first edition after the execution) also was published by Thomas and Samuel Green in New Haven: *A Brief Account of the Life, and Abominable Thefts, of the Notorious Isaac Frasier, Who was Executed at Fairfield, Sept. 7th, 1768*. In addition to the narratives, Thomas and Samuel Green also tried to take advantage of Frasier's execution by publishing his execution sermon, delivered by Noah Hobart: *Excessive Wickedness, the Way to an Untimely Death* (New Haven, 1768). The copy text used for the anthology is taken from the third edition.

Frasier indeed was notorious. Along with the several texts published by the Green family, he received ample notice in many of New England's newspapers. *The Connecticut Journal*, *The Connecticut Courant*, *The New London Gazette*, *The Massachusetts Gazette*, *The Boston Post-Boy*, and *The Boston Evening Post* all carried progressive accounts of Frasier's burning down the Fairfield jail, his trial, his escape and recapture, and his execution. According to *The Connecticut Journal:*

> *NEW-HAVEN, April 8.*
>
> *One Isaac Frasier, (a notorious Offender, who has already been crop't, branded and whip't twice, in this Colony, for Burglary) was last Friday committed to the Goal in Fairfield, for breaking open, and robbing the Shop of Samuel Bradley, Esq; of that Place. Last Monday he by some Means procured Fire, with an Intention as he says, of burning a Hole, large enough, in the Side of the Goal, to make his Escape at, but the Fire soon getting the Mastery of him, and it being dead Time of Night, he was, with one Hoyt, a Prisoner for Debt, (they being the only Persons in Goal) in great Danger of being suffocated, but their Cries being heard by a young Woman who happened to be up, in the Goaler's Family, she gave the Alarm just Time to take them out alive, but the Fire had got to so great a Head, that it could not be stop't, but soon communicated itself to the Court-House, that adjoined the Goal, and soon reduced them both to Ashes. Mr. Camp, the Goaler, who liv'd with his Family in Part of the Court-House, sav'd the chief of their Furniture. Several of the neighbouring Houses were much exposed, but the Night being calm, and the Inhabitants of the Town very active, prevented the Flames from spreading any further. The Goal was newly built, at a great Expence, and was reckoned the strongest Place of confinement in the Colony.*
>
> *Last Tuesday, the above mentioned Prisoners were both brought to the Goal in this Town* [New Haven].

Less than a month later (April 29, 1768), the *Journal* published the following notice:

> Last Wednesday, at a special Superior Court, holden at Fairfield, Isaac Frasier, was Indicted for Burglary and setting Fire to Fairfield Goal, . . . to which Indictments he plead not guilty.—But after a fair Trial on both Indictments, he was found guilty; and is sentenced to be hang'd; but the Time of his Execution is not yet determined. He is now in our Goal [New Haven].

During the summer (July 29, 1768), the *Journal* reported:

> Last Night broke out of his Majesty's Gaol in New-Haven, one Isaac Frasier, under Sentence of Death for Burglary; he is of middling Stature, black Hair, pitted with Small-Pox, has both his Ears cropt, and branded Twice on his Forehead with the Capital Letter B, his Fore-Teeth gone, aged Twenty-Eight Years; had on a brown Great Coat, A Pair of old Homespun Breeches, and a Check Shirt.
>
> Whoever shall take up said Frasier, and secure him in any of his Majesty's Gaols, or bring him to the Subscriber, in New-Haven, shall receive TWENTY DOLLARS Reward, and all necessary charges paid by STEPHEN MUNSON, Gaoler.

About a month later (August 26, 1768), the Journal related his recapture:

> Last Wednesday Evening, the notorious FRASIER, who was under Sentence of Death, for Burglary . . . was brought from Worcester, (where he was taken up for Theft, and whipt) and re-committed to the Goal in this Town [New Haven], from where he escaped about a Month since—in which Time he has committed Five or Six Burglaries and Thefts, and travelled near 500 Miles. The next Night but one, after his escape, he broke open no less than Three Shops of Middletown, from one which he stole £.70. Value in Goods and Cash. The Superior Court, now sitting in Fairfield, have given strict Orders, that he should be loaded with Chains, and the Goal guarded every Night, till the Time of his Execution, which is appointed to be at Fairfield. on Wednesday the Seventh of next Month.

The final notice of Frasier appeared in the Journal on September 9, 1768:

> *Last Wednesday,* Isaac Frasier, *was executed at Fairfield, pursuant to the Sentence of the Superior Court, for the Third Offence of Burglary; the lenient Laws of this Colony, only Punishing the first and second Offences with whipping, cropping, and branding. He was born at North-Kingston, in the Colony of Rhode Island, It is said, he seem'd a good deal unconcerned, till a few Hours before he was turn'd off—and it is conjectured, by his Conduct, that he had some secret Hope of being cleared, some Way or other.*

A few lines below this last notice, the *Journal* advertised Frasier's *Account* as "*Just published, and to be sold by the Printers hereof.*"

THE

# Confeſſion and Dying Words

OF

# JOHN JUBEART,

Who was Executed at NEW-YORK, upon Wedneſday the Sixth of September, 1769;

## For Coining and Paſſing Counterfeit Dollars.

JOHN JUBEART, the unhappy Criminal, who was executed this Morning, was Sixty-Eight Years of age; ſaid he was born upon Staten-Iſland, that his Father came over from England to this City, with, and in the employ of Governor Dungan. He was bound an Apprentice to his elder Brother, who had ſerved a regular Apprenticeſhip to a Black-Smith in this City, learnt that buſineſs from him, and became ſo great a proficient therein, that he not only knew every part of it, but was alſo capable of repairing Clocks and Watches. His Parents were induſtrious honeſt People, and gave him as genteel an Education as their circumſtances would allow; they early inſtilled into his mind, the principles of Virtue and Piety, and exhorted him, both by Precept and Example, to fear and love his Creator.---During their lives he conducted himſelf entirely to their ſatisfaction; and, at the age of Twenty-Four Years, was married to a young Woman of a reputable Family, in New Jerſey, whoſe name he did not chuſe to mention, leſt ſome evil minded Perſons, whoſe malice is as inſatiate, as their hearts are corrupt, ſhould unjuſtly reproach her family with his unhappy fate. By this Woman he had ſeveral Children, all of which are dead, except Two Daughters, whoſe virtuous deportment, and, the then unexceptionable character of their Parents, recommended them to the eſteem of every perſon who had the pleaſure of their acquaintance; and induced Gentlemen of family and character, to commence an alliance with *their* family, by joining with them in the bands of Matrimony. Soon after this alliance their Mother died: this misfortune threw him [Jubert] into a deep melancholy, which preyed upon him a conſiderable time; and ever ſince, he found himſelf quite unſettled, and even at ſome times, a little delirious: the place of his former reſidence became very diſagreeable to him; and the uncomfortable ideas with which he was perpetually haunted, he imagined, could only be aleviated by keeping himſelf in continual agitation of body, by removing from one place to another. Purſuant to this determination, he ſettled his Eſtate, which was not inconſiderable, upon his Children, and rambled about the Country, working at his buſineſs wherever he came, for his ſupport, and he had always the happineſs to gain the eſteem of thoſe who employed him; he followed his vocation for a conſiderable time, at Saliſbury, Kent, Canaan, and Hartford and moſt of the towns and villages in New-England, he then came to the Fiſh-kill, where he reſided three years with an unblemiſh'd character; he then removed to a place called Quaker-Hill, in the great Nine Partners, at which place he heard there was a ſilver mine, which he viſited, and from whence, with great aſſiduity and hard labour, he extracted a ſmall quantity of baſe ſilver from the oar he found there; this ſilver he melted down with five Spaniſh Dollars, and from that compoſition he fabricated ten counterfeit ones; but he declared upon the word of a dying man, that it was more for the ſake of trying an experiment than any fraudulent intention he had to impoſe upon the public, but his ſimplicity, and being badly paid for his work, had reduced him ſo low that he was greatly in want of linen and ſeveral other neceſſaries, and although he might have been ſupplied by his children and friends, yet he did not chuſe to apply to them while he was able to earn a ſubſiſtence for himſelf; in fine, his neceſſities urged him to endeavour to paſs the dollars he had coined: he came to New-York for that purpoſe; was detected in the act, carried before a magiſtrate, and after examination committed to goal. At the Supreme court held in July laſt, he was tried, convicted, and ſentenced to be hang'd on Wedneſday the 23d of Auguſt; he was reſpited by his Excellency the Governor untill Wedneſday the 30th of ſaid month, and then obtained a further reſpite till this day.

His behaviour during his confinement, and when upon his trial, was decent, and while under ſentence of death, penitent and reſigned; he ſeem'd to have a due ſenſe of the henouſneſs of the offence for which he ſuffered, ſaid he had no accomplices, and that he died in peace and charity with all mankind, whom he had never defrauded preceding this unfortunate attempt for which he now ſuffered.—— Since his receiving ſentence of death he has been duly attended by the gentlemen of the clergy, to whoſe pious exhortations he gave the greateſt attention, and ſeriouſly lamented that poverty had urged him to deviate from the paths of virtue; yet notwithſtanding the ignominy of his death, he hoped, through the merits of JESUS CHRIST, to awake to a bleſſed immortality.

†+† Printed for the *Sober* JOHN STEWART, Eſq; and C°. and ſold from their Fiſts, in every Quarter of this City.

[ JOHN JUBEART ]

# *The Confession and Dying Words of John Jubeart*

[ 1769 ]

JOHN JUBEART, the unhappy Criminal, who was executed this Morning, was Sixty-Eight Years of age; said he was born upon Staten-Island, that his Father came over from England to this City, with, and in the employ of Governor Dungan. He was bound an Apprentice to his elder Brother, who had served a regular Apprenticeship to a Black-Smith in this City, learnt that business from him, and became so great a proficient therein, that he not only knew every part of it, but was also capable of repairing Clocks and Watches. His Parents were industrious honest People, and gave him as genteel an Education as their circumstances would allow; they early instilled into his mind, the principles of Virtue and Piety, and exhorted him, both by Precept and Example, to fear and love his Creator.—During their lives he conducted himself entirely to their satisfaction; and, at the age of Twenty-Four Years, was married to a young Woman of a reputable Family, in New Jersey, whose name he did not chuse to mention, lest some evil minded Persons, whose malice is as insatiate, as their hearts are corrupt, should unjustly reproach her family with his unhappy fate. By this Woman he had several Children, all of which are dead, except Two Daughters, whose virtuous deportment, and, the then unexceptional character of their Parents, recommended them to the esteem of every person who had the pleasure of their acquaintance; and induced Gentlemen of family and character, to commence an alliance with *their* family, by joining with them in the bands of Matrimony. Soon after this alliance their Mother died; this misfortune threw him (Jube[a]rt) into a deep melancholy, which preyed upon him a considerable time; and ever since, he found himself quite unsettled, and even at some times, a little delirious: the place of his former residence became very disagreeable to him; and the uncomfortable ideas with which he was perpetually haunted, he imagined, could only be alleviated by keeping himself in continual agitation of body, by removing from one place to another. Pursuant to this determination, he settled his Estate, which was not inconsiderable, upon his Children, and rambled about the Country, working at his business wherever he came, for his support, and he had always the happiness to gain the esteem of those who employed him; he followed his vocation for a considerable time, at Salisbury, Kent, Canaan, and Hartford and most of the towns and villages in New-England, he then came to the Fish-kill, where he resided three years with an unblemish'd character; he then removed to a place called Quaker-Hill, in the great Nine Partners, at which place he heard there was a silver mine, which he visited, and from whence, with great assiduity and hard labour, he extracted a small quantity of base silver from the oar he found there; this silver he melted down with five Spanish Dollars, and from the composition he fabricated ten counterfeit ones; but he declared upon the word of a dying man, that it was more for the sake of trying an experiment than any fraudulent intention he had to impose upon the public, but his simplicity, and being badly paid for his work, had reduced him so low that he was greatly in want of linen and several other necessaries, and although he might have been supplied by his children and friends, yet he did not chuse to apply to them while he was able to earn a subsistence for himself; in fine, his necessities urged him to endeavour to pass the dollars he had coined: he came to New-York for that purpose; was detected in the act, carried before a magistrate, and after examination committed to goal. At the Supreme court held in July last, he was tried, convicted, and sentenced to be hang'd on Wednesday the 23d of August; he was respited by his Excellency the Governor untill Wednesday the 30th of said month, and then obtained a further respite till this day.

His behaviour during his confinement, and when upon his trial, was decent, and while under sentence of death, penitent and resigned; he seem'd to have a due sense of the heniousness of the offence for which he suffered, said he had no accomplices, and that he died in peace and charity with all mankind, whom he had never defrauded preceding this unfortunate attempt for which he now suffered.—Since his receiving sentence of death he has been duly attended by the gentlemen of the clergy, to whose pious exhortations he gave the greatest attention, and seriously lamented that poverty had urged him to deviate from the paths of virtue; yet notwithstanding the ignominy of his death, he hoped, through the merits of JESUS CHRIST, to awake to a blessed immortality.

## Source Notes

According to information supplied at the bottom of the broadside, *The Confession and Dying Words of John Jubeart* was "Printed for the *Sober* John Stewart, Esq; and Co. and sold from their Fists in every Quarter of this City [New York]." The short broadside account of Jubeart's life and death was not reprinted and little notice of Jubeart was taken in the newspapers. On July 31, 1769, *The New-York Gazette* mentioned Jubeart in a list of cases tried before the state's Supreme Court: "Saturday last the Supreme Court ended here, when John Hennesey, for Felony and Sacrilege, in stealing the Sattin Covering of the Cushions of St. Paul's in this City, and John Jubeart, on two Indictments, for passing Counterfeit Dollars, knowing them to be such, were found guilty, received Sentence of Death, and are to be executed the 23d of August." A brief notice in the September 4, 1769, issue of *The New-York Gazette* stated that Jubeart's execution was "respited until next Wednesday the 6th of September." A week later (September 11, 1769) *The New-York Gazette* published a final notice: "Wednesday last John Jubeart, late of Staten-Island, was executed at the Gallows near this City, for passing counterfeit Dollars. He died with great Appearance of Penitence, and denied having any Accomplices." In his comprehensive *Counterfeiting in Colonial America* Kenneth Scott did not mention Jubeart as belonging to any of the counterfeiting gangs operating in and around New York.

THE

# LIFE

AND

# CONFESSION

OF

*HERMAN ROSENCRANTZ*;

Executed in the City of *Philadelphia*, on the 5th Day of *May*, 1770, for Counterfeiting and Uttering the Bills of Credit of the Province of *Pennſylvania*.

In which is an ACCOUNT who were his CONFEDERATES.

Taken from his own Mouth, in one of the Cells of the Goal, a ſhort Time before he was Executed; and, by his Requeſt, Publiſhed, as a Warning to all others.

---

*Better is a Little, with the Fear of the* LORD, *than great Treaſure, and Trouble therewith.* Prov. xv. 16.

---

*PHILADELPHIA:*

Printed for JAMES CHATTIN, and Sold by him at Mr. GRAHAM's, in *Second-ſtreet*, the ſecond Door from *Market-ſtreet* Corner, and next Door to Mr. MILNE's, Jeweller.

[ HERMAN ROSENCRANTZ ]

# *The Life and Confession of Herman Rosencrantz*

[ 1770 ]

I HERMAN ROSENCRANTZ was born in the county of *Ulster*, in the government of *New-York*, on the 4th day of *April*, 1716; my parents were *Low-Dutch*, and bred me up religiously; they being pious, good people, of the *Presbyterian* persuasion. I liv'd with them until I was 22 years of age; I then made a purchase of WILLIAM ALLEN, Esq; of *Philadelphia*, of a tract of land in *Northhampton* county, in *Pennsylvania*; to which I moved, and continued there one year; when I returned to my Father's, near *Delaware*.

The 27th of *December* following, I married into a honest, reputable family, and continued with my parents, after marriage, two years. In this time I join'd myself to the *Presbyterians*.

For nine years after my marriage, things prospered in my hands, and I was blest with *the dew of heaven, and the fatness of the earth.*

After this time I mov'd to *Bethlehem*, in *Pennsylvania*, and resided there seven years; during which I met with many losses and misfortunes; which, instead of bringing me to *remember the rock from whence I was hewn, and the hole of the pit from whence I was dug,* had quite a contrary effect upon me.

I gave myself over to an uneasy and restless mind, with an undue desire of gaining riches; which disposition, pushed on by the enemy of my soul, has been a means of my downfal.

With this distemper of mind, I moved myself and family over the river *Delaware*, to land belonging to *Richard Stevens*, in *Bucks* county; here I liv'd two years.

When at this place, *D____d R_____lds* and *J___h B_____gs* came to me, and introduced themselves by some frivolous excuses to a further acquaintance.

Much discourse passed between us, at length *R_____ds* called me on side, and shewed me two Thirty Shilling bills, of *New-Jersey* currency, which he said they had made.

This was the first of my knowledge of their concerns in Counterfeiting of money.

Here I had a fair opportunity of being of service to the community, by discovering these pests of civil government, and bringing them to justice: But *the love of money, the root of all evil*, blinded my eyes, so that I received at their hands two of these counterfeit bills.

*R_____lds* parted with us at my house; but I accompanied *B____ngs* to one widow *Kelly's*, at whose house we parted.

Four weeks after this *B____ngs* and myself met at *Tulpahocken*. Here I received of him Forty Pounds of the same sort of money. As I came homewards I passed nine of the bills; but it was not long after, this counterfeit money was advertised. I was then under great apprehensions of being discovered, in passing the nine bills above-mentioned; wherefore, as speedily as I could, I went and took up all but two of them, which I could not get. In consequence of passing these two, I was apprehended, and *Timothy Smith* and _______ *Parowl* were my securities for my appearance at the Quarter Sessions at *Newton*, in *Bucks* county, in order for trial. When the time came, I employed JOSEPH GALLOWAY and JOHN ROSS, Attornies at Law, who laboured the point for me so effectually, that I got acquitted.

After I was discharged at *Newtown*, I went into the *Jerseys*, where I was apprehended for passing the same bills I had stood my trial for in *Bucks*.

The constable took me to Col. *H____t's*; but he was not at home. He then took me to *D_____ R____lds's*, and when there, I told *R____lds*, that if they did proceed against me, I would blow them all, meaning Col. *H____t, D_____d R____lds*, and a certain *J___n D____k*, who afterwards made his escape to Ireland.

*D_____ R____lds* and myself were commited, tried and acquitted.

I then removed myself and family to the place I had formerly lived at, in *Bucks* county.

At this time, as I had not much apprehension of further prosecution, I ought to have made a full stop; and it would have been happy for me, if I had. But instead of these difficulties I had gone through, being a warning to me, they rather, as will appear in the end, made me more venturesome. But here I must confess, what with the continual stings of my own conscience, and the reflexions I made from whence I had fallen, even from being considered as a religious good member of society, to that of the companion of the worst sort of men, had such an effect upon me at times, that I had little comfort of my life.

It was not long after this, before *D____d R______ds* came to me, and wanted me to join with him in passing fifteen hundred pounds, bills of *New-Jersey*, and Twenty Shilling bills of *Pennsylvania*, upon this condition, that I should advance him some good money. I denied him. He then told me, he would shew me the whole plan, and the person that did counterfeit the money; which was one *J_____s L_____g*, that lived at Carlisle.

The next day I went to *R____ds'* s house, where I met with *J____s L____g* and *R____ds*. They shewed me the plates, and a large number of bills. *L____g* said, that we all might live a gentleman's life, as he had done for twenty years past; yet I did not then accept of their offer.

The next day I met *L_____g* and *R_____ds* seven miles from my home. Here it was I resolved to join them

It was now concluded among us, that *R____ds* and myself should meet *L____g* soon after this at *Shippenstown*, and that we were to make ourselves strangers to each other in all companies we should fall in with.

At the place appointed *R____ds* and myself met; but no *L_____g* was there. Concluding in my mind, that we should be disappointed, I returned home to *Shrewsbury*, whither by this time my family had removed.

It was not long after this *J____s L_____g* came to me at *Shrewsbury*, and staid three weeks. On parting with me, he gave me 274 l. of the 1500 l. before-mentioned. Some time after this I went in company with one *J____ H____a* to *Elizabeth Town*, and bought four horses with part of the said bad money. The same day both of us were apprehended and committed. Upon trial *H____a* was condemned to be pillored and to have his ears cropped; my sentence was to be pillored and fined. Which punishments were executed upon us.

From thence *H____a* and myself were moved to *Amboy*, where we were both tried for stealing a piece of cloth, which I here declare I had no hand in. However we were both convicted, and sentenced to be pillored, which was executed. We then were moved back to *Elizabeth-Town*, where he was confined for his fees, and myself for fine and fees.

After my discharge I returned home to *Shrewsbury*, to the great joy of my family. I industriously set myself to work, and might have lived comfortably, if it had not been for what follows.

My wife and son *Alexander* went in a slay to *Hopewell*. When they returned, they said they had heard a report, that I was one that was concerned with *B____gs* and *M_____ C____tz* in making counterfeit money. I was much terrified at this piece of news, and hastily moved myself and family to *Egg-Harbour*. In this remove I verified the Scripture, where it says, *that the wicked flee, when no man pursues.*

I had not been above three months at *Egg-Harbour*, when *G____er S____t* and *J____n Le F____e* came there with a stolen mare, which they swapped with *John May.* They went home, and in about a month after, they returned with one *J___ M__re.* They came to my house, and in the evening several things not material were discoursed of; but they brought a report, that I was concerned in concealing stolen horses, which I denied; for I never had one left in my care. Hearing this, I was again put in great fear, and went off immediately as far as *George Town*, on *Potowmack* river. I there staid in company with one *B___t,* at the house of one *Graves,* a tavernkeeper. Here I met with *J______n B______s,* an old acquaintance, who had with him some bad money, part of which he put into my pocket when in bed, unknowingly to me. The next day we were both apprehended, but made our escapes; we were pursued, and I was retaken, and confined in *Fredrickstown* goal. After sometime I had my trial, and was acquitted. The judges of *New-Jersey* sent for me from this goal, to receive my trial in *Middlesex*, where I was charged with uttering counterfeit money, and was acquitted.

While I was in *Middlesex* goal, my wife and family moved to her friends at *Hopewell.* After my discharge I went home to them, and was received with unspeakable joy.

Now I had a second opportunity of taking up, and becoming a new man; as I had in each place where I had committed offence, been tried, and acquitted, or received punishment according to sentence. But that fatality which always attended me, or the evil disposition of my own heart, still pushed me on to my ruin. So harrassed as I had been, sometimes having to labour through cold, nakedness and want, with pockets full of bad money, and afraid to use it; yet I could not help returning *like the dog to his vomit, and as the sow that is washed to her wallowing in the mire,* to my old *sin that so easily beset me.*

I remained sometime with my family at *Hopewell*; then removed to *Delaware*, to the place I formerly lived on.

I was there three years as a farmer, with great uneasiness of mind, on account of my former conduct. While I lived there, one *B____et* and *J___e A____son* came to me with two horses they had stolen, as they informed me. *A____son* lay off in the woods with the horses, while *B____et* came to my house for victuals: But they did not stay long before they departed.

A rumour soon spread abroad through the country, that I was confederate with them. I declare myself innocent, except in the knowledge of what they had done. Warrants were issued for apprehending me upon that occasion: Upon this, and several other accounts, I set off for *Virginia*, in order to procure a place for my family.

In *April*, 1769, I passed through the city of *Philadelphia*, on my journey there.

When I arrived in *Virginia,* I soon found a place to my mind. I returned, and immediately set forward with my family to the place I had procured.

In my journey with my family, I met with *J____h B____ngs,* on *Shennadore* mountains; but no conversation material then happened between us.

After fixing my family, I staid there nine days, and then returned back as far as *Charles McCormick's*. On my journey to *Charles McCormick's,* I met with *J____h B____ngs.* I asked him what brought him there? He told me, that he was going to make tavern money, that is, as he explained himself, Eighteen Penny bills. I was not then joined with the party that I shall hereafter mention.

After this I passed on my journey to a place called *Deep-Run*, to receive some money due to me there.

From thence I went to *Allen-Town*, in *Northampton* county; and was at many other places, accomplishing business I had to settle, which I compleated.

On my return home, I stopped at one *M_____an'* s, in *Carlisle.* He invited me to be concerned with him in Counterfeiting money. I gave him no satisfactory answer; but pro[c]eeded on in my journey.

I got as far as *M'C____k'* s, where I stopped, and staid all night. In the morning he invited me to ride with him to look for some beeves, in company with *W____m C_____n.* We proceeded on in hunt for the beeves about twenty miles, and came to a cabbin, in an unfrequented place, in the woods: Here we met with *J____h B___ngs, S_____l P______n* and *G______e* __________. They comforted us by setting before us such things as they had. They disclosed to me no matters of consequence that night. In the morning they all concluded, that I must stay and assist them; which I did. They shewed me and *M'C___k* several bills. *M'C____k,* after looking at them, said, They were not fit for him, and threw them in the fire. *M'C____k* soon after went home, leaving me with the rest of them.

A few days after I was sent off for provisions; I procured what I wanted, at the nearest place in my power, and returned with flour, meat and butter.

During eight days that I staid with them, I saw them make, and assisted in making, a number of Three Pound bills, *Pennsylvania* currency. After this was compleated, we all quit our cabbin; first destroying the press we made use of in counterfeiting.

We all went to *C______s M'C_____k'* s. At *M'C_____k'* s we had a great frolic; drinking and carousing the chief part of the night.

Next morning I received part of the money we had been counterfeiting. *B__ngs* gave me two bills that he had signed, the rest were blanks.

I proceeded from thence to *Carlisle* to the fore-mentioned *M____n's*. When I got to *M____n's*, I told him that I had got some blanks: he replied to me, that he would sign them, and pay himself with some of them.

I staid at *M____n's* two days, and then set off towards *Philadelphia*.

On my way down nothing happened particular till I came to *Michael Stadleman's*, tavernkeeper, on *Lancaster* road; to him I past one of my counterfeit bills, and got my change in good money.

The next I passed was to *William Stadleman*, of him I likewise got my change in good money.

From *William Stadleman'* s I came into *Philadelphia* ; the next day I passed one of these bad bills to *Hannah Lithgow*, and got the value of it to my satisfaction in the same manner as if the bill had been good.

The day following I passed another of the same sort to *Robert Taggart*; on his looking on the bill, I thought that he suspected that it was bad; he told me he would go and enquire about the bill; he staid a considerable time. *A guilty conscience needing no accuser*, I got so uneasy about it, that I quit the house; and in the quickest manner set about preparing to leave the city: But before I could get ready, I was apprehended, and carried before JOHN GIBSON, Esq; here I was searched, and a large number of bad bills were found in the seat of the breeches I had on, where I had put them for my better security. Upon this I was commited to goal that evening.

The next day but one I was taken before Judge ALLEN: He examined me; but I gave him small satisfaction.

I was then returned to goal, and the next day took before him again. The Judge advised me to confess the whole, as the most likely way to influence the Governor to mercy. I still remained obstinate and fearful; and told him, that was no surety for me. I then asked him if he would give me any assurance of safety if I did confess? Upon his answering, that it was out of his power, I concluded to give him but little account of the affair; and was remanded back to prison again.

The next day I was taken before JOHN GIBSON, Esq; and there *Hannah Lithgow* confronted me; to whom I had passed one of the counterfeit bills, as aforesaid. Finding that I was now further hampered, and concluding in my mind that it could be of no use to me to stand out any longer, upon examination, I confess'd my confederacy with others, in making and uttering the aforesaid counterfeit money, mentioning the names of all the confederates, except *M______an.*

I was returned to goal, and some few days after was had before Judge ALLEN; he shewed a letter from *M_____an* to me, about some of our affairs, and told me that *M_____an* was apprehended for uttering counterfeits; the Judge then asked me if *M______an* was concerned? I told him no, except in signing my blanks. I then gave him a more full account than I had done before; I was remanded back to prison.

Some days after I heard that our whole gang was taken. I then thought that if Judge ALLEN would please to hear me, I would give him an additional account to what I had already done. He sent for me, when before him, I informed, that they (meaning the gang I was concerned with) had got stamps for making of dollars, and that *M'C_____k* was the man that procured a Three Pound bill at *York-Town*, by which *B______ngs* cut the plate, as they told me.

I was remanded back to prison, where I continued close confined till *April*, 1770, when I was arraigned for Counterfeiting and Uttering the bills of credit of the government of *Pennsylvania*: To which I confessed myself *Guilty*. The reason of my pleading guilty was, that as I had before made a full discovery of my confederates, by giving the Court little trouble, I should stand the better chance to find mercy.

Sentence of death was passed upon me, and I confess that I deserved the same sentence before.

It has been rumoured, that in the *Jerseys* I had been concerned in stealing of horses; but declare myself innocent of the accusation:—-*The command in my heart was*, THOU SHALT NOT STEAL; which I always kept.

I knew of persons that were concerned in stealing horses, as already mentioned, and I hope they will repent, and do so no more. As my time is short, it is taken up in preparing for my final change. I have been careful, only to relate such things as concerned myself, or knew by certain knowledge.

And as I have here made this open confession to the world professing my sorrow and true penitence (as my life is to be taken for my faults) I hope all people whom I have injured, will *forgive me my trespasses.*

My conscience convicts me, that I have imposed on the world, by uttering counterfeit money for good, in confederacy with others; which I candidly and openly confess. And if this dying and open confession should fall into the hands of any of my old confederates, I would have them solemnly reflect, that though they may escape the hands of man, they cannot screen themselves from the swift justice of Almighty God. Consider, O my companions! that I am made a spectacle to the world; involved my innocent wife, and four children, in the disgrace; I have offended them that were most dear to me; I have offended man, and, more than all, I have offended God! Let this be a warning to you all; and may God grant you repentance and amendment of life, is the last prayer of your dying companion.

I now stand a candidate for happiness or misery to all eternity, the charitable prayers of all good Christians, I ask.—To the Supreme Creator I appeal, to rectify me in my last moments. My wife and children I beg may not be treated ill on my account.

I leave the world in true charity, forgiving all men; acknowledging myself a sinner; I resign my soul to God, hoping that He, through the merits of our Lord and Saviour Jesus Christ, will accept my life as a sacrifice, and receive my soul into bliss. AMEN.

WHEREAS it has been reported that several reputable people in the county of *Hunterdon* have been brought in by H. ROSENCRANTZ in his Confession, it is thought necessary, for the clearing of the character of such persons, to publish the following List, and to insert the Certificate signed by the said ROSENCRANTZ, annexed to the said List.

David Reynolds
Joseph Billings
Col. Hacket
John Dick
James Long
James Hanna
Michael Contz
Grover Stout
John Le Fevere
John Moore
_____ Bennet
Jesse Anderson
_____ Mooran
Charles M'Cormick
William Culbertson
Samuel Pelton
George _____.

AT present, to my knowlege, in my dark Cell, I cannot remember any others of my Associates.

HERMAN ROSENCRANTZ.

*Philadelphia* goal, *May* 4, 1770.

## Source Notes

*The Life and Confession of Herman Rosencrantz* was printed in Philadelphia by Joseph Crukshank at the request of James Chattin "and Sold by him at Mr. GRAHAM's, in *Second-street*, the second Door from *Market-street* Corner, and next door to Mr. MILNE's Jeweller" (title page). In his *History of Printing in America*, Isaiah Thomas included information concerning both Crukshank and Chattin (i, 246–7, 252, 262). Kenneth Scott's account of Rosencrantz in *Counterfeiting in Colonial America* agreed with the *Life and Confession* on all major points (216–18). Scott, however, located the dates of Rosencrantz's various arrests and trials and thus was able to piece together the counterfeiter's career more accurately. Moreover, according to Scott, Rosencrantz was less of a reluctant counterfeiter than his narrative portrayed him to be. Several times Rosencrantz declared that he was coaxed into the counterfeiting business by "Doctor" Joseph Billings and David Reynolds. While Scott found evidence that Billings certainly was one of the primary counterfeiters in the mid-Atlantic region, he established that Rosencrantz had lured Reynolds into counterfeiting. Scott stated: "It is known that Reynolds was a farmer. In an evil hour he chanced to make the acquaintance of the notorious Herman Rosencrantz and by him was led into the scheme of making and passing counterfeit money" (244). When Rosencrantz was apprehended for the last time in 1770, he was "a rather corpulent man of about sixty [54], some five feet ten inches tall" (217).

On December 21, 1769, *The Pennsylvania Gazette* reported that Rosencrantz had been arrested:

> On Saturday Night last, One ROSEY GRANT, was taken up, and committed to the Goal of this City, on Suspicion of counterfeiting the THREE POND Bills of this Province, dated March 1, 1769. On Searching him 68 of the above counterfeit Bills were found upon him. They are in general badly engraved on Copper-plate, the Letters very irregular, and may easily be distinguished from the true Bills, which are done with common Printing Types. Both the Back and the Face of the Counterfeits are blacker than the true Bills; the Signers Names, and Number, all wrote with the same Ink, very pale, and seem to be done by the same Hand; the Paper thinner, smoother and whiter than the genuine Bills; and we think after this Notice, no Person, acquainted with the Money of this Province, can be deceived by them.

One week later (December 28, 1769), *The Pennsylvania Gazette* corrected its first report: "The Person's Name, committed on Suspicion of counterfeiting the Three Pound Bills of this Province, is HARMAN ROSENCRANTZ." Undoubtedly due to Rosencrantz's cooperation, *The Pennsylvania Gazette* soon printed an official proclamation calling for the apprehension of Billings (January 18, 1770), and two months later the paper announced that he had been arrested: "We hear from Carlisle, that an Account is received there, that the notorious Billings (the principal Person concerned in counterfeiting the Three Pound Bills of this Province) was lately taken up, with another Man, after a long and obstinate Resistance, at Winchester, and committed to the Goal of that Place" (March 29, 1770). Despite what he might have hoped for, Rosencrantz's cooperation did not change the outcome of his trial; on April 19, 1770, *The Pennsylvania Gazette* reported: "Last Week, at a Court of Oyer and Terminer, held in this City, came on the Trials of Thomas and David Jones, and Mary-Ann Bryan, for Burglary, who were all convicted, and received Sentence of Death. Herman Rosencrantz, was indicted for uttering Counterfeit Three Pound Bills of Credit of this Province, to which he plead Guilty, and also received Sentence of Death." A month later the paper announced: "Last Saturday Harman Rosencrants, and David and Thomas Jones, were executed here pursuant to their Sentence. Mary Brian, who also received Sentence of Death, is reprived."

Brief notices mentioning Rosencrantz's trial and execution also were published in *The Pennsylvania Chronicle* on April 16 and May 7, 1770.

# The laſt WORDS and Dying SPEECH of LEVI AMES,

Who was Executed at BOSTON, on Thurſday the 21ſt Day of *October*, 1773, for BURGLARY.

Taken from his own Mouth, and Publiſhed at his deſire, as a ſolemn Warning to all, more particularly Young People.

*There is a Way that ſeemeth right unto a Man, but the End thereof are the Ways of Death.* Prov. 14. 12.

I LEVI AMES, aged twenty-one years, was born in *Groton*, in *New-England*, of a credible family, my father's name was *Jacob Ames*, who died when I was but two years old. I am the firſt of the family who was ever diſgraced. My prevailing ſin, and that for which I am ſoon to ſuffer death was *Thieving*; to practice which I began early and purſued it conſtantly; except at certain intervals when my conſcience made me uneaſy, and I reſolv'd to do ſo no more.

My firſt thefts were ſmall. I began this awful practice by ſtealing a couple of eggs, then a jack-knife, after that ſome chalk. But being detected and reproved for the crime, I thought to repent and reform; but found myſelf powerfully urged to repeat this wickedneſs, by the temptations of the devil; with which I again complied. My tender Mother ſeeing me take ſuch horrid courſes, and dreading the conſequences, often entreated and pleaded with me to turn from my evil ways, and I as often aſſured her that I would. Had I followed her good advice and counſel, I ſhould never have come to this ſhameful and untimely end. But I am now made to feel the anger of God againſt me, for my diſobedience to my parent! God will not let diſobedient children paſs unpuniſhed.

Having got from under my mother's eye, I ſtill went on in my old way of ſtealing; and not being permitted to live with the perſon I choſe to live with, I ran away from my maſter, which opened a wide door to temptation, and helped on my ruin; for being indolent in temper, and having no honeſt way of ſupporting myſelf, I robbed others of their property.

About this time I ſtole a gun at *Woburn*, from *Joſiah Richardſon*, and a large ſilver ſpoon from one Mr. *Howard* of the ſame town. I then broke open the ſhop of Mr. *Edward Hammond*, in the county of *Plymouth*, and took out a piece of broad-cloth, and ſome money. I ſtole between twenty and thirty dollars from another perſon, whoſe name I have forgot. I broke open the ſhop of Mr. *Jonas Cutler*, of *Groton*, and took from him a good piece of broad-cloth, a quantity of ſilk mitts, and ſeveral pieces of ſilk hankerchiefs. I alſo ſtole a quantity of money from *Jonathan Hammond*, of *Waltham*, and a hat from *Jonas Dix*, Eſq; of the ſame place; and when in goal at *Cambridge*, I ſtole a ſilver ſpoon which was brought from Mr. *Bradiſh*'s the goal-keeper for me to eat with. I robbed the Rev. Mr. *Clark* of *Lexington*, of a tankard, twelve tea ſpoons, one large dit. a pepper-box, and two pair of ſugar tongs. I alſo ſtole from Mr. *Keith* at *Natick*, two coats and jackets, with which I dreſſed myſelf when I came to *Boſton*; I gave *John Battle* twenty dollars to make up the matter with Mr. *Keith*, being part of the money I ſtole from Mr. *Hammond* of *Waltham*. I ſtole ten or eleven dollars from Mr. *Symonds* of *Lexington*, whoſe ſon in law Mr. *Meriam*, while I was in priſon, informed me where the money was and how to get it, but he never received any of it; I ſuppoſed he gave me this information thro' envy againſt his father in law, thro' whoſe means he was then confined for debt. I ſtole a pair of ſilver buckles, and a pair of turned pumps out of a pair of ſaddle bags at *Leaſon*'s tavern in *Waltham*; the buckles were marked I. D. which I delivered to a man at *Marlborough*, a blackſmith, to make up with him for ſome ſtockings I took from him; his name I do not remember. I twiſted a padlock and enter'd the cellar of a Miniſter's houſe at *Marlborough*, I then went up the cellar ſtairs, lighted a candle in order to get ſome victuals. I have ſeveral times taken ſundry articles off of lines, hedges, fences, buſhes, apple-trees, graſs, &c. but cannot recollect the owners. *Tho. Cook* and I ſtole two great coats and ſold them. I have left three ſhirts and ſeveral pair of ſtockings at *Scipio Burnam*'s at *Newbury-Port*: I then went by the name of *Iſaac Lawrence*. I ſtole an ax out of a cart and hid it in a ſtone wall between *Watertown* and *Boſton*, (the night before I took the money from Mr. *Hammond*) in *Little-Cambridge*, near to Mr. *Dana*'s tavern, there I left it with a deſign to ſell it when I came back. I broke open the houſe of Mr. *Rice* in *Marlborough*, on the Lords day, while the people were gone to public worſhip, having been adviſed to it by *Daniel Cook*, when we were in *Concord* Goal; was taken in the houſe, and returned the things to the [illegible]ner.

Some[illegible] fall I ſaw *Tho. Cook* who told me he had ſeven pou[illegible] he hid, viz. a tankard, a number of table ſpoons, [illegible] ditto; theſe he dug up while I was with him; we [illegible] away from that place and hid them in a ſtone wall, [illegible]arn, cloſe to the ſign of the bull on *Wrentham* road, but [illegible]er informed me where he got them, or how he came by them; he offered me half if I would diſpoſe of them, but I was affraid to do it.

Laſt *June* an Iriſhman who called his name *Thomas Smith*, of middle ſtature, much marked with the ſmall-pox, told me that he knew of a watch which was taken from his excellency ſome time ago, and I ſuſpected that he was the perſon who ſtole it, becauſe he ſaid he knew the governor's houſe well: He alſo aſſured me that his Excellency had a conſiderable quantity of money in the houſe, and aſked me to go with him to get it. I denied, knowing that the governor had many ſervants, which I urged as a reaſon why I would not join him. He ſaid he had one to aſſiſt him, whoſe name he would not tell me, unleſs I would be one of the party. He farther declared that he ſhould go well armed with ſwords and piſtols. Upon this I abſolutely refuſed, becauſe I never thought of murdering any man, in the midſt of all my ſcene of theiving. He thought to prevail on me by telling me that there was a cheſt of dollars in the houſe but I would not go with them.

In the ſame month (*June*) I lodged at a tavern in *Killingsley* or *Pomfret* in *Connecticut* government, on the Lord's day, where eat and drank and went off without paying. A few evenings after, I returned ſhoved up the window, and put in my hand and ſtole a box with a johannes, ſome ſmall change, a pair of knee buckles, and ſleeve buttons, for which I was apprehended, confeſſed the fact, returned the goods, was puniſhed and ſet at liberty. The ſame night as above I took a horſe out of *Killingsley*, and rode him down to the county of *Worceſter*, where I broke a ſhop open about day light, and took a quantity of coppers, and a remnant of ſattin: The owners have got them again. I alſo robbed a baker at *Rhode-Iſland* of a quantity of coppers which I found in three baſkets, and ſpent them.

As for *Atwood*, in company with whom I committed that theft for which I am ſoon to die, my acquaintance with him began in the following manner—I was ſtanding at a countryman's cart, in the market at *Boſton*, aſking the price of a turkey; *Atwood* came up to me, and we fell into converſation, he aſked me to walk with him to Beacon-Hill, which I did—We aſked each other about the place of reſort. I told him that I lodged at Capt. Dickey's. He ſaid his money was all ſpent except one copper, which he had in a ſnuff-box. I aſked him where he belonged? He ſaid he was born in an Iſland in the Weſt-Indies, and that his parents lived in Rhode-Iſland. I aſked him where he had been? he told me that he lately came from *Portſmouth*. I told him that ſince he had no money, if he would go with me to my lodgings, I would give him ſome dinner—I aſked him what he would do with ſome ſilver plate, if he had any to diſpoſe of? He told me he knew of a goldſmith who would take it, becauſe he had ſold ſome to him before. I told him I knew where there was ſome, and if he would go with me, we would get it; to which he conſented. We then went to *Menotomy*, and found it hid in a ſtone wall. We kept it about us till next Morning. He told me he knew of a Vendue maſter in *Boſton*, with whom he had lived, who had a large ſum of money by him, and if I would join him, we would get it. I aſked who it was; he ſaid Mr. *Bicker*. We accordingly agreed to ſteal it. At night, after we had ſlept, we went to a joiner's ſhop, into which I entered and took out three chizels; we then went to Mr. *Bicker*'s Houſe, and on the way were hailed by a watchman, to whom we anſwered, Friends. Having come to Mr. *Bicker*'s houſe, we found a front chamber window open; we pulled off our ſhoes, and *Joſ. Atwood* with my aſſiſtance climed up to the window, and entered the houſe, and opened the doors for me; we then went together to the deſk, which we broke open with the chizels. *Atwood* pulled out the firſt drawer, and ſaid there was ſmall change in it, which was all he could find. As he was going away, I pulled out another drawer, in which I found a bag of ſilver coin.—After that we came out, and went to fox-hill, near the powder-houſe, there we hid the plate, which we had kept in our pockets while we were at ſupper, and when we entered Mr. *Bicker*'s houſe. The ſmall change in ſilver, which *Atwood* took were equally divided, tho' the gold which *Atwood* had then ſecreted I knew nothing of, nor did he ever give me any of it. Before ſunſet I ſaw him at Mr. *Bell's*, when he informed me that a warrant was out for me; he went with me to *Winiſimit*, and adviſed me to go over the ferry, promiſing to meet me at *Portſmouth* the Wedneſday following at the houſe in which he was taken. I returned again to *Boſton* to ſee if any of my cloaths were done, which I had beſpoke; on Saturday I was taken by Mr. *Bicker* and committed to goal, and ſaw *Atwood* no more till I ſaw him in the priſon yard after he was apprehended.

Thus have I given an account of that ſhocking manner in which I have filled up a ſhort life, and of which I am now aſhamed. May God forgive me my dreadful wickedneſs, committed both againſt him, and many worthy men, of whom alſo I would aſk forgiveneſs, it being not in my power to make reſtitution, which if it was I would readily do it—I alſo forgive from my heart *Joſeph Atwood*, who ſwore on my tryal that I entered the houſe of Mr. *Bicker* firſt, and let him in, when he knows in his conſcience, that he entered firſt and let me in. I die in charity with all mankind. But though I lived ſuch a wicked life, it was not without ſome ſevere checks of conſcience. For after I had ſtolen, I have been ſo diſtreſſed at times, as to be obliged to go back, and throw the ſtolen goods at the door, or into the yard, that the owners might have them again——And not long before I was taken for this laſt robbery, I paſſed the gallows on *Boſton* neck with ſome ſtolen goods under my arm; when my conſcience terribly ſmote me, and I tho't I ſhould ſurely die there, if I did not leave off this courſe of life. What I then feared, is now come upon me.———

Having thus given an account of my dreadful life of wickedneſs, I would alſo mention the manner in which I have conducted, and my mind has been exerciſed during my confinement in goal, ſince the awful ſentence of DEATH was paſs'd upon me.

At firſt I had ſecret hopes of eſcape; that I ſhould by ſome means get out of priſon. When I ſaw that it was impoſſible, I endeavoured to reconcile myſelf as well as I could. My conſcience made me uneaſy—I thought I had been ſo wicked that I ſhould certainly go to Hell. And when I conſidered how ſhort my time was, I knew I could not do good works to go to Heaven. To Hell then I was ſure I ſhould go. And I ſeemed to have ſuch an awful ſight of Hell and the Grave, that I was very much terrified indeed—I then took to drinking ſtrong liquor in order to drown my ſorrow. But this would not do—I left that off and took to reading my bible; my conſcience became ſo uneaſy, that I could have no reſt, O! a wounded conſcience who can bear? I tried to pray; but it came into my mind that the prayers of the wicked would not be heard. Yet I could not help crying for mercy. I was at times ready to deſpair of the mercy of God. But the miniſters who viſited me, aſſured me that the blood of Chriſt was ſufficient to cleanſe me from all ſin, which gave me a little encouragement to go on crying to God. I now began to underſtand ſomething of that law of God which I had broken, as condemning me for the wickedneſs of my heart as well as life—I ſaw that I was undone, that my heart and life were bad beyond all account. I ſaw that if God ſhould damn me a thouſand times he would be juſt, and I ſhould have nothing to ſay. In this condition I was a week before the time firſt fixed for my execution—The loſs of body and ſoul made me tremble; though I could not freely tell all that I felt to all who came to ſee me. I thought that if I ſhould be executed in this condition, I muſt be dragged like a bullock to the ſlaughter.

But God's name be bleſſed forever; that on Friday evening, the 8th inſtant, I turned over a little book which was put into my hands, in which I ſaw, Ezek. 36. 26, 27. *A new heart will I give you, and a new ſpirit will I put upon you: and I will take away the ſtony heart out of your fleſh, and I will give you a heart of fleſh. And I will pour out my ſpirit upon you*, &c. This at once ſurprized me: I knew that I wanted this new heart; and could not help looking on this as God's gracious promiſe to me: and I tho't that as I knew God could not lie, if I would not believe this, I would believe nothing: my mind at once felt eaſy. I now ſaw that I had ſinned againſt God all my life with as much envy, as ever I killed a ſnake; which I always hated.

After this I had, and now have ſuch a view of the way of ſalvation by Chriſt, that I felt and do feel my ſoul reſt on him as my only hope of ſalvation. Since which I have found peace of mind, anger againſt myſelf for ſin, and a deſire to be made holy. At times the terrors of death ſeem to be removed: at other times I am full of fears leſt I ſhould deceive myſelf. Yet I cannot but hope that Chriſt has freely pardoned me. On him I deſire to reſt living and dying; and to give him all the praiſe.

And now as a dying man I mention the following things, viz.

1. To keep your doors and windows ſhut on evenings, and ſecured well to prevent temptation. And by no means to uſe ſmall locks on the outſide, one of which I have twiſted with eaſe when tempted to ſteal. Alſo not to leave linnen or clothes out at night, which have often proved a ſnare to me. Travellers I adviſe to ſecure their ſaddle bags, boots, &c. in the chambers where they lodge.

2. Parents and maſters I entreat who have any concern for and connection with children, to have an eye over their actions; and to take ſpecial care for their precious and immortal ſouls.

3. All Perſons whether old or young, who may ſee theſe lines, ſpoke as it were by a poor, dying, ſinful man, now bound in chains, and who has but a ſhort ſpace of time before he muſt launch into an endleſs eternity; guard againſt every temptation to ſin. If at any time you are tempted to do any thing like the poor ſoul who now ſpeaks to you, earneſtly pray to God for ſtrength to reſiſt the temptation; as well as for repentance for your paſt ſins.

The youth more eſpecially I would ſolemnly caution againſt the vices to which they are moſt inclin'd.—Such is *bad Women*, who have undone many, and by whom I alſo have ſuffered much; the unlawful intercourſe with them I have found by ſad experience, leading to almoſt every ſin. I alſo warn them to guard againſt the firſt temptation to *diſobedience to parents*. Had I regarded the many kind intreaties and reproofs of my tender Mother, I had never come to this ſhameful and untimely death.

Profane *curſing and ſwearing* I alſo bear my dying teſtimony againſt, as a horrid ſin, and very provoking to God.

Nor muſt I omit to mention *gaming*, to which young people are much inclin'd, and which at this day prevails to the ruin of many. For when a youth hath gamed away all his money, he will be tempted even to ſteal from his maſter or parents, in order to get at it again. Beſides, this ſin leads to *drunkenneſs* another dreadful vice.

There is one ſin more that I muſt warn all perſons againſt, and that is, *a profanation of the Lord's day, and of public worſhip*. Oh! how many ſuch days have I deſpiſed, and while others have been engaged in ſerving God, I have been employed in wickedneſs, which I now confeſs with grief of heart.

4. I have one requeſt more to make from the borders of the grave, a compliance with which is earneſtly deſired by a poor dying mortal: which is, That no perſon, old or young, would ever reflect on my poor dear Mother, or Brother, or any of my relations, on account of my ſhameful and untimely death, who could not prevent my wickedneſs, and have trouble too much to be borne, by the life I have lived, and the death I am to die.

I deſire ſincerely to thank all the good miniſters of the town, who have taken great pains with me ever ſince the ſentence of death was paſt upon me, to convince me of my unhappy ſituation, of my loſt and undone condition by nature, of my aggravating ſins by practice, and of the infinitely free rich grace and mercy of God, only thro' the merits and mediation of my dear ſaviour Jeſus Chriſt. I alſo thank all the good people both of town and country, who, I have reaſon to think, have offered up many prayers at the throne of grace for me. I alſo thank Mr. *Otis*, the goal-keeper and his family, who have all been very kind to me during my confinement in Goal.

And now may Jeſus Chriſt forgive me, the worſt of ſinners, as he did the thief on the croſs, if he does not, I am forever undone in ſoul and body!

Atteſt, JOSEPH OTIS,
Dept. Goal-Keeper.

*Levi Ames.*

BOSTON: Printed and Sold at the Shop oppoſite the Court-Houſe in Queen-Street.

[ LEVI AMES ]

# *The Last Words and Dying Speech of Levi Ames*

[ 1773 ]

I LEVI AMES, aged twenty-one years, was born in *Groton,* in *New-England,* of a credible family, my father's name was *Jacob Ames,* who died when I was but two years old. I am the first of the family who was ever disgraced. My prevailing sin, and that for which I am soon to suffer death was *Thieving*; to practice which I began early and pursued it constantly; except at certain intervals when my conscience made me uneasy, and I resolved to do so no more.

My first thefts were small. I began this awful practice by stealing a couple of eggs, then a jack-knife, after that some chalk. But being detected and reproved for the crime, I thought to repent and reform; but found myself powerfully urged to repeat this wickedness, by the temptations of the devil; with which I again complied. My tender Mother seeing me take such horrid courses, and dreading the consequences, often entreated and pleaded with me to turn from my evil ways, and I as often assured her that I would. Had I followed her good advice and council, I should never have come to this shameful and untimely end. But I am now made to feel the anger of God against me, for my disobedience to my parent! God will not let disobedient children pass unpunished.

Having got from under my mother's eye, I still went on in my old way of stealing; and not being permitted to live with the person I chose to live with, I ran away from my master, which opened a wide door to temptation, & helped on my ruin; for being indolent in temper, and having no honest way of supporting myself, I robbed others of their property.

About this time I stole a gun at *Woburn*, from *Josiah Richardson,* and a large silver spoon from one Mr. *Howard* of the same town. I then broke open the shop of Mr. *Edward Hammond*, in the county of *Plymouth,* and took out a piece of broad-cloth, and some money. I stole between 20 and 30 dollars from another person, whose name I have forgot. I broke open the shop of Mr. *Jonas Cutler*, of *Groton*, and took from him a good piece of broad-cloth, a quantity of silk mitts, and several pieces of silk handkerchiefs. I also stole a quantity of money from *Jonathan Hammond*, of *Waltham*, and a hat from *Jonas Dix*, Esq; of the same place; and when in goal at *Cambridge*, I stole a silver spoon which was brought from Mr. *Braddish*'s, the goal-keeper, for me to eat with. I robbed the Rev. Mr. *Clark*, of *Lexington*, of a tankard, twelve tea-spoons, one large ditto, a pepper-box, and two pair of sugar tongs. I also stole from Mr. *Keith*, at *Natick*, two coats and jackets, with which I dressed myself when I came to *Boston*; I gave *John Battle* 20 dollars to make up the matter with Mr. *Keith*, being part of the money I stole from Mr. *Hammond*, of *Waltham*. I stole ten or eleven dollars from Mr. *Symonds*, of *Lexington*, whose son in law, Mr. *Meriam*, while I was in prison, informed me where the money was and how to get it, but he never received any of it; I supposed he gave me this information thro' envy against his father in law, thro' whose means he was then confined for debt. I stole a pair of silver buckles, and a pair of turned pumps out of a pair of saddle bags at *Leason*'s tavern in *Waltham*; the buckles were marked I. D. which I delivered to a man at *Marlborough*, a blacksmith, to make up with him for some stockings I took from him; his name I do not remember. I twisted a padlock and entr'd the cellar of Minister's house at *Marlborough*, I then went up the cellar stairs, lighted a candle in order to get some victuals. I have several times taken sundry articles off of lines, hedges, fences, bushes, apple trees, grass, &c. but cannot recollect the owners. *Tho. Cook* and I stole two great-coats and sold them. I have left three shirts and several pair of stockings at *Scipio Burnam*'s, at *Newbury-Port*: I then went by the name of *Isaac Lawrence*. I stole an ax out of a cart and hid it in a stone wall between *Watertown* and *Boston*, (the night before I took the money from Mr. *Hammond*) in *Little Cambridge*, near to Mr. *Dana*'s tavern, there I left it with a design to sell it when I came back. I broke open the house of Mr. *Rice* in *Marlborough*, on the Lords Day, while the people were gone to public worship, having been advised to it by *Daniel Cook*, when we were in *Concord* Goal; was taken in the house, and returned the things to the Owner.

Some time last fall I saw *Tho. Cook* who told me he had seven pounds of plate hid, viz. a tankard, a number of table spoons, and one soup ditto; these he dug up while I was with him; we carried them away from that place and hid them in a stone wall, near a barn, close to the sign of the bull on *Wrentham* road; but he never informed me where he got them, or how he came by them; he offered me half if I would dispose of them, but I was afraid to do it.

A

# Solemn Farewell to *LEVI AMES,*

Being a POEM written a few Days before his EXECUTION, for *Burglary, Oct.* 21, 1773.

HOW black the diſmal Day appears
To *Ames's* anxious Heart!
His Eyes o'erflow with conſcious [Tears
He quakes in every Part.

See! round the Priſon how the Throng
From every Quarter pour;
Some mourn with ſympathiſing Tongue,
The ruder Rabble roar.

How can the human Heart refuſe
Pity to deep Diſtreſs,
To ſee a Soul Immortal looſe
Itſelf in Wretchedneſs?

What Anguiſh heaves the dying Breaſt
When rack'd with laſt Diſpair?
The Wicked find no Shade of Reſt,
When GOD proclaims the War.

Slow rolls the Cart with ſolemn Pace,
The Ladder ſhows on high;
See the poor pinion'd Priſoner paſs
On to Eternity.

The Officers of Juſtice round,
The Miniſter intent;
The Priſoner fix'd in Awe profound,
Attends the dire Event.

The Crowds preſs on, the Windows full
Gaze keen on every Side;
O! may the Sight on every Soul
In laſting Thoughts abide.

But oh! the diſmal Place he ſpies,
The fatal Gallows Tree:
Hark how the Malefactor cries
"What will become of me?"

O Son of Death, thy Sins lie hard,
But do not thou Diſpare:
The Thief upon the Croſs was heard,
*JESUS* the *GOD* was there.

*Manaſſah* in his Fetters pray'd,
His *GOD* regards his Cry:
A perſecuting *Saul* is made
Poſſeſſor of the Sky.

There *Peter,* who his *LORD* deny'd,
There murdering *David* view;
Bleſs'd Saints! to Angels near alli'd,
Such! Such were ſome of you!

O *JESUS* how thy Merits plead!
How full thy Righteouſneſs!
Can he who knows how *JESUS* bled,
E'er doubt the *FATHER*'s Grace?

All Heaven is purchas'd by His Croſs,
For ſuch vile Souls as thine:
You leave this Earth; it is no Loſs,
If you in Heaven may ſhine.

The dying Pangs you'll now ſuſtain;
How ſhort a Scene is this,
Compar'd with Hell's Eternal Pain,
And Heaven's Eternal Bliſs!

But O, admoniſh'd by his Fate,
Warn'd by a dying Man—
" Repent before it be too la
" *Your* Life is but a Spar

" I ſeldom pray'd: I ſeldor
" Or heard *GOD*'s hol
" From Righteous Paths
" And Holineſs abhor'

" Soon learnt to lye, and
" With little Thefts b
" And ſtill went on fror
" From Childhood up

" Convictions oft and
" Me never could
—" *Sin ends in Sorro*
" By this my fearf

*BOSTON:* Printed and Sold at DRAPER's Printing-Office, in N

Last *June* an Irishman who called his name *Thomas Smith*, of middle stature, much marked with the small-pox, told me that he knew of a watch which was taken from his excellency some time ago, and I suspected that he was the person who stole it, because he said he knew the governor's house well: He also assured me that his Excellency had a considerable quantity of money in the house, and asked me to go with him to get it. I denied, knowing that the governor had many servants, which I urged as a reason why I would not join him. He said he had one to assist him, whose name he would not tell me, unless I would be one of the party. He farther declared that he should go well armed with swords and pistols. Upon this I absolutely refused, because I never thought of murdering any man, in the midst of all my scene of thieving. He thought to prevail on me by telling me that there was a chest of dollars in the house but I would not go with them.

In the same month (June) I lodged at a tavern in *Killingsley* or *Pomfret*, in *Connecticut* government, on the Lord's-day, where I sat and drank and went off without paying. A few evenings after, I returned, shoved up the window, and put in my hand and stole a box with a johannes, some small change, a pair of knee buckles, and sleeve buttons, for which I was apprehended, confessed the fact, returned the goods, was punished and set at liberty. The same night as above I took a horse out of *Killingsley*, and rode him down to the county of *Worcester*, where I broke a shop open about day light, and took a quantity of coppers, and a remnant of sattin: The owners have got them again. I also robbed a baker at *Rhode-Island* of a quantity of coppers which I found in three baskets, and spent them.

As for *Atwood*, in company with whom I committed that theft for which I am soon to die, my acquaintance with him began in the following manner—I was standing at a countryman's cart in the market at *Boston*, asking the price of a turkey; *Atwood* came up to me, and we fell into conversation, he asked me to walk with him to Beacon-Hill, which I did—We asked each other about the place of resort. I told him that I lodged at Capt. Dickey's. He said his money was all spent except one copper, which he had in a snuff-box. I asked him where he belonged? He said he was born in an Island in the West-Indies, and that his parents lived in Rhode-Island. I asked him where he had been? he told me that he lately came from *Portsmouth*. I told him that since he had no money, if he would go with me to my lodgings, I would give him some dinner—I asked him what he would do with some silver plate, if he had any to dispose of? He told me he knew of a goldsmith who would take it, because he had sold some to him before. I told him I knew where there was some, and if he would go with me, we would get it; to which he consented. We then went to *Menotemy*, and found it hid in a stone wall. We kept it about us until next Morning. He told me he knew of a Vendue-master in *Boston*, with whom he had lived, who had a large sum of money by him, and if I would join him, we would get it. I asked who it was; he said Mr. *Bicker.* We accordingly agreed to steal it. At night, after we had slept, we went to a joiner's shop, into which I entered and took out three chizels; we then went to Mr. *Bicker's* House, and on the way were hailed by a watchman, to whom we answered, Friends. Having come to Mr. *Bicker's* house, we found a front chamber window open; we pulled off our shoes, and *Jos. Atwood* with my assistance climbed up to the window, and entered the house, and opened the doors for me; we then went together to the desk, which we broke open with the chizels. *Atwood* pulled out the first drawer, and said there was small change in it, which was all he could find. As he was going away, I pulled out another drawer, in which I found a bag of silver coin.—After that we came out, and went to fox-hill, near the powder-house, there we hid the plate, which we had kept in our pockets while we were at supper, and when we entered Mr. *Bicker's* house. The small change in silver, which *Atwood* took were equally divided, tho' the gold which *Atwood* had then secreted I knew nothing of, nor did he ever give me any of it. Before sunset I saw him at Mr. *Bell's*, when he informed me that a warrant was out for me; he went with me to *Winisimit,* and advised me to go over the ferry, promising to meet me at *Portsmouth* the Wednesday following at the house in which he was taken. I returned again to *Boston* to see if any of the cloaths were done, which I had bespoke; on Saturday I was taken by Mr. *Bicker* and committed to goal, and saw *Atwood* no more until I saw him in the prison-yard after he was apprehended.

Thus have I given an account of that shocking manner in which I have filled up a short life, and of which I am now ashamed. May God forgive me my dreadful wickedness, committed both against him, and many worthy men, of whom also I would ask forgiveness, it being not in my power to make restitution, which if it was I would readily do it—I also forgive from my heart *Joseph Atwood*, who swore on my trial that I entered the house of Mr. *Bicker* first, and let him in, when he knows in his conscience, that he entered first and let me in. I die in charity with all mankind. But though I lived such a wicked life, it was not without some severe checks of conscience. For after I had stolen, I have been so distressed at times, as to be obliged to go back, and throw the stolen goods at the door, or into the yard, that the Owners might have them again.—And not long before I was taken for this last robbery, I passed the gallows on *Boston* neck with some stolen goods under my arm; when my conscience terribly smote me, and I tho't I should surely die there, if I did not leave off this course of life. What I then feared, is now come upon me.—

Having thus given an account of my dreadful life of wickedness, I would also mention the manner in which I have conducted, and my mind has been exercised during my confinement in goal, since the awful sentence of DEATH was pass'd upon me.

At first I had secret hopes of escape; that I should by some means get out of prison. When I saw it was impossible, I endeavored to reconcile myself as well as I could. My conscience made me uneasy—I thought I had been so wicked that I should certainly go to Hell.—And when I considered how short my time was, I knew I could not do good works to go to Heaven. To Hell then I was sure I should go.—And I seemed to have such an awful sight of Hell and the Grave, that I was very much terrified indeed—I then took to drinking strong liquor in order to drown my sorrow. But this would not do—I left that off and took to reading my bible; my conscience became so uneasy, that I could have no rest. O! a wounded conscience who can bear? I tried to pray; but it came into my mind that the prayers of the wicked would not be heard. Yet I could not help crying for mercy. I was at times ready to despair of the mercy of God. But the ministers who visited me, assured me that the blood of Christ was sufficient to cleanse me from all sin, which gave me a little encouragement to go on crying to God.—I now began to understand something of that law of God which I had broken, as condemning me for the wickedness of my heart as well as life—I saw that I was undone, that my heart and life were bad beyond all account. I saw that if God should damn me a thousand times he would be just, and I should have nothing to say. In this condition I was a week before the time first fixed for my execution—The loss of body and soul made me tremble; though I could not freely tell all that I felt to all who came to see me. I thought that if I should be executed in this condition, I must be dragged like a bullock to the slaughter.

But God's name be blessed forever; that on Friday evening, the 8th instant I turned over a little book which was put into my hands, in which I saw, Ezek. xxxvi. 26, 27. *A new heart will I give you, and a new spirit will I put upon you: and I will take away the stony heart out of your flesh, and I will give you a heart of flesh. and I will pour out my spirit upon you*, &c. This at once surprized me: I knew that I wanted this new heart, and could not help looking on this as God's gracious promise to me: and I tho't that as I knew God could not lie, if I would not believe this, I would believe nothing: my mind at once felt easy. I now saw that I had sinned against God all my life with as much envy, as ever I killed a snake; which I always hated.

After this I had, and now have such a view of the way of salvation by Christ, that I felt and do feel my soul rest on him as my only hope of salvation. Since which I have found peace of mind, anger against myself for sin, and a desire to be made holy. At times the terrors of death seem to be removed; at other times I am full of fears lest I should deceive myself. Yet I cannot but hope that Christ has freely pardoned me. On him I desire to rest living and dying; and to give him all the praise.

And now as a dying man I mention the following things, viz.

1. *To keep your doors and windows shut on evenings, and secured well to prevent temptation. And by no means to use small locks on the outside, one of which I have twisted with ease when tempted to steal. Also not to leave linnen or clothes out at night, which have often proved a snare to me. Travellers I advise to secure their saddle bags, boots, &c. in the chambers where they lodge.*

2. *Parents and masters I entreat you who have any concern for, and connection with children, to have an eye over their actions, and to take special care for their precious and immortal souls.*

3. *All Persons whether old or young, who may see these lines, spoke as it were by a poor, dying, sinful man, now bound in chains, and who has but a short space of time before he must launch into an endless eternity; guard against every temptation to sin. If at any time you are tempted to do any thing like the poor soul who now speaks to you, earnestly pray to God for strength to resist the temptation, as well as for repentance for your past sins.*

*The youth more especially I would solemnly caution against the vices to which they are most inclin'd—Such as* bad Women, *who have undone many, and by whom I also have suffered much; the unlawful intercourse with them I have found by sad experience, leading to almost every sin. I also warn them to guard against the first temptation to* disobedience to parents. *Had I regarded the many kind intreaties and reproofs of my tender Mother, I had never come to this shameful and untimely death.*

Profane cursing and swearing *I also bear my dying testimony against, as a horrid sin, and very provoking to God.*

*Nor must I omit to mention* gaming, t*o which young people are much inclined, and which at this day prevails to the ruin of many. For when a youth hath gamed away all his money, he well be tempted even to steal from his master or parents, in order to get at it again. Besides, this sin leads to* drunkenness, *another dreadful vice.*

*There is one sin more that I must warn all persons against, and that is,* a profanation of the Lord's day, and of public worship. *Oh! how many such days have I despised, and while others have been engaged in serving God, I have been employed in wickedness, which I now confess with grief of heart.*

4. *I have one request more to make from the borders of the grave, a compliance with which is earnestly desired by a poor dying mortal; which is, That no person, old or young, would ever reflect on my poor dear Mother, or Brother, or any of my relations, on account of my shameful and untimely death, who could not prevent my wickedness, and have trouble too much to be borne, by the life I have lived, and the death I am to die.*

# The SPEECH of DEATH
## TO
# *LEVI AMES.*

Who was Executed on *Boſton*-Neck, *October* 21, 1773, for the Crime of Burglary.

I DEATH, Poor *Ames*, pronounce your Fate,
Thus grining grimly through your Grate.
Remember all the Crimes you've done,
And think how early you begun.
Loſt in the grand Apoſtacy,
You were at firſt condemn'd to die;
In adding Guilt you ſtill went on:
I doubly claim you for my own.
How often you the Sabbath broke!
GOD's Name in vain how often took!
A filthy Drunkard you have been,
And led your Life with the Unclean:
No Thoughts of GOD you ever choſe,
But chas'd them from you when they roſe:
In Idleneſs you did proceed,
And took ſmall pains to learn to read:
With vile Companions, your Delight,
You often ſpent the guilty Night:
Your Lips ſcarce ever breath'd a Prayer,
You gave your Tongue to curſe and ſwear:
You've been to all your Friends a Grief,
And from your Infancy a Thief;
You know the Truth of what I tell,
No Goods were ſafe that you could ſteal;
How many Doors you've open broke!
And windows ſcal'd, and Money took:
Round Houſes you all Day have been,
To ſpy a Place to enter in;
Thence in the Night, all dark and late,
You've ſtole their Goods and Gold and Plate.
Impriſon'd, whip'd, yet you proceed,
The Life you led you ſtill would lead.
Your Conſcience cry'd, "you'll be undone."—
You ſtifi'd Conſcience and went on.
And now, behold! my poiſon'd Dart,
I point directly at your Heart.
The Halter and the Gallows view,
Death and Damnation is your due.
Darkneſs, and Horror, Fire, and Chains,
Almighty Wrath, and endleſs Pains.
—But lo! I ſee the Preacher come,
Salvation ſpeaks——I muſt be dumb.

The Preacher ſpeaks—Behold I come,
A voice from Heaven to call you home.
Though you the chief of Sinners were,
I bring the Goſpel; don't Deſpair.
Nor death, nor Hell, ſhall do you hurt,
Be JESUS only your Support.
To you he holds His Righteouſneſs,
He bled and dy'd to buy your Peace.
Pardon and Life are His to give,
'Tis thine, Poor Sinner, to believe.
Let Death in all it's Dread appear,
Though public Execution's near,
Of Wrath Divine He bore the Weight,
*He* ſuffer'd too without the Gate,
*He* betwixt Heaven and Earth was hung,
He conquer'd Hell, and death unſtung.

Now let the Guilty ſee and hear,
And all the Congregation fear;
This Spectacle your Hearts impreſs,
And do no more ſuch Wickedneſs;
Hear ſuch important Truths as theſe,
Ruin advances by Degrees:
The youth with leſſer Crimes begins,
And then proceeds to groſſer Sins,
From Step to Step he travels on,
And ſees himſelf at once undone:
Surpriz'd! unthought on! finds his Fate,
His Ruin final, and compleat.

*I desire sincerely to thank all the good ministers of the town, who have taken great pains with me ever since the sentence of death was past upon me, to convince me of my unhappy situation, of my lost and undone condition by nature, of my aggravating sins by practice, and of the infinitely free rich grace and mercy of God, only thro' the merits and mediation of my dear Saviour Jesus Christ. I also thank all the good people both of town and country, who, I have reason to think, have offered up many prayers at the throne of grace for me. I also thank Mr.* Otis, *the goal-keeper and his family, who have all been very kind to me during my confinement in goal.*

*And now may Jesus Christ forgive me, the worst of sinners, as he did the thief on the cross, if he does not, I am forever undone in soul and body.*

*Attest.* JOSEPH OTIS, *Levi Ames.*
*Dept. Goal Keeper*

[The following final account is taken from Samuel Mather's execution sermon, *Christ Sent to Heal the Broken Hearted.*]

[*Ames* was attended to the place of execution by the rev. *Samuel Stillman,* one of the baptist-ministers in this town, who constantly visited and prayed with him while he was under confinement, and spared no pains to reform and bring him to a just sense of his unhappy condition and guilt; in short, such was the assiduity of that reverend and pious Gentleman, that his utmost efforts were not wanting, in season and out of season, to sit and prepare him for a future state: So great affection and concern did he shew for the future welfare of this unfortunate young creature, that while he was accompanying him to the fatal tree, with tears in his eyes, he clasped this young convert round his waist, and seemed to take the greatest satisfaction in conversing with him about the things that concerned his everlasting happiness; to sum up the whole in a few words, his whole deportment, in his agreeable moments spent in his travel, seemed to bespeak, *Come, ye blessed of my Father, inherit the kingdom prepared for you.* The Prisoner was turned off just at four o'clock, having first given a short but pathetic exhortation to the vast concourse of people, who attended this awful scene, supposed to consist of seven or eight thousand persons, and particularly the YOUTH, who he earnestly entreated to avoid *Stealing*, the crime which he was most addicted to, and for which he was to suffer an ignominious death. He took by the hand Mr. *Edward Ranger*, housewright, (a member of Mr. *Stillman's* church) and returned him and Mrs. *Ranger* thanks for their kindness to him. After which he made a short prayer, and seemed to die a true penitent, without scarce a struggle.]

## Source Notes

Levi Ames was the most widely publicized criminal in early America. In addition to the many notices carried in Boston's newspapers concerning his crime, arrest, trial, and execution, thirteen separate publications appeared during a four-month period (from September to December 1773). Nine of these publications were broadside ballads, five of which were published before Ames reached the gallows on October 21, 1773: *A Prospective View of Death: Being, A solemn Warning to inconsiderate Youth, occasioned by the Trial and Condemnation of Levi Ames*; *A few Lines wrote upon the intended Execution of Levi Ames*; *A Solemn Farewell to Levi Ames, Being A Poem written a few Days before his Execution*; *Theft and Murder: A Poem on the Execution of Levi Ames*; *The dying Penitent; or, the affecting Speech of Levi Ames*. The ballads published after the execution were *The Dying Groans of Levi Ames*; *An Exhortation to young and old to be cautious of small Crimes*; *The Speech of Death to Levi Ames*; *An Address to the Inhabitants of Boston, (Particularly the thoughtless Youth:)*. Also, a broadside, the tenth Ames publication appeared as the burglar's first person account: *The last Words and Dying Speech of Levi;* first published in Boston, Ames's *last Words* was published a second time in Salem.

The remaining three publications were execution sermons: Samuel Stillman's *Two Sermons*; Andrew Eliot's *Christ's Promise to the penitent Thief*; and Samuel Mather's *Christ sent to heal the Broken Hearted*. In addition to the sermons, the Stillman text advertised on its title page *An Account of the Exercise of his Mind, from the Time of his Condemnation, till he left the World; together with the Conversation the Author had with him as he walked with him from the Prison to the Gallows*. A popular commodity, the Stillman text was published four times by two different printers and two different booksellers. Two of the editions were printed by John Kneeland and sold by Philip Freeman, while the remaining two were printed by Ezekiel Russell and sold by A. Ellison. Apparently the Kneeland/Freeman edition was the original (totalling sixty-seven pages), while the Russell/Ellison edition was an edited version of thirty-two pages. Both the Eliot and the Mather texts included Ames's first person account as supplements (retitled as *The Life, last Words, and Dying Speech of Levi Ames*. The Eliot text received two editions; the first was printed by John Boyles and the second by William M'Alphine.

In all, nineteen different texts and editions were published concerning Ames during the last few months of 1773. The copy text used in the anthology is taken from the original edition of *The last Words and Dying Speech of Levi Ames*.

Notices of Ames's crime, arrest, trial, and execution appeared in all of Boston's newspapers: the *Boston Gazette*, the *Massachusetts Gazette*, the *Boston Post-Boy*, and the *Boston Evening Post*. The first notice was published in the *Boston Gazette*, August 30, 1773:

> On Thursday Night last, the House of Mr. Martin Bicker was broke open, and Robb'd of about £ 60 L. M. On the Saturday following one Levi Ames, was taken up on Suspicion, who confess'd he was one of the Party, had about 30 l. of the Cash with him. One other of the gang he says is named Joseph Atwood, who is absconded; and for the apprehend-

> ing of whom Mr. Bicker has offered a Reward of TEN DOLLARS.— These are the Villains who broke open the Rev. Mr. Clark's House of Lexington, last Spring, some of whose Plate were found upon them.

A few days later the *Massachusetts Gazette* (September 2, 1773) printed the same notice but added further information concerning Atwood:

> the said Atwood had hid some Plate in the [Boston] Common near the Powder-House, upon which Searching was found, and it proved to be the Tankard, Spoons, &c. stolen from the Rev'd Mr. Jonas Clark of Lexington, the 22d of May last, as advertised at that Time. Mr. Bicker went to Portsmouth in Pursuit of the said Atwood: He was taken at the House of one Davis, and brought to Town last Evening; after an Examination before a Magistrate, he was committed to Goal on Suspicion of being concerned with Levi Ames in entering and robbing the House of Mr. Bicker: There was found upon him five Johannes, seven Dollars and some small Silver Changes hid in a Pocket provided for that Purpose under the Crotch of his Breeches.

The trials of Ames and Atwood took place shortly after their arrests. According to the *Boston Post-Boy* (September 13, 1773):

> At the Superior Court of Judicature, Court of Assize and General Goal Delivery held at the Court-House in this Town, on Monday last one Joseph Attwood was tried for Burglary, by breaking into the House of Mr. Martin Bicker, as mentioned in our last, when the Jury brought in their Verdict, *Guilty in Part*;—Guilty of Theft, but not of Burglary.— The next Day Levi Ames was also tried for the same Crime, when the Jury brought in their Verdict,—*Guilty*. And on Friday afternoon, after a very pathetic Speech from the Chief Justice, he received Sentence of Death, agreeable to a Law of this Province, for the Crime of Burglary. Thursday, the 14th of October next, is the Day appointed for his Execution.
>
> It evidently appeared that Ames entered the House and stole the Money, while Attwood watched in the Street.—Attwood was admitted as an Evidence against him.
>
> Attwood was sentenced to receive 20 Stripes at the Public Whipping Post, to pay Costs and treble Damages; but signifying to the Court that he had nothing to discharge that Sum, he was ordered to be at Mr. Bicker's Disposal for ten Years.

After a week's reprieve, Ames was executed on October 21, and in their next issues the newspapers reported the event. The *Boston Evening-Post* stated:

> Last Thursday Afternoon Levi Ames, aged 21 Years, was executed here for Burglary, pursuant to his Sentence.—He was born at Groton, of a credible Family; his Father's Name was Jacob Ames, who died when he was about two Years old; He said he was the first of the Family that was ever disgraced, and died very penitent.

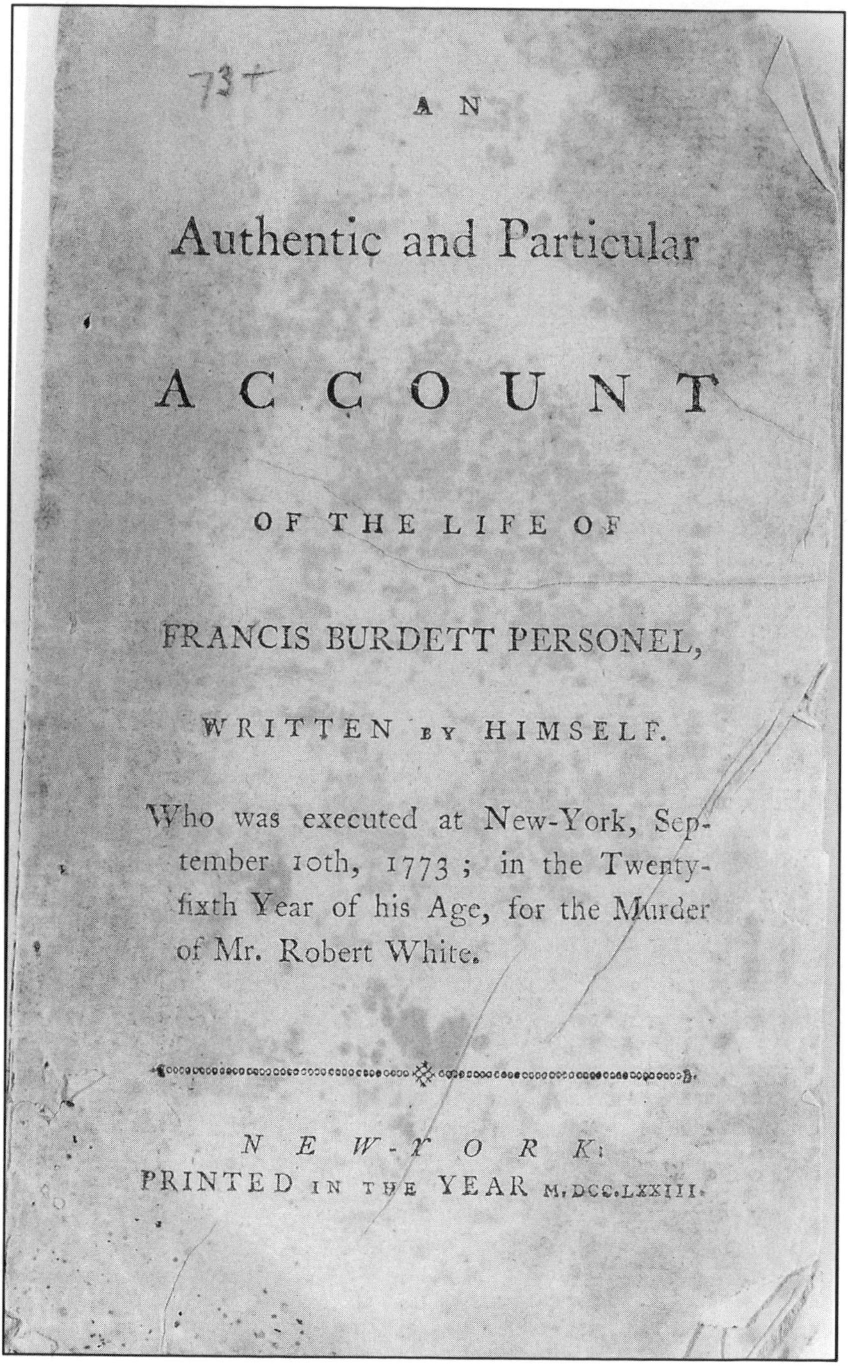

AN

Authentic and Particular

ACCOUNT

OF THE LIFE OF

FRANCIS BURDETT PERSONEL,

WRITTEN BY HIMSELF.

Who was executed at New-York, September 10th, 1773; in the Twenty-fixth Year of his Age, for the Murder of Mr. Robert White.

*NEW-YORK:*
PRINTED IN THE YEAR M,DCC,LXXIII.

# *An Authentic and Particular Account of the Life of Francis Burdett Personel, &c.*

[ 1773 ]

I FRANCIS BURDETT PERSONEL, was born in Ireland, tenderly raised by careful and industrious parents, who took all care imaginable of me in my education. Tho' eight years schooling were laid out upon me, I did not improve it, so as to answer the design of my parents, they finding that I had not so much learning as they expected I might have had in that time, bound me an apprentice, according to my own desire, to a good trade: When master of my trade I went to England; but on my voyage thither, put into Wales, went from thence to Bristol, in England, tarried there some time, and went from thence to Shepton-Mallet, in Somersetshire, where I also abode a considerable while, and was regarded by all who knew me for my sober deportment. My mother hearing where I was, continually importuned me, by letters, to come home; which I accordingly did. My father being now dead, I began to be very careful about worldly affairs, and was remarkably sober; yet, my mother being a passionate woman, could never be content with me; do what I could, I might have done it better. She often said to others, that being an only child, she loved me beyond measure; yet it grieved me that she was of such a temper. I now became acquainted with a young man, who knew her temper, and desired me to go with him to a frolic; which I accordingly did: He espied a young woman walking along, whom he knew; he spake to her, and desired her to go with us to take a glass of liquor, which she did, and was in company with us, till it was so late, that I dreaded to go home. She was the first lewd woman I was ever in company with: But sin and Satan strove so much with me, that I left my mother's house to be at liberty. While from under her eye, I was guilty of pleasing the sinful appetites of the flesh many times; she hearing of me, never rested, till she got me home again. I then lived with her six or eight months; but soon growing weary of her continual admonitions, was resolved to get out of her reach: Accordingly, came to America, where I staid eighteen months; I then returned to Ireland, was very much distressed when I got home, and was resolved never to leave home again. I came to my mother in a poor and miserable condition; but she received me tenderly, and kept me concealed, lest the neighbours should see me before she had provided cloathing for me. I then lived with her one year very comfortably; but, she fearing that I would leave her again, advised me to marry: I was glad of this proposal, and said, if she was willing, I would seek me a wife as soon as possible; she answered, she had one already provided, of an honest family, who had seven sisters already married to creditable men, and that none of the family ever had the least blemish in their characters; she said, that the one she had provided for me, was the youngest, and I might get a handsome dowry with her: I asked her name; when I heard who she was, I said I must have some time to think of it, (not that ever I designed to have her) but was unwilling to put my mother in a passion: She said, I might have time to make love to her, but have her I must, or never be a penny the better at her death. Thinking the young woman not handsome enough, nor fancying her in the least, knowing myself to be but young, I resolved not to have her, let what would happen. My mother was at me day after day to have her, but to no purpose. Being rid of this importunity by the young woman's being married to another; through disobedience I came off to America a second time, and have never since returned. I lived in Baltimore county, in Maryland, for eighteen months, as a servant, and served but so much of four years due for my passage. Being now in want of clothes, as those I brought from home were wore out, and those I had of my master but indifferent, though far better than what other servants got for common. At length, I took a thought to run away, and accordingly did in a foolish manner; one morning, after breakfast, my master came home, and shewed me what was to be done; I worked a little after his departure, then took my ax with me, went about a mile through the woods, and seated myself on the top of a hill till night, it being then the spring of the year, though the trees were not yet green. I travelled that night but slowly, my shoes being bad and the roads very deep, as it had rained. I got within a mile of Baltimore by day-light, and then, for fear of being discovered, went and laid me down in the woods; but, having only a shirt, jacket, and a pair of trowsers upon me, and it raining very much, I could not sleep, being cold, wet and hungry. I now repented of my running away, and would have returned home, had I not recollected that I had heard my master say, he would treat a runaway that returned, worse than one that used his endeavour to get off; therefore, I would not go home, nor tell that I was a runaway, but wished to be taken up; and, with an expectation of being taken, came on the high road at midday, and went into Baltimore Town. As nobody questioned me, I enquired for a certain tavern, where I had heard my master say he used to put up at; coming there, I mentioned my master's name, and said, that he desired me to get a dinner there; the landlord asked me if my master had given me a note. I said, no: Then said he, I cannot let you have dinner. I wished to be taken up, yet would not inform him I was a runaway.

I then walked through the town, and came to a road that leads to Annapolis, I reached the river by sun-set, where I waited till two Gentlemen came who wanted to get over; they asked me to whom I belong? I said to Squire Carroll of Annapolis, which was false; but he living in Annapolis, and I wanting to get there if possible: They examined me no farther, knowing that whom I called my master had several farms, and his servants continually going from one to another: I travelled with this lie in my mouth till I came to Annapolis; it was evening when I came to town, and I had neither money, friends, nor clothes, I walked about hoping somebody would take me up, but nobody noticed me. Going to a Gentleman's house, I laid me down under the stoop, hoping that some one from within would examine me, but there came none. The next morning I walked out of town very feeble and hungry not having eat for a long time. I then wandered I know not where, steering partly by the sun, travelled by day on the high road, caring not much whether I was then taken up or no, but was resolved to keep going whilst I was able. I met several people, and saluted them, and so passed on: At length, I saw a Gentleman on horseback coming towards me, which daunted me, fearing he was in pursuit of me, I saluted him, passed on, and sometime after met his brother, who questioned me; I told him I was just free, and my master was such a villain, that he would not give me my freedom dues, and that I came to Annapolis, in search of a friend, to acquaint him how my master served me. But unhappily, I told him, my friend had left town before I came, and having no money I left town, with an intent to get work in the country; he replied his brother wanted a workman but could get none this while past, therefore, desired me to call at his brother's house, told me his name, and gave proper directions, and desired me to tarry there till his brother came home, where I went, and spoke to the Gentlewoman, who ordered me a dinner, which was very welcome to me just then: When the Gentleman came home, I engaged with him for four months under the name of James Alkins, having been with him a week or two, pleasing him, being handy at any sort of plantation work, he let me have necessary apparel; with him I lived till after harvest, but he not letting me have my earnings, lest I should leave him before my time was expired, and I fearing my master would hear of me, borrowed a coat, hat, and other necessaries suitable, under a pretence of visiting a friend, and went off, being provided with a pass I had written myself, and signed a Magistrate's name to it, changing my name to Patt Percy; having now some money, I delayed not till I got into Virginia; and, being well dressed, could write a passible hand, and understood some figures, I set up for a Schoolmaster, accordingly I got a school, where I taught for some time, was very well regarded by my neighbours, some gave me credit for one thing and some for another. I lived very happy, as I thought, just then, and could go out on a evening after school and serve the devil with delight. I continued this practice for some time, till I went to hear the Baptists called by some New Lights. I went more out of curiosity then anything else, having heard much of them: The first sermon I heard pricked my heart. I went to hear them often, wrestled against sin in a measure, and would not commit such as appeared base in the world, and as few others as possible.

I had a desire to leave off all sin; but depended on the broken staff of my own strength, therefore could not do it: I obtained the name of being a religious young man by some, who knew not what it was; and I myself was deceived, thinking I was converted when only convicted, and wanted to join the church, but was not accepted, upon which the young men derided me: yet I continued to hear preaching, and, to appearance, had I staid there, should have been brought to the knowledge of God through Christ: But two men, who suspected me to be a run-away, saying they would take me up, occasioned my leaving this place, being unwilling to return to Maryland to my master. I went to a widow, whom I was bound in oath to be married unto, borrowed a mare, bridle and saddle of her, under a pretence to go to town for some things; from whence I went, calling myself Francis Personel, *alias* Burdett Personel, and never returned. About an hundred miles therefrom I sold the mare, bridle and saddle, and travelled to Pittsburg, nigh which I tarried sometime.

Thus you may see I have been a hypocrite, and what sin have I not committed, except the sin against the Holy Ghost? And, I may thank God for restraining me by his grace from that, for my heart was bad enough.

*After I came to New-York, I took a wife; and notwithstanding I knew she had followed a loose way of life, I loved her. In short the next morning after I had been married and beded to her, I consented to her going to her old habitation, till she could pay some debts which she said she owed, and for which otherwise I would be sued, but she could pay them very soon: She was not long there before I took her away, as I could not bear to think of her following that course any longer. I did not let her want whilst I was

*It has been said, that he was tried at Lancaster, after he left Virginia, for horse-stealing, in company with another, which he did not mention in the account of his life; but, as the true state of the affair cannot be justly ascertained, at present, it must be omitted.

able to work, and could get it to do; but, unfortunately, I had not been long married before I was taken so ill, as to be unable to work; and, as we saw no other way, rather than be beholden to the people we lived with, we concluded unanimously, that we must either perish, or she take to her old course; accordingly, she prostituted her body as usual. The first night she went on this occasion, she returned somewhat cheerful, and said she had met with a young woman that lent her some money, and declared she had no conversation with any man that night. I answered, it was no matter if she had, I would never tell her of it. Next night she went and brought home some cash, which she said was lent her in like manner. Sometime after I was ill, she went out every night she could, to which I still encouraged her, even so much as to go with her some nights part of the way, and would pass the evening at some neighbour's house till nine or ten o'clock, then meet her at the place appointed, and come home, as though we had been together all the time we were out. This abominable practice we followed until the 16th of May, when I went to her father's, not expecting to return that night, neither did she expect me, according to her own confession, otherwise she would not have staid out so late. Upon my coming home that night, I sat down contentedly, knowing what she was after. I waited for her till after nine o'clock, and she not returning, I proposed to go to bed; and my landlady said she would lock the doors. As I was unwilling she should be shut out all night, I said to my landlady, if she would sit up fifteen minutes, I would go and see if I could find her; but if I did not return in that space she might shut the doors and go to bed. I went in quest of her, and came to the house where she was, and notwithstanding that she was there, as I learnt by hearing her laugh, she was denied to be there; and, as I was going out of the house, through the entry, I heard her speak in a room, the door being shut; going to the room window, I heard two Gentlemen speak, but knew not who they were at that time: Mr. Gl—r came out of the room and returned in about fifteen minutes, after which they shortly came out, as I was standing near the room window. I expected that the Gentlemen would depart from her, and then intended to go home with her; but the Gentlemen took her one by the one arm, and the other by the other arm, and so went away. It is not easy for me to relate how I felt. As I had given her liberty before that time to act in such a manner, according to the proverb, *What the eye don't see the heart don't grieve at;* yet, I confess, I had no right to meddle with the Gentlemen; but the devil whom I faithfully served at that time, drew near and tempted me to get a weapon, making me believe if I could strike one or both of them and take away my wife it would appear in the eyes of some of my neighbours that I was an honest man, and innocent of her doings; with this resolution I went into the house where they had been, and seeing no other weapon, unfortunately took the wooden bar of the door, and having pursued and overtaken them, made a blow which struck Mr. Robert W—te on his head, and by it he fell to the ground. My wife ran off: Upon recovering the weapon to defend myself, Mr. Gl—r enclosed me, letting the bar fall to the ground, I fought with my hands. After a short combat; Mr. Gl—r begged his life; I said it was granted: Whereupon he asked me, why I had struck Mr. Wh—te? For being in company with my wife, in a bad house at an unseasonable hour, said I: Upon my honour said he, I had no connection with her, nor have I reason to believe that Mr. Wh—te had? I replied, if they were innocent I was sorry that I struck them. In the fray I lost my hat, and so did Mr. Gl—r his. While seeking for them, I considered, as Mr. Wh—te did not stir, that he might be dangerously wounded; therefore, finding Mr. Gl—r's hat and my own, and seeing some people approach, I made immediately off with them both. I was at home some time before my wife came, and told my landlady what happened, in order to make her believe that I was innocent of what my wife followed. I went to bed that night, and after rising in the morning, took Mr. Gl—r's hat, and gave it to a neighbour to keep, where I suppose it remains.*

Herein God is glorified for putting a stop to the sinful course that my wife and I followed, (as it was altogether abominable in his sight, who is of purer eyes than to behold iniquity) by detecting, apprehending and executing of me; for though I did not intend to kill Mr. White, when I struck him; yet, as it proved the cause of his death, I confess I am guilty of the murder of him, inasmuch as I had given my wife the liberty before-mentioned. Some people have said, that it was a made up thing between my wife and me; but it is false, neither do I blame her in the least, as I am the sinful wretch, and really guilty, and none else: Why then should I strive to conceal that from the world, which is well known unto God?

Thus you may read how great a sinner I have been. I have provoked God times without number, procured his wrath daily, served the Devil faithfully, deserved nothing, had I my deserts, but everlasting damnation; several other heinous, soul damning sins have I committed, which are not here mentioned; and yet, after serving the Devil so long, having been guilty of so many crimes of the deepest dye, yet God was pleased to draw me from the mouth of the pit, to pluck me out of everlasting burnings, and to receive me even at the eleventh hour, and to give me the knowledge of himself in and through Jesus Christ. Oh! the riches of the free grace of God to such a sinful wretch as I am, as I shall endeavour to make appear as well as I am

*After committing the crime of killing Mr. White, he went off, (having informed his landlady, as before mentioned, of that action) and, as he said, when coming back to get his effects, which were in New-York, was apprehended.

able, being assisted by the grace of God. The last day of July I received sentence of death; I knowing that I was then out of Christ, prayed for a long day for repentance, and six weeks were granted me. Certainly, if I had been put to death at that time, I should have been a lost soul, for my conscience was a hell to me, and witnessed against me: I then saw hell open, as it were, to receive me, and could then see no way of escape, for I was almost in despair, and was in dread that the holy Spirit of God was withdrawn from me, never more to return. The condition I was then in I am unable to express. I came to prison, was put in the condemned room, where I sat very melancholy, and expected some of the Clergy to come and see me. I sent for a Divine of the Church of England, but he did not come just then. I then sent for Mr. Pilmore, a Methodist Minister, but he did not come that day, which made me almost think that I was forsaken of God and his Ministers too. I was advised to send for Mr. L—le—d, a Methodist; I accordingly did: He came, with two others, and advised me much; I declared that I was a great sinner, and that I had transgressed God's holy laws, despised his counsels, and grieved his holy Spirit, and was not worthy to take his holy name into my polluted lips: He counselled me not to despair, and made mention of several great sinners whom the Lord had made monuments of his mercy, which are recorded in the holy Scriptures. He came three or four times, advised me much, prayed and sung whenever he came, and I must say, the Lord was pleased to make him an instrument in his hands, of some good to me. Perhaps, the reader will be glad to know how I was delivered from the fear of hell: It was done in so short a time, that I can scarce tell; this I know, I prayed earnestly to God, after I was awakened and alarmed, that he would be pleased to pluck me as a brand from the burning: The Lord shewed me the danger I was in, the follies and madness of my past life, in living so many years without God in the world, he was pleased to shew me that I was under the curse of a broken law, and that if I departed this life, without an interest in Jesus Christ, that I must be eternally lost; therefore, seeing Christ the Saviour, and none else, I prayed him to be merciful to me for his own Name's sake, plead his own most gracious promises, which he hath left on record, desired him to save me, else I perish, importuning him constantly until he was pleased to hear me and grant my request. The first mark or instance I had of it, was this, my troubled conscience was at ease, my slavish fears were taken away; I now no more dreaded hell; Christ Jesus was altogether lovely to me: I could see that my sins crucifyed him, which grieved me: My imprisonment, my death, and the punishment due to me did not move me; now nothing troubled me, but the thought of having offended so good a God so often as I had done. The Lord was pleased to give me so much of his divine presence, that I was so lifted up, that I thought it was all well, imagining that I was quite out of danger, I almost forgot how nigh I was to everlasting damnation; but the Lord being willing to let me see and know that of myself I was nothing, permitted Satan to tempt me, I being a poor weak creature when left to myself, and not calling on the Lord to assist me, was soon overcome; after Satan got that advantage of me, I was cast down so low that he made me believe all my former peace was a delusion; I was between hope and despair, was in dread to pray, lest it should be an abomination to the Lord; at this time Mr. L—le—d came into the room, and was instrumental in leading me to prayer.

I was visited at different times by the Rev. Dr. Oglesby, the Rev. Mr. Page, the Rev. Dr. Rogers, the Rev. Mr. Levingston, the Rev. Mr. Fering, the Rev. Mr. Mason, the Rev. Mr. Gano, Mr. Pilmore and Mr. Rankin; who, though of different denominations, are, in my opinion, each of them experienced Ministers of the Gospel, some more, some less, according to the measure of the gift of Christ; and I acknowledge their kindness in frequently attending me, whilst under condemnation, in the prison; I hope the Lord blessed, a word, from each of them to me; therefore to his name be the glory ascribed.

I am just going to depart to an eternity, and would have all sinners to take warning, by my shameful ignominious, tho' most happy end: It is no matter of joy to me when I think that it is my sins brought me to it; yet it yields me comfort and consolation to die; when I think what God had done for me, even in my last hours. Oh! how happy should I have been, if I had known so much of God in time past, as I do now: but blessed be God, that he was pleased to reveal his Son Jesus Christ to me, even in prison. O Lord God was not I the chief of sinners, the most vile wretch on earth; and as thou, O God, has been pleased to forgive me for thy Son's sake, so for his sake, and for the honour and glory of thy holy name, do thou enable me to set forth a few lines, as a caution to sinners, and, O God, do thou be pleased to bless them, though weak, that thy holy name may be glorified by my death, and that it may redound to the honour of the ever-blessed Trinity, Father, Son, and Holy Ghost.

## To The Public.

GOOD people and bad: But, Why did I say good? There is none good, no not one. Whatever you are, whither rich or poor, learned or not, that read this, be assured that you must taste death as well as I, and in a short space of time. Your delicate bodies must be meat for worms, must lay rotting in corruption as well as mine. You are all certain of death, but uncertain when you must die; and there is nothing more sure, than that you must appear before the judgment-seat of the Lord Jesus Christ, to give an account of the deeds done in the body. Knowing, therefore, that all this is true, there are three things which should make a sinner, out of Christ tremble: The first is, When the soul is to depart from his body. The second, When it is to appear before God to receive judgment: And the third, When sentence is pronounced. Oh! how terrible then will death be to a sinner. O dreadful moment, which cuts the thread of time, and begins the web of eternity. It is not the most terrible consequence of death, to leave this world; but it is, to give an account of our actions unto the Creator of the world, especially in such a time, when you cannot look for mercy. The thoughts of appearing before a holy God, made even Job tremble, who was so just, that the Almighty himself rejoiced in having such a servant. If Job trembled, then, methinks, sinners out of Christ, have greater cause to tremble; for, if they depart out of this life in an unconverted state, how will it amaze them, to behold the Lord Jesus Christ himself alive; not a dead image, nor in that state of humiliation when he suffered on the cross; but upon a throne of majesty, and seat of justice: Not in a time of mercy, but in the hour of vengeance: Not naked, tho' with pierced hands, but armed against sinners with the sword of justice, when he will come to judge and revenge the injuries which they have done him: God is as righteous in his justice, as in his mercy; and, as he hath allotted a time for mercy, so he will for justice. O sinners, think of these great truths, and consider the things that belong to your everlasting peace, before it is too late. Remember, O sinners, that you were born into this world under the wrath of God, by reason of the original transgression committed by your forefather Adam, and see that every sin which thou committest, deserves nothing but God's wrath and everlasting damnation. Perhaps, some think that they are already Christians, and converted to God, because they have been baptized in their infancy, and brought up in such a church: But, my friend, whoever thou art, that harbours this opinion, without being born anew of the Spirit of God, you are as yet mistaken; for that was the very thought that I built my profession upon for many years, to my grief, and if I had departed this life in that state, I should have been infallibly lost: therefore, as I am a dying man, I tell you with love to your souls, as Jesus Christ himself said and confirmed it with an oath, saying, "Verily, verily, Except a man be born again, he cannot see the kingdom of God." Thou drunkard, thou bold blasphemer, thou thief, thou whoremaster, thou Sabbath breaker, thou adulterer, thou fornicator, thou extortioner, thou unjust dealer, thou liar, and thou daughters of hell, that are bond slaves, both you and your guests, to the Devil; you, I say, that take delight in prostituting your bodies as common whores, rather than work for an honest living; do any, or either of you, here mentioned, think that you are Christians, or that if death was to cut you off this day, that you would be received into the heavenly Jerusalem, where no unclean thing can enter. O! says the foolish sinner, death is not so near me, I am yet young and hearty, but when I arrive at such an age, then will I repent: If I were to become serious in my young days, I should lose all the pleasures of this life. O! be it known to you, that if this is the language of your heart, you are deluded by your master, the Devil, whose you are, and whom you serve, whilst carnally minded. Long was I deluded by him in the same manner, until he made me commit the crime for which I justly die; and, if the Lord was not pleased to make me a monument of his mercy and free grace, I should suffer in hell to all eternity. O sinners! consider how my sins brought me to this end; and remember my words, your sins, if not repented of, will bring you to eternal torments. Consider, you are ever dying while in the body, still drawing nigher the grave; therefore, you should always be ready. O young people! do ye seek the Lord while he may be found, call upon him while he is near, for the Lord has made a gracious promise unto you; he has said in his word, that they that seek him early, shall find him: let old hardened sinners go on to serve the Devil, if they are so minded; but, you young sinners, seek ye the Lord in your youthful days, and you shall find him, and you old hardened sinners, whose heads are gray, whose locks of hair may be called the blossoms of the grave; methinks you have been slaves to the Devil long enough, if you could but know it; beg of the Lord, therefore, to shew you what you are by nature and by practice. Here is encouragement for all sinners, old and young, be their sins ever so numerous, ever so heinous, or of ever so deep a dye, yet the blood of Christ Jesus is able and all-sufficient to cleanse from all sin and iniquity; and seeing that the Lord is gracious unto me at the eleventh hour, in a prison room, to me that has been the vilest of wretches; methinks, every sinner ought to come and try the Lord. Oh! the goodness of God, the riches of free grace in and through Jesus Christ. Now, if you seek the Lord, you'll certainly find him; his promises are such, that the heavens and the earth shall pass away, but one jot or title of his word shall not fail. If you neglect it, and obey not the sound of the Gospel, now in your day, be it known unto you, that you must obey the sound of the trump of God at the last day, when the angel of the Lord shall sound it, and cry aloud, Arise ye dead and come to judgment; then, O Sinners, ye must come whether you will or no; as you die judgment will find you; as the tree falleth, so it doth lie: If death sweep you off this day, in your sins, where do you think you will find yourself; certainly in torments, never to cease. O then, flee from the wrath to come unto the city of refuge, unto a crucified Jesus, unto the Lamb of God, who taketh away the sins of the world of believers; confess your sins unto him, for he alone is able to cleanse you from them by his atoning blood, and is ever ready and willing to do it, if you should think yourselves unworthy by reason of your many offences; remember me, the chief of sinners, that as the Lord was gracious to me, so will he be to you, if you diligently seek him. Is not the blood of Christ sufficient to cleanse from all sins? and, is not God able and willing to save all that come unto him in and through Jesus Christ? But, if you that are filthy remain filthy still, till death comes unawares, and cuts you off. Alas! for your poor souls, it were better for you never to have been born. The day of judgment will be an awful, shocking, dreadful day to you; when the Lord Jesus Christ will come in the clouds of heaven, in power and great glory, with his holy angels, in flaming fire, to take vengeance on them who know not God, and have not obeyed the Gospel. Who will be able to bear everlasting burnings? How will it grieve you, when you see them that were greater sinners than you, placed at the right hand of the Judge, waiting for a crown of immortal glory, and you yourselves at the left hand, waiting for the word, Depart! ye cursed! into everlasting fire, prepared for the Devil and his angels! O terrible sentence! depart! alas dread Sovereign, whereto? Into hell! into everlasting torments! where the God of heaven will pour forth his wrath on the damned souls to all eternity! Oh sinners! of all ranks and conditions tremble! And ye harlots of the city of New-York, and you inn-keepers, that entertain such in your houses; and you married or young men that are so led by the Devil, tremble, for you are all in danger of dropping into hell every moment, and certainly will if death overtakes you before you have got an interest in the Lord Jesus Christ, then if you intend to escape the wrath to come; if you seek or desire the salvation of your own souls, fly from sin, shun every appearance of evil; shun gaming, drinking, lying; shun bad company of all sorts; keep holy the Sabbath of the Lord, attend to hear the word of God preached with an earnest desire to benefit thereby, forsaking all your former sins and iniquities, and praying to the Lord constantly, and then no doubt the Lord will bless a word from one or another of his ministering servants to your hard hearts, to the breaking of them in pieces. The word of God is like unto a hammer, sharper then a two-edged sword when it comes with power, and if the Lord is pleased to bless a word unto you, then will you see the danger you are in; and if God so begins that work, the Lord Jesus will certainly give you repentance, and will take away the heart of stone, and give you a heart of flesh. Then thus much being done by the grace of God, your mind, your will, and the powers of your soul will be changed by the Spirit of God from darkness unto light, and from the power of Satan unto the everliving and true God; your feet, formerly so nimble to run into destruction, will now be employed in going to the house of God, and attending on his ordinances; your eyes that lusted after all manner of vanities, will be now fixed on the words of salvation, the testimony of his will, the sacred Scriptures. Christ Jesus whom you so long rebelled against, will be now more precious to you then ten thousand worlds. This is something of regeneration or of the new birth, which Christ spake of, and is what I wish you may attain to for Christ's sake, that your precious, everlasting and never dying souls may be found worthy of the promises of Christ, and of the glory, and those joys which no tongue can express, and which are laid up for all who truely love and serve the Lord; and the glory thereof shall be to God the Father, God the Son, and God the Holy Ghost, for ever and ever. Amen.

## Of My Experience.

When I was condemned, I saw myself out of Christ. I saw that I was under the curse of a broken law, that I was a child of hell, a bond slave to the Devil for many years, which threw me almost into despair. Knowing that God was just, and that my sins had overtaken me. My neglecting the calls of mercy so often in my past life, made me think that the Lord would not hear me now. The day after I was condemned, I had but little hopes; my past life being in my view, was a great shock to me. The 2d day of August, my burden was great, and my troubled conscience was a hell to me. But, happily, before a week was expired, the fear of hell was taken away from me, and my troubled conscience was at rest. I saw that the blood of Christ was fully sufficient to cleanse from all sin and iniquity. When the Ministers of Christ came to see me, I did not let them know that I enjoyed this peace, for, I was in dread least I should be deceived. After I enjoyed this peace two or three days, then I made it known, and was so lifted up with inward frames and feelings, that I almost forgot what God had done for me, in plucking me like unto a brand out of the burning: Then I thought that I was past all danger; but God was pleased to let me see that I was nothing of myself, in the following manner: Satan tempted me to sin, and I not being on my guard, was overcome: Satan remained near me a long while, and overcame me a second time, then he wanted to make me despair: He conquered me so far, that he made me believe, all my former peace was a delusion; then I was in dread to go to prayer, lest it should be an abomination to the Lord. I was in great distress for some time, until I was told of the goodness of God in different manners, which, when I had heard, I burst into tears; then was I slain. After that, I could draw nigh to God in Prayer, in an humble manner, but had many wrestlings with Satan, yet the Lord helped me to resist. I then again enjoyed inward peace, but it was a considerable time before I could see Christ suffered for me. This I knew, that I could not be saved without a Saviour. I knew and believed that Christ Jesus was the promised Messiah, the Anointed of God, and I trusted on him, his blood and righteousness, and on none else. The Lord shewed me, that I had nothing in me that could commend me to God, therefore I continually pleaded the promises of Christ, until he was pleased to give me faith, that I could say he suffered for me. I always gained ground by the instructions of the Ministers; yet was tempted by Satan, after all this, to unbelief; but the Lord gave me to know it was a temptation, and helped me to overcome. I saw that I was given much to spiritual pride at times, which made me pray God to humble me. The week before my death, I was so lifted up at times, and to that degree, that the approaching death seemed a comfort to me; yet, at one time I could find my faith stronger than at another. I could say, that Christ Jesus raised me from death to life. Nay, I was twice dead; dead in sin, and dead by the laws of man, agreeable to the justice of God. Before I was brought to life savingly by God, in and through Jesus Christ; and as I am shortly to die a shameful death, which I brought upon myself, by reason of living so long without God in the world; yet I would die this death, in the condition I am now in, rather than live in this world, to be carnally minded, as usual. I die now to live eternally. Glory be to God for his free gift, bestowed on me a vile sinner. I die, though most unworthy of the title, one of the Israel of God, and an heir of glory.

## *Vide* WATTS'S HYMNS, *B.* II. *H.* LXXXII. &c.

1 Arise, my soul, my joyful pow'rs,
And triumph in my God;
Awake, my voice, and loud proclaim
His glorious grace abroad.

2 He rais'd me from the deeps of sin,
The gates of gaping hell,
And fix'd my standing more secure
Than 'twas before I fell.

3 The arms of everlasting love
Beneath my soul he plac'd,
And on the Rock of ages set
My slipp'ry footsteps fast.

4 Now shall my body faint and die,
And thou my soul remove:
Oh! for some guardian angel nigh,
To bear it safe above.

5 He is a God of sov'reign love,
That promis'd heav'n to me,
And taught my thoughts to soar above,
Where happy spirits be.

6 Jesus, to thy dear faithful hand,
My naked soul I trust;
Now, my flesh waits for thy command,
To drop into my dust.

7 Prepare me, Lord, for thy right hand,
Now is the joyful day;
Come death, and some celestial band,
To bear my soul away.

8 Thus finish I my parting song,
And now I close my eyes.
Receive me, Lord, into thy arms:
Its thou alone I prize.

The above Francis Burdett Personel, towards the close of his life, appeared very cheerful and resigned to the will of God. When he was told by the officers, that they came to wait upon him, we are informed, he said smiling, That he was ready; and when at the gallows, gave an exhortation with much composure, and resigned himself to the King of Terrors.

## Source Notes

*An Authentic and Particular Account of the Life of Francis Burdett Personel* was first published in New York shortly after Personel was executed on September 10, 1773. A second edition was published in New Haven, and, although no date appeared on the title page, was probably printed in 1773 soon after the original New York text. In his *Supplement to Evans' American Bibliography* (1970), Roger P. Bristol listed a third edition but without a place of publication or a date. The copy text used in the anthology is taken from the original New York edition.

In the narrative, Personel moved directly from the attack that resulted in the death of Robert White to his penitential state just before his execution. Whoever helped to shape Personel's statements for publication was not quite satisfied with the abrupt shift from crime to conversion and added a footnote stating that the fugitive "went off" after the attack; he was later apprehended when he returned to New York "to get his effects" (194). New York readers might have encountered lengthier accounts of Personel's attack, escape, and capture in the newspapers. On June 21, 1773, *The New-York Gazette* published an official proclamation calling for Personel's apprehension:

BY HIS EXCELLENCY
**WILLIAM TRYON, ESQ;**
CAPTAIN GENERAL AND GOVERNOR IN CHIEF,
IN AND OVER THE PROVINCE OF NEW-YORK, AND THE TERRITORIES DEPENDING THEREON IN AMERICA, CHANCELLOR AND VICE-ADMIRAL OF THE SAME.

*A Proclamation.*

WHEREAS Francis Personel, otherwise called Francis Parsells, stands charged by the Coroner's Inquest, with the Murder of Robert White, late of the City of New-York, Gentleman, by a Wound which the said Robert White, on the sixteenth day of May last, received from the said Francis Personel, who hath since fled, and is supposed now to live concealed in this or in one of the neighbouring Colonies: In order therefore to bring the said Criminal to condign Punishment, I have thought fit, with the Advice of his Majesty's Council, to issue this Proclamation; hereby commanding, and strictly enjoining all Magistrates, Justices of the Peace, Sheriffs, Constables, and other Civil Officers of this Province, to make, and cause diligent Search and Inquiry to be made within their respective Districts or Bailiwicks, for the said Francis Personel; and being found, him to apprehend, and cause to be committed to the next public Goal, there to remain until delivered by due Course of Law. And if discovered within any of the neighbouring Governments, hereby requesting such Government to issue Orders for the immediate apprehending and securing the said Francis Personel; and on his Commitment, to give Directions for his Delivery over to the Officers of this Government, the Charges whereof shall be satisfied to the Person authorized to receive the same.

Given under my Hand and Seal at Arms, at Fort-George, in the City of New-York, the ninth Day of June, One Thousand Seven Hundred and Seventy Three, in the thirteenth Year of the Reign of our Sovereign Lord George the Third, by the Grace of God, of Great Britain, France, and Ireland, King, Defender of the Faith, and so forth.

**WM. TRYON.**
By His Excellency's Command,
GOLDSBROW BANYAR, D. Secry.
GOD save the KING.

(The Corporation have agreed to give the Sum of TWENTY FIVE POUNDS, as a Reward for apprehending and bringing to Justice, the Person that murdered Mr. White. The same to be paid on Conviction.)

Exactly one week later (June 28, 1773), *The New-York Gazette* published a report that Personel had been apprehended:

> Francis Personel, alias Parsells, for apprehending whom a Proclamation was inserted in our last, was taken up at New-Haven by Mr. Van Gelder, having been sent by Order of the Mayor and Corporation of this City for that Purpose, was brought to Town Yesterday, and committed to our Goal: He stands charged with the Murder of Robert White, Esq; having knocked him down with a Club in the Street, near St. Paul's church in this Place about 6 Weeks since, of which Blow he never recovered.

A few days later (July 1, 1773) *The New-York Journal* included a lengthier account of Personel's crime, flight, and arrest:

> On Sunday last was brought to Town and committed to our Gaol, Francis Personel, alias Parsells, who stands charged with the Murder of Robert White, Esq; by coming behind him in the Night Time as he was walking the Street, near St. Paul's Church, about 6 Weeks ago, and knocking him down with a Club, said to be the Bar of a Door, by which his Scull was fractured in many Places, and he remained speechless and deprived of his Senses till his Death, which happened some Days after. The Murderer absconded, a Proclamation was issued for apprehending him, and Notice being soon after received, that he was at New Haven, in Connecticut, a Messenger was by the Mayor and Corporation dispatched in Quest of him. Before Mr. Van Gelder, the Messenger, arrived at New Haven, the Criminal, anxious to know what was passing at New-York relating to himself, was come off for this Place, and arrived here about the same Time of Mr. Van Gelder's arrival at New-Haven, Who after a fruitless Search there, was about to set out on his Return, when the Criminal finding himself unsafe in New-York, got on board a Vessel that was just setting out from hence for New-Haven, and had a remarkable short Passage to that Place, where he arrived just in Time to be taken by Van Gelder, who conducted him safely to our Gaol, where he remains for Trial.

Notice of Personel's trial and conviction were printed in *The New-York Journal* on August 5, 1773, and a month later (September 9) the newspaper also mentioned that two sermons were delivered "before the unhappy Prisoner."

Both the *Gazette* (September 13) and the *Journal* (September 16) printed brief notices of Personel's execution; according to the *Journal*: "Friday last, Francis Burdett Personel, was executed here, pursuant to his Sentence, for the Murder of Robert White, Esq; in the Night of Sunday the 16th of May last, on the Green near the Liberty Pole, in this City." Probably few, if any, of the spectators paused to consider the ironic juxtaposition between the gallows and liberty pole, but the two symbols could have been interpreted to represent entirely different social orders, one a repressive mechanism of the elite, the other an icon of those dissatisfied with the political hegemony. As he was presented, the humble and repentant Personel went to his death affirming the order that condemned him. Such a conventional portrayal was necessary, since Personel's attack did convey revolutionary implications. In both the narrative and in the newspaper accounts, the social differences between Personel and his victim were made apparent. White was an "Esquire," a "Gentleman," and in being struck from behind and knocked down in the street by someone socially his inferior, his death represented an attack on the social hierarchy. While overlooking the symbolic implications of his wife's prostitution to "Gentlemen," Personel's narrative denied all possible political interpretations or justifications. Once Personel was branded as a "criminal" by both the newspapers and the narratives, his actions were voided of revolutionary significance.

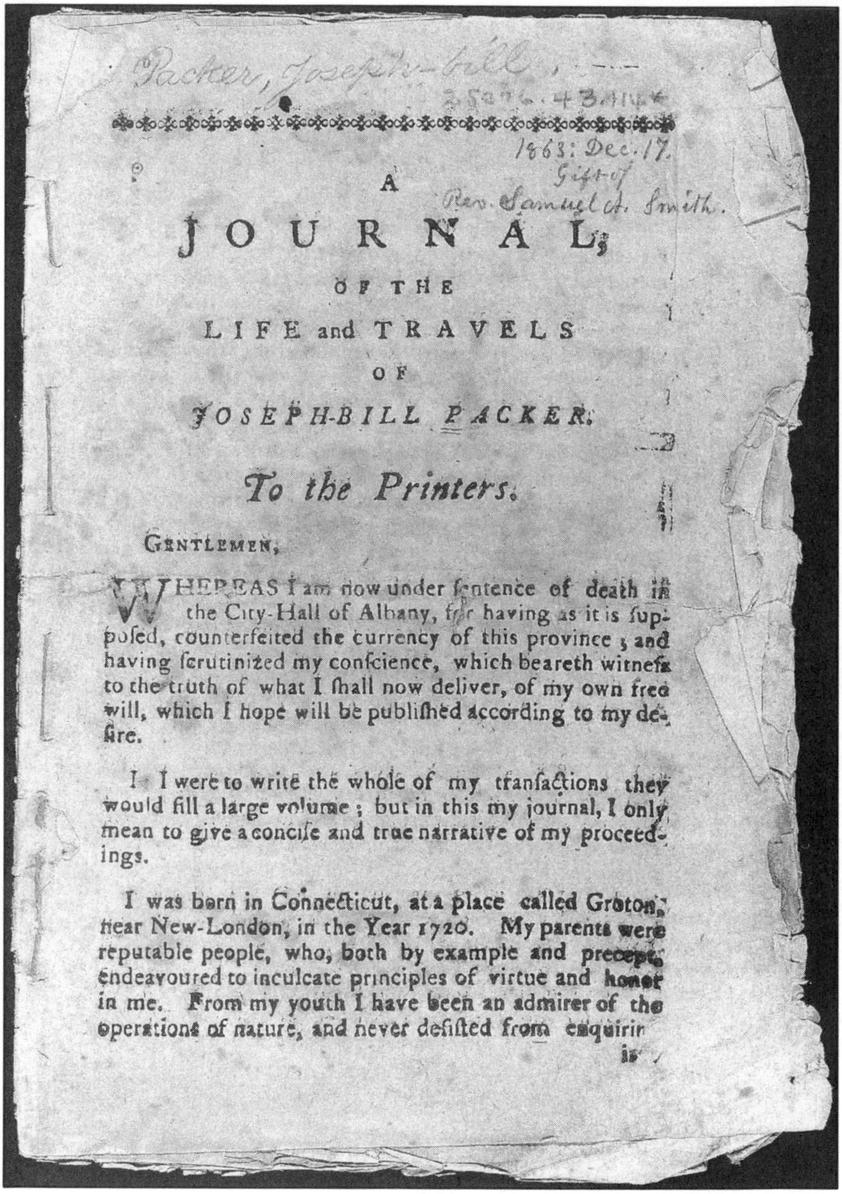



A

# JOURNAL,

OF THE

LIFE and TRAVELS

OF

*JOSEPH-BILL PACKER.*

## *To the Printers.*

GENTLEMEN,

WHEREAS I am now under ſentence of death in the City-Hall of Albany, for having as it is ſuppoſed, counterfeited the currency of this province; and having ſcrutinized my conſcience, which beareth witneſs to the truth of what I ſhall now deliver, of my own free will, which I hope will be publiſhed according to my deſire.

If I were to write the whole of my tranſactions they would fill a large volume; but in this my journal, I only mean to give a conciſe and true narrative of my proceedings.

I was born in Connecticut, at a place called Groton, near New-London, in the Year 1720. My parents were reputable people, who, both by example and precept, endeavoured to inculcate principles of virtue and honor in me. From my youth I have been an admirer of the operations of nature, and never deſiſted from enquirin

is

[ JOSEPH-BILL PACKER ]

# A Journal of the Life and Travels of Joseph-Bill Packer

[ 1773 ]

## To the Printers.

GENTLEMEN,

Whereas I am now under sentence of death in the City-Hall of Albany, for having as it is supposed, counterfeited the currency of this province; and having scrutinized my conscience, which beareth witness to the truth of what I shall now deliver, of my own free will, which I hope will be published according to my desire.

If I were to write the whole of my transactions they would fill a large volume; but in this my journal, I only mean to give a concise and true narrative of my proceedings.

I was born in Connecticut, at a place called Groton, near New-London, in the Year 1720. My parents were reputable people, who, both by example and precept, endeavoured to inculcate principles of virtue and honor in me. From my youth I have been an admirer of the operations of nature, and never desisted from enquiring into any thing that I thought an arcanum until I had obtained some idea of it, my thirst after knowledge being insatiable.

When I arrived at the twenty second year of my age, my inclination prompted me to visit the southern colonies, I traveled into Virginia, where I resided near sixteen years: The principal part of my business was curing cancers; of this art I may justly call myself master, as I have cured every species of them except the sanguine cancer, and even that some times when the blood was not too much infected. I understand the seperation of metals, and was often called upon to examine minerals. In Virginia,

Colonel Cheswell, who had lead mines, employed me to work upon lead and copper ore: He died, and Colonel James Bird, who became sole owner of the mines, declined having them worked. From these works, which are situate at a place called New-River, near the line which divides North Carolina from Virginia, I went to Dan River, which I crossed and came to a place called Salisbury, in Roan county, North-Carolina. After spending a few days there I steered my course to Meclinburgh, which lies upon the Calava River. This seemed to be a good place for my business; and, as the county was young and the court house then building, I resolved to make that the place of my residence.

Having agreed for my board and lodging, and being informed that several persons in the neighbourhood were afflicted with cancers, I published an advertisement, the purport of which was, that I would undertake to cure them, and if I did not succeed, no money should be demanded. This had the desired effect, for in a few days I had several patients.

The first that I cured was Colonel Lewison, of a cancer on his lip, the second, the Widow Canada, who had been grievously afflicted for four years with a cancer near her nose; the next was one James Mac, he had been distressed with a cancer for upwards of twenty two years, and was, indeed, a miserable spectacle to look upon; three months elapsed before I could cure him. I cannot forbear relating an incident that happened to this man while he was my patient: After I caused the cancer to fall out, and the place nearly healed, a cow broke into his corn-field which put him in a violent passion; he loaded a pistol almost full with powder and salt, went into the field to frighten the cow, and snapped the pistol several times, but it missing fire, he held it carelessly in his hand; however, some sparks having remained in the pan, it went off at a time when he did not expect it; the cock flew up, cut his under lip two thirds off, struck through his nose, and broke up the cancer: I was obligated to sew his lip and heal that wound, which required nearly as much time as the cancer had done. This happened in Tryon County, near Broad River, that falls into Santee on the south border of North-Carolina.

In that country I became acquainted with several gentlemen, who desired me to make their houses my home, when I came near them; they declared it should not cost me any money if I would tarry with them all that winter.—I accepted their kind invitation; and, as I understand watch work, I constantly employed myself at that business, unless when called abroad.

In that situation I remained several years, but having a strong desire to visit my brethren in New-England, I made application to my patients, and got in part of the money they owed to me; those who could not pay I did not distress, nor would I accept of any reward from those persons who required my help and were in low circumstances, being always apprehensive that if I accepted a fee it might disenable them to provide necessaries for their children; nor did I turn away poor people who applied to me for help, but constantly exerted my abilities for their relief.

While I remained in North Carolina, at the house of a gentleman who was a Justice of the peace, there came a poor woman driving a cow before her; my landlord enquiring where she was driving the cow, she answered, to the doctor, that it was the last she had, and that her children must now be deprived of milk. I asked what was her disorder; she replied a cancer in her nose; I desired to see it, and to know how long she had been in the doctor's hands; she said (to the best of my remembrance) a year or a year and a half. My landlord informed me that she was a poor widow who lived about four miles distant from his house; that her name was Clark, and that she had a great many poor naked children. My heart then felt a melting charity for the distressed widow: —I told her, that with the assistance of God, I would cure her, and desired her call upon me when she returned from the doctor. She complied, and I applied my medicine, and told her, that by the time she got home the cancer would drop out, which accordingly happened, and in less than three weeks she was perfectly cured. The poor creature was willing to give me all she had in the world, but I would accept of nothing; for God gave me the cure, not to oppress widows, or make fatherless children cry for bread, but to relieve the afflicted; and this duty corresponds with my natural disposition.

In the month of September, 1770, I began my journey into from North-Carolina, to New-England. No remarkable event happened in my travels until I came to Wyoming, on Susquehanna, where I found several of my relations, but we did not know each other till I told them my name; then they remembered that they had heard their fathers speak of me. Upon the road to Wyoming, I had obtained intelligence that a company of Pennsylvanians were coming to drive off the settlers there; and, as I always was a lover of my countrymen, I warned them of the approaching danger.

At Wyoming I continued with my relations four days, and then proceeded on my journey to Delaware River; there I was informed that Captain Ogden and his company had marched to East-Town, after having lain in wait for some time to intercept such New-England people as might pass between Susquehanna and New-England. There was a man and a woman with me, the man's name was John Wickisine, we were well armed and resolved not to be imposed upon whatever might be the event. We went on unmolested, came to Fish Kill Ferry, and crossed Hudson-River, we travelled on the post road until we arrived at De Bois's Tavern, there we continued two days, as my companion Wickisine wanted to hire a house for himself and family, but the landlord and him could not agree upon the terms. At this Tavern I met with one Doctor Smith, he informed me that he lived near Groton River, and that he had been at New-York upon affairs of importance: He was a man of affability and a good orator; we entered into an argument, and I found him to be a man of sense and learned in the sciences. I was so charmed with his discourses upon philosophy, that I could have spent the remainder of my days with him: He desired me to ride along with him, I complied, and the subject of our conversation was nature, the productions of nature, and the primary causes of such surprising effects. The Doctor conducted me to his own house, which was a tavern, and there I lodged that night: During the evening we talked about various matters, but now a word was mentioned about counterfeiting money. Among other things our conversation turned upon the transmutation of metals; the Doctor told me that he was master of that art, but that his extensive practice of physick would not permit him to prosecute his discoveries in alchymy. I informed him that I intended to begin a course of experiments if I could get a convenient place to carry it on the process: He recommended me to Capt. Hard of New-Millford, who, he said, had for several years been carrying on operations of that nature.

Having taken leave of Doctor Smith, I proceeded to New-Millford, enquired for Capt. Hard, and was very courteously received by him; I found him to be a gentleman of strict honor and integrity, and I had a very cordial esteem for him.

I had not remained long there until I received a visit from Doctor Smith; he requested that I would cut his coat of arms, which he told me he wanted to put into his books and gave me a precedent that was done in England. I cut the plate and sent it to him by one David Thar, whom he sent to receive it; soon after the Doctor favoured me with another visit, and after a long prefatory discourse, informed me that he wanted more work done, and that if I would take it in hand to execute it I should be handsomely rewarded. I enquired what he wanted engraved, he said he would show me a pattern, and soon after brought me a ten shilling bill and asked if I could imitate it. I answered him in the affirmative, but told him I did not choose to do such work, being then engaged in philosophic studies: I represented to him the enormity of the crime, and endeavoured to disuade him from persisting in it: his reply was, that the great men are guilty of greater frauds, and that for his part he did not mean to enrich himself by emitting a large number of bills, his principal motive being curiosity to know how near he could imitate the true bill. I told him it was impossible to do it so exact as not to be distinguishable from the genuine bill: He said that a little difference was not material, with sundry other words to that effect. Capt. Hard, understanding his errand, gave him a sharp reprimand, and told me that if I worked for the Doctor I should not stay one hour longer in his house: I promised that I would not, but one word brought on another, we differed, and I left him. —Oh! unhappy day! —for having no overseer to watch for my good I met again with Mr. Smith; who, taking advantage of my weak capacity, debauched my judgment with sophistical reasoning and made me err.

Anxious to improve myself by philosophic studies, naturally inclined to learning, remarkably inquisitive about the secrets of nature and science, I travelled to Saratoga, with an intention to set up my works; and accordingly built a shop for that purpose at the house of John Davis. I agreed with Capt. Garrison to bring me stills, glasses, and other materials from New-York. When these things arrived I prepaired to begin my operations, but a misunderstanding happening between the woman of the house and me, I resolved to leave that place.

I went down to New-Britian, but it being the winter season and the cold very intense, I could not erect my works, but embraced that opportunity to transcribe my philosophy book, which I did at the house of Samuel Wheeler.

As I understood that Doctor Whiting kept potters works, and having occasion for some earthen stills, I went to his house and gave him directions about them; it required some time before they could be finished, and in the interim I employed myself in preparing medicines at Samuel Wheeler's house.

I went again to Doctor Whiting's, expecting my stills were done, but found they were not. This circumstance retarded my business, and because I applied closely to my studies and spent the greatest part of my time in my shop, a report was circulated about the country that I was counterfeiting bills and coining money. I declare, before God! that the said report, was *false*! for I did not make nor offer to pass any bad money, nor never had any thoughts on that subject. Conscious of my innocence, I gave myself no trouble about their surmises, until I heard that they had applied for and obtained a warrant, either at Kinderhook or Clavarack, against me. This made me very uneasy and confirmed my determination of abandoning a place where the people were so censorious and malicious.

I then resolved upon a recluse way of life, and erected a house in a solitary place, where intended to carry on my chymical process; but having made an excursion from my habitation, I met with one Hulburt, who informed me that he had been long searching for me, and that he was employed by Daniel Lewis of Sheffield.

When he acquainted me with his business, I told him that nothing could induce me to be concerned in his Scheme; that being now an old man, and my eye-sight much decayed, I had given over engraving nice work; and that being then engaged in other business, I had neither time nor inclination to comply with his requisition; but he persisted to persuade and make me large offers.

I am now tried, convicted and condemned, on suspicion of having counterfeited the currency of this province; but, if the word of a dying man can be taken, I am innocent of the crime imputed to me. I never did make, sign or pass counterfeit Bills; nor had I any hand in the scheme further than what I have related. In my manner of living I always studied not to give offence, even to Children; and as I practiced no deceit, it never occured to me that others would use it. In the days of prosperity Gold and Silver was not too precious for me; but no sooner did adversity appear, than those whom I formerly imagined to be my best friends, having obtained their ends and glutted their mischievous appetites; they compassed me about like a troubled sea, and having the poison of asps under their tongues they have done their utmost to destroy their fellow creatures in hopes to clear their own characters. Alas! the strongest castle may be taken when besieged by superior force; and if a man is assailed by large offers and insinuation, it is not surprising if he surrenders, especially if his poverty and good nature are taken the advantage of. By over persuasion I engraved, to gratify those who are now cleared and have got their pardon, but it plainly appearth that I never coined, dispersed, nor passed one penny of bad money; but it seems that I must be an *Escape Goat* to bear their transgressions into the other world. LORD strengthen me to bear their burden in this world, and be merciful to my soul in that which is to come.

As it is appointed for all men once to die, and it seems that the time of my dissolution draweth near, I desire that these my transactions may be published for the satisfaction of the public; for that reason, Messrs. Printers, I have sent these manuscripts to you; print them with all convenient speed, and you will greatly oblige your humble servant,

JOSEPH BILL P———

*City Hall, Albany, March 9, 1773,*

Messrs. ROBERTSONS,

Since I wrote the preceding pages, I have recollected the following material occurrences of my Life, which you will be pleased to add as a postscript to what I formerly sent. I would most willingly communicate my recipe for curing cancers to the world, but I have very strong reasons, to be silent on that topic; I am very sorry that this is the case, for, notwithstanding the hardships put upon me, my heart is warm with universal good will and benevolence to my fellow creatures.

I am,
Gentlemen,
your's, &c.
J. B. P.

City-Hall, Albany.
March 16, 1773.

## Postscript.

*In the course of my peregrinations through Virginia, I came to a certain gentleman's house, which I made my home for upwards of four years. During that time I became acquainted with one of his daughters, and at last we thought proper, and indeed it was high time, to marry; accordingly we entered into the connubial state. About half a year after, my wife and me held a consultation upon the posture of our affairs; and, after a good deal of confabulation, we concluded that living with her parents did not suit our convenience. I proposed to go and seek a place that would be more agreeable to us, and observed to my wife, that as I had two good horses, she might, if she pleased, take a ride along with me; she acquiesced, and, having made some necessary preparations for our journey, we set off together.*

*We rode about eighty miles up into the country, and came to a quaker settlement called Opechen Creek, where we put up at a* friend's *house; the gentleman was extremely civil, and we discoursed very jocosely together. He asked where we were journeying: —we answered, to seek our fortune, and enquired if they wanted to have a School master at that settlement? He said they did, and would be very fond of a good one. His reply pleased me exceeding well, and we determined to abide with them; the* friends *being a very good people to live with, especially if they find that those whom they employ are honest and have merit.*

*I engaged with them a year. They built a house for me and my wife, and a school house adjacent. When the buildings were finished, the* brothers *and* sisters, *as they call them, presented us with every utensil necessary for house keeping. We then made as respectable an appearance as any of our neighbours. I opened my school, went on extraordinary well, and had the universal applause of my constituents.*

GENERAL BRADDOCK's *defeat happening about four months after our settlement at Opechen, threw a damp upon our happiness; I was in my school house when the sad news arrived; the whole settlement was alarmed, being apprehensive that the victors would follow their blow and ravage the country with fire and sword. I still continued my school, but, in about two months after, the murder shout was heard in our neighbourhood; numbers of people were killed and scalped, and the miserable fugitives who escaped with life were at a loss where to fly for protection! At last I was obliged to abandon my happy settlement, and, with my wife, repair to a fort; there we remained near two months, but the place being much crouded, by the multitude who came there for protection and we having our two horses with us, made it very incomodious for us to stay there. My wife and me came to a resolution to leave the fort, and not choosing to settle again in a country so open to the incursions of a merciless enemy, we prepared for a journey into the province of Pennsylvania; we arrived safe there, rented a room, and I resumed my practice of surgery and curing cancers. I had surprising good success, and obtained the name of an experienced practitioner in physic, but the tide of fortune again turned and set hard against me; I catched the infection of the small-pox; the eruption was copious and the symptoms very unfavourable. I entreated my wife to leave my room and keep at a distance from me, but her tenderness for me would not permit her to comply with my request. I was under violent apprehensions, that if she got infected, in the condition she was then in, that the consequence would be fatal. Alas! my imaginary distress was very soon realized; she sickened, the pustles appeared, and on the sixteenth day of her illness, to my inexpressible grief, expired.*

*I had a boy three years of age, who was dangerously ill of the same distemper that had been fatal to his mother; at the same time, I was not sufficiently recovered to quit my bed; my situation was truly pitiable, I was sick, dejected, and forlorn, among strangers; my expence for attendance, nursing, and indeed I may say for every thing, amounted to a considerable sum, and I was then in a place where something could not be had for nothing.*

Upon *my recovery I proposed to visit my old friends the Quakers, but hearing that times were altered, much for the worse, in their settlement, I declined it. Having agreed with an old welch widow for my boy's board and lodging, I continued my practice of surgery and had tolerable success. As soon as my boy was able to go, I sent him to school, and he became a very good scholar — I fervently implore the Almighty to preserve, govern and bless him.*

The War still continuing, I was, by the recommendation of several gentlemen who interested themselves in my behalf, appointed surgeon's mate to the garrison of Augusta; there I continued until a detachment of our men were draughted to go against Fort Du Quesne; our principal doctor went with them, but before his departure he wrote to the commissioners in my behalf, without informing me of the favour he had conferred upon me. In consequence of his recommendation I was sent for to Philadelphia, and there received a commission to be chief surgeon to the garrison of Augusta; at the same time I got a chest of medicines and then went back to my station, where I continued seven years. At the conclusion of the war I was discharged at Lancaster, in Pennsylvania: Being then out of employment, I went down to Virginia to visit my father in law, and continued in these parts. My transactions, after that time, I have mentioned in my Journal, to which I refer the reader hereof.

I would willingly write a more minute detail of the various vicissitudes of my life; which would make a large volume, but my time is much too short for such an undertaking; if I could obtain a Reprieve for two months, the work might be finished. What time I can spare, from my more weighty concerns, shall be devoted to the above purpose; and if my sentence is executed, at the time appointed, I shall leave what manuscripts I have, in the hands of the Printers hereof.

When from the World I take my Flight,
To Fields and Regions of Delight;
My cruel Foes need not Exult,
For they'll be punish'd for their Fault.
And those who brought on my Distress,
Will never Taste of Happiness;
Sunk in Despair and lost to Hope,
Their only Remedy's a Rope.
Me quite unwary, for their Sake,
Put Character and Life to Stake;
Deceiv'd, I did the Law transgress;
Words cannot utter my Distress.
I from a Brother ask'd relief,
He only laughed at my Grief;
Oh! may no Brother in Distress,
Be forc'd to ask of him Redress!
To Bliss they can have no Pretence,
Whose Heart disclaims Benevolence;
To me the Needy welcome were,
I gave them what I had to spare.

*Finis.*

## Source Notes

In his *American Bibliography*, Charles Evans listed two editions of *A Journal of the Life and Travels of Joseph-Bill Packer*; both published in Albany during 1773. According to Evans, the first was printed by Alexander and James Robertson, but no copy of this edition has been located. The copy text used in the anthology is taken from the second edition listed by Evans. Although lacking a title page, the narrative began with Packer's address "*To the Printers.*"

By his own account, Packer was an innocent man. Throughout the narrative he maintained that he was accused falsely. In *Counterfeiting in Colonial America*, however, Kenneth Scott's historical investigation failed to exonerate Packer. According to Scott, Packer, under his alias Joseph Bill, was first arrested for counterfeiting in 1747 at the age of twenty-seven in New Haven, Connecticut. Although first claiming his innocence, he confessed after counterfeit bills and engraving tools were found among his possessions. After escaping from the New Haven and Hartford jails, he journeyed to Boston, where he set up a counterfeiting ring with several accomplices, and for the next several years he printed and distributed his bogus currencies throughout New England. During this time Packer adopted the name of Doctor Wilson and "pretended to be a famous physician" (176). In 1751 he was arrested in New York City for counterfeiting but, when his accomplice—on whose testimony he had been arrested—hung himself in his jail cell, he was released on a lack of evidence. Scott lost track of the counterfeiter after this but did mention that, despite having a wife and daughter in New England, Packer married again in Virginia, where his second wife bore him a son. According to the narrative, Packer arrived in Virginia when he was twenty-two (1742) and remained in the South until 1770. If Scott's research is correct, Packer then journeyed south sometime after his release from the New York jail and remained there for nearly two decades. In the narrative Packer did mention working as a physician ("curing cancers") and the birth of a son.

According to Scott, in addition to a life devoted to counterfeiting, the most sensational part of Packer's life was his death. Arrested late in 1772 in White Plains, New York, Packer was placed in custody in the Albany jail along with nine or so of his accomplices. On November 12, 1773, *The New-York Journal* reported: "We hear, that a few Days ago no less than 9 Men were committed to Gaol in Albany, on Suspicion of concerned in counterfeiting our last commission of Paper Money, as a Quantity of the same, and many bad Dollars, with Instruments for operating on both, were found in their Possession." Shortly after his arrest Packer and his fellow counterfeiters attempted to escape. A notice in *The New-York Gazette* (December 12, 1772) stated: "By a gentleman from Albany, we learn, that the Court was opened there on Friday the 11th Inst. for the Trial of the Money Makers confined in Goal at that Place; and that on the Night of Wednesday the 9th, the said Prisoners intended to have a general Goal Delivery, having nearly effected an Escape by breaking out of the Prison near the Chimney, but being heard by the Guard that had been kept over the Goal ever since their being committed, they were prevented, and more closely confined." Despite being "closely confined," Packer was still not ready to surrender his life. Appropriately, on April 1, 1773, the day before his execution, the "famous physician" and two other counterfeiters escaped but were soon retaken and once more chained up. Still defiant, the three soon freed themselves of the chains, barred the door to their cell, and threatened to kill anyone who entered. Although the city militia was called to arms, the counterfeiters kept everyone back for several hours. Vowing to make their own exit, the three set fire to the jail, "expecting to die in the conflagration" (221). The fire, however, was put out, but the three had one final trick. Previously "some mischievous fellows" had given them two pounds of gunpowder, which was put in a bottle (221). One of Packer's two conspirators, John Wall Lovey, held a match to the bottle and threatened to blow everyone up if anyone attempted to take them. Again there was a stand off. Finally a group rushed in, and Lovey set the match to the bottle. Miraculously, the powder did not explode, and the three "were carried off to the gallows, singing psalms on the way" (222). Scott's account of the affair closely followed the report published in several newspapers. For an example, see the "*Extract of a Letter from* Albany, *dated April 3*" printed in the *The New-York Journal* (April 15, 1773) and in the *Boston News-Letter* (April 22, 1773).

The Joseph-Bill Packer presented in the narrative differed drastically from Scott's characterization of the counterfeiter not only in action but also in personality. While Packer exclaimed his virtues and denied his vices throughout the text, Scott's counterfeiter boasted of his skills and justified his craft. After stating that he had engraved counterfeit plates in North Carolina, Virginia, Pennsylvania, the Jerseys, and New York, "he declared that he never considered it criminal for a mechanic to finish any piece of work that he was employed to execute, whatever mischievous purposes the instrument might be applied to after the artist delivered it out of his hands" (173).

Two of the counterfeiters arrested and imprisoned with Packer also published narratives: John Wall Lovey (the same who threatened to blow up the Albany jail with a bottle of gun powder) was presented to the public in *The Last Speech, Confession and Dying Words of John Wall Lovey* (Albany, 1773), and John Smith also became a published figure in *The Last Speech, Confession and Dying Words of John Smith* (Albany, 1773; reprinted Hartford, 1773, and New Haven, 1773). Smith, who was executed a month before Packer and Lovey, wrote two letters to Alexander and James Robertson, Packer's original printers. In the first letter he stated: "I am very much obliged to you for your offering to serve me in publishing some few Lines under my unhappy Circumstances" (Hartford 3). In all probability the Robertsons, anticipating a popular market, similarly approached Packer, offering him the same opportunity to publish "some few Lines."

THE

*DYING DECLARATION*

OF

JAMES BUCHANAN, EZRA ROSS,

AND WILLIAM BROOKS;

*Who were executed at Worcester, July 2, 1778;*

*FOR THE MURDER OF*

***Mr. Joshua Spooner.***

ON February 8th, 1778, we, *James Buchanan* and *William Brooks* left Worcester with an intent to go to Springfield to work. In passing Mr. Spooner's we were called in by *Alexander Cummings*, who we thought was a British soldier. Having stood some time by the fire, he told us his master was gone from home, but he would go and call his mistress, for she had a great regard for the army, as her father was in it and one of her brothers. He called her; and she came down, and appeared glad to see us. She asked us whether we came from the Hill? We told her we did, and were going to *Canada*, as I, *Buchanan*, had left my family there. She ordered Breakfast for us, and as soon as it was ready we were desired to go into the sitting-room. We were very much surprised at this, for we should have thought ourselves well dealt by to have received any favours she might see fit to bestow on us in the kitchen. However, we all breakfasted together. The weather being very bad, we were asked to stay till it cleared up. As we had but little money, we accordingly stayed. The weather continuing very bad, we stayed there that day and night. I (Buchanan) am not positive whether it was the first or second day, she told me, when by ourselves, that she and her husband did not agree—that he was gone a journey to Prince-

[Worcester? n.d.]

[ BUCHANAN, ROSS, & BROOKS ]

# *The Dying Declaration of James Buchanan, Ezra Ross, & William Brooks*

[ 1778 ]

ON February 8th, 1778, we, *James Buchanan* and *William Brooks* left Worcester with an intent to go to Springfield to work. In passing Mr. Spooner's we were called in by *Alexander Cummings*, who we thought was a British soldier. Having stood sometime by the fire, he told us his master was gone from home, but he would go and call his mistress, for she had a great regard for the army, as her father was in it and one of her brothers. He called her; and she came down, and appeared glad to see us. She asked whether we came from the Hill? We told her we did, and were going to Canada, as I, Buchanan, had left my family there. She ordered Breakfast for us, and as soon as it was ready we were desired to go into the sitting-room. We were very much surprised at this, for we should have thought ourselves well dealt by to have received any favour she might see fit to bestow on us in the kitchen. However, we all breakfasted together. The weather being very bad, we were asked to stay till it cleared up. As we had but little money, we accordingly stayed. The weather continued very bad, we stayed there that day and night. I (Buchanan) am not positive whether it was the first or second day, she told me, when by ourselves, that she and her husband did not agree—that he was gone a journey to Princetown, and that he would not be home soon—that we should not go from thence until the weather was fair, there being a great fall of snow at this time.

We very readily consented, and stayed from day to day, expecting Mr. Spooner home. Mrs. Spooner getting very free in discourse with me (Buchanan) one day told me that she never expected Mr. Spooner to return, as there was one Mr. Ross gone with him, who had an ounce of Poison, which he had promised her he would give to Mr. Spooner the first convenient opportunity.

The reader must needs think this a very strange circumstance, that she should make such a discovery to an entire stranger. She said at the same time, we should stay till we saw whether Mr. Spooner returned or not. Accordingly we stayed, and were never in better quarters, little thinking of the bait the seducer of souls was laying for us; we were then in a disposition to catch at it, having no fear of God before our eyes, and being entirely forsaken of him.

Having tarried ten or eleven days as nearly as can be recollected, her husband came home, and seeing us there asked her who we were. She told him that I (Buchanan) was cousin to Alexander Cummings. He took no further notice of it, but going out among his neighbours, it is likely he was informed how long we had been there, and probably heard at the tavern, of the quantity of liquor he had to pay for, since his going on his journey. Be that as it may, at night he came home, and seeing we were not gone, he desired us to go immediately. We begg'd he would let us stay till morning. He after some time consented that we should stay by the fire all night. He was in the sitting-room by himself, and Mrs. Spooner went to bed. There was one *Reuben Old* came upon some business with Mr. Spooner, and after some time came out and told us that Mr. Spooner told him he was afraid we should rob him, adding that he had lost a silver spoon, and a great deal of pewter. This vexed us, as we were conscious we had no thought of stealing from him. Had we been so inclined, we had as much opportunity as we could have desired. The spoon he found where he lay it, and Cummings convinced him that there was none of the pewter missing.

Mr. Spooner went up stairs and brought down a box, which he had his money in, and laid down on the floor with it under his head. Every thing Mr. Spooner did or said, *Old* came and told us, and was with us all the time he was asleep, and we were all merry together, sitting by the kitchen fire. Said *Old* declared in court, that I, *Buchanan*, said if Mr. Spooner came out, I would for two coppers put him into the Well, which is false. In the morning, it not being convenient to see Mrs. Spooner, to take our leave of her, we, *Buchanan*, *Brooks* and *Cummings* went to Mrs. Stratten's to pass the day, till we could get an opportunity to bid Mrs. Spooner farewell. We stayed at Mrs. Stratten's the best part of the day, Cummings having received five dollars from Mr. Spooner, to treat his pretended cousin with, we went to Mr. Conley's tavern and had some drink, from thence to Doctor Foxcroft's, stayed there until Cummings came and told us Mr. Spooner was in bed. We then went to the house, and had supper and liquor, retired to the barn and tarried all night. In the morning had breakfast sent to the barn for us. And as Mrs. Berry and Mrs. Tufts had been there the day before and wanted to see me, (*Buchanan*) I said I would go and see them. Mrs. Spooner said she would also go, which was agreed upon. Buchanan and

Brooks went there, and we all stayed at Mr. Green's, drinking until late; some distance from thence, she said she had given a handkerchief to a British soldier that had some words in anger with me, Buchanan, upon which Brooks went back on the horse, and she and I went home. Brooks missed his road on his return, but got to the house some time after us; but he did not get the handkerchief, as the soldier would not deliver it, until he saw Mrs. Spooner. Buchanan and Brooks stayed that night in the barn; in the morning went to Mr. Gilbert's tavern and stayed there some time, and on coming out from his house we saw Cummings approaching on one of Mr. Spooner's horses; he told us his master was gone to the tavern, and that his mistress desired we would come there, which we did, and had supper; we went to the barn that night, and in the morning she sent us word that her husband was gone abroad into the country to get some oats.

The boy Parker had proposed to Brooks, if he would come and meet Mr. Spooner and himself, on their return, the said Parker said he would help take Mr. Spooner's life. We went over from the barn to the house, and found he was gone, and stayed there all day, and lived on the best the house afforded of meat and drink.

Mr. Spooner came home in the dusk of the evening, so that we had like to have been seen; but we heard him come with the sleigh to the door and Brooks ran into the cellar, and I went and stood on the back stairs, until he went into the sitting-room. We then came out, and went to the barn, there stayed all the next day, and at night when Mr. Spooner was in bed, we were sent for to the house and received supper and some liquor to encourage another plan, which Cummings and Parker (who have for this time escaped punishment,) proposed to poor Brooks, which was, they all three to go up stairs, and Brooks to take his life from him; for which he was to receive one thousand dollars, Mr. Spooner's watch, buckles, and as much cloth as would make a suit of cloathes; but Brooks heart failed him; and Mrs. Spooner said she did not think he was so faint hearted. Had this been done he was to be put into the Well as he was taken out of bed; for she observed it would be thought he had fallen in, while drawing water in the night; next day we had breakfast brought us by Cummings. He informed us there was another plan formed by her, which was as follows. Either Cummings or Parker were to tell Mr, Spooner one of the horses was sick; and as he came to the barn to kill him; and put him amou[n]gst the horse's feet, to make people believe when he was found that the horses had killed him. But Brooks told Parker not to tell him, but to make her believe he would not go over. The boy conducted accordingly. We stayed all that day and night. The next day being Sunday, we stayed there; she came over at night; we told her we should go away the next morning; she desired we would not; but we would not stay. We set out to go to Springfield, as we went through Western on that road, we engaged to work with one Mr. Marks a smith; I Buchanan worked there two days; but as he had no files fit for the branch of trade Brooks followed, we proposed to go to Worcester to get some, which was agreed to.

We set off on Wednesday about noon, and in going by Mr. Spooner's we called and told her where we were going; she said she would follow us down the next day as she wanted to see her sister, saying she was glad we had got work so near; and further added, that she had got two notes one of 20 pounds, lawful, and another of 300 dollars, which she would endeavour to get changed, and let me, Buchanan, have one hundred dollars, to purchase any thing I might want.

We stayed in the barn till morning, and then set out for Worcester, and she followed us the same day and called at Mrs. Walker's for us, according to agreement; she came in and stayed some time, and gave me, Buchanan, a note, as much cloth as made a shirt, and 6 or 7 dollars, observing that they came from one M'Donald, an acquaintance of hers; she then went to see her sister, and desired us to stay till she came back, which we did; she returned on Friday morning about ten o'clock, and stayed till night; she told me, Buchanan, at parting, that she had no more paper money, but what she had given me; but begged I would procure her some poison to give Mr. S*pooner*; I accordingly that day got one drachm of Calomel, and made it into 20 papers. I desired her to give one in the morning; she told me she never gave him any; she went to her sister's late that night and called on us in the morning, about ten o'clock. I went to the door; she would not come in, but desired me to come up to Mr. Nazro's shop, and she would get files for us, as we had not money sufficient to get what we wanted; she asked me, when we would come through Brookfield. I told her if she would set up, we would call on Monday night at eleven o'clock, she said she would; I parted with her and sent Brooks up to the shop. But as he came in sight he saw her ride from the door, and therefore did not go there; we stayed at Walker's until Sunday afternoon, and then left Worcester, and about 8 o'clock at night got to Mr. Spooner's; we saw Mrs. Stratten at the Well, Buchanan spoke to her, she told me there was company in the house, but she would let Mrs. Spooner know we were there; Mrs. Spooner came out, and told us that one Mr. Ross was in the house, who had a brace of pistols loaded, and that he had promised her he would kill Mr. Spooner as he came home from the tavern, she desired us to come in, which we did, he shewed us a pistol, and said Mr. Spooner should die by that to night. Either Brooks or Buchanan said it would alarm the neighbours.

Brooks said if Ross would help him he would knock him down, accordingly it was agreed on, and there was a look out kept at the sitting room door for his coming, in the mean time there was some supper brought by Mrs. Stratten to us, we had had some flip before, and there was now some rum brought, which we drank, each of us by turns giving a look out. We are certain Mrs. Stratten could not but know what was going forward. That we leave the public to judge of. Mr. Spooner was at length seen coming, and then was the time for the Devil to shew his power over them who had forsaken God.

An account of the murder as it was committed.

William Brooks went out and stood within the small gate leading into the kitchen, and as Mr. Spooner came past him he knocked him down with his hand. He strove to speak when down, Brooks took him by the throat and partly strangled him. Ross and Buchanan came out; Ross took Mr. Spooner's watch out and gave it to Buchanan; Brooks and Ross took him up and put him into the well head first; before they carried him away, I, Buchanan, pulled off his shoes: I was instantly struck with the horror of conscience, as well I might; I went into the house and met Mrs. Spooner in the sitting room; she seemed vastly confused: She immediately went up and brought the money which was in a box. She not having a key desired me to break it open which I did; At the same time Brooks and Ross came in: She gave two notes of 400 dollars each to Ross to change and give the money to Brooks; But there was found some paper money, which Brooks received (243 dollars) and the notes were returned. At the same time she gave Ross four notes, each of them ten pounds, to purchase camblet for a riding dress. Ross gave Brooks his waistcoat, breeches and a shirt. She went and brought Ross a waistcoat, breeches and a shirt of Mr. Spooner's[;] when they were shifted, she gave me, Buchanan, three eight dollar bills, and asked me when she should see me again, I told her in fourteen days, but it pleased God to order it sooner, and in a dreadful situation. Had we all been immediately struck dead after the perpetration of so horrid a murder, and sent to Hell, God would have been justified and we justly condemned.

About 11 o'clock at night, we set off for Worcester. About 4 o'clock in the morning we reached Mrs. Walker's house; Mary Walker and a Negro girl were within; we told them a parcel of lies to excuse our sudden return; in the morning we went to drinking to endeavour to drown the thoughts of so horrid action we had been guilty of; we stayed there all day with a view to go off at night, but it pleased God to order it otherwise; for Brooks being in liquor, went down to Mr. Brown's tavern; there shewing Mr. Spooner's watch, and the people seeing him have silver Buckles, became suspicious of him, and one Ensign Clark going to Mrs. Walker's and seeing what passed there gave information concerning us. The news of the murder had now reached the town, and we were all taken, and brought before the Committee, examined, and committed to gaol. On the 24th of April last we were brought to trial before the Superior Court, found guilty and received sentence of death.

JAMES BUCHANAN,
EZRA ROSS,
his
WILLIAM ✠ BROOKS,
mark.

James Buchanan was a Serjeant in the army under Gen. Burgoyne born in Glascow in Scotland aged 30 years. William Brooks, a private in said army, born in the parish of Wednesbury in the county of Statford, in England, aged 27. Ezra Ross a soldier in the continental army, born in Ipswich in the parish of Lyndebrook, New England, aged 18.

We, Buchanan, Brooks and Ross, are conscious to ourselves that we are indeed guilty of the above murder, and that hereby we have forfeited our lives into the hands of public justice, and exposed ourselves to have our part in the lake which burneth with fire and brimstone. We desire to give glory to God by free and full confession of our heinous guilt[.] We trust we have with deep penitence and contrition of soul, confessed it to God, hoping an infinite mercy and compassion, through the atoning blood of his son Jesus that our scarlet and crimson guilt may be done away, that we may be saved from eternal damnation which we know we justly deserve, and obtain eternal life and salvation. We would as dying men, who have been made to feel what an evil and bitter thing sin is, earnestly warn all, especially young people, that they would avoid the vices we have been addicted to, and which prepared the way for our committing the heinous wickedness for which we are to suffer a premature and ignominious death: That they would avoid bad company, excessive drinking, profane cursing and swearing, shameful debaucheries, disobedience to parents, the prophanation of the Lord's day, &c. That they would be pious, sober and virtuous, that so they may be in favour with God and man.

And now we commend our departing souls into the hands of a merciful God and Saviour, earnestly desiring that all who may be spectators or hearers of our tragical end, while we are the subjects of prayer, would lift up their hearts in fervent supplications for us, that God would receive us to his everlasting mercy.

## Source Notes

James Buchanan, Ezra Ross, and William Brooks were involved in the most sensational American criminal case in the late eighteenth century. Soon after Joshua Spooner was murdered on March 2, 1778, publications began to appear relating the grisly facts of the crime. Following Spooner's burial, the Boston printers Thomas and Timothy Fleet published Nathan Fiske's funeral sermon: *A Sermon Preached at Brookfield March 6, 1778.* While the minister made indirect references to the "bloody Tragedy" throughout his text, the title page stated that Spooner "was most barbarously murdered at his own Gate, on the LORD's Day Evening . . . by three Ruffians, who were hired for the Purpose by his Wife (5). Fiske further heightened the indignant tone of his rhetoric by declaring: "So premeditated, so aggravated, so horrid a murder was never perpetrated in America, and is almost without parallel in the known world" (6). Evidently Fiske's sermon was popular; two more editions appeared in 1778. Ezekiel Russell printed an edition in "Danvers, near Boston" (no copy located), and Green and Spooner printed another edition in Norwich, Conn. (Ritz 210).

Two ballads also appeared sometime between March 2 and July 2 (the execution): *The Cruel Murder Or. a Mournful Poem Occasioned by Sentence of Death being pass'd upon William Brooks, James Buchanan, Ezra Ross and Bathsheba Spooner* (Boston: Gross and Dozen, 1778) and *A mournful POEM: Occasioned by Sentence of Death being pass'd upon William Brooks, James Buchanan, Ezra Ross and Bathsheba Spooner* (Boston, 1778). Since no separate copy of *The Cruel Murder* has been located, Ritz listed the two ballads as separate publications, yet given the nearness of the titles, it seems likely that *A mournful POEM* is a reprint. Moreover, since *A mournful POEM* made no specific reference to the Spooner case, it seems likely that the ballad was recycled through several cases and broadside editions. The first stanzas, in fact, are nearly identical to *A Mournful POEM on the Death of John Ormsby and Matthew Cushing* (Boston: Thomas Fleet, 1734).

With slight differences (notably in the titles and arrangement of sections) six editions of the condemned murderers final confession were published. The first edition was probably Isaiah Thomas' broadside, *The dying Declaration of James Buchanan, Ezra Ross and William Brooks* (Worcester, 1778). A second edition, believed also to have been published in Worcester during 1778, was published as an eight-page chapbook: *The Dying Declaration of James Buchanan, Ezra Ross, and Willam Brooks.* With the exceptions of the title and form, the two texts are virtually the same. The former, however, stated that Buchanan's age was thirty-six, while the latter stated that it was thirty. The *Declaration* soon was turned into the *The last Words and dying Speech of James Buchanan, Ezra Ross and William Brooks*, a broadside printed and sold in Boston by Draper and Folsom in 1778. A second edition of this broadside, bearing the exact same title and form but with slight variations of fonts and graphics, also is believed to have been printed in Boston during 1778. The primary difference between the *Declarations* and the *last Words* is that a concluding footnote stating that Buchanan was a "Serjeant in the army under Gen. Burgoyne" and that Brooks was "a private in said army" was transferred to the beginning of the text as an opening statement: "I JAMES

BUCHANAN was a serjeant in the Army under General Burgoyne . . . I WILLIAM BROOKS was a private in the said army." Apparently, Draper and Folsom used Thomas' original broadside, since their text gave Buchanan's age as thirty-six. Two more editions of the *last Words* were published as broadsides, but without date or place of publication (although both were probably 1778 editions as well). The only difference between these editions and the Draper and Folsom text was an addition to the title: "Bathsheba Spooner, who was convicted of being an accessary to the Murder of her Husband, was also executed at the same Time." Possibly this addition was made to remind readers of Bathsheba Spooner's involvement in the affair, thus making the text more marketable. The edition of the condemned men's final confessions was printed in chapbook form as *The Lives, Last Words, and Dying Speech of Ezra Ross, James Buchanan, and William Brooks*; while no place of publication or date was included, the American Antiquarian Society's copy bears a handwritten note that the text was possibly printed in Worcester during 1778. Along with the addition of a lurid engraving of an execution scene on the title page, the only difference in *The Lives* was the inclusion of the original ballad, *The CRUEL MURDER: Or, a MOURNFUL POEM*; the text of this ballad and *A mournful POEM* are the same.

The copy text used in the anthology is taken from the original broadside, *The dying Declaration of James Buchanan, Ezra Ross and James Brooks.* Due to the imperfect condition of the Readex imprint, the second chapbook edition was used as a reference. When both texts proved unreadable, the copy was checked against the several editions of *The last Words and dying Speech.*

Unlike Buchanan, Ross, and Brooks, Bathsheba Spooner was never presented to the public in the convention of a dying speech. But Thaddeus Maccarty, the minister who attended the prisoners during their final days, included an *ACCOUNT of those PRISONERS in Their LAST STAGE* when he published his execution sermon, *The Guilt Of Innocent Blood Put Away* (Worcester: Isaiah Thomas, 1778). Maccarty devoted several pages to Spooner, who was described in terms strikingly similar to those of Esther Rodgers. Moments before the gallows procession began, Spooner was baptised in a "very solemn and affecting" scene (39). When the sheriff placed the rope around her neck to begin the procession, "she told him she esteemed it as much as though he had put on a necklace of gold or diamonds" (39). After mounting the scaffold, she exclaimed, "with a serene countenance, *that it was the happiest day she ever saw*" (39–40). Both Maccarty's sermon and account proved marketable; a second edition of the sermon, complete with the supplementary account, was published by John Trumbull in Norwich, Conn. in 1778. About the same time, Maccarty's description of Spooner was excerpted and published as *The Rev. Mr. Maccarty's Account of the Behaviour of Mrs. Spooner after her Commitment and Condemnation for being Accessary in the Murder of her Husband at Brookfield* (n.p. 1778?).

In addition to the various broadsides and chapbooks, New England readers were presented with information concerning the notorious case in the newspapers. One of the first announcements was printed by Isaiah Thomas in *The Massachusetts Spy*, March 5, 1778:

> On Sunday night last a most horrid murder was committed in Brookfield,

> on the person of Mr. Joshua Spooner. From the long premeditation of the murder, the number of persons concerned (there being no less than seven capitally concerned) and the methods made use of to accomplish their designs, it is supposed to be the most extraordinary crime ever perpetrated in New-England.
>
> Monday evening three of the villains concerned in the murder of Mr. Spooner were taken up in this town [Worcester]. On examination they impeached their accomplices, in consequence of which Mrs. Spooner, (the inventor of the murder) and the rest of her associates were seized, and on Tuesday evening brought to this town and confined in goal.

On April 30, 1778, *The Massachusetts Spy* printed a brief notice of the trial: "*On Friday last came on before the Hon. Superior court for this county, the trial of William Brooks, James Buchanan, Ezra Ross, and Bathsheba Spooner, for the cruel and deliberate murder of Mr. Joshua Spooner, as mentioned in this paper some time since; of which crime they were found guilty and received sentence of death.*"

Still exploiting the case's notoriety, one week later (May 7, 1778) Thomas printed a much longer account of the crime, and in this sensational relation readers were encouraged to feel a sense of outrage. As it was reported, the murder involved a double social sacrilege, that it desecrated the boundaries of rank and status, and that it profaned the sanctity of a man's family and home. Placed at the center of such apostasy, and thus held up for public condemnation, was Bathsheba Spooner:

> The following is a particular account of the trial of the persons mentioned in our last. *William Brooks, James Buchanan*, and *Ezra Ross*, were indicted for the murder of Mr. JOSHUA SPOONER of Brookfield, and *Bathsheba*, his late wife, was indicted as accessary thereto, by causing, procuring, aiding, and abetting the same. They were set at the bar, and severally pleaded, *not guilty*; having council assigned them the trial came on, and lasted 16 hours, wherein every legal indulgence were granted them. They were all found guilty and received sentence of death accordingly.
>
> It appeared by the course of the evidence, that Mrs. Spooner had, for some time, conceived a great aversion to her husband, with whom she had lived near about 14 years: His only fault appears to be his not supporting a manly importance as head of his family, and not regulating the government of it. It is very uncertain what this aversion in Mrs. Spooner's mind at first arose from, but from the general tenor of her conduct, it is probable that she cherished a criminal regard for some other persons, until, having followed the blind impulses of wicked and unchaste desires, she lost all moral sensibility, discarded reason and conscience from her breast, and gave herself up to infamous prostitutions, and finally became determined to destroy the life of her husband, who seemed to check her wanton career in no other way than by preventing her wasting his whole estate as she pleased, in pursuance of this horrid design, she, at various times, procured poison, but never gave

it to him; and sometime before the commission of this cruel fact, she became acquainted with Ross, to whom she made some amorous overtures, and told him, that if he would kill her husband, she would become his lawful wife: It appears, by the examination of Ross, before the Justices, that his conscience at first started at the appearance of so much guilt; but upon her persuasions and the fancied happiness of marrying a woman so much above his rank in life, and the allurements of wallowing in Mr. Spooner's wealth he fatally consented. Previous to this, Ross had been sick at Spooner's house, and was kindly treated there, and that after these guilty overtures, tarried there some time, with freedom, as one of the family, when Mr. Spooner treated him with great civilities, and many marks of particular friendship; that while he was there, he put poison in his drink, which was discovered; and that he rode with him to Oakham and Lancaster, and had engaged to poison him on the road; that he bought arsenic to affect his death, but never gave it to him.

Mrs. Spooner, tired of the delays of Ross, made like overtures to Serjeant Buchanan, of the convention troops, whom she directed to be called in, as he was passing in the road. Buchanan and she engaged one William Brooks, of the same troops, to commit the murder, promising him the deceased's watch, buckles and a thousand dollars. Buchanan and Brooks came to Spooner's about a fortnight before his death, and stayed in his kitchen all night: He then being afraid they would rob him, brought his money from the chambers and procured one of his neighbours to stay with him, and set up all night; but on his ordering them to go away in the morning, they went to the barn, and layed concealed there two days and two nights, in which time Mrs. Spooner sustained them with victuals and drink. That on the Thursday next before the first day of March, which was the day her husband was murdered, she met them at one Widow Walker's in Worcester, where, although she was a stranger to the house, she tarried with them the greater part of that and two following days—was often alone with them, treated them very familiarly, and suffered them to use great familiarities with her, to the astonishment of Walker's family, who knew her rank in life. On Saturday, when she went away from Walker's, some words passed between her and Buchanan, at parting, which leaves no doubt of their having agreed to meet at Brookfield, the next day, to effect the death of Mr. Spooner.

While she was absent on Saturday, Ross came in the house, and concealed himself till evening, when he looked through a window and spoke to one Widow Stratton, who was ironing in the kitchen, and told her that he was exceeding cold but could not come in because he wanted to conceal himself from Mr. Spooner, whose horse he had borrowed to go to Ipswich, to see his father, and which he had abused. This woman concealed him in the buttery until Mrs. Spooner came home, who was received pleasantly by her husband: She concealed Ross all the next day, being the Sabbath, on the evening whereof, the deceased went out, and spent an hour or two with one of his neighbours, as he usually did; while he was gone, Buchanan and Brooks came to his house, and, after a great

> deal of conversation of the killing of Mr. Spooner, she stimulated them to the murder, sometimes by promises of reward, and [at] others by upbraidings of cowardice, until it was agreed that the three men should stand sentry by turns to watch his returning to his own house. About nine o'clock he left his company, in a cheerful humour, and great calmness of mind, without the least suspicion of villainy. As he came near his own door, Brooks met him and knocked him down; he asked what was the matter, and cried murder (as appears by the examination of Brooks, before the Justices) but that three fell upon, and presently dispatched him, with repeated blows, and unparalleled cruelty, and then threw him into the well. After this they came into the house to Mrs. Spooner, with the cloathes of Brooks wet with the blood of her innocent husband. She went up to his bed chamber to get his money to pay Brooks, according to her promise, and to distribute his wealth amongst his murderers; but while she was there, she told the Widow Stratton who was in the kitchen when the murder was done (and whose conscience must witness whether she was before, privy to this hellish design against the life of a man who found her bread) that she hoped Mr. Spooner was in heaven, and seemed much affected. She however, came down, brought the money, and distributed it amongst the ruffians. She then sent a Scotch servant, whom [s]he had often invited to kill her husband, to the well to get water to wash the bloody cloaths; he knowing of the murder was afraid to go alone, and Stratton went with him; but, when he put the bucket down into the well, he felt his master, dropped the poles and they both ran into the house, where Stratton took down the bible, went to reading, and cried. They then agreed to burn the bloody cloaths; Ross gave Brooks his breeches and put on Spooner's. She gave Brooks 200 dollars, the watch and buckles; and the three murderers set off in the dead of night for Worcester, with Spooner's horse and goods. They were there overtaken on Monday and apprehended. The next morning after the murder, Mrs. Spooner and the Scotch servant went to the well, and saw her husband there, and, after some proposals of sinking him, she sent the servant on horse back, to inquire for him, that she might not be suspected; when the neighbours were collected they discovered the strongest marks of guilt in the whole family.
>
> She appeared to be little affected either on the trial or when sentence of death was passed upon her; and it is wished, that there may be, in the other convicts, more signs of repentance, before their execution, than has been observed in her.

To inform even more readers of the sensational crime, and as well boost sales, two Boston papers printed this same account (*The Independent Chronicle*, April 30, and *The Continental Journal*, May 7).

As the execution approached, *The Massachusetts Spy* inserted a couple of brief notices, the first on May 28 announcing that on the previous Sabbath Ezra Ross had been publicly baptized, and the second on June 25 warning the anticipated large number of spectators to beware of smallpox:

> The selectmen of the town of Worcester, taking into consideration the large concourse of people that will probably attend at the execution of the unhappy persons under sentence of death here, as also that there are several hospitals, in this county, for the reception of persons having the small pox, DO, in behalf of the PUBLIC, caution and request all Physicians and Nurses, concerned in such Hospitals, and persons having lately had the small-pox, not to appear in the assembly of spectators unless sufficiently CLEANSED. Otherwise their attendance may prove fatal to many, and render the execution, which is intended for the warning and benefit of ALL, a public detriment.
>
> By order of the Select Men,
>
> WILLIAM CHAMBERS, Town-Clerk.
>
> *Worcester, June* 24, 1778.

On July 9, a few days after the execution, *The Massachusetts Spy* included a brief announcement stating that it had taken place and that "a Sermon was preached by the Rev. Mr. MACCARTY of this place from Deut. XIX, 13. 'THINE EYE SHALL NOT PITY HIM, BUT THOU SHALL PUT AWAY THE GUILT OF INNOCENT BLOOD FROM ISRAEL, THAT IT MAY GO WELL WITH THEE.'" Within a week (July 12) Isaiah Thomas inserted an advertisement in the paper announcing the publication of *The dying Declaration*, and on July 23 the Worcester printer inserted another advertisement announcing the publication of Maccarty's sermon (complete with the sensational "Account of those Prisoners in their Last Stage").

The last notice of this notorious crime in *The Massachusetts Spy* was printed on August 6, a month after the execution. To explain its late inclusion, the paper stated: "The following paragraph would have been published in season, had it not been for the necessary absence of the Printer at that time; and since omitted by reason of its being mislaid":

> On the 2d ult. were executed in this town, James Buchanan, Ezra Ross, William Brooks, and Bathsheba Spooner, for the murder of Mr. Joshua Spooner, late of Brookfield. At about half past two in the afternoon, the criminals were brought out of prison, and conducted to the place of execution, under a guard of about an hundred men. The three male prisoners went on foot, Mrs. Spooner was carried in a chaise, being, as she had been for a number of days, exceedingly unwell. The procession was regular and solemn. Just before they reached the place of execution a black thunder cloud arose and darkened the Heavens; here followed an awful half hour! The loud hallooings of the officers, amidst a crowd of five thousand, to *Make way! Make way!* the horses pressing upon those on foot; the shrieks of women in the confusion; the malefactors slowly advancing to the fatal tree, preceded by their dismal urns; the fierce coruscations athwart the darkened horizon, quickly followed by loud peals of thunder, conspired together, and produced a dreadful compound scene of horror! It seemed as if the author of nature was determined to add such terrors to the punishment of the criminals, as

> must stagger the stoutest heart of the most abandoned. While the sheriff was reading the Death Warrant, Buchanan, Brooks, and Ross were on the stage; Mrs. Spooner, being excessively feeble, was permitted to sit in the chaise; she heard the warrant read with as much calmness as she would the most indifferent matter: she was frequently seen to bow to many of the spectators with whom she had been acquainted. When called to ascend the stage, with a gentle smile she stepped out of the chaise and crept up the ladder upon her hands and knees. The halters being fastened; the malefactors pinioned, and their faces covered, the sheriff informed them that he would drop the stage immediately; upon which Mrs. Spooner took him by the hand, and said, "My dear sir! I am ready! in a little time I expect to be in bliss: and but a few years must elapse when I hope to see you and my other friends again." They were all calm and smiled at the approach of death, considering the king of terrors but as a kind messenger to introduce them to the regions of eternal joys.

Bathsheba Spooner and her accomplices were thus depicted as going to their deaths as saints, but few readers would have forgotten, or forgiven, their sins.

*The Massachusetts Spy*, of course, was not the only newspaper to condemn Bathsheba Spooner and her accomplices with the rhetoric of damnation. *The Boston Gazette*, for example, carried a couple of notices referring to the murder and as well mentioning that Spooner was the daughter of a well known Tory:

> The Week past the most cruel, inhumane and unheard of Murder was committed on the Body of Mr. Joshua Spooner of Brookfield, (formerly of this town [Boston]) at the instigation of his Wife, a daughter of the well known Mandamus Counsellor, Timothy Ruggles. She, with her Accomplices, we hear, are committed to Worcester Goal. — The Particulars of this diabolical Plot, we hope, we shall be able to give our Readers the next Week. (March 9)

> Thursday last was executed at Worcester, agreeable to their Sentence, Mrs Bathsheba Spooner (a daughter of the noted Timothy Ruggles, one of the Mandamus Counsellors) prime Conspirators of the Death of her Husband, Mr. Joshua Spooner, formerly of this Town; together with her Accomplices, James Buchanan, Ezra Ross and William Brooks, whom she hired to perpetrate the hellish Plot. (July 6)

Because it was the first capital trial held in the Commonwealth of Massachusetts, and because of Bathsheba Spooner's involvement as an accessary, the case has attracted the attention of several legal historians. The first account was Peleg W. Chandler, ed., "Trial of Mrs. Spooner and Others," *2 American Criminal Trials* (Boston, 1844), 1-58. A second account was Samuel Swett Green, "The Case of Bathsheba Spooner," *5 American Antiquarian Society Proceedings, New Series* (Worcester, 1889), 430-36. A third account was John D. Lawson, ed., "The Trial of Bathsheba Spooner, William Brooks, James Buchanan and Ezra Ross for the Murder of Joshua Spooner, Massachusetts, 1778," *2 American State Trials* (St. Louis, 1914), 175-201.

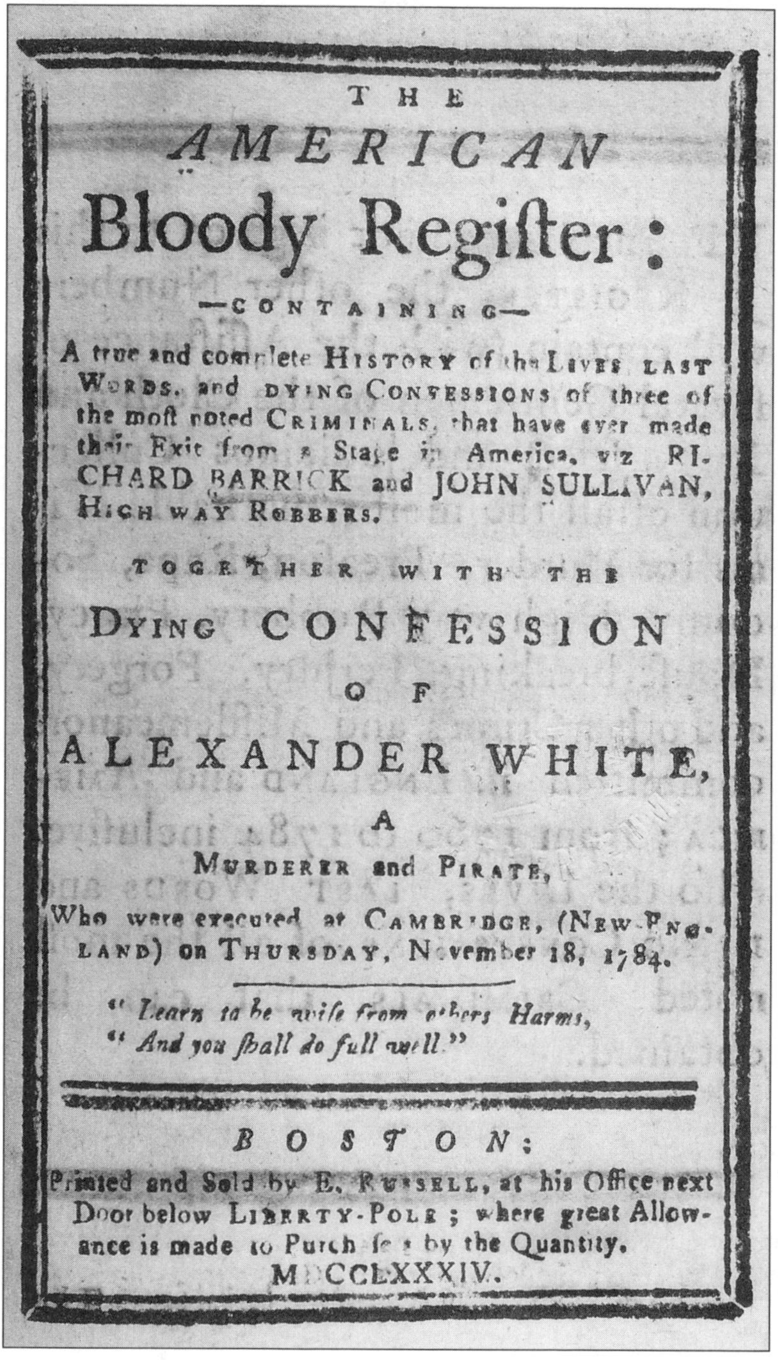

THE

*AMERICAN*

Bloody Regiſter:

—CONTAINING—

A true and complete HISTORY of the LIVES, LAST WORDS, and DYING CONFESSIONS of three of the moſt noted CRIMINALS, that have ever made their Exit from a Stage in America, viz RICHARD BARRICK and JOHN SULLIVAN, HIGH WAY ROBBERS.

TOGETHER WITH THE

DYING CONFESSION

OF

ALEXANDER WHITE,

A

MURDERER and PIRATE,

Who were executed at CAMBRIDGE, (NEW-ENGLAND) on THURSDAY, November 18, 1784.

*" Learn to be wiſe from others Harms,*
*" And you ſhall do full well."*

*BOSTON:*

Printed and Sold by E. RUSSELL, at his Office next Door below LIBERTY-POLE; where great Allowance is made to Purchaſers by the Quantity.

MDCCLXXXIV.

# *The American Bloody Register*

## [ 1784 ]

*A* LETTER *to* JOHN SULLIVAN, *one of the unhappy Criminals, who were executed on Thursday,* Nov. 18, 1784, *for Highway Robbery, on* Winter-Hill. Boston Goal, *Nov.* 10, 1784.

I Received your Letter of the sixth, and should have sent you an answer the same day, but Mr. *Bradish* was in a hurry. My dear souls, I am heartily sorry for You and *Richard Barrick* both.—Likewise *Thomas O'Neil* and *Cornelius Airy* heartily sympathize with me on your unhappy situation.—We are all well, my dear souls, and heartily pray Almighty GOD to receive your souls in glory. We sincerely beseech you to give yourselves into the hands of Almighty GOD, for he is the only friend you have now to seek to and confide in.

I am your Well-wisher,
JAMES DENNIS.

*To Mr.* JOHN SULLIVAN, *under sentence of Death, in* Cambridge Goal.

IF Encouragement is given to this REGISTER, the other Numbers will contain (with the Assistance of several Gentlemen of the Cloth and Bar) a select and judicious Collection of all the most remarkable Trials for Murder, Treason, Rape, Sodomy, High-way Robbery, Piracy, House-breaking, Perjury, Forgery, and other Crimes and Misdemeanors committed in ENGLAND and AMERICA; from 1760 to 1784 inclusive. Also the LIVES, LAST WORDS and DYING CONFESSIONS of the most noted CRIMINALS that can be obtained.

The SECOND EDITION of BICKERSTAFF's true and genuine BOSTON ALMANACK for the Year of our REDEMPTION 1785, is now selling by the PRINTER, either by the thousand, groce, or lesser quantity, containing a great variety of entertaining matter in prose and verse—The Public may rely on the correctness of the *Courts* in this Almanack, (they having been carefully revised by a Gentleman learned in the law) notwithstanding the *false* and *ungenerous* assertion of a PRINTER to the contrary. Large allowance to Travelling-Traders, Country-Shop-keepers and others who purchase by the quantity.

THE
LIFE AND DYING CONFESSION OF
RICHARD BARRICK, HIGH-WAY ROBBER.

I *RICHARD BARRICK*, was born in *Ireland*, in the month of February, in the year 1763, and brought up in the Foundling-Hospital: I never could read nor write. At ten years of age I went as apprentice to *James Saunders*, a Silk-weaver in *Spittlefield* Parish, lived with my master about three years, but he starved and froze me almost to death, for which I left him, and roved through the streets, and frequently stole small things from shop-windows.

I WENT to *Salt-petre Bank* and joined a gang of thieves. We stole from many people for a space of a year; when I was taken up for stealing a handkerchief, and carried before the Lord Mayor of *London*, who sent me to goal. I was tried and found not *innocent*; was complimented with thirteen stripes, *which is Continental colours*, signifying, that I should be honoured in *America* with the *Hibernian* coat of arms, i.e. two sticks *rampant*, one couchant, a string *pendant*, and an *Irishman* at the end of it.

I JOINED my old gang again, and continued picking pockets for one year, and then was taken up and committed to goal, and lay there eleven weeks for trial; then tried and found guilty. They told me they would pardon me if I would enter on board one of his Majesty's ships; this I consented to, but made my escape before I got to the ship. I returned back to *Salt-petre Bank*, where I joined my old companions in iniquity; went on picking pockets for six months, and was apprehended on suspicion of robbery, and was sent on board a vessel in which I came to *New-York*.

THEN I deserted and went to *Long-Island*, and lived with Mr. *Volentine Williams*; I left him and lived with Mr. *Kirk*, fifteen months, intending to learn Paper-Making. *During this time I was as honest as the times would allow.* I left Mr. *Kirk*, and went to *Horse-Neck*, intending to return to the place from whence I came, and follow my old trade of *Basket-Making*.

SOON after this, I and my comrades went to *Long Island*, with an intent to rob *James Ulits*; but the weather being very severe, we turned back. On our return, we met a *British* vessel which we boarded, and carried her into *Stanford*. We then went back to Mr. *Ulit's* in the night, and told him he must get up, for his brother's child was very sick.—He supposing us to be robbers, call'd for his firelock: We then forced in at the windows, and demanded his money. He said he had none; but his wife asked us how much we wanted? I answered one hundred pounds, Mr. *Ulit* went down cellar with a light in his hand, and we followed him; he took a horn from under a hogshead, which contained one hundred and ninety odd guineas. He then atempted to count out our hundred pound which we demanded; but we told him that as he made some resistance at first, we would take all he had. He then gave us another horn, which contained about forty guineas: Then he gave us a number of dollars. We went out of the house, but soon concluded that if he had so many guineas, it was more than probable he had some other sort of gold; therefore we went back and demanded the remainder. Then he gave us another horn, containing thirty-two half joes. We also took his plate and cloathing, to the value of one hundred dollars. We ordered him to give us some liquor; he obeyed us. Then we went back to our boat unmolested, and gave the man who took care of the boat two guineas.

AFTER this we went to *Copt-Island*, where we divided our booty.

FROM thence we went to *Greenwich*, and tarried there until our money grew short: Then we went over to *Long-Island*, to the house of one *Allberson*, where we knocked at the door and demanded a light: We then demanded his money: He gave us money and plate to the amount of two hundred dollars: We eat and drank in his house, and then ordered him to keep the matter secret for three weeks, which I have reason to think he was fool enough to comply with. After dividing the booty, I returned to *Stanford*, and tarried there until my money grew short.

I AND my comrades went to *Long-Island*, and order'd one *Peter Sniffing* to open his door, which he did; we then made a civil demand upon him, which was, *Give us all your money*; he said he had none. (Take notice that as *Sniffing* knew me, I did not enter the house:) After his refusal one of our gang came out to me for advice: I told him to flash a pistol in *Sniffing's* face, and then he would comply; but this had not the desired effect; for *Sniffing* had two pistols and other weapons: However, we disarmed and robbed him of money and cloathing.

WE went from there to *Cow-Neck*, and attacked the house of Mr. *John Mitchel*; his wife saw us coming, upon which she blew out the candles and bar'd the doors: We ordered him to open the door, which he refused; then we burst the door open with a stone. One of *Mitchel*'s family fired at us and wounded one of our gang. *Mitchel* fell upon the wounded man who cried for mercy. We retired a little way and held consultation: Our leader said that one man was wounded and should not be left behind; then we made the second attack upon the house, but was obliged to retreat again; then we made the third attack, upon which they left the room: We then brought off the wounded man, who (like a true christian) begged us to retaliate upon *Mitchel*, as he was unable to do it himself. All we took from the house was the firearms: Then we went to our boat; one of our party said he wanted some retaliation; that one returned back and met *Mitchel*'s son at the door, whom he instantly shot dead. After he had shot the young man he said he had got satisfaction in behalf of his wounded partner. We made the best of our way to the boat and went to *New-Rochel*, where we was hailed by the guard: We told them we had a man wounded by the Refugees. We ran away from the guard, leaving our boat and all behind except our fire-arms.

WE went to *Greenwich* and gave relief to our wounded partner; there I parted with my comrades. From thence I went to *New-Haven*, intending to get some employment. I got no work there, and went to *Norwich*—No employment there, I returned to *Greenwich*, where I met with the wounded man, in company with a well man. The well man went with me to *Long-Island*. We intended to rob the house of Mr. *Titus*; but a guard being kept at his house, we hid in a swamp, and went from thence to *Sand's-Point*.

AFTER this I and others broke open the house of Mr. *James Mots*, and took from him fifty guineas, besides plate and cloathing, to the amount of two hundred pounds. We went to *Greenwich* and divided the booty: Then we parted and met again in a fortnight. Then we went to the house of Mr. *John Sands* on *Long-Island*. Mr. *Sands* let us in, I demanded his money: He denied having any. I made a search and found fourteen dollars, one silver spoon, twenty-three guineas and one half joe, together with cloathing and plate, to the amount of ten pounds: Then we made off, but was pursued so close that one of our party was taken. We rescued him; but the pursuers pressed so hard upon us, that they took two more of our party, and brought them to trial; but they availed themselves of a stratagem, and told a false story; for they told the pursuers that they were not in our gang; but were endeavouring to take us prisoners. I escaped myself and kept concealed some time. I hid in a hollow rock. After this I went to *Hog-Island*, in company with other sinners. We robbed one Mr. *Ledlow* of six dollars and a watch, and a quantity of cloathing. We returned to *Greenwich*, from thence to *Heton's-Neck*; There we broke open a house and robbed the master of one hundred and sixty dollars, and cloathing to the amount of thirty dollars.

AFTER that we went to *Greenwich*; and from thence to *Long-Island*, and broke open Mr. *Allberson's* house, and robbed him of twenty-four dollars. (It may not be amiss to notice here, that I had robbed this man once before.) The next night we went into the house of one Mr. *Parsons*, and demanded his money; but there being fifteen or sixteen folks in the house, we could not collect them all together. The man of the house went on the roof and sounded an alarm. We went into the chamber and found an iron chest, but could not break it open, nor get it out of the room: The neighbours raised a party who fired upon us; but we made our escape.

AFTER this we went to *Long-Island* and were discovered; therefore we hid ourselves several days. Then we went with an intent to rob one *Henry Post*, but were discovered, and ran into the woods. We went to a house that night and demanded a supper; they gave us one.

SOON after this we set out for *New-York*, but were taken and carried before a *British* Colonel and examined; they asked my name, and told me they wanted to catch *Barrick*: (They did not know I was the man.) I told them my name was *Richard Willis*. The Colonel ordered a party to escort me out of the lines; but unluckily for me we met with a party of about twenty. They asked our party if they had got *Barrick*? The answer was, They had not; but one of their party knew me and called me by my right name, and says, *Now we have you we will keep you*. Then they bound me and kept me in that situation for almost five weeks.

THE people I had robbed came to see me, to know whether they could swear to me out of the whole gang, There were but two of the spectators could swear to me, viz. *Allberson* and *Robbins*.

(****For the remainder of* BARRICK's *Life*, (*which contains a series of heinous crimes perpetrated in* Philadelphia, New-York, Hartford, New-Haven, *in* Boston *Market, at the vendues and on* Winter-Hill) *we must refer our Readers to the Second Number of our* REGISTER, *which we shall publish immediately. In the same Number we intend to publish the remarkable conver-*

*sion of* Alexander White, *the Pirate; as we could not possibly procure the copy time enough for this Publication—In the subsequent Numbers will also be published the remarkable lives and dying confessions of a number of pirates, murderers, high-way robbers, house-breakers, &c. which can be obtained from* England *and* America. *We acknowledge the receipt of the remarkable trial, life and dying behavior of* Earl Ferrers, *convicted in England for murder; and the trial, life, and dying confession of* William Corbett, *who was born at* Portsmouth, *in* New-Hampshire; *who was also convicted in* England *of the most atrocious and cruel murder of a man and his wife; for which he was executed and his body afterwards hung in chains, as a warning to others to avoid the crime.*)

In the Press at Printing-Office hereof, and in a few Days will be published,

A excellent SERMON, entitled, "Paradise promised by a dying SAVIOUR, to the penitent Thief on the Cross." Delivered at *Cambridge*, on Thursday the Eighteenth of November, immediately preceding the Execution of ALEXANDER WHITE, RICHARD BARRICK and JOHN SULLIVAN, the former for Piracy, the latter for High-way Robbery. With an APPENDIX, exhibiting some Account of their Conversation and Behaviour in Prison, &c.

By TIMOTHY HILLIARD, A. M.

Pastor of the First Church in *Cambridge*.

## THE

## LIFE AND DYING CONFESSION OF

## JOHN SULLIVAN, HIGH-WAY ROBBER.

I *JOHN SULLIVAN*, was born in *Ireland* in the town of *Limrick*, and was eighteen years old last April. I shall minute down my crimes in the order I committed them.

Crime 1. I inlisted as a soldier in the *British* service in the year 1777, and took five pounds bounty; the Captain's name was *Thomas*, of the thirty-sixth regiment. Went to *Bristol*, in order to join the army, but deserted.

Crime 2. Went to *Wales* with an intent to inlist the second time, but alter'd my mind and enter'd on board the *Saris* frigate, in the King's service, bound to *New-York*: I staid on board near three weeks, and then deserted. I went to *Long-Island*, and there was press'd on board a vessel, staid on board eleven weeks and then deserted.

Crime 3. I enter'd on board a sloop bound to *New-York*, but hawl'd in at *Loyd's-Neck*: When I landed I was discover'd and pursued by the Doctor of my former vessel; he was on horseback, and drove me into the water, but

NUMBER I. of the

BLOODY REGISTER.

REPRESENTATION of the MURDER of Capt. WHITE, on board his Schooner, by ALEXANDER WHITE, the PIRATE.

MURDER, though it has no Tongue will speak with most miraculous Organs. SHAKESPEAR.

was obliged to come on shore and surrender; I then received thirty-nine lashes.

Crime 4. The same night I deserted and swam to another vessel commanded by one *Kelley*: The master and I combined together, and stole the vessel, carried her into *Stonington* and sold her: I received about three hundred dollars for my share.

Crime 5. From *Stonington* I went to *New-London*, and entered on board a privateer *John Buckley* commander: tarried on board three months; took some prizes. I then entered on board another privateer, commanded by *James Woodworth*; after a months cruise was taken by the *British* and carried into *New-York*, and put on board the guardship, where remained three days, and then was put on board the Lesophe, where I remained 11 weeks: I came to *Staten-Island*, where I deserted. I went from thence to *Marrineck* where I was hailed by a small party, and ordered to stand: I had a firelock with me and fired on them, but they took me prisoner, and carried me to *Horse-Neck*, where Col. *Camfield* commanded; the Colonel examined me and gave me a pass to go to *Stanford*, where I became acquainted with *Barrick*, who is condemned to die with me.

Crime 6. In August one thousand seven hundred and eighty two, I happened in company with a young lad; he and I laid down to take rest. After he got to sleep I searched his pockets and stole one guinea and one crown. After this I entered on board a whale-boat with the person I stole the money from, we went a cruise and came into *Stonington*, where I was accused of stealing the guinea and crown, but denied it: They searched me and found the money tied up in the tail of my shirt; they cut off my shirt-tail and left me. I went to Col. *Davenport* and he gave me a pass to go to *New-London*: I there entered on board a privateer commanded by *Isaac Wherar*. We went about eight days cruise, and by distress of weather got dismasted: Our vessel being a wreck and unable to defend ourselves, we were taken by a *British* vessel and carried to *Bermudas*. I then engaged with the Captain who took me prisoner to go to sea with him. I took twenty dollars bounty. I never went on board after I received the money and cloaths; but rode off on my ten toes and left them.

Crime 7. I went about seven miles to a place called *Cole-Lane*, and engaged to go on board a privateer, took twenty-four dollars from the Captain and then bid them good night. I next went to *St. Georges;* there I enter'd on board another privateer, Capt. *Hall* commander, and took twenty-four dollars in bounty: We went five weeks cruise and returned to *Bermudas*. Being destitute of all things, I endeavoured to help myself to that which *Soloman* says *will answer all things;* and knowing that one *Gutheridge* kept a store there, I took a partner with me and broke open his store, where we found a barrel of dollars; we took our pockets and hats full, and then went to a place called *Salt-Kittles* and changed the silver for gold.

Crime 8. Three weeks after this I entered on board Capt. *Vezey*, bound to *St. Thomas's:* Peace being proclaimed, I went to *North-Carolina*. I went from thence to *Portsmouth*, where I went to work three weeks: Then I and my partner broke open a store in the day-time, and took out twenty-four half-joes and some silver; my comrade was taken up on suspicion and carried before a Justice, but made his escape; and as I was not suspected, was sent to catch him; I followed on until I overtook him, and he and I contrived the matter between us, so that he gave me his shoes and buckles to carry, and tell the injured people that I pursued him so close that he was obliged to drop his shoes and buckles, and for this piece of villainy they rewarded (what they falsely called) my fidelity with two dollars.

Crime 9. I then went to *Baltimore* and entered on board a pilot-boat and went to *Philadelphia*: Then went from thence to *New-York*. I then entered myself on board a transport bound to *Scotland*. I suspected there was money on board, nor was my suspicion groundless, for I and one more found a chest, and breaking it open took out forty pounds: Then made our escape to *New-York*.

Crime 9. [sic] Soon after this I got a new comrade, and we broke open a shop and took out the value of a hundred pounds in money and watches. I then went to *Newbury-Port*, where I entered on board Capt. *Wheelwright* bound for the *West-Indies*: When I arrived there I went into a trader's shop and took to the value of forty pounds, in goods. Soon after this I took another comrade and walking out we met a man in the road: We told him we wanted some money, and some we would have; the man gave us three crowns. After this I returned to *Boston*.

Crime 10. On Friday night before Commencement, *Barrick* and I went to *Roxbury* with an intent to rob any person, but we were disappointed. The next Monday night we went upon the old errand but no booty. Soon after this we went to *Winter-Hill*, and there we fell in with one Mr. *Baldwin*. *Barrack*, and I stopt said *Baldwin*, and rob'd him of his watch and money. I took the watch out of *Baldwin*'s pocket, but *Poor* was the man that abused and gave him heavy blows. For this last crime I am to suffer death.—These are the most capital crimes I have committed, and I sincerely wish that others may avoid the rock I have split upon.

*JOHN SULLIVAN.*

Compiled from the Prisoner's mouth by ELISHA BREWER, of *East-Sudbury*.
Transcribed by WILLIAM BILLINGS, of *Boston*.
Attest, ISAAC BRADISH, Goaler.

## THE CONFESSION OF ALEXANDER WHITE, PIRATE.

THIS is to give satisfaction to all enquiring Friends, that I *ALEXANDER WHITE*, was born in *Ireland*, in the County of *Tyrone*, in the year of our Lord one thousand seven hundred and sixty-two, and was brought up in said place, and got what education my Parents thought necessary. After I grew up, my mind being inclined to see strange countries against my Parent's will. I took my departure from *Ireland*, and went to *England* and bound myself apprentice to learn the Mariner's art, and served my Master faithfully until it pleased him to give up my indentures.

I STILL followed the occupation of a Mariner, and improved my education 'till I thought myself fit to take the command of a vessel. I have been through many scenes of life, and always endeavoured to support the character of an honest man, and I believe I was harmless to any body but myself. It is needless for me to give an account of how I spent my life; for I have been in many parts of the world, but never did any thing that would cause me to blush or be ashamed before I transacted this heinous crime that I am to suffer for.

If you are desirous to know what this temptation did arise from; with shame I will endeavour to inform you: At first when I met with Capt. *White*, it was in *Philadelphia*. My money being almost spent I agreed to go to *Nova-Scotia* with him. Accordingly we pursued our intended voyage as far as *New-York*, and there we took on board our cargo, and came to a place called *Cow-Harbour*, in *Long-Island*, and there tarried some days and took on board the passenger *John Vail*, and sailed quickly from thence.

MY mind being very uneasy on account of a young lady who I proposed to marry, and only the want of money prevented our being married. Being below her degree, and being ashamed to own my necessity, prolonged our being joined in wedlock. But Love began to burn my poor and wounded heart; and being resolved to go through any difficulty that might impede us, I intended to take the life of my fellow-creature; one evening seeing a good opportunity, I took up an ax, and with it struck Capt. *White* over board, and attempted to murder the passenger also; but when I found I could not accomplish my purpose, surrendered myself a prisoner.

I was confined for some time. Towards morning we fell in with a vessel, who carried me into *Plymouth* as a prisoner, and remained there for a considerable time, which I spent in anguish, imploring mercy from GOD, for the crime I had committed. Then I was sent to *Cambridge*, and condemned to die by my own confession; And, agreeable to my inclination, (chusing rather to die than to live.) Time would fail me to give a particular account of this affair; but this is the truth that I have set forth, which I declare as a dying criminal.

ALEXANDER WHITE.

Compiled from the Prisoner's mouth by ELISHA BREWER, of *East-Sudbury.*
Transcribed by WILLIAM BILLINGS, of *Boston.*
Attest, ISAAC BRADISH, Goaler.

(*For a concise and accurate Account of the behaviour and conversation of the Prisoners [particularly of* White *the Pirate] while in prison and in their last moments; also a pathetic and affectionate Address to the Prisoners, we must refer our Readers to Number II. of this* REGISTER, *or to the* APPENDIX *of an excellent* SERMON, *preached at their Execution, by the Reverend Mr.* HILLIARD, *of* Cambridge, *who attended them during their Confinement—We should have readily gratified our Readers with the above interesting particulars, but it was out of our power, as the copy was handed to us but a few hours before this Publication. We shall endeavour (on suitable encouragement to this infant Work) to furnish Number II. with an elegant copperplate engraving, executed by an ingenious Artist.*)

## NUMBER II. of the AMERICAN BLOODY REGISTER:

*THE kind and generous Reception of the* First Number *of this* REGISTER *has induced the Publisher to continue the Work, and hopes to lay before the Publick, from Time to Time, a Number of curious and useful Pieces, which has been handed to him by several Friends.*

*THE curious* TRIAL *of Lady* NEWTON *for* ADULTERY *with her Groom, &c. came too late for this Number, but shall be inserted in our next.*

*THE bloody and cruel History of The* KING *of* ROBBERS *and* MURDERERS: *Being a most surprising and shocking Account of the horrid Massacre of more than Twelve Hundred Men, Women and Children in Twenty-five Years, will be in our next.*

*THE Confession of the barbarous* MARGARET STILLWELL, *executed in* New-York *for the Murder of a Child; with several others are received, and shall be attended to.*

*THE Gentleman who promised to furnish some Confessions from* Philadelphia *and* New-York, *would oblige the Publisher by sending them as soon as possible.*

*SOME shocking Accounts receiv'd from* England, &c. *must be deferred for the present.*

> Rejoice, O young Man in thy Youth, and let thy Heart chear thee in the Days of thy Youth; but know ye that for all these Things GOD will bring thee into Judgment.
>
> SOLOMON.

## THE LIFE AND DYING CONFESSION OF RICHARD BARRICK, HIGH-WAY ROBBER.

[ *Continued from No. II. P.* 16. ]

THE Colonel ordered me from *Long-Island* to *New-York* goal for trial; where I remained three weeks, and then broke goal.

I RETURNED to *Greenwich,* and was there re-taken for the same crime, and carried back to *New-York* goal.

I BROKE out the second time and returned to *Greenwich.*

THEN I went to *Philadelphia* and there I was taken up and committed to goal for *Burglary,* and tried for my life; but was acquitted. I was sent back to goal and had another trial and found guilty of theft. Then I was sent back to the work-house, to pick oakum for a month and pay fifteen pounds fine. *(It may be noted here, that I had been confined in the dungeon in* Philadelphia *six weeks before.)* I tarried in the work-house one fortnight and then ran away to *New-York.* There I found some companions in iniquity; they assisted me to break open a house, out of which we stole about six pounds worth in cloathing.

AFTER this I attempted to break open a house in *New-Haven,* but was prevented.

I THEN set out for *Hartford;* and on my way I broke open a house and stole a necklace and some cloathing; but I was apprehended, carried before a justice, and ordered to pay a fine, which I did.

FROM thence I set out for *Boston,* and on my way I took some small matters. When I arrived there I was short of money, so that I stole a pocket-book out of a man's pocket: The book contained about three hundred pounds in consolidated notes. I attempted to sell them, but the person I first offered them to, told me the notes were cried by the common Cryer: Well, said I, that is true, and I have found them; upon which the man went and informed the owner, who gave me ten dollars for what he (falsely) called my trouble. Soon after this I stole a bag out of a man's pocket at vendue; but the sum did not answer my expectation; for it did not exceed eight dollars. Then I went to another vendue and stole a man's pocket-book, containing about sixty pounds. Then I went to another vendue and also robbed a man of his pocket-book, containing about ninety pounds in consolidated notes, together with some other notes; I threw the notes away. Then I robbed *Peter Hays* of his pocket-book, but found it of no service to me, therefore I ordered the Cryer to cry, in consequence of which the owner recovered it again. The Reader may here observe, that my intention was to take his money, but failed in the attempt. Soon after this I robbed a man in *Boston*-Market of a silk purse, containing about four dollars. Then I went to a vendue and robbed a man of his purse, containing about two dollars. Then I went to the Market and robbed a *Frenchman* of his pocket-book; he had it cried, offering two dollars reward: I carried it to the Cryer and received the reward. Next I robbed a man in State-Street of a purse, containing ten dollars. Next I robbed a man of his pocket-book, but observing I was discover'd by a by-stander, I drop'd the pocket-book and cry'd out, *Who has lost a pocket-book?* The right owner claimed it and gave me a dollar for picking it up. Then I went to the Market and robbed a man of one crown. Then I went to a vendue and robbed a man of two crowns. Then I went to the Market and stole two dollars.

THEN I went to *Roxbury,* intending to break open a store: I attempted to undermine the same, but failed in the design.

THEN I went to *Boston,* and from thence to *Winter-Hill,* near *Charlestown,* and being in company with *John Sullivan,* we met with one Mr. *Baldwin. Sullivan* and I stopped said *Baldwin* and robbed him of his watch and money. *Sullivan* took the watch out of *Baldwin*'s pocket, but

*Poor* was the man that gave him the severe blows. For this crime we are shortly to suffer death.

AND now to conclude, I declare that there is scarcely a crime in nature but what I have been guilty of (except murder, and that never entered my heart.) I have been (according to the best of my remembrance) in every goal in *London,* and I acknowledge very justly, and nothing but my youth excused me from the halter: And as far as my memory serves, I have been guilty of three times as many crimes as I have related.

BUT one thing I must not omit, *viz.* I know a number of my fellow-sinners, who live within six or eight miles of this place, who are as bad or worse than myself (the number I mention is from six to ten;) but I have made such solemn promises to secret them, that I had rather die than betray them.

FOR myself as well as for my fellow-prisoners, I sincerely return thanks to the Gentlemen of the Clergy, and Friends of every denomination, for their kind and tender admonitions, warnings and counsels; and for their liberality to us, whilst in Prison. We also return our unfeigned thanks to Mr. BRADISH and Family, who have at all times shewn their kind regard to us all during our confinement; Mr. Goaler having treated us more like children than criminals under sentence of death. May Almight GOD reward them all infinitely more than we can ask for.

RICHARD BARRICK.

Compiled from the Prisoner's mouth, by ELISHA BREWER, of *East-Sudbury.*
Transcribed by WILLIAM BILLINGS, of *Boston.*
Attest, ISAAC BRADISH, Goaler.
CAMBRIDGE-GOAL,
*Nov.* 17, 1784.

*An exact* COPY *of a* LETTER *indited by* ALEXANDER WHITE, *Pirate, directed to Mrs.* PHEBE BARRICK, *the unhappy and disconsolate Wife and Parents of the unfortunate* RICHARD BARRICK, *Robber.*

TAKE these as the last lines from Your undutiful Husband, and may GOD be a Husband to You and direct you for the best, as I shall soon be no more.

MY Dear, I am very sorry to inform You of my disagreable situation of being under sentence of Death, which grieves me to leave You and my dear Child behind me: But I leave you in the hands of GOD, who will be a Husband and Father to you. My Dear altho' I am going to eternity I shall leave my heart with You.

AT my departure from You I promised to return in a short time, but

GOD has otherwise ordered it, and you must be content. My Dear, although Death approaches, and the time draws near that I must appear before the Great Tribunal of GOD, and there give an Account of all my life that I have spent, pursuing the vanities and follies of this world; for which I have to stand before the Great JUDGE of the Universe, and I hope to have a favorable Sentence passed on my poor immortal soul.

*My Dear* FATHER *and tender* MOTHER,

I BEG that You would take care of my Child, and bring him up in the fear of GOD, and give him such an education as you may see requisite.

*Dear* FRIENDS *and* NEIGHBOURS,

I BEG that no reflections may be cast on the innocent Child hereafter, for the untimely death of his unhappy Father.

*My dear* PHEBE,

I THANK You for Your tenderness to me, and may GOD reward You accordingly. It is the prayer of Your unfortunate Husband, that GOD may bless You forevermore.

*I remain your dying* HUSBAND,
*RICHARD BARRICK.*

*P. S.* You will oblige me to write as soon as this comes to hand, and direct to me at *Cambridge,* to the care of Mr. ISAAC BRADISH.

*Some* ACCOUNT *of the Trial, Religious Conversation and Dying Behaviour of* ALEXANDER WHITE: *Also, many Particulars relating to* RICHARD BARRICK *and* JOHN SULLIVAN; *which is kindly handed to us by a Reverend* CLERGYMAN, *who constantly attended them in Prison and in their last Moments.—This Narrative of Facts is now inserted in our* REGISTER, *with a View to inforce good Government and Piety among Children and Servants, and to shew the Necessity of restraining them from Vice and Immorality in their Youth.—GOD grant it may have the desired Effect.*

ALEXANDER WHITE, when brought upon his Trial before the Honourable Supreme Judicial Court, for Murder and Piracy on the High Seas, pleaded GUILTY. The Court seemed much affected with his plea and the rehearsal of his story. They did not direct his plea to be recorded, but remanded him to prison, informing him that they would consider further of his case the next morning. Upon his appearing at the Bar the second time he pleaded as before. The Court were so tender of his case, that they proceeded to examine sundry witnesses; and after they had gone through their evidence, *White* declared that they had related the circumstances of the affair as nearly as possibly could be expected.

AT the first Pastoral Visit, which was made him in *Cambridge,* it was particularly enquired, Why he accused himself before the Court in a trial for his life? He answered, that his conscience informed him that he was guilty, and that as his life was forfeited, he wished not to retain it.—It was then observed, that pleading *not guilty* amounted to nothing more than putting one's self upon trial.—He said he was sensible of that, but knowing that he had murdered an innocent man, it appeared to him his duty to confess it before GOD and men; he added, that he believed the evidence was not sufficient to convict him, but he chose to suffer the punishment due to his crime.—It was then observed to him, that Death was a solemn and important event, and that the fear of it is a passion deeply implanted in human nature; and particular enquiry was made upon what grounds he was so reconciled to it? He said, that he had, soon after the commission of his crime, framed a story, in which he endeavoured to throw the guilt upon the Passenger; but that after he was committed to prison at *Plymouth,* he was brought under deep conviction of the evil of sin, and was for several weeks in the utmost anguish and distress; that he read the Word of GOD and other books of devotion with the utmost attention and care, and frequently received visits from Mr. *Robbins* and other Ministers and Friends, who gave him the best advice in their power; and also that he heard sundry Sermons which were well adapted to his case. He further said, that as he was mourning on account of his crimes with penitential sorrow, he had a very lively and affecting view of the mercy of GOD through JESUS CHRIST, and that he found in himself a strong and ardent desire to submit to CHRIST in the character of a Saviour. There appeared to him to be a great change in his sentiments and views. He thought that he found in his heart a real love to GOD and JESUS CHRIST, and true benevolence to mankind.

WHEN it was observed to him, that he must be destitute of the most satisfactory evidence of a real change, *viz.* the fruits of righteousness and true holiness in the life; he said, he was aware of that, but that he felt in himself such a divine temper and disposition, and such an hearty approbation of the ways of GOD and religion, that he had strong hope of final acceptance and everlasting life.

EVERY time he was visited, he appeared very humble, serious and prayerful. He spake of death with great calmness and composure, and declared himself perfectly reconciled to it, from a strong persuasion of his interest in the favour of GOD, and a confident hope of a better life. When he was asked whether he wished for a *Reprieve?* He replied that he did not on his own account; but as his Fellow-sufferers were very desirous of it he would acquiesce in it. He added, that if the prison-doors were opened to him, and he might have his liberty and life, he should rather wish to die.

SEVERAL Ministers who saw and conversed with him, were at first very apprehensive that he was a mere *Enthusiast* and that as death approached, he would change his stile: But upon further conversation, when the time of execution was at hand, they seemed more satisfied of his sincerity. It is worthy of notice, that he took great pains to enlighten his Fellow-sufferers, by reading to them the Scriptures and other good books, by counsels and exhortations, and that he often prayed with and for them.

AS he was going to the place of execution, he was asked, Whether he now heartily approved of the method of salvation through JESUS CHRIST, and could trust in his merits and mediation for pardon and eternal life? He said, that it appeared to him most wise and excellent, and that he had not the least wish for any other way of life than that through JESUS CHRIST, and that he did entirely depend on the rich grace and mercy of GOD, through him, for pardon and salvation. When enquiry was made, Whether his faith and hope continued as strong and vigorous as ever? He said they really did, and that he viewed death with the utmost complacency and satisfaction; and further said, that if these graces should fail him to his last moments, he would openly declare it: He added, that he ardently wished the prosperity and success of the kingdom of the Redeemer among men: He prayed very earnestly with his last breath and died commending his soul into the hands of GOD.

IN this recital, the stile of the Prisoner could not be exactly recollected; but his ideas are represented as nearly as possible. Many other questions were proposed to him, the recording of which would too far protract this Narrative.—These facts are submitted, leaving every one to form his own judgment upon so singular a case.

*Richard Barrick* and *John Sullivan* appeared exceedingly ignorant, and owned that they had never been taught to read. *Barrick* said that he never knew his Parents, but was sent very young to the Foundling-Hospital. It was observed to him that proper provision was made there for the instruction of children. He said that this was the case in some parts of it, but not in others.—*Sullivan* said, that his Parents were solicitous for the education of their children, and that of eleven he was the only one which was not taught; and that this was owing to his refractory temper and disobedience to his Parents. When enquiry was made, Whether they believed the being and perfections of GOD, and that men would be happy or miserable after death according to their conduct in this life? They answered in the affirmative. They were asked, Whether they were sensible of the exceeding evil of sin, as it is opposite to a holy GOD, and their need of pardon and mercy through JESUS CHRIST? They seemed at a loss for an answer, and said they did not understand it. No small pains was taken by sundry Ministers to lead them to a proper sense of their state, and to open to them the way of salvation through CHRIST.

AT the first visit they pretended to deny that they were guilty of the Robbery at *Winter-Hill,* for which they had been convicted; but after sentence of Death was pronounced by the Court, they both owned the fact.

HAVING formed an inveterate habit of vice in early life, and been destitute of instruction and discipline, it was extremely difficult to make any impression upon them. They said they were afraid to die, sensible that they were unprepared, and wished for more time.—As the day of execution approached, they seemed considerably affected, and said they were heartily sorry for all their sins, and wished for mercy through JESUS CHRIST. As they advanced to the Gallows, they seemed much distressed and continued crying to GOD through CHRIST, until the moment arrived which ushered them into eternity.——Thus much is mentioned with respect to these unhappy Men, to shew the extreme danger of neglecting the proper Education and Government of Children, and the necessity of restraining them, while young, from sinful excesses.

*A true and faithful* ACCOUNT *of the Life, dying Behaviour and last Words of* JOHN DIXON, *who was executed, agreeable to his Sentence, at* TAUNTON, *in the County of* Bristol, *on Thursday, Nov.* 11, 1784, *for* BURGLARY. *His last Words was delivered to a crouded Auditory, whilst standing on his Coffin under the Gallows: Which Account is handed to us by a respectable* GENTLEMAN, *who was very near the Prisoner in his last Moments, and is as follows,* viz.

TAUNTON, NOVEMBER 15, 1784.

THURSDAY last, between the hours of eleven and three, JOHN DIXON was executed here, agreeable to his sentence.—DIXON said he was born in the town of *East-Haddam,* in the State of *Connecticut,* in the year one thousand seven hundred and sixty-two: He said he had a Mother, Brother and Sister, now living in good credit in the above Place.

DIXON's conduct in prison, previous to his trial, was intermixt with profanity and dissoluteness, gratifying every lust which his close confinement would possibly admit of. But after his trial, and receiving his sentence, the poor deluded man was, in some measure, brought to a sense of his sorrowful situation, and conducted himself with a decency becoming a person under sentence of Death: He was frequently attended by the several Ministers of this and the neighbouring towns, who, with prayers, tears and solemn admonitions, discharged their duty to GOD and the unhappy Prisoner, as faithful Ambassadors and Servants of JESUS CHRIST.

HE was taken from the prison-house in the morning by the Sheriff and his Under-Officers, attended by a Guard of one hundred men, decently equipped, under the command of Col. Crossman, together with between two and three thousand Spectators, and conducted to the Meeting-House, where a Sermon pertinent to the occasion was preached by the Reverend Mr. FORBES, of *Roynham,* from the following words, to *Luke* xxiii. 41, 42: *And be said unto* JESUS, LORD *remember me when thou comest into thy kingdom.* JESUS *said unto him, Verily I say unto thee, to-day shall thou be with me in Paradise.*—From the Meeting-House the Prisoner was taken to the place of execution, by the Sheriff and his Guards, where a concluding Prayer, suitable and affectionate, was made by the Reverend Mr. JUDSON, of *Taunton.*

AFTER the usual ceremonies of reading the process and warrant, the unhappy Criminal stept into the cart, and standing upon his coffin, addressed the audience, nearly in the following words:

My BRETHREN and FRIENDS,

I WOULD solemnly warn and caution you all against hard drinking, gaming and keeping bad company: for following these practices is what has brought me to this untimely end. And I desire you all to take warning by me, and avoid the bad practices I have run into.——As I was brought an entire stranger into this place, and there was no person knew me, neither had I knowledge of any of you, I return my sincere and hearty thanks to all my Friends and Acquaintance in *Taunton* for the many favours they have bestowed upon me. I also acknowledge the many kindnesses shewn to me by Mr. DEAN, Ostler his Family, during my confinement in prison; if I had been their child they could not have shewn more respect; they never denied me any thing for my comfort by night or day.——And all you People of *Taunton*, I thank you for your respect to me, and hope GOD will bless and prosper you all. AMEN.

The cart moved off about two o'clock, and after the Criminal had hanged about twenty-five minutes, he was taken down, put into his coffin and decently buried.

The Sheriff, his Under-Office[r]s and the Guards behaved themselves well, and to the universal satisfaction of all present.

## Source Notes

*The American Bloody Register* was first printed in Boston by Ezekiel Russell shortly after the executions of Barrick, Sullivan, and White on November 18, 1784. In his *History of Printing in America*, Isaiah Thomas referred to Russell as primarily a printer of ballads and pamphlets, which were sold to street peddlers. According to Thomas, "in these small articles his trade principally consisted, and afforded him a very decent support" (I, 155). Apparently, Russell indeed catered to a popular audience; his *American Bloody Register* was the first attempt to publish a criminal magazine in the United States,` and from the beginning he projected a series of "Numbers" that would narrate "the LIVES, LAST WORDS and DYING CONFESSIONS of all the most noted CRIMINALS that can be obtained" (233). Following the title page of his first "Number," he advertised that, "If Encouragement is given to this REGISTER," he would publish further accounts of "the most remarkable Trials for Murder, Treason, Rape, Sodomy, High-way Robbery, Piracy, House-breaking, Perjury, Forgery, and other Crimes" (233). But Russell did not wait for "Encouragement" to publish his second "Number." The narratives of his first issue were divided so that they would continue into the next issue; specifically, both the Barrick and White material were carried over from the first into the second "Number." A third (much shorter) narrative, "A true and faithful ACCOUNT of the Life, dying Behaviour and last Words of JOHN DIXON," also was included in "Number II." In an editorial note included on page sixteen of the first issue, directly after the Barrick narrative abruptly stopped, Russell announced: "*For the remainder of* BARRICK's *Life . . . we must refer our Readers to the Second Number of our* REGISTER, *which we shall publish immediately.*" However, in all probability, the second issue was printed at the same time as the first and then bound separately. Not only was pagination between the two issues continuous, but also the events in the Dixon narrative occurred simultaneously with those of Barrick, Sullivan, and White. Dixon was executed on November 11, a week before the two highwaymen and the pirate.

Although no copies are extant, there evidently were at least three more issues of Russell's *Register.* In several of the advertisements included in the first two issues, the printer announced to his readers those narratives intended for future "Numbers." For example, in the advertisement following the abrupt suspension of Barrick's life included on page sixteen of the first issue, Russell offered:

> *In the subsequent Numbers will also be published the remarkable lives and dying confessions of a number of pirates, murderers, high-way robbers, house-breakers, &c. which can be obtained from* England *and* America. *We acknowledge the receipt of the remarkable trial, life and dying behavior of* Earl Ferrers, *convicted in* England *for murder; and the trial, life, and dying confession of* William Corbett, *who was born at* Portsmouth, *in* New-Hampshire; *who was also convicted in* England *of the most atrocious and cruel murder of a man and his wife; for which he was executed and his body afterwards being hung in chains, as a warning to others to avoid the crime* (238).

Also, in an advertisement in beginning of *Number II*, the printer declared:

> *THE kind and generous Reception of the* First Number *of this* REGISTER *has induced the Publisher to continue the Work, and hopes to lay before the Publick, from Time to Time, a Number of curious and useful Pieces, which has been handed to him by several* Friends.
>
> *THE curious* TRIAL *of Lady* NEWTON *for* ADULTERY *with her Groom, &c. came too late for this Number, but shall be inserted in our next.*
>
> *THE bloody and cruel History of The* KING *of* ROBBERS *and* MURDERERS: *Being a most surprising and shocking Account of the horrid Massacre of more than Twelve Hundred Men, Women and Children in Twenty-five Years, will be in our next.*
>
> *THE Confession of the barbarous* MARGARET STILLWELL, *executed in* New-York *for the Murder of a Child; with several others are received, and shall be attended to* (243).

Despite his promises and projections, Russell might not have received as much copy as he needed. In the same announcement, he added:

> *THE Gentleman who promised to furnish some Confessions from* Philadelphia *and* New-York, *would oblige the Publisher by sending them as soon as possible.*
>
> *SOME shocking Accounts receiv'd from* England, &c. *must be deferred for the present* (244).

Quite possibly, the narratives of Ferrers, Corbett, Newton, and Stillwell were published in a third issue. However, other than the above announcements, no copies, references, or advertisements have been located for this third issue. But the narrative of the "KING of ROBBERS" (a reference to the sensational story of Sauny Beane, variously published in a number of popular sources) had to wait for the fourth issue.

There was, however, evidently a fourth issue. According to Charles Evans, sometime in the fall of 1789 Russell printed *The Prisoner's Magazine. Or malefactor's bloody register. No. IV.* This issue was advertised as *Containing the life and confession of Rachel Wall, William Durogan, and William Smith.* No copies of this fourth issue have been located, but there were at least two other narratives printed about the same time dealing with the three highway robbers. According to an advertisement published with his *Elegy &c.* (Boston, date unknown), Russell also intended "to insert in *Number Four* . . . the whole of the shocking and tragical Affair" of Elizabeth Wilson, including a "particular *Account* of *Miss* WILSON'S *Religious Exercises, Dying Sayings* and *Hymn of Death.*" Furthermore, in the same advertisement Russell once again announced the sensational story of the "KING of ROBBERS":

> In the REGISTER will also be published, a true and faithful Narrative of the horrid, bloody and cruel Murders (amounting it is said, to no less than twelve hundred persons, men women and children) which were perpetrated in Scotland, by those noted and audacious Murderers, Rob-

> bers and Man-eaters, SAWNEY BANE and Family, for which shocking and unheard of Deeds, they were all executed in a manner equal to their deserts, by being burnt alive.

Seeking to attract the notice of "his *Friends*, who are *Country Shop-keepers, Travelling-Traders or Town-Flys*," Russell announced "that the BLOODY REGISTER is in Press, and will be published as soon as the necessary Plates can be engraved for the pages, which will consist of near forty pages, at the very moderate price of eight pence single, with large allowance for those who buy by the hundred[,] groce or dozen."

For the narrative of Rachel Wall and related information concerning it and other publications, see below, the *Life, Last-Words and Dying Confession, of Rachel Wall* (Boston, 1789). For the narrative of Elizabeth Wilson and related information concerning it and other publications, see below, *A Faithful Narrative of Elizabeth Wilson*.

The only other reference to the continuation of Russell's series was an announcement in the November 12, 1790, issue of *The Boston Herald of Freedom* that *The Bloody Register, No. V* was "this day published." At the very least, America's first criminal magazine was published sporadically over a period of six years.

Russell borrowed more than simply his title and format from an English original. In 1764 two London booksellers, E. and E. Viney, marketed *The Bloody Register*. The sensational list of crimes that Russell advertised ("Murder, Treason, Rape, Sodomy, High-Way Robbery, Piracy, House-breaking, Perjury, Forgery, and other Crimes and Misdemeanors") was taken directly from the original's title page. Moreover, at least two of the accounts that Russell later promised (those of Earl Ferrers and William Corbett) first were published in the London original.

The Boston newspapers included several accounts of Barrick, Sullivan, and White. In the July 26, 1784, issue of *The Boston Gazette*, the following account was given describing the final crime that led to the capture, conviction, and execution of Barrick and Sullivan:

> Last Tuesday evening, about one hour after Sunset, as Mr. Cyrus Baldwin, was returning from Boston for Woburn, he was attacked near the top of Winter Hill, in Charlestown, by three Ruffians, who instantly rushed on him and robbed him of his Watch and about 14£ in Money, being all he had with him, and several other Articles; during [the] greatest part of the time they were stripping him[,] one of the Villains was dealing very heavy Blows with a Club on the left side of his Head, and cut his Scalp in several Places: his Wounds are very sore, but 'tis hoped they'll not prove Mortal—The Watch was a Pinchbeck one, with a Turtle-shell Case, and China face, with the words *Brown, Boston*, on it; a double Steel Chain, compos'd of long narrow crinkled Links, connected together with small Rings, a Brass and Steel Key, and an oval Silver Seal, not very large, [also] the Stem on the handle, a Dolphin; the Impression, an Anchor and Cable; or Hope, (as it is called). Said Seal hath a narrow Dent on one Limb of its outer Circle, which prevents its

> giving a true oval Impression. One of the Ruffians in endeavoring to twitch the Watch from the Fob, broke the Chain—so that its probable it will be furnish'd with a new Chain or String.

A week later (August 2) T*he Boston Gazette* reported: "The three Villains mentioned in our last to have robbed Mr. Cyrus Baldwin, and attempted to rob Major Swain, have since been apprehended, and committed to Goal for Tryal. Their Names are Richard Barrick, John Poor, and John Sullivan."

Three weeks later (August 23) *The Boston Gazette* referred to Alexander White for the first time: "The Mate of one Capt. White in a small Schooner, bound from New-York to Nova-Scotia, rose upon and kill'd the Captain.—He is an Irishman, and now confin'd in Plymouth Goal. This is all the Particulars we have as yet learned."

On November 1, 1784, *The Boston Gazette* mentioned the trials of the three. No mention of John Poor was included, but, in view of the accusations both Barrick and Sullivan made in their narratives against Poor, it seems probable that he turned state's evidence in return for his life:

> Last Week at the Superior Court held at Cambridge, in and for the County of Middlesex, one Alex White plead guilty to his Indictment, for the Murder of the Skipper of a Shallop bound from New-York to Nova-Scotia, as formerly mentioned.
>
> Dirik Grout and Frances Coven were executed last Thursday, agreeable to their Sentence for Burglary.
>
> This day is appointed for the Trial of the two Persons who robb'd Mr. Baldwin on Winter Hill in Charlestown in July last.

Two weeks later (November 15) Th*e Boston Gazette* announced the executions: "Thursday next Barrack & Sullivan, who robbed Mr. Cyrus Baldwin on Winter hill, and who attempted to rob Major James Swan on Boston neck, as lately mentioned, are to be executed at Cambridge—As is also Alexander Wight [sic], for murder and piracy." Finally, a week later (November 22) the paper reported that the executions had taken place: "Thursday last agreeable to their Sentence Richard Barrick and John Sullivan, for high-way robbery, and Alexander Wight, for piracy and murder, were executed at Cambridge——The High-Sheriff of the County of Middlesex, and his Deputies performed the several duties, with the utmost decorum, and without any expense to the Community."

At the same time the Boston newspapers included accounts of the two highwaymen, several notices appeared concerning John Dixon (also spelled Dixson). In the November 1, 1784, issue of *The Boston Gazette* (the same issue mentioning Barrick and Sullivan's trial), an account of Dixon's trial and courtroom behavior appeared:

> Thursday the 21st ult. came on before the Supreme Court at Taunton, the trial of John Dixon, for breaking open the shop of Mr. James Daggett, of Rehoboth, and stealing from thence sundry articles. The Jury bro't him in guilty; and the next morning he received sentence of death. He appeared previous to and at his trial a most hardened wretch—

> making a jest of death, judgment, and eternity, in such an extraordinary manner, that the Judges and spectators were very much affected.

Apparently the description of Dixon's blasphemy disturbed at least one reader. Two weeks later (November 15) Th*e Boston Gazette* printed a rebuttle:

> Mess'rs Printers, please insert the following in your text.
>
> I saw an account in your paper, representing on John Dickson, under sentence of Death, Burglary, now in Taunton prison, "as a hardened wretch[.]" The representation is not just; he appears to be greatly disturbed; death appears to him solemn; the bible and eternal things infinite realities. He has been a wicked inconsiderate youth, but not that hardened infidel that he is represented to be. He believes [in] a future state of rewards and punishments and is greatly affected with it. All this can be attested to by some who have had the opportunity of repeated visits. (He is now no more.)

Perhaps the person who had the most "opportunity of repeated visits" was Peres Fobes, the minister who attended Dixon in prison and who delivered the final execution sermon. Along with the sermon, which was soon published by Bennett Wheeler of Providence, Fobes included "A SKETCH of JOHN DIXSON's Life," a brief two page account that resisted depicting him as either saint or sinner. According to Fobes, Dixon was a particularly "hardened wretch" in life:

> His mouth was full of cursing and swearing, of oaths and blasphemies of the most horrible sound, that his imagination could invent. He shewed no regard for the holy sabbath; rarely ever read the scriptures, or attended public worship, and never gave any attention to the word preached when present. ("Appendix" 13-14)

Fobes added, however, that imminent death did alter Dixon's attitude, and his final description tends to support the account presented in The *Bloody Register*:

> Before he received the sentence of death, he was in prison jovial, dissolute, and prophane; but afterwards he appeared, at times, full of anxiety and remorse.—His attention and behaviour, the last times he attended public worship, were very serious. In a short speech made at the gallows, he warned others, by himself, against drinking, gameing, and evil company: He then expressed his thanks to the sheriff, and to all of who he had received kindnesses, while in prison; and as soon as the appointed moment of execution arrived, he leaped into the cart, assisted in adjusting the rope about his own neck, and even in turning himself off, with an appearance of fortitude, which surprized every spectator; but this, whether from principles of infidelity, stupefaction, or christianity, we dare not pronounce. ("Appendix" 14)

Also, what is especially interesting about the Fobes text is the inclusion of a twelve-page defense of capital punishment in general and of Dixon's execution in particular. Indicative of the larger debate concerning the death penalty, Fobes stated that

> a considerable number, chiefly of the populace, manifested their doubts and dissatisfaction concerning the lawfulness of the intended execution; others "raged and were confident," that it would be a murderous bloody deed, and wished he might escape. This suggested the propriety of offering in public a short vindication of his punishment. ("Appendix" 1)

In order to vindicate "his punishment," Fobes then drew upon Biblical sanctions and examples of capital punishment.

# The Life and Confeſſion of JOHNSON GREEN,

Who is to be Executed this Day, Auguſt 17th, 1786, for the

## Atrocious Crime of BURGLARY;

Together with his

# LAST and DYING WORDS.

I JOHNSON GREEN, having brought myſelf to a ſhameful and ignominious death, by my wicked conduct, and as I am a dying man I leave to the world the following Hiſtory of my Birth, Education, and vicious Practices, hoping that all people will take warning by my evil example, and ſhun vice and follow virtue.

I was born at Bridgwater, in the County of Plymouth, in the Commonwealth of Maſſachuſetts, was twenty-nine years of age the ſeventh day of February laſt. My father was a negro, and a ſervant to the Hon. Timothy Edſon Eſq; late of ſaid Bridgwater, deceaſed. My mother was an Iriſh woman, named Sarah Johnſon, ſhe was a widow, and her maiden name was Green. I have been called Joſeph-Johnſon Green. When I was five years of age my mother bound me as an Apprentice to Mr. Seth Howard of ſaid Bridgwater, to be inſtructed in Agriculture. I was uſed very tenderly, and inſtructed in the principles of the Chriſtian Religion. Whilſt I was an apprentice my mother gave me much good advice, cautioned me againſt keeping company with thoſe that uſed bad language and other vicious practices. She adviſed me not to go to ſea nor into the army, foretold what has come to paſs ſince the commencement of the late war, and ſaid it would not come to paſs in her day. She died about ſixteen years ago, and if I had followed her good advice I might have eſcaped an ignominious death.

When I was eighteen years of age (contrary to my mother's advice) I inliſted into the American ſervice, and remained in the ſame for the duration of the war. I would juſt obſerve to the world, that my being addicted to drunkenneſs, the keeping of bad company, and a correſpondence that I have had with lewd women, has been the cauſe of my being brought to this wretched ſituation.

In March, 1781, I was married at Eaſtown, to one Sarah Phillips, a muſtee, who was brought up by Mr. Olney, of Providence. She has had two children ſince I was married to her, and I have treated her exceeding ill.

When I began to ſteal I was about 12 years old, at which time I ſtole four cakes of gingerbread and ſix biſcuit, out of a horſe cart, and afterwards I ſtole ſundry ſmall articles, and was not detected.

When I was about fourteen, I ſtole one dozen of lemons and one cake of chocolate, was detected, and received reproof. Soon after I ſtole ſome hens, and my conduct was ſo bad that my maſter ſold me to one of his couſins, who uſed me well.

I continued the practice of ſtealing, and juſt before I went into the army I took my maſter's key, unlocked his cheſt, and ſtole two ſhillings; he diſcovered what I had done, gave me correction, but not ſo ſeverely as I deſerved.

Sometime after I was engaged in the American ſervice, at a certain tavern in Sherburne, I ſtole fifteen ſhillings, one caſe bottle of rum, one dozen of biſcuit, and a pillow caſe with ſome ſugar.

In April, 1781, I ſtole at the Highlands, near Weſt-Point, a pair of ſilver ſhoe buckles, was detected, and received one hundred laſhes.

In October, the ſame year, when I was at Weſt-Point, and we were extremely pinched for the want of proviſions, three of us broke open a ſettler's market, ſtole three cheeſes, one ſmall firkin of butter, and ſome chocolate. I only was detected, and puniſhed by receiving one hundred ſtripes.

Sometime in the winter of 1783, at Eaſton, I broke into a griſt mill, belonging to Mr. Timothy Randall, and ſtole about a buſhel of corn, and at ſundry times the ſame year I broke into a cellar belonging to Mr. Ebenezer Howard, of the ſame place, and ſtole ſome meat and tobacco; and I alſo broke into a cellar and a corn houſe belonging to Mr. Abiel Kinſley, of the ſame place, and ſtole ſome meat and corn; and at Eaſt-Bridgewater, the ſame year, I broke open a griſt mill, and ſtole near a buſhel of meal; and at the ſame time I ſtole three or four dozen herrings out of a corn houſe. I alſo went to a corn houſe belonging to Mr. Nathaniel Whitman, of Bridgwater, and ſtole two cheeſes out of it.

Auguſt 1ſt, 1784, I broke open a houſe in Providence, and ſtole goods to the value of forty dollars. Soon after I broke open a ſhop near Patuxet Falls, ſtole one pair of cards, two cod fiſh, and ſundry other articles.

In 1784 I alſo committed the following crimes, viz. I broke into a cellar about a mile from Patuxet Bridge, ſtole about thirty weight of ſalt pork, one caſe bottle, and ſeveral other articles. About the ſame time I ſtole out of a waſhing tub in Patuxet, a pair of trowſers, three pair of ſtockings, and a ſkirt; and at Seaconk I ſtole two ſhirts and ſome ſtockings through an open window. I ſtole at a barn between Seaconk and Attleborough, a woollen blanket, and through an open window near the ſame place, I ſtole two ſheets, one gown, and one ſhirt. At Mr. Amos Shepherdſon's, in Attleborough, I ſtole out of a waſh-tub, one ſhirt, two ſhifts, one ſhort gown, and one pair of ſtockings.

At Norton, I broke into a cellar belonging to Col. George Leonard, and ſtole a quarter of mutton. The ſame night I broke into another cellar near that place, and ſtole between twenty and thirty weight of ſalt pork.

About the ſame time, I broke into a tavern near the ſame place, and ſtole near two dollars in money, and one caſe-bottle of rum.

Between Providence and Attleborough, I broke open two cellars, and ſtole ſome meat.

I broke into a houſe in Johnſton, and ſtole betwixt twenty and thirty wt. of ſalt pork and beef, and one broom.

Some of the things I ſtole this year, I ſold at the market in Providence.

April 23d, 1785, I was impriſoned at Nantucket, for ſtriking a truckman, and ſome other perſons, at a time when I was intoxicated with liquor: The next day I was releaſed upon my paying a fine and the coſt of proſecution.

I broke open a houſe in Stoughton, ſtole ſeveral aprons, ſome handkerchiefs, and ſome other apparel.

I ſtole about two yards and an half of tow cloth from Col. David Lathrop, of Bridgewater; and the ſame night I ſtole a ſhirt from a clothier, in the ſame town; and I alſo ſtole one apron, one pocket-handkerchief, one pair of ſtockings, and one ſhift from Thomas Howard, of Eaſt-Bridgewater, upon the ſame night.

The next week I ſtole a piece of tow-cloth, in Halifax, and at the ſame time I broke into a houſe, and ſtole about twenty pounds of ſalt beef, and three pounds of wool.

October 15th, 1785, I broke open a ſhop in Walpole, and ſtole ſeven pair of ſhoes.

Nov. 1785, I broke open a ſtore in Natick, and ſtole a quantity of goods from the owner, viz. Mr. Morris.

At Capt. Bent's tavern, in Stoughtonham, I went down chimney, by a rope, opened a window and faſtened it up with my jack-knife; immediately after, a man came to the houſe for a gallon of rum; he called to the landlord, and his daughter (as I took her to be) aroſe and waited upon him. She diſcovered the open window, with the jack-knife, and ſaid it did not belong to the houſe; it was concluded that it belonged to ſome boys who were gone to a huſking, and had called there that evening.—It was my deſign to have made my eſcape out at the window, when I opened it, in caſe I ſhould be diſcovered by any perſon in the houſe: But when the man came up to the houſe, I fearing I might be diſcovered, drawed myſelf up chimney and ſtood on the croſs-bar until he was gone and all the people were aſleep; I then deſcended again, and ſtole near three dollars out of the bar; then aſcended the chimney and eſcaped without being diſcovered.

The ſame month I hid a quantity of goods which I had ſtole (part of them being the goods I had ſtolen at Natick) in a barn, belonging to Mr. Nathaniel Foſter, in Middleborough, and I engaged to come and work for the ſaid Foſter: It happened that I was taken up on ſuſpicion that I had ſtolen a horſe (which I had taken and rode about four miles) and committed to gaol in the county of Plymouth, but as no ſufficient evidence appeared, I was ſet at liberty. In the mean time the ſaid Foſter found the goods and advertiſed them. I ſent my wife to him, ſhe owned and received the goods, and I eſcaped undiſcovered, by her telling him that I came to his houſe in the evening preceding the day I had promiſed to work for him; that as it was late in the night, and the weather rainy, I did not chooſe to diſturb him and his family, by calling them up; that I was obliged to leave the goods and return home, and being taken up on the ſuſpicion aforeſaid, I could not take care of the goods, &c.

April 1ſt, 1786, I broke into a houſe, in Medford, and ſtole two pair of ſtockings, one ſcarf, one gown, and one pair of buckles.

The ſame month I broke into the houſe of one Mr. Blake, innholder, oppoſite the barracks in Rutland, and ſtole a bottle of bitters, and three or four dollars in money.

Soon after I broke into Mr. Chickery's houſe, in Holden, and ſtole about thirty dollars worth of clothing. The next day I lodged in the woods, and at evening Mr. Chickery took me up after I had got into the high-way, ſearched my pack, and found his things. On his attempting to ſeize me, I ran off, and made my eſcape.—I left my pack, and the money I had ſtolen from Mr. Blake.

Not long after, I went to Mr. Jotham Howe's in Shrewſbury, and opened a window, and ſtole a blanket.

I then went to another houſe, broke in, and ſtole a fine apron out of a deſk. The ſame night I went to a barn belonging to Mr. Baldwin, in ſaid Shrewſbury, and lodged in it the next day, and at evening I broke into his houſe, and ſtole about three ſhillings and three pence in money, and about nine dollars worth of clothing, for which crime I am now under ſentence of death.

The ſame night I broke open the houſe of Mr. Farrar, in ſaid Shrewſbury, and ſtole in money and goods, to the value of near ſix dollars.

I alſo broke into the houſe of Mr. Roſs Wyman, of the ſame town, and upon the ſame night, and ſtole from him near two dollars.

Moreover, I ſtole a pair of thread ſtockings at a houſe juſt beyond ſaid Wyman's, and hid myſelf in the woods, where I lay all the next day, and at evening I ſat off towards Boſton, and was taken up by a guard that was placed by a bridge in the edge of Weſtborough. I was taken before General Ward, confeſſed the crimes alledged, was committed to gaol, and in April laſt, I received ſentence of death, for the crime aforementioned.

Upon the evening of the firſt day of June, I cleared myſelf of all my chains, and made an eſcape from the gaol: And notwithſtanding all the admonitions, counſels and warnings that I had received from the good miniſters and other pious perſons who had viſited me under my confinement, I returned again to my vicious practices, "like the dog to his vomit, and the ſow that is waſhed, to her wallowing in the mire;" for the very ſame evening I ſtole a cheeſe out of a preſs in Holden: And the next Saturday I broke into the houſe of Mr. James Caldwell, in Barre, and ſtole near twenty five dollars worth of clothing.

I tarried in Barre about twelve days, and then ſet off for Natick, and on the way I broke into a cellar, in Shrewſbury, and ſtole ſome bread and cheeſe.—Whilſt I tarried in Barre, I lived in the woods all the time—when I had got to Natick, I ſtole two pair of ſtockings and two pocket handkerchiefs, that were hanging out near a houſe.

From Natick I went to Sherburne, and broke open a ſtore belonging to Mr. Samuel Sanger, and ſtole between four and five dozen of buttons.

From thence I went to Mr. John Sanger's houſe, in the ſame town, broke it open, and ſtole a caſe bottle of rum, one bottle of cherry rum, ſix cakes of gingerbread, and as many biſcuits: I ſearched for money, but found none.

At another tavern in the ſame town, I took out a pane of glaſs, and opened the window, but I was diſcovered by the landlord, made my eſcape, and went back to Natick, and tarried there two days.

From Natick I went to Stoughtonham, and at Capt. Bent's (the place where I went down the chimney) the cellar being open, I went through it, and in the bar-room I ſtole fifteen ſhillings in money, one caſe bottle of rum, and one half dozen of biſcuits.

Afterwards I went to Eaſton, and on the way I broke open a houſe, and ſtole ſome cheeſe, and two pair of ſhoes, and two pair of ſhoe-buckles. At Eaſton I tarried two days, and then made my eſcape from two men who attempted to take me up on ſuſpicion that I had broken gaol. From thence I went to Attleborough, and through a window I ſtole two cheeſes, and at a tavern near the ſame place, I ſtole ſix ſhillings and eight pence, one caſe bottle of rum, a ſailor's jacket, and one pair of ſilver knee buckles.

I then ſat off for Providence, and by the way I opened a window, and ſtole one cotton jacket, one jack-knife; and at another houſe on the ſame way, I ſtole through a window, one fine apron, one pocket handkerchief, and one pillow caſe.

I came to Providence the 26th day of June, and not long after, I broke open a cellar, and ſtole one bottle of beer, ſome ſalt fiſh, and ten pounds of butter.

A few nights after, I went to Col. Manton's, in Johnſton, and the cellar being open, I went into it, and ſtole twenty pounds of butter, near as much ſalt pork, one milk pail, one cheeſe cloth, and one frock.

A few nights after, I went to Juſtice Belknap's, in the ſame place, and broke into his cellar, and ſtole about thirty pounds of ſalt pork, one neat's tongue, one pair of nippers, one box of awls, and one bag.—It remarkably happened on the 13th ultimo (the day that had been appointed for my execution) that I was committed to gaol in Providence, on ſuſpicion of having ſtolen the things laſt mentioned, and on the 18th ult. I was brought back and confined in this gaol again.—Many more thefts and other vicious practices have I been guilty of, the particulars of which might tire the patience of the reader.

Some of the things I have ſtolen I have uſed myſelf—ſome of them I have ſold—ſome have been taken from me—ſome I have hid where I could not find them again—and others I have given to lewd women, who induced me to ſteal for their maintenance. I have lived a hard life, by being obliged to keep in the woods; have ſuffered much by hunger, nakedneſs, cold, and the fears of being detected and brought to juſtice—have often been accuſed of ſtealing when I was not guilty, and others have been accuſed of crimes when I was the offender.—I never murdered any perſon, nor robbed any body on the highway. I have had great dealings with women, which to their and my ſhame be it ſpoken, I often too eaſily obtained my will of them. I hope they will repent, as I do, of ſuch wicked and infamous conduct. I have had a correſpondence with many women, excluſive of my wife, among whom were ſeveral abandoned Whites, and a large number of Blacks; four of the whites were married women, three of the blacks have laid children to me beſides my wife, who has been much diſtreſſed by my behaviour.

Thus have I given a hiſtory of my birth, education and atrocious conduct, and as the time is very nigh in which I muſt ſuffer an ignominious death, I earneſtly intreat that all people would take warning by my wicked example; that they would ſhun the paths of deſtruction by guarding againſt every temptation, that they would ſhun vice, follow virtue, and become (through the aſſiſtance of the ALMIGHTY) victorious over the enemies of immortal felicity, who are exerting themſelves to delude and lead nations to deſtruction.

As I am ſenſible of the heinouſneſs of my crimes, and am ſorry for my wicked conduct, in violating the laws of the great Governour of the Univerſe, whoſe Divine Majeſty I have offended, I earneſtly pray that He would forgive my ſins, blot out my multiplied tranſgreſſions, and receive my immortal ſpirit into the Paradiſe of never ending bliſs.

I aſk forgiveneſs of my wife, and of all perſons whom I have injured. I return my ſincere thanks to the Miniſters of the Goſpel, and others, who have viſited me under my confinement, for their counſels and admonitions, and for the good care they have taken of me: God reward them for their kindneſs, and conduct us all through this troubleſome world to the regions of immortal felicity in the kingdom of Heaven.—AMEN.

his
JOHNSON † GREEN.
mark.

*Worceſter Gaol, Auguſt 16, 1786.*

*The following POEM was written at the requeſt of JOHNSON GREEN, by a priſoner in Worceſter Gaol, and is at ſaid GREEN's ſpecial requeſt, added to his Life and Confeſſion, as a PART of his DYING WORDS.*

LET all the people on the globe
  Be on their guard, and ſee
That they do ſhun the vicious road
  That's trodden been by me.
If I had ſhun'd the paths of vice;
  Had minded to behave
According to the good advice
  That my kind mother gave,
Unto my friends I might have been
  A bleſſing in my days,
And ſhun'd the evils that I've ſeen
  In my pernicious ways.
My wicked conduct has been ſuch,
  It's brought me to diſtreſs;
As often times I've ſuffer'd much
  By my own wickedneſs.
My lewdneſs, drunkenneſs, and theft
  Has often times—(behold)
Caus'd me to wander, and be left
  To ſuffer with the cold.
Hid in the woods, in deep diſtreſs,
  My pinching wants were ſuch,
With hunger, and with nakedneſs
  I oft did ſuffer much.
I've liv'd a thief; it's a hard life;
  To drink was much inclin'd;
My conduct has diſtreſs'd my wife,
  A wife both good and kind.
Though many friends which came to ſee
  Me, in theſe latter times,
Did oft with candour, caution me
  To leave my vicious crimes;
Yet when I had got out of gaol,
  Their labour prov'd in vain;
For then, alas! I did not fail
  To take to them again.
If I had not conducted ſo;
  Had minded to refrain;
Then I ſhou'd not have had to go
  Back to the gaol again.
Thus in the Devil's ſervice, I
  Have ſpent my youthful days,
And now, alas! I ſoon muſt die,
  For theſe my wicked ways.
Repent, ye thieves, whilſt ye have breath,
  Amongſt you let be wrought
A reformation, leſt to death,
  You, like myſelf, be brought.
Let other vicious perſons ſee
  That they from vice abſtain;
Leſt they undo themſelves, like me,
  Who in it did remain.
I hope my ſad and diſmal fate
  Will ſolemn warning be
To people all, both ſmall and great,
  Of high and low degree.
By breaking of the righteous laws,
  I to the world relate,
That I thereby have been the cauſe
  Of my unhappy fate.
As I repent, I humbly pray
  That God would now remit
My ſins, which in my vicious way
  I really did commit.
May the old TEMPTER ſoon be bound
  And ſhut up in his den,
And peace and honeſty abound
  Among the ſons of men.
May the great GOD grant this requeſt,
  And bring us to that ſhore
Where peace and everlaſting reſt
  Abides for ever more.

his
JOHNSON † GREEN.
mark.

Printed and Sold at the Printing-Office in Worceſter.

## [ JOHNSON GREEN ]

# *The Life and Confession of Johnson Green*

## [ 1786 ]

I *JOHNSON GREEN,* having brought myself to a shameful and ignominious death, by my wicked conduct, and as I am a dying man I leave to the world the following History of my Birth, Education, and vicious Practices, hoping that all people will take warning by my evil example, and shun vice and follow virtue.

I was born at Bridgewater, in the County of Plymouth, in the Commonwealth of Massachusetts, was twenty-nine years of age the seventh day of February last. My father was a negro, and a servant to the Hon. Timothy Edson Esq; late of said Bridgewater, deceased. My mother was an Irish woman, named Sarah Johnson, she was a widow, and her maiden name was Green. I have been called Joseph-Johnson Green. When I was five years of age my mother bound me as an Apprentice to Mr. Seth Howard of said Bridgewater, to be instructed in Agriculture. I was used very tenderly, and instructed in the principles of the Christian Religion. Whilst I was an apprentice my mother gave me much good advice, cautioned me against keeping company with those that used bad language and other vicious practices. She advised me not to go to sea nor into the army, foretold what has come to pass since the commencement of the late war, and said it would not come to pass in her day. She died about sixteen years ago, and if I had followed her good advice I might have escaped an ignominious death.

When I was eighteen years of age (contrary to my mother's advice) I inlisted into the American service, and remained in the same for the duration of the war. I would just observe to the world, that my being addicted to drunkenness, the keeping of bad company, and a correspondence that I have had with lewd women, has been the cause of my being brought to this wretched situation.

In March 1781, I was married at Eastown, to one Sarah Phillips, a mustee, who was brought up by Mr. Olney, of Providence. She has had two children since I was married to her, and I have treated her exceeding ill.

When I began to steal I was about 12 years old, at which time I stole four cakes of gingerbread and six biscuit, out of a horse cart, and afterwards I stole sundry small articles, and was not detected.

When I was about fourteen, I stole one dozen of lemons and one cake of chocolate, was detected, and received reproof. Soon after I stole some hens, and my conduct was so bad that my master sold me to one of his cousins, who used me well.

I continued the practice of stealing, and just before I went into the army I took my master's key, unlocked his chest, and stole two shillings; he discovered what I had done, gave me correction, but not so severely as I deserved.

Sometime after I was engaged in the American service, at a certain tavern in Sherburne, I stole fifteen shillings, one case bottle of rum, one dozen of biscuit, and a pillow case with some sugar.

In April, 1781, I stole at the Highlands, near West-Point, a pair of silver shoe buckles, was detected, and received one hundred lashes.

In October, the same year, when I was at West-Point, and we were extremely pinched for the want of provisions, three of us broke open a settler's markee, stole three cheeses, one small firkin of butter, and some chocolate. I only was detected, and punished by receiving one hundred stripes.

Sometime in the winter of 1783, at Easton, I broke into a grist mill, belonging to Mr. Timothy Randall, and stole about a bushel of corn, and at sundry times the same year I broke into a cellar belonging to Mr. Ebenezer Howard, of the same place, and stole some meat and tobacco; and I also broke into a cellar and a corn house belonging to Mr. Abiel Kinsley, of the same place, and stole some meat and corn; and at East-Bridgewater, the same year, I broke open a grist mill, and stole near a bushel of meal; and at the same time I stole three or four dozen herrings out of a corn house. I also went to a corn house belonging to Mr. Nathaniel Whitman, of Bridgewater, and stole two cheeses out of it.

August 1st, 1784, I broke open a house in Providence, and stole goods to the value of forty dollars. Soon after I broke open a shop near Patuxet Falls, stole one pair of cards, two cod fish, and sundry other articles.

In 1784 I also committed the following crimes, viz. I broke into a cellar about a mile from Patuxet Bridge, stole about thirty weight of salt pork, one case bottle, and several other articles. About the same time I stole out of a washing tub in Patuxet, a pair of trowsers, three pair of stockings, and a shirt; and at Seaconk I stole two shirts and some stockings through an open window. I stole at a barn between Seaconk and Attleborough, a woollen blanket, and through an open window near the same place, I stole two sheets, one gown, and one shirt. At Mr. Amos Sheperdson's, in Attleborough, I stole out of a wash-tub, one shirt, two shifts, one short gown, and one pair of stockings.

At Norton, I broke into a cellar belonging to Col. George Leonard, and stole a quarter of mutton. The same night I broke into another cellar near that place, and stole between twenty and thirty weight of salt pork.

About the same time, I broke into a tavern near the same place, and stole two dollars in money, and one case-bottle of rum.

Between Providence and Attleborough, I broke open two cellars, and stole some meat.

I broke into a house in Johnston, and stole betwixt twenty and thirty wt. of salt pork and beef, and one broom.

Some of the things I stole this year, I sold at the market in Providence.

April 23d, 1785, I was imprisoned at Nantucket, for striking a truckman, and some other persons, at a time when I was intoxicated with liquor: The next day I was released upon my paying a fine and the cost of prosecution.

I broke open a house in Stoughton, stole several aprons, some handkerchiefs, and some other apparel.

I stole about two yards and an half of tow cloth from Col. David Lathrop, of Bridgewater; and the same night I stole a shirt from a clothier, in the same town; and I also stole one apron, one pocket-handkerchief, one pair of stockings, and one shift from Thomas Howard, of East-Bridgewater, upon the same night.

The next week I stole a piece of tow-cloth, in Halifax, and at the same time I broke into a house, and stole about twenty pounds of salt beef, and three pounds of wool.

October 15th, 1785, I broke open a shop in Walpole, and stole seven pair of shoes.

Nov. 1785, I broke open a store in Natick, and stole a quantity of goods from the owner, viz. Mr. Morris.

At Capt. Bent's tavern, in Stoughtonham, I went down chimney, by a rope, opened a window and fastened it up with my jack-knife; immediately after, a man came to the house for a gallon of rum; he called to the landlord, and his daughter (as I took her to be) arose and waited upon him. She discovered the open window, with the jack-knife, and said it did not belong to the house; it was concluded that it belonged to some boys who were gone to a husking, and had called there that evening.—It was my design to have made my escape out at the window, when I opened it, in case I should be discovered by any person in the house: But when the man came to the house, I fearing I might be discovered, drawed myself up chimney and stood on the cross-bar until he was gone and all the people were asleep; I then descended again, and stole near three dollars out of the bar; then ascended the chimney and escaped without being discovered.

The same month I hid a quantity of goods which I had stole (part of them being the goods I had stolen at Natick) in a barn, belonging to Mr. Nathaniel Foster, in Middleborough, and I engaged to come and work for the said Foster: It happened that I was taken up on a suspicion that I had stolen a horse (which I had taken and rode about four miles) and committed to gaol in the county of Plymouth, but as no sufficient evidence appeared, I was set at liberty. In the mean time the said Foster found the goods and advertised them. I sent my wife to him, she owned and received the goods, and I escaped undiscovered, by her telling him that I came to his house in the evening preceding the day I had promised to work for him; that as it was late in the night, and the weather rainy, I did not choose to disturb him and his family, by calling them up; that I was obliged to leave the goods and return home, and being taken up on the suspicion aforesaid, I could not take care of the goods, &c.

April 1st, 1786, I broke into a house, in Medford, and stole two pair of stockings, one scarf, one gown, and one pair of buckles.

The same month I broke into the house of one Mr. Blake, innholder, opposite the barracks in Rutland, and stole a bottle of bitters, and three or four dollars in money.

Soon after I broke into Mr. Chickery's house, in Holden, and stole about thirty dollars worth of clothing. The next day I lodged in the woods, and at evening Mr. Chickery took me up after I had got into the high-way, searched my pack, and found his things. On his attempting to seize me, I ran off, and made my escape.—I left my pack, and the money I had stolen from Mr. Blake.

Not long after, I went to Mr. Jotham Howe's in Shrewsbury, and opened a window, and stole a blanket.

I then went to another house, broke in, and stole a fine apron out of a desk. The same night I went to a barn belonging to Mr. Baldwin, in said Shrewsbury, and lodged in it the next day, and at evening I broke into his house, and stole about three shillings and three pence in money, and about nine dollars worth of clothing, for which crime I am now under sentence of death.

The same night I broke open the house of Mr. Farror, in said Shrewsbury, and stole in money and goods, to the value of near six dollars.

I also broke into the house of Mr. Ross Wyman, of the same town, and upon the same night, and stole from him near two dollars.

Moreover, I stole a pair of thread stockings at a house just beyond said Wyman's, and hid myself in the woods, where I lay all the next day, and at evening I sat off towards Boston, and was taken up by a guard that was placed by a bridge in the edge of Westborough. I was taken before General Ward, confessed the crimes alledged, was committed to gaol, and in April last, I received sentence of death, for the crime aforementioned.

Upon the evening of the first day of June, I cleared myself of all my chains, and made an escape from the gaol: And notwithstanding all the admonitions, counsels and warnings that I had received from the good ministers and other pious persons who had visited me under my confinement, I returned again to my vicious practices, "like the dog to his vomit, and the sow that is washed, to her wallowing in the mire;" for the very same evening I stole a cheese out of a press in Holden: And the next Saturday I broke into the house of Mr. James Caldwell, in Barre, and stole near twenty five dollars worth of clothing.

I tarried in Barre about twelve days, and then set off for Natick, and on the way I broke into a cellar, in Shrewsbury, and stole some bread and cheese.—Whilst I tarried in Barre, I lived in the woods all the time—when I had got to Natick, I stole two pair of stockings and two pocket handkerchiefs, that were hanging out near a house.

From Natick I went to Sherburne, and broke open a store belonging to Mr. Samuel Sanger, and stole between four or five dozen of buttons.

From thence I went to Mr. John Sanger's house, in the same town, broke it open, and stole a case bottle of rum, one bottle of cherry rum, six cakes of gingerbread, and as many biscuits: I searched for money, but found none.

At another tavern in the same town, I took out a pane of glass, and opened a window, but I was discovered by the landlord, made my escape, and went back to Natick, and tarried there two days.

From Natick I went to Stoughtonham, and at Capt. Bent's (the place where I went down the chimney) the cellar being open, I went through it, and in the bar-room I stole fifteen shillings in money, one case bottle of rum, and one half dozen of biscuits.

Afterwards I went to Easton, and on the way I broke open a house, and stole some cheese, and two pair of shoes, and two pair of shoe buckles. At Easton I tarried two days, and then made my escape from two men who attempted to take me up on suspicion that I had broken gaol. From thence I went to Attleborough, and through a window I stole two cheeses, and at a tavern near the same place, I stole six shillings and eight pence, one case bottle of rum, a sailor's jacket, and one pair of silver knee buckles.

I then sat off for Providence, and by the way I opened a window, and stole one cotton jacket, one jack-knife; and at another house on the same way, I stole through a window, one fine apron, one pocket handkerchief, and one pillow case.

I came to Providence the 26th day of June, and not long after, I broke open a cellar, and stole one bottle of beer, some salt fish, and ten pounds of butter.

A few nights after, I went to Col. Manton's, in Johnston, and the cellar being open, I went into it, and stole twenty pounds of butter, near as much salt pork, one milk pail, one cheese cloth, and one frock.

A few nights after, I went to Justice Belknap's, in the same place, and broke into his cellar, and stole about thirty pounds of salt pork, one neat's tongue, and one pair of nippers, one box of awls, and one bag.—It remarkably happened on the 13th ultimo (the day that had been appointed for my execution) that I was committed to gaol in Providence, on suspicion of having stolen the things last mentioned, and on the 18th ult. I was brought back and confined in this gaol again.—Many more thefts and other vicious practices have I been guilty of, the particulars of which might tire the patience of the reader.

Some of the the things I have stolen I have used myself—some of them I have sold—some have been taken from me—some I have hid where I could not find them again—and others I have given to lewd women, who induced me to steal for their maintenance. I have lived a hard life, by being obliged to keep in the woods; have suffered much by hunger, nakedness, cold, and the fears of being detected and brought to justice—have often been accused of stealing when I was not guilty, and others have been accused of crimes when I was the offender. I never murdered any person, nor robbed any body on the high-way. I have had great dealings with women, which to their and my shame be it spoken, I often too easily obtained my will of them. I hope they will repent, as I do, of such wicked and infamous conduct. I have had a correspondence with many women, exclusive of my wife, among whom were several abandoned Whites, and a large number of Blacks; four of the whites were married women, three of the blacks have laid children to me besides my wife, who has been much distressed by my behaviour.

Thus have I given a history of my birth, education and atrocious conduct, and as the time is very nigh in which I must suffer an ignominious death, I earnestly intreat that all people would take warning by my wicked example; that they would shun the paths of destruction by guarding against every temptation; that they would shun vice, follow virtue, and become (through that assistance of the ALMIGHTY) victorious over the enemies of immortal felicity, who are exerting themselves to delude and lead nations to destruction.

As I am sensible of the heinousness of my crimes, and am sorry for my wicked conduct, in violating the laws of the great Governour of the Universe, whose Divine Majesty I have offended, I earnestly pray that he would forgive my sins, blot out my multiplied transgressions, and receive my immortal spirit into the Paradise of never ending bliss.

I ask forgiveness of my wife, and all persons whom I have injured. I return my sincere thanks to the Ministers of the Gospel, and others, who have visited me under my confinement, for their counsels and admonitions, and for the good care they have taken of me: God reward them for their kindness, and conduct us all through this troublesome world to regions of immortal felicity in the kingdom of Heaven.—AMEN.

his
JOHNSON ✠ GREEN
mark.

*Worcester Gaol, August* 16, 1786.

*The following POEM was written at the request of JOHNSON GREEN, by a prisoner in Worcester Gaol, and is at said* GREEN's *special request, added to his Life and Confession, as a PART of his DYING WORDS.*

LET all the people on the globe
Be on their guard, and see
That they do shun the vicious road
That's trodden been by me.
If I had shun'd the paths of vice;
Had minded to behave
According to the good advice
That my kind mother gave,
Unto my friends I might have been
A blessing in my days,
And shun'd the evils that I've seen
In my pernicious ways.
My wicked conduct has been such,
It's brought me to distress;
As often times I've suffer'd much
By my own wickedness.
My lewdness, drunkenness, and theft
Has often times—(behold)
Caus'd me to wander, and be left
To suffer with the cold.
Hid in the woods, in deep distress,
My pinching wants were such,
With hunger, and with nakedness

I oft did suffer much.
I've liv'd a thief; it's a hard life;
To drink was much inclin'd;
My conduct has distress'd my wife,
A wife both good and kind.
Though many friends which came to
Me, in these latter times,
Did oft with candour, caution me
To leave my vicious crimes;
Yet when I had got out of gaol,
Their labour prov'd in vain;
For then, alas! I did not fail
To take to them again.
If I had not conducted so;
Had minded to refrain;
Then I shou'd not have had to go
Back to gaol again.
Thus in the Devil's service, I
Have spent my youthful days.
And now, alas! I soon must die,
For these my wicked ways.
Repent, ye thieves, whilst ye have breath,
Amongst you let be wrought
A reformation, lest to death,
You, like myself, be brought.
Let other vicious persons see
That they from vice abstain;
Lest they undo themselves, like me,
Who in it did remain.
I hope my sad and dismal fate
Will solemn warning be
To people all, both small and great,
Of high and low degree.
By breaking of the righteous laws,
I to the world relate,
That I thereby have been the cause
Of my unhappy fate.
As I repent, I humbly pray
That God would now remit
My sins, which in my vicious way
I really did commit.
May the old TEMPTER soon be bound
And shut up in his den,
And peace and honesty abound
Among the sons of men.

May the great GOD grant this request,
And bring us to that shore
Where peace and everlasting rest
Abides for ever more.

his
JOHNSON ✠ GREEN
mark

## Source Notes

*The Life and Confession of Johnson Green* was "Printed and Sold at the Printing-Office at Worcester" by Isaiah Thomas on August 17, 1786, the same day that Johnson was executed. The five-column broadside included a fairly detailed engraving of an execution scene. Such engravings often were reused, and Thomas previously had printed this particular engraving at least twice before: *The Last Words and Dying Speech of Robert Young* (Worcester, 1779) and *The Last Words of William Huggins and John Mansfield* (Worcester, 1783). Seven years later Thomas again recycled the engraving in both of his Samuel Frost publications (see Frost note below). Evidently, there were no reprints of the Johnson narrative.

Notices of Green's trial, escape, recapture, and execution were printed in the newspapers throughout the spring and summer of 1786, including Isaiah Thomas' *The Worcester Magazine* (formerly *The Massachusetts Spy*). In issue IV of April 1786, the following notice was printed:

> At the Supreme Court now sitting in this town [Worcester], Johnson Green, a Mulatto, or Mustee, was convicted of Burglary. It clearly appeared in evidence on trial that he broke open and entered three dwelling houses in Shrewsbury, viz. Mr. Baldwin's, Mr. Farror's, and Mr. Wyman's, and stole and carried off goods from each of them, on the night of the 14th instant. (50)

In the next issue of *The Worcester Magazine* (V, May), notice of Green's conviction was reported:

> *Johnson Green*, indicted for three Burglaries, committed in one night, within the space of about half a mile, was tried on one of those indictments only, and convicted, and received sentence of death according to law, on Friday last. (62)

Green did not resign himself to his official fate, and within a month he made his escape from the Worcester jail. Shortly thereafter a rather specific notice of his abrupt departure was printed in *The Boston Gazette* (June 12)

> WORCESTER, June 7.
>
> Last Thursday evening Johnson Green, a negro, under sentence of death, made his escape from the goal in this town, being then in the care of an Under-Sheriff. Some workmen had been repairing the goal, and the Under-Sheriff had a few minutes before secured him, as he supposed, to the floor; the door being unlocked, as the workmen were going in and out, he by some means freed himself of his irons, and went off undiscovered, among a number of people who were in and about the goal—This fellow broke open three houses in one night, and carried off a number of articles from each. The goaler has offered a reward of Thirty Dollars, to be paid on delivering said Green to him. The time affixed for Green's execution is the 13th of July next.

In another notice, dated July 15 from Providence, the July 24 issue of *The Boston Gazette* reported Green's recapture:

> On Thursday a man by the name of Johnson Greene, charged with committing two robberies in the town of Johnston, was apprehended here and secured in goal. He is said to be the same person, who some time since robbed three houses at Worcester in one night, where he broke goal, and was to have been executed the day he was taken here.

About the same time, *The Worcester Magazine* (XVII, July) offered a similar account:

> Johnson Green, who was to have been executed in this town on the 13th inst. for Burglary, but avoided it by breaking gaol, a few days previous to this time, was on the day sat apart for his execution apprehended and secured at Providence for several robberies committed after he had broken gaol as aforesaid. On application he was delivered up to the Sheriff of this County, and is again confined in the gaol in this town. (206)

On August 17, as Green trudged to the gallows, *The Worcester Magazine* advertised "a particular account of his crimes" as it announced the execution:

> Johnson Greene is to be executed here this day for Burglary. It is supposed that he has been as great a villain for house-breaking and stealing as ever was hung in this Commonwealth. A particular account of his crimes, with his last words, &c. are this day published.

Perhaps Thomas actually believed that Green was "as great a villain . . . as ever was hung"; nevertheless, his rhetorical indictment obviously served to attract readers and thus to help market his broadside narrative. In the August 21 issue of *The Boston Gazette*, Thomas' words (with a slight Bostonian revision) were repeated:

> On Thursday last, Johnson Greene, was executed at Worcester, for Burglary—It is supposed he was as great a villain as ever was hung in that county.

Although *The Worcester Magazine* offered nothing about the execution, it published advertisements announcing the sale of the Johnson broadside in two more issues (XXI, XXII):

> Just Published, and to be sold at the Printing-Office in Worcester, THE LIFE and CONFESSION of *JOHNSON GREEN*, who was executed at WORCESTER, August 17th, 1786, for the atrocious Crime of BURGLARY, together with his LAST and DYING WORDS.

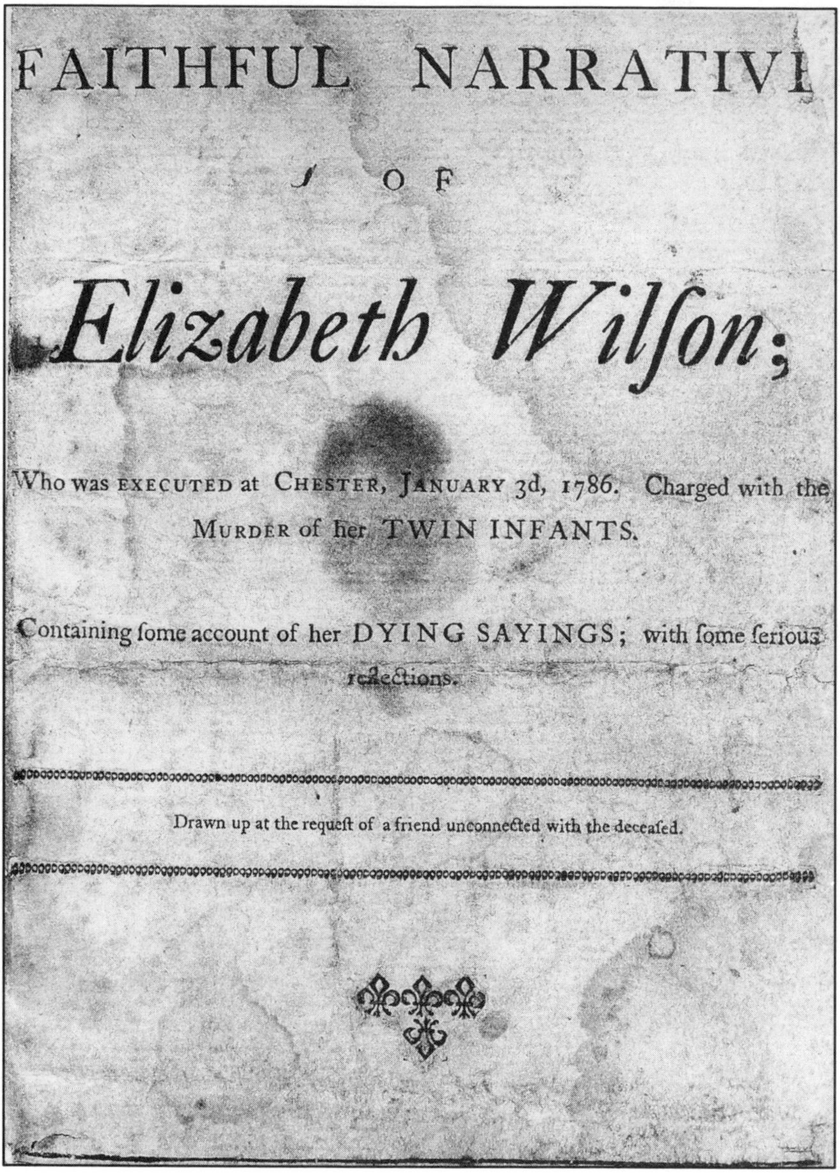

FAITHFUL NARRATIVE

OF

*Elizabeth Wilſon;*

Who was EXECUTED at CHESTER, JANUARY 3d, 1786. Charged with the MURDER of her TWIN INFANTS.

Containing ſome account of her DYING SAYINGS; with ſome ſerious reflections.

Drawn up at the requeſt of a friend unconnected with the deceaſed.

[ ELIZABETH WILSON ]

# *A Faithful Narrative of Elizabeth Wilson*

[ 1786 ]

Borough of Chester, Jan. 5, 1786.

*ON the third instant was executed here, pursuant to her sentence,* ELIZABETH WILSON; *charged with the murder of her twin illegitimate infants, on the 12th of October,* 1784.

*As the case of this woman is of a singular nature, has engrossed the public attention; and as there are various reports circulating respecting her, the following narrative, drawn up at the request of a person unconnected with her, may be acceptable at this time.*

WAS found, by a person with a dog, crossing the fields, in a piece of woods a little distance from the road leading from Brandywine to the Turk's Head, two dead infants. Upon enquiry, and from concurring circumstances, there was reason to conclude, they were Elizabeth Wilson's; who some time before was delivered of two children, not far from the place where they were found, and who about eight weeks before, had left the house with the children; having a design, as she said, of going to Philadelphia. She was accordingly apprehended, and after examination before Justice Taylor, was ordered to this jail.

She was brought to trial the last court of Oyer and Terminer, which commenced on the 17th of October last, before the Honorable Judge Atlee; circumstances were so strong against her, that she was brought in guilty, and received sentence of death.

Before, at, and after her trial, she persisted in denying the fact; her behaviour was such, in general, as gave reasons to conclude she was innocent of the murder of which she was charged, or was an insensible, hardened creature, and did not expect to die for this crime.

It was some time after she was sentenced, before she could be prevailed upon to make a discovery of the person that committed the horrid murder. A great deal of pains were taken to make her sensible that a promise of concealment, under the circumstances she was in when made, and in a matter of such consequence, was not binding. She was very desirous of seeing her younger brother.* When he came to visit her, she proposed to him the making a real discovery of the truth; he refused hearing it, until he had called several persons of character as witnesses. The account she gave them, or the confession she then made, and which was similar to the following one, together with their proceedings thereon, in finding the person charged with the murder, were presented to the Honorable the President and Council; who were pleased to grant her a respite for one month; with the respite came her death warrant, ordering her execution on Tuesday the 3d of January, 1786.

During her confinement she was visited by serious people of different religious denominations, and appeared amazingly ignorant respecting her spiritual state, until some time after she was sentenced, when many were much affected at the relation she gave of her religious exercises, and the apparent concern and distress of her mind. She said the dungeon was the happiest place she ever was in in her life.

The night before she was to be executed, she was visited, at her request, by two ministers of the Baptist persuasion; and who, besides visiting her, came to attend the execution. After some time spent in serious devotion, she made the following confession: dated

Chester, Dec. 6, 1785, Tuesday Evening, 10 o'Clock.

I *Elizabeth Wilson, Daughter of John and Elizabeth Wilson, was born in East-Marlborough, Chester County, of honest, sober parents. From sixteen to twenty-one years of age, I had a religious concern, but thro' the subtilty of Satan and corruptions of nature was led away to the soul-destroying sin of fornication, which I believe to be my predominant evil. I had three children in an unlawful way before I fell into the wretched company of* †*Joseph Deshong. At the time I fell in company with him I lived in Philadelphia at the sign of the Cross-Keys, in Chesnut-street, at the corner of Third-street. In the beginning of the year 1784,*

*This note, in her own hand-writing, was found on her table——O could I but see my own brother! to speak just a few words to him, to ease my broken heart that is so distressed. Oh how hard a thing it is that I cannot see him! Was he in my place and I in his, I would go to him, was't on my hands and knees; but he will not come to me, to speak one word to me, before I depart this life and see man no more: so I just give myself up to the Lord, begging that he would hear my crie[s], and give me life everlasting.

†From her account and description of the man, and from some persons who used Mr. Bogart's house, (the Cross Keys) 'twas found that the name he pass'd by with her, Joseph Deshong, was not his proper name.

*he insinuated himself into my company, under pretence of courtship, declaring himself a single man, and by repeated promises of marriage deceived and persuaded me to consent to his unlawful embraces. In a short time after I proved with child of the two dear innocents, for which I must shortly suffer an ignominious death. I told him of my situation, and then he dropt entirely his purpose of marriage; but told me, I must stay in town until I was delivered, and promised to bear all the expences, declaring I should not want for any thing. Accordingly I rented a room of Joseph Rhoods in Union-street. I stayed there a few weeks, and provided for myself; in which time he never came near me. And the time of my delivery drawing near, I was in great want of money, and after repeated inquiries after him I found that he had left me in that unhappy condition. I then found, I could not live in town; so proceeded to the house of Josiah Wilkinson, in East Bradford township, Chester County, where I was delivered of my dear infants. I continued at said house, 4 or 5 weeks, and then I went to Philadelphia and left the children at Mr. Wilkinson's in order to find my deceiver, where I met with him and told him my deplorable situation. When I told him, I had two children, he looked me in my face, saying, "the devil! you have?["] I requested him to do something for my by fair means, assuring him, if he did not consent, I should apply to the law: He answered, I need not go to law, for he would do for me, and seemed to sympathize with me in my pitiful case. I then requested him to put one of the dear children to nurse, the other I proposed to keep, on condition of his giving me a supply of money. To which he consented, and gave me a small trifle to bear my expenses back to the aforesaid Wilkinson's. He then appointed a day for me to return back to the city with my children, in order for him to fulfil his promise. The fatal appointed day being come, I, according to promise, set off to meet him at the appointed place (Newtown-Square); but, contrary to my expectations, he met me within two miles of the aforesaid Wilkinson's house. When we met he kindly accosted me, and getting off his horse, he jumped him over the fence, and requested me to go into the woods with him. Accordingly I went with him, and sat down on a rotten log, with both my children in my arms. He asked me to let him look at one of the children, in order to see if it look'd like him. He holding it in his arms, asked me what I thought I would do with them? I told him I thought it was his place, according to promise, to do for them. After a little pause he laid the dear infant on the ground, taking the other out of my arms, and laid it beside its dear little fellow sufferer, making this reply to my requesting him for money: I have no money for you, nor your bastards neither. He then requested me to take their dear lives; which I would by no means consent to, but requested him to let me have them, and I would beg for them. He then arose up, putting a pistol to my breast, forbidding me to make any noise; then he wickedly stamped on their dear little breasts, upon which the dear infants gave a faint scream and expir'd; he still keeping the pistol to my breast, forcing me most solemnly to vow, that I would never discover the dreadful act; to which I, thro' fear, consented. He then requested me to strip my dear dead infants naked. Thro' fear I took off each of their little gowns, but could proceed no further; my bowels yearning over my dear children. He then took them up, and made a place with his feet and covered them with leaves, and throw'd a piece of brush over them, and took me to Philadelphia. To the truth of this relation, I appeal to the eternal God to witness, before whose dreadful bar I expect to appear the ensuing day. A guilty rebel I acknowledge myself to be. My sins are more in number than the hairs of my head; but my Righteous Judge doth know my innocence in respect of that cruel murder. I know I deserve not only death, but hell; yet, nevertheless, I hope to obtain mercy, through the blood and righteousness of the Adorable Redeemer, to whose boundless mercy I commend my poor naked soul; venturing into that unknown world, only depending (I trust) on the all-sufficient merits of that precious God-Man, who died on the tree.*

Lord Jesus! accept thy sinning creature! and receive my spirit! So prayeth the dying

*ELIZABETH WILSON.*

*Taken from her own mouth, the evening before she suffered, by JOHN STANCLIFF, Minister.

Present—Mr. Thomas Taylor, Sub-sheriff,
Revd. Thomas Fleeson,
Joshua Vaughan.

This confession she signed; afterwards the ministers were preparing to go to Philadelphia to lay it before the Council, which was about two o'clock in the morning: they were informed her brother had come down from Philadelphia that evening, stopt at Mr. Kerlin's, and said he would be in Chester early in the morning. It was thought proper to see him before the ministers went up; two persons went for him to his place, two miles from Chester; when he came, he informed he had a respite for her, which superseded the necessity of going that night. We are the more particular in this part of the relation, as we are of opinion, neither the prisoner, minister, nor any person in or about the jail, knew that she was respited. This confession was put into the hands of one of the Council.

During the time of her respite her behaviour was in general consistent with her situation; but not appearing at all times so deeply affected, as when the ministers visited her, some reports of the prisoners, intimating the insincerity of her profession, gave uneasiness to her friends: but when she was informed of these reports she was greatly distressed, and accounted for them in such a manner, as to remove all scruple of her sincerity.

*Her respite was brought by her brother about an hour after this confession was wrote, and the execution put off to January 3d.

January the 3d, the morning of her execution, she was again visited by one of the before-mentioned ministers, and other serious persons, who spent some time with her in religious exercises. The minister exhorted her to a steadfast faith in the Son of God, who was not ashamed to be called the "friend of sinners," and who came into the world to "seek and save that which was lost," endeavouring to impress on her mind the solemnity of death, and an eternal state, the necessity of a real change of heart and holiness of nature, as a meetness for the kingdom of God. Her behaviour was serious, solemn, and devout.

When informed there was no respite for her, and was desired to prepare for death, she received the awful summons with a considerable degree of composure; and, after a short space, said, "she did not expect to live." Hearing that her brother was gone in haste to Philadelphia, she was much moved and said, "My poor brother is gone to Philadelphia with an aching heart, he has been concerned about me, kind and tender to me; I hope the Lord will reward him for all his care." After some more serious conversation with her, she was taken with a fit, the women attended her, and the minister left the room.

She was attended to the place of execution by the before-mentioned minister, and a preacher of the Methodist order. On the way the sheriff put her in mind where she was going, and that if she had charged any person wrongfully, now was the time to retract. She said she had not, and seemed uneasy at her sincerity being called in question. At the place of execution, after exhortation and prayer, she requested her confession might be read: leave being obtained of the sheriff, it was read accordingly. She stood up and confirmed what was therein related, on the testimony of a dying woman; appeared penitent, resigned, and engaged in prayer; prayed that others might take warning from her to shun those sins that brought her to this shameful end; said she freely, and from her heart forgave all that had injured her, and prayed for forgiveness of her sins, and that the Lord would have mercy on her; once more declared her innocence of some things, as before mentioned, and seemed uneasy that she should be suspected of insincerity. Being asked the state of her mind, she said her burden was in a great measure removed; seemed easy at the thoughts of death: frequently expressing her confidence in the adorable Redeemer and Saviour of sinners.

The execution was prolonged to give time for her brother's return from Philadelphia.

The Sheriff reminded her that she had but a few minutes to continue, and to make the best use of her time, and appeared much affected.

In her last moment she appeared perfectly calm and resigned; took an affectionate leave of the minister, no longer able to bear the sight, and said "she hoped to meet him in a better world." The moment before she was to be turned off the sheriff asked her if with her dying breath she sealed the confession she had made? When she understood who spoke to her, she moved her hand and said: "I do, for it is the truth." And in a moment was turned off, and quickly left the world, in exchange, we hope, for a better.

But here we must drop a tear! What heart so hard, as not to melt as human woe!

Her brother came in all haste from Philadelphia, with a respite or letter from the Honorable the President and Council, to delay the execution, but through unexpected and unavoidable hindrances on the road, did not arrive until twenty-three minutes after the solemn scene was closed. When he came with the respite in his hand, and saw his sister irrecoverably gone, beheld her motionless, and sunk in death,—who can paint the mournful scene?

Let imagination if she can!

He took her body home, and some efforts were made to restore her to life, but in vain. The day following she was decently enterred, and a large number of respectable people attended her funeral. The minister that attended her in her last moments attended her to the grave. The exercise was solemn; a deep concern was conspicuous on the face of many, if not all that were present.

Thus ended the life of Elizabeth Wilson, in the 27th year of her age; innocent, we believe, of the crime for which she suffered, but guilty in concealing, or rather attempting to conceal, a crime of so horrid a nature, which she was privy to.

May others reflect, that a few years past she was esteemed having a virtuous character.

May they, agreeably to her dying request, take warning from her sufferings and shameful end; and shun the paths of vice, which lead to endless woe: and as the sin that brought her to this shameful end is so predominant, may they in an especial manner guard against it, and be kept from it.

May they consider that sin is hateful to God, contrary to his pure and holy nature, and that he cannot look on it, but with the utmost abhorrence.

May they seriously reflect on its malignant nature! and dreadful! dreadful! consequences. The wages of sin, says an inspired apostle, is death. Painful idea!

Death, natural or corporal, a separation of the soul from the body. Death spiritual, a separation of the soul from God. Death eternal, a separation of soul and body from God; the absence of all good; the presence of all evil; unspeakable torments in soul and body for ever and ever, where our Lord says, their "worm dieth not, and the fire is not quenched."

May they fly from sin to HIM that bled, and groaned, and died the painful, shameful and accursed death of the cross for sinners; that they may have healing by his wounds and life by his death: so shall they be saved from sin and its dreadful consequences here, and for ever hereafter.

Which God of his mercy grant, for the sake of his beloved co-equal, and co-eternal Son, the Lord Jesus Christ. Amen.

The following are taken from papers wrote by her own hand in the latter part of her confinement, as appears by the dates.

ELIZABETH WILSON her hand, the 2d. day of November, 1785, under whose eyes those lines may come, I pray they may take warning by me, a poor distressed prisoner, that is begging for mercy. O Lord! turn not thyself from me! Oh my Heavenly Father! But let me intreat thee to shew mercy to me, a poor distressed sinner. O God! thou knowest my heart is broken within me! O Blessed Lord! help thou my poor begging soul, in the day that I leave this world; and give me life everlasting. World without end. Amen.

I will pray to thee, O my God! while I have breath to breathe. O Lord! have mercy on me a poor sinner! wash me clean, O my God! and make me fit for thy kingdom, where I can have rest and peace for my poor soul! for here I have none! Amen to this world.

ELIZABETH WILSON, in Chester goal, 11th day of November, 1785, under sentence of death, cries for mercy to God. Oh Lord! have mercy on me a poor begging sinner, that is now pleading. O Lord! be merciful unto me! heal my soul! for I have sinned against thee, blot out my iniquity, O my Heavenly Father! and give me to feel thy power more and more! for my poor soul's sake. O Lord! I remember thy blessed promise: They that seek thee with their whole heart is sure to find. O my dear Redeemer! look down with an eye of pity on thy poor unworthy servant, that can do nothing of myself without thy help, O Lord of life and glory! hear thou my cries! pity my poor distressed soul! O my dear Redeemer! wash me, purge me, from all my dross; and make me fit for thy kingdom: where all glory is. O Lord! I regard not what I suffer here on earth, to go to thee above, where all tears are wiped away, and there is no more sorrow. And so farewel to all this world, hoping that God will shew mercy to my poor begging soul in Heaven; where there is joy and peace, for ever and ever more. World without end. Amen, and Amen.

ELIZABETH WILSON, in Chester goal, under sentence of death, on the 22d. day of October, in the year of our Lord 1785. O Lord! help my poor soul, and shew an eye of pity to thy distressed servant, that is begging at thy door for mercy, for her never dying soul! O Lord of life and glory! turn not thy ear from me! O my heavenly father! but grant me mercy! mercy! mercy! O Lord! that I may say in peace. Amen to this world.

Psalm 55, verse 21. The words of his mouth were smoother than butter; but war was in his heart: his words were softer than oil; yet were they drawn swords.

Cast thy burthen upon the Lord, and he shall sustain thee; he shall never suffer the righteous to be moved; but thou, O God! shalt bring them down into the pit of destruction; bloody and deceitful men shall not live out half their days; but I will trust in thee.

## Hymn on Death.

*VAIN man thy fond pursuit forbear,*
*Repent, thy end is nigh——*
*Death at the farthest can't be far,*
*Oh think before you die!*
*Reflect thou hast a soul to save,*
*Thy sins how high they mount,*
*What are thy hopes beyond the grave?*
*How stands that dark account?*
*Death enters and there's no defence,*
*His time there's none can tell;*
*He'll in a moment call thee hence,*
*To heaven or to hell.*
*Thy flesh perhaps thy chiefest care*
*Shall crawling worms consume;*
*But ah, destruction stops not there,*
*Sin kills beyond the tomb.*
*To-day the gospel calls to-day,*
*Sinners it speaks to you,*
*Let every one forsake his way,*
*And mercy will ensue.*
*Rich mercy dearly bought with blood,*
*How vile soever he be,*
*Abundant pardon, peace with God,*
*All given entirely free.*

*Finis.*

## Source Notes

*A Faithful Narrative of Elizabeth Wilson* originally was published in Philadelphia shortly after Wilson's execution occurred on January 3, 1786, in the town of Chester. The narrative made an obvious impact on both printers and readers. Before the year was out at least three (possibly four) other editions were published. One of these editions was printed by Ashbel Stoddard in Hudson, New York, and another appeared in New Haven. A third edition was included in Isaiah Thomas' *The Worcester Magazine* IV, which appeared in April (44–46). Although no copies could be located, both Evans and Ritz listed several "ghosts" as possible publications. One of these "ghosts" was catalogued as having been "Printed and sold" in Carlisle, Pa., by Kline and Reynolds. A second was listed as being "Printed and sold at the Printing-Office, No. 22 Water-Street" in New York. A third spurious edition similarly was listed: "Printed and sold by Hudson and Goodwin" in Hartford, Conn. And a fourth edition supposedly appeared in Middletown, Conn: "Printed by Woodward and Green." All of these "ghosts" appeared, or at least were advertised as appearing, in 1786. Ritz, who has made the most systematic effort to trace the narrative's publishing history, located a copy of the Carlisle edition in the Harvard University Law School Library but was unable to discover either copies or the sources for the Evans entries. In 1807, twenty-one years after the original, a final Wilson edition appeared in Philadelphia, which—according to the title page—was "Printed for the Purchaser."

Two other related works also should be mentioned. In 1786 Ezekiel Russell printed an *ELEGY &c.*, a doggerel broadside ballad that presented the sensational details concerning the murder of Wilson's ten-week old twins. Since the only known existing copy is damaged, the full title cannot be known, and of some thirty-four alternating quatrains, only sixteen remain undamaged. After announcing that "In *Chester-Town* there liv'd a Maid/ . . . [who was] caught in snare deep laid," the "POETESS" condemned Wilson's lover as a "Hard-hearted Wretch! a Monster sure"; as "O Bloody Wretch! infernal Fiend!"; and as "this inhuman Beast!" Such hyperbolic rhetoric, of course, was meant to heighten the sensational impact of the story. Along the same lines, the murder itself was presented as one of Satan's "hellish schemes." But, aside from tantalizing readers, the poet was not interested in describing anything so "hellish"; on the contrary, she spent much of the ballad describing her inability to paint "the PICTURE." She stated that

> A Crime more shocking sure I think
> I never heard the name,
> My pen would take a sea of ink,
> Should I record the same.

A few stanzas later, she similarly exclaimed:

> This solemn Scene! ah who can paint?
> Of skill I'm sure despair,
> Had I a pen of adamant,
> And seas of ink to spare!

O had I pens in both my hands,
And floods of ink to spare!
My pens would fail, my ink grow dry
With anguish and despair.

While in all probability "seas of ink" were not necessary, Russell certainly intended to make further use of the sad events concerning Wilson. In fact, his *Elegy &c.* was nothing more than an elaborate advertisement for the fourth issue of his crime magazine, *The American Bloody Register.* Nearly one-fourth of the three-column broadside was devoted to a long description of Russell's next issue, which would include the full text of the original *Faithful Narrative.*

The "POETESS" herself, in fact, while lamenting her inability to paint "this solemn Scene!," directly referred readers to Russell's "REGISTER" in stanza fifteen. In the advertisement, supposedly included as a footnote to the reference in stanza fifteen, the printer declared:

> Our kind POETESS may, perhaps, be gratified in her wishes, as the *Publisher* hereof proposes, at the earnest request of many, to insert in *Number Four* of his AMERICAN BLOODY REGISTER, the whole of the shocking and tragical Affair, which will include a true and particular *Account* of *Miss* WILSON's *Religious Exercises, Dying Sayings* and a *Hymn* on *Death,* with some *serious moral Reflections* and many other *interesting Particulars. . . .*

The printer stated that he received the "*Particulars*" of "this most melancholy TRAGEDY" from a correspondent in Baltimore, "the Reverend ISAAC STORY," who desired that the Wilson narrative "might be re-printed in the REGISTER for the benefit of the "*Rising Generation.*" Yet like the *Elegy &c.*, neither the advertisement nor *Number Four* entirely were dedicated to saving the "Rising Generation." After a few words from the Reverend Story, urging readers "*to restrain the lusts of the* gay *and* thoughtless," the advertisement then promised readers that "in this REGISTER will also be published" the wildly sensational tale of Sauny Beane. For further information concerning Russell's crime magazine, see above, *The American Bloody Register.* Russell's *Elegy &c.* must be seen as one of the most clever advertising gimmicks of early America.

The last publication relevant to the Wilson case was presented to the public as *The victim of seduction! Some interesting particulars of the life and untimely fate of Miss Harriot Wilson, who was publicly executed in the State of Pennsylvania in the year 1802, for the murder of her infant child . . .* (Boston: J. Wilkey, n.d.). According to Thomas M. McDade in *The Annals of Murder,* the Wilkey narrative "is undoubtedly a fictional treatment of the Elizabeth Wilson case" (328). Aside from changing the date and the number of victims, the Wilkey text generally resembled the Wilson original, including a description of Elizabeth/Harriet Wilson's brother arriving five minutes too late with a pardon for his sister.

Wilson was taken into custody a full year before she finally was executed. The grisly announcement of Wilson's arrest, published in both *The Pennsylvania Journal* (January 5, 1785) and *The Independent Gazetteer* (January 8, 1785), contradicted the later account in the narrative, making no mention of Deshong and denying knowledge of the murders:

> About a week ago a woman was committed to Chester goal, on suspicion of murdering her two sucking infant twins, whose bodies were found under some brush. A traveller passing by, observed his dog scratching among the brush, and presently after brought out the head of a child, in his mouth. This induced his master to light, and examine further, when he found the bodies of two innocent babes, who had been put to death not long before. The woman was charged with the murder, which she denies, but acknowledged having placed the children by the road side, in order that any person passing that way, and who had humanity enough, might take them up. The head which the dog brought out, had been cut off; and the woman was seen sucking the children near the spot but a little time before the bodies were discovered. (*The Independent Gazetteer*)

A year later both *The Pennsylvania Journal* (January 14, 1786) and *The Independent Gazetteer* (January 14, 1786) again included identical announcements concerning Wilson:

> On Tuesday, the 3d instant, the woman who was tried and convicted at Chester, of murdering her two bastard children, ten weeks after birth, was hanged at that place, pursuant to her sentence, the respite given by the honorable the Council having expired. (*The Independent Gazetteer*)

# Life, Laſt Words and Dying *CONFESSION*,

OF

# RACHEL WALL,

Who, with ***William Smith*** and ***William Dunogan***, were executed at BOSTON, on Thurſday, October 8, 1789, for

HIGH-WAY ROBBERY.

*BOSTON-GOAL*, WEDNESDAY EVENING, *October* 7, 1789.

I RACHEL WALL, was born in the town of *Carliſle*, in the ſtate of Pennſylvania, in the year 1760, of honeſt and reputable parents, who were alive and in good health not long ſince: They gave me a good education, and inſtructed me in the fundamental principles of the Chriſtian Religion, and taught me the fear of God; and if I had followed the good advice [illegible] I ſhould never have come to this untimely fate. When I left home I had three brothers and two ſiſters alive and well.

Without doubt the ever-curious Public, (but more eſpecially thoſe of a ſerious turn of mind) will be anxious to know every particular circumſtance of the Life and Character of a perſon in my unhappy ſituation, but in a peculiar manner thoſe relative to my birth and parentage.

With regard to my Parents, I have only room in this ſhort Narrative to obſerve, that my father was a Farmer, who was in good circumſtances when I left him. Both my parents being of the Preſbyterian, or rather Congregational Perſuaſion, I was educated in the ſame way. My father was of a very ſerious and devout turn of mind, and always made it his conſtant practice to perform family-prayers in his houſe every morning and evening; and was very careful to call his children and family together every Sabbath-day evening, to hear the holy ſcriptures, and other pious books read to them; each one being obliged, after reading was over, to give an anſwer to ſuch queſtions in the Aſſembly's Catechiſm as were propoſed to them.

I left my parents without their conſent when I was very young, and returning again was received by them, but could not be contented; therefore I tarried with them but two years, before I left them again, and have never ſeen them ſince.

I came away with one *George Wall*, to whom I was lawfully married: If I had never ſeen him I ſhould not have left my parents. I went with him to *Philadelphia*; we tarried there ſome time, but left that place and went to *New-York*, where we ſtaid about three months.—From thence we came to *Boſton*, where he tarried with me ſome time, and then went off, leaving me an entire ſtranger: Upon which I went to ſervice and lived very contented, and ſhould have remained ſo, had it not been for my huſband; for, as ſoon as he came back, he enticed me to leave my ſervice and take to bad company, from which I may date my ruin. I hope my unhappy fate will be a ſolemn warning to him. He went off again and left me, and where he is now [illegible] forgive him, as I expect forgiveneſs at the bar of God, through the merits of my dear Saviour and Redeemer JESUS CHRIST, who is able to ſave all thoſe that, by faith, come unto him, not refuſing even the chief of ſinners.

I hope my awful and untimely fate will be a ſolemn warning and caution to every one, but more particularly to the youth, eſpecially thoſe of my own ſex.

I acknowledge myſelf to have been guilty of a great many crimes, ſuch as Sabbath-breaking, ſtealing, lying, diſobedience to parents, and almoſt every other ſin a perſon could commit, except murder; and have not lived in the fear of God, nor regarded the kind admonitions and counſels of man.

In ſhort, the many ſmall crimes I have committed, are too numerous to mention in this ſheet, and therefore a particular narrative of them here would ſerve to extend a work of this kind to too great a length; which crimes I moſt ſincerely deſire to confeſs to Almighty God, humbly hoping forgiveneſs thro' his dear Son.

But as I could heartily wiſh that the innocent may not ſuffer with the guilty, I ſhall, in ſome degree, deviate from my firſt intention, by relating the particulars of ſome material tranſactions of my life, which, perhaps, may ſerve as a ſolemn warning to the living, of my ſex at leaſt; eſpecially to thoſe whom they may more immediately concern: They are as follow, viz.

In one of my nocturnal excurſions, when the bright goddeſs Venus ſhined conſpicuous, and was the predominant Planet among the heavenly bodies, ſometime in the ſpring of 1787, not being able to aſcertain the exact time, I happened to go on board a ſhip, lying at the Long-Wharf, in Boſton;—the Captain's name I cannot recollect, but think he was a Frenchman: On my entering the cabin, the door of which not being faſtened, and finding the Captain and Mate aſleep in their beds, I hunted about for plunder, and diſcovered, under the Captain's head, a black ſilk handkerchief containing upwards of thirty pounds, in gold, crowns, and ſmall change, on which I immediately ſeized the booty and decamped therewith as quick as poſſible; which money I ſpent freely in company as lewd and wicked as myſelf, fully proving the old adage, "*Light come light go.*"

At another time, I think it was about the year 1788, I broke into a ſloop, on board of which I was acquainted, lying at Doane's Wharf, in this town, and finding the Captain and every hand on board aſleep in the cabin and ſteerage, I looked round to ſee what I could help myſelf to, when I eſpied a ſilver watch hanging over the Captain's head, which I pocketed. I alſo took a pair of ſilver buckles out of the Captain's ſhoes: I likewiſe made free with a parcel of ſmall change for pocket-money, to make myſelf merry among my *evil companions*, and made my eſcape without being diſcovered.

I would beg the patience of the public for only a few minutes, while I relate another adventure that happened in the courſe of my life, which, were it not for the novelty thereof, might be thought too trifling to mention in this ſheet; but with a view of gratifying the curioſity of ſome particular friends, who have been very kind to me under ſentence, I have conſented to give it to the publiſher for inſertion, which is as follows:

Sometime about the year 1785, my huſband being confined in the Goal in this place for theft, I had a mind to try an expedient to extricate him from his impriſonment, which was to have a brick-loaf baked, in which I contrived to encloſe a number of tools, ſuch as a ſaw, file, &c. in order to aſſiſt him to make his eſcape, which was handed to him by the goaler in perſon, who little ſuſpected ſuch a trick was playing with him; however, it like to have had the deſired effect the crafty contriver intended; for, by means of this ſtratagem, the poor culprit, *Wall*, had buſily employed himſelf with the implements that his kind help-mate had in this curious manner conveyed to him, and had nearly effected his deſign before it was diſcovered.

I do now, in the preſence of God, declare Miſs Dorothy Horn, a crippled perſon in Boſton Alms-Houſe, to be entirely innocent of the theft at Mr. Vaughn's in Eſſex-Street, tho' ſhe ſuffered a long impriſonment, was ſet on the gallows one hour, and whipped five ſtripes therefor.

As to the crime of Robbery, for which I am in a few hours to ſuffer an ignominious death, I am entirely innocent; to the truth of this declaration I appeal to that God before whom I muſt ſhortly appear, to give an account of every tranſaction of my life.

With regard to the above Robbery, I would beg permiſſion to relate a few particulars, which are, that I had been at work all the preceding day, and was on my way home in the evening, without deſign to injure any perſon: in my way I heard a noiſe in the ſtreet; what it was I knew not, until I was taken up; I never ſaw Miſs *Bendar* (the perſon I was charged with robbing that evening.) and was quite ſurpriſed when the crime was laid to my charge. The witneſſes who ſwore againſt me are certainly miſtaken; but as a dying perſon I freely forgive them.

I return my ſincere thanks to the Hon. gentlemen who were my Judges, for aſſigning me counſel, and to them for their kindneſs in pleading my cauſe.

I likewiſe return my hearty thanks to the ſeveral Miniſters of the town, who have attended me ſince I have been under ſentence: alſo to a number of other kind friends, for the care they have ſhewn to me, both for ſoul and body, which gratitude obliges me to acknowledge. May God reward them all for their kindneſs to me.

And now, into the hands of Almighty God I commit my ſoul, relying on his mercy, through the merits and mediation of my Redeemer, and die an unworthy member of the Preſbyterian Church, in the 29th year of my age.

Taken from the priſoner's mouth, a few hours before her execution, and ſigned by

*Rachel Wall.*

JOSEPH OTIS, Deputy-Goaler.

WM. CROMBIE, Aſſiſtant.

## [ RACHEL WALL ]

# *Life, Last Words, and Dying Confession of Rachel Wall*

## [ 1789 ]

*BOSTON-GOAL,* WEDNESDAY
EVENING, *October* 7, 1789.

I RACHEL WALL, was born in the town of *Carlisle*, in the state of Pennsylvania, in the year 1760, of honest and reputable parents, who were alive and in good health not long since: They gave me a good education, and instructed me in the fundamental principles of the Christian Religion, and taught me the fear of God; and if I had followed the good advice, and pious counsel they often gave me, I should never have come to this untimely fate. When I left home I had three brothers and two sisters alive and well.

Without doubt the ever-curious Public, (but more especially those of a serious turn of mind) will be anxious to know every particular circumstance of the Life and Character of a person in my unhappy situation, but in a peculiar manner those relative to my birth and parentage.

With regard to my Parents, I have only room in this short Narrative to observe, that my father was a Farmer, who was in good circumstances when I left him. Both my parents being of the Presbyterian, or rather Congregational Persuasion, I was educated in the same way. My father was of a very serious and devout turn of mind, and always made it his constant practice to perform family-prayers in his house every morning and evening; was very careful to call his children and family together every Sabbath-day evening, to hear the holy scriptures, and other pious books read to them; each one being obliged, after reading was over, to give an answer to such questions in the Assembly's Catechism as were proposed to them.

I left my parents without their consent when I was very young, and returning again was received by them, but could not be contented; therefore I tarried with them but two years, before I left them again, and have never seen them since.

I came away with one *George Wall*, to whom I was lawfully married: If I had never seen him I should not have left my parents. I went with him to *Philadelphia*; we tarried there some time, but left that place and went to *New-York*, where we staid about three months.—From thence we came to *Boston*, where he tarried with me some time, and then went off, leaving me an entire stranger: Upon which I went to service and lived very contented, and should have remained so, had it not been for my husband; for, as soon as he came back, he enticed me to leave my service and take to bad company, from which I may date my ruin. I hope my unhappy fate will be a solemn warning to him. He went off again and left me, and where he is now I know not. As a dying person, I freely forgive him, as I expect forgiveness at the bar of God, through the merits of my dear Saviour and Redeemer JESUS CHRIST, who is able to save all those that, by faith, come unto him, not refusing even the chief of sinners.

I hope my awful and untimely fate will be a solemn warning and caution to every one, but more particularly to the youth, especially those of my own sex.

I acknowledge myself to have been guilty of a great many crimes, such as Sabbath-breaking, stealing, lying, disobedience to parents, and almost every other sin a person could commit, except murder; and have not lived in the fear of God, nor regarded the kind admonitions and counsels of man.

In short, the many small crimes I have committed, are too numerous to mention in this sheet, and therefore a particular narrative of them here would serve to extend a work of this kind to too great a length; which crimes I most sincerely desire to confess to Almighty God, humbly hoping forgiveness thro' his dear Son.

But as I could heartily wish that the innocent may not suffer with the guilty, I shall, in some degree, deviate from my first intention, by relating the particulars of some material transactions of my life, which, perhaps, may serve as a solemn warning to the living, of my sex at least; especially to those whom they may more immediately concern: They are as follow, viz.

In one of my nocturnal excursions, when the bright goddess Venus shined conspicuous, and was the predominant Planet among the heavenly bodies, sometime in the spring of 1787, not being able to ascertain the exact time, I happened to go on board a ship, lying at the Long-Wharf, in Boston;—the Captain's name I cannot recollect, but think he was a Frenchman: On my entering the cabin, the door of which not being fastened, and finding the Captain and Mate asleep in their beds, I hunted about for plunder, and discovered, under the Captain's head, a black silk handkerchief containing upwards of thirty pounds, in gold, crowns, and small change, on which I immediately seized the booty and decamped therewith as quick as possible; which money I spent freely in company as lewd and wicked as myself, fully proving the old adage, "*Light come light go.*"

At another time, I think it was about the year 1788, I broke into a sloop, on board of which I was acquainted, lying at Doane's Wharf, in this town, and finding the Captain and every hand on board asleep in the cabin and steerage, I looked round to see what I could help myself to, when I espied a silver watch hanging over the Captain's head, which I pocketed. I also took a pair of silver buckles out of the Captain's shoes: I likewise made free with a parcel of small change for pocket-money, to make myself merry among my *evil companions*, and made my escape without being discovered.

I would beg the patience of the public for only a few minutes, while I relate another adventure that happened in the course of my life, which, were it not for the novelty thereof, might be thought too trifling to mention in this sheet; but with a view of gratifying the curiosity of some particular friends, who have been very kind to me under sentence, I have consented to give it to the publisher for insertion, which is as follows:

Sometime about the year 1785, my husband being confined in the Goal in this place for theft, I had a mind to try an expedient to extricate him from his imprisonment, which was to have a brick-loaf baked, in which I contrived to enclose a number of tools, such as a saw, file, & c. in order to assist him to make his escape, which was handed to him by the goaler in person, who little suspected such a trick was playing with him; however, it like to have had the desired effect the crafty contriver intended; for, by means of this stratagem, the poor culprit, *Wall*, had busily employed himself with the implements that his kind help-mate had in this curious manner conveyed to him, and had nearly effected his design before it was discovered.

I do now, in the presence of God, declare Miss Dorothy Horn, a crippled person in Boston Alms-House, to be entirely innocent of the theft at Mr. Vaughn's in Essex-Street, tho' she suffered a long imprisonment, was set on the gallows one hour, and whipped five stripes therefor.

As to the crime of Robbery, for which I am in a few hours to suffer an ignominious death, I am entirely innocent; to the truth of this declaration I appeal to that God before whom I must shortly appear to give an account of every transgression of my life.

With regard to the above Robbery, I would beg permission to relate a few particulars, which are, that I had been at work all the preceding day, and was on my way home in the evening, without design to injure any person: in my way I heard a noise in the street; what it was I knew not, until I was taken up; I never saw Miss *Bendar* (the person I was charged with robbing that evening) and was quite surprised when the crime was laid to my charge. The witnesses who swore against me are certainly mistaken; but as a dying person I freely forgive them.

I return my sincere thanks to the Hon. gentlemen who were my Judges, for assigning me counsel, and to them for their kindness in pleading my cause.

I likewise return my hearty thanks to several Ministers of the town, who have attended me since I have been under sentence: also to a number of other kind friends, for the care they have shewn to me, both for soul and body, which gratitude obliges me to acknowledge. May God reward them all for their kindness to me.

And now, into the hands of Almighty God I commit my soul, relying on his mercy, through the merits and mediation of my Redeemer, and die an unworthy member of the Presbyterian Church, in the 29th year of my age.

Taken from the prisoner's mouth, a few hours before her execution, and signed by

*Rachel Wall.*

JOSEPH OTIS, Deputy-Goaler.
WM. CROMBIE, Assistant.

## Source Notes

Wall's broadside narrative, the *Life, Last Words and Dying Confession, of Rachel Wall*, was published in Boston shortly after her execution on Thursday, October 8, 1789. Although the full title advertised that Wall was accompanied to the gallows with William Smith and William Dunogan, the text was concerned only with the woman, but in order to exploit the sensation caused by the triple hanging, the broadside included an engraving depicting the three as they were "turned off." According to the newspaper accounts, the three were each executed for "High-Way Robbery," but their crimes were unrelated. Two other publications did combine the lives and confessions of the three. About the same time that the broadside was printed, Ezekiel Russell published the fourth issue of his "register": *THE PRISONER'S Magazine. Or the MALEFACTOR'S BLOODY REGISTER. No. IV. CONTAINING THE LIFE AND CONFESSION OF RACHEL WALL, WILLIAM DUNOGAN AND WILLIAM SMITH* (Boston, 1789). Also sometime during the fall of 1789, there was published *The Lives and Confessions of Rachel Wall, William Smith, and William Denosse, executed in Boston. Neither of the above had arrived to the age of thirty years, but have been old offenders—The woman in particular.* (Keene, NH: James D. Griffith). Although no copies of these last two have been located, Charles Evans listed them because both Russell and Griffiths advertised their respective narratives as "just published." The copy text used in the anthology is taken from the original broadside.

Several newspapers listed the trials and execution of Wall, Smith and Dunogan (whose name was variously spelled). In the September 14, 1789, issue of *The Boston Gazette*, mention of the trials was included in a long list of indictments and convictions:

> At the the Supreme Judical Court began and held at Boston, in and for the County of Suffolk, on the last Tuesday of August, A.D. 1789.
>
> John Cambell and William Smith were indicted for robbery. Smith was convicted and sentenced to be hanged; and Cambell acquitted.
>
> Rachel Wall, indicted for robbery, convicted and sentenced to be hanged.
>
> William Dennossee, convicted for robbery, and sentenced to be hanged.

*The Massachusetts Centinel* (September 12) also simply listed the convictions: "At the Supreme Judical Court lately held here, *William Smith*, *Rachel Wall*, and *William Dennosse*, were severally convicted of *robbery*, and sentenced to be *hanged*." After listing the other trials and convictions, the paper further announced: "The Supreme Executive of this State has been pleased to order, that the execution of the sentence of death pronounced on *William Smith*, *William Dennosse*, and *Rachel Wall*, for robbery, shall be on Thursday the 8th of October next."

According to both newspapers, the executions took place on schedule. The *Gazette* (October 12) reported that "Thursday was executed William Dennossee, William Smith, and Rachel Wall, pursuant to their sentence, for highway robbery," while the *Centinel* (October 10) offered its readers: "On Thursday were executed *William Denosse*, *William Smith*, and *Rachel Wall*, pursuant to their sentence for highway robbery."

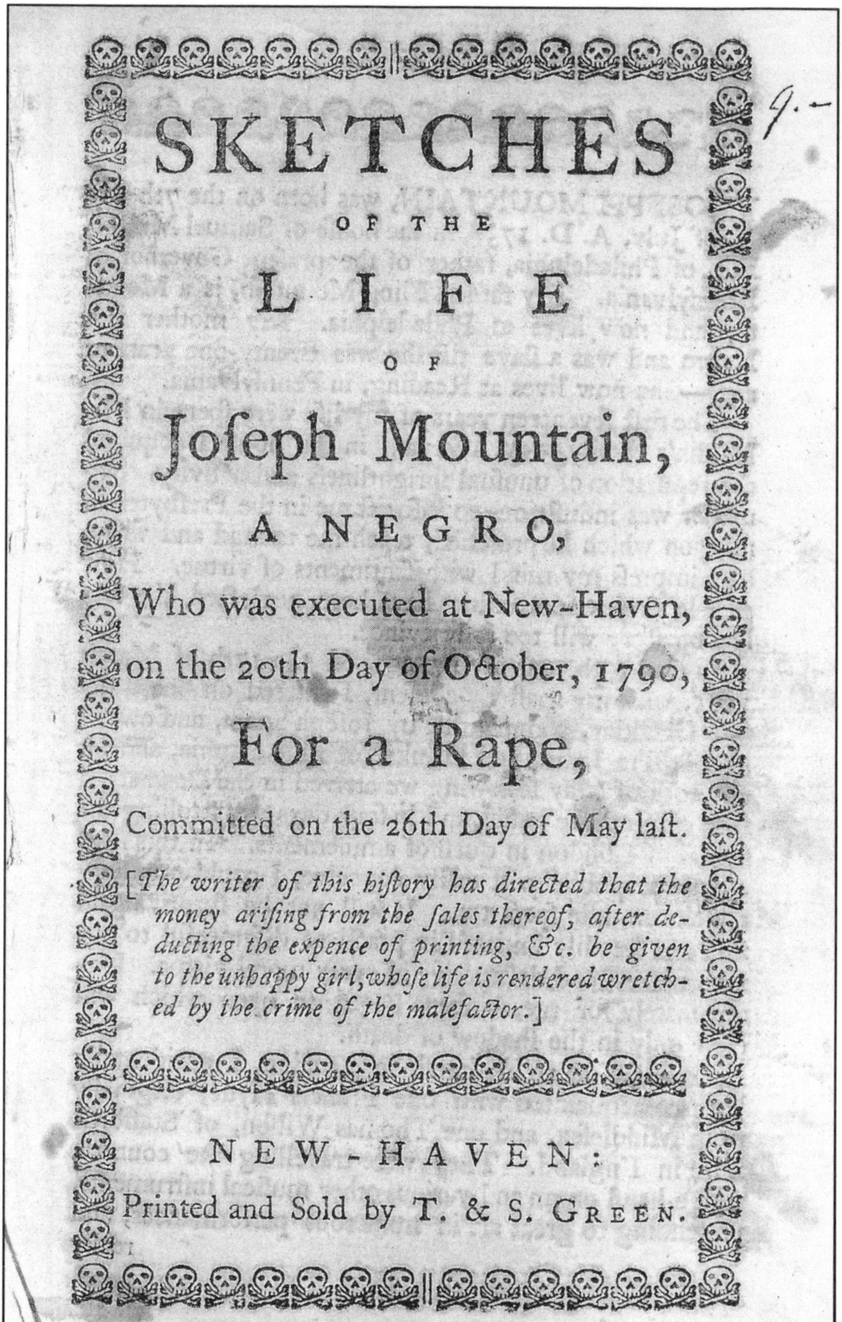

SKETCHES

OF THE

LIFE

OF

Joſeph Mountain,

A NEGRO,

Who was executed at New-Haven, on the 20th Day of October, 1790,

For a Rape,

Committed on the 26th Day of May laſt.

[*The writer of this hiſtory has directed that the money ariſing from the ſales thereof, after deducting the expence of printing, &c. be given to the unhappy girl, whoſe life is rendered wretched by the crime of the malefactor.*]

NEW-HAVEN:

Printed and Sold by T. & S. GREEN.

[ JOSEPH MOUNTAIN ]

# *Sketches of the Life of Joseph Mountain, a Negro*

[ 1790 ]

I JOSEPH MOUNTAIN, was born on the 7th day of July, A.D. 1758, in the house of Samuel Mifflin, Esq. of Philadephia, father of the present Governor of Pennsylvania. My father, Fling Mountain, is a Molatto, and now lives at Philadelphia. My mother is a Negro and was a slave till she was twenty-one years of age.—She now lives at Reading, in Pennsylvania.

The first seventeen years of my life were spent in Mr. Mifflin's family.—As a servant in the house I acquired the reputation of unusual sprightliness and activity. My master was industrious to instruct me in the Presbyterian religion which he professed, teach me to read and write, and impress my mind with sentiments of virtue. How grossly these opportunities have been neglected, the following story will too fully evince.

In the 17th year of my age, on the 17th of March 1775, with my master's consent, I entered on board the ship Chalkley, commanded by Joseph Spain, and owned by Mess'rs. James and Drinker of Philadelphia, and on the 20th of May following we arrived in the Downs. I soon quitted the vessel, and in four days was strolling the streets of London in quest of amusements. In this situation, the public will easily conceive, I could not long remain an idle spectator. It will not be surprizing to find me speedily initiated in practices disgraceful to human nature, and destructive of every moral virtue. Unfortunately for me, a scene began to open which will close only in the shadow of death.

One day, at an ale-house in London, I accidentally became acquainted with one Francis Hyde, originally from Middlesex, and one Thomas Wilson, of Staffordshire in England. They were travelling the country, with a hand organ and various other musical instruments, pretending to great art in numerous performances, and really possessing surprizing knowledge in every species of juggling. This was their employment in the day time, for the purpose of executing more effectually the principal business of their lives, viz.* highway robbery. They soon found me susceptible of almost any impressions, and neither incapable of, nor averse to, becoming a companion in their iniquity. We all sat out from London about 8 o'clock in the evening after I had joined them, each armed with a hanger and a brace of pistols. We had also suitable dresses and a dark lanthorn. Our landlord, who kept tavern at the sign of the black horse, at Charing-cross, furnished us with every requisite for the expedition. His name was William Humphrys. The plan this evening was to attack the mail-coach, which would start at 12 o'clock at night, from the ship tavern, between Woolwich and Graves-end, about 9 miles from London.

We were on the spot at the hour agreed upon, and disguised ourselves for the adventure. Hyde and Wilson were dressed in white frocks and boots, with their faces painted yellow to resemble Molattoes. Mountain was dressed in the same manner, with the addition of a large tail wig, white gloves and a black mask over his face. When the stage arrived, I started, and caught the leading horses by their bridles, while Hyde and Wilson each presented a brace of pistols in at the coach window, and demanded of the passengers their money. There were four gentlemen and one lady in the coach. They denied having any money. Wilson said, "Deliver, or death." They then gave us a bank note of 50 l. one other of 20 l. and about 60 guineas in cash. We then retired to an unfrequented place, shifted our dresses, and prepared to prosecute our journey to Chatham in the county of Kent.

In the day time, Hyde and Wilson commonly played upon their instruments, and performed various feats of slight of hand, as tho' that was their sole occupation. We were also very particular in making observations upon all travellers, to learn if they might be *touched;* (for that was our word for *robbed.*)

In four days after the former robbery, we met a Capt. Hill at the foot of Rochester bridge near Chatham—He was a captain of the marines, and we had seen him in the day time at Brumpton barracks, about half a mile from the bridge. We walked directly before his horse. Wilson asked him the time of night. He made no reply. Hyde then caught the bridle. I, his left hand, and Wilson presented a pistol to his breast, and said, "Deliver, or death." He assured us that he had no money worth taking. Wilson said, "then give us your watch," which he did. The watch was gold, and valued at 50 guineas. We then walked off about 300 rods towards Graves-end, and

*The reader will note, that when we use the term *foot-pad*, we mean him who robs on foot only; *highway-man* intends one who rides on horse back.

immediately tacked for Rochester, where we lodged at the mariner's inn. There was great *hue and cry* for us; but the pursuers, supposing from Capt. Hill's information, we had gone for Graves-end, entirely mistook our rout. The next morning we took post-chaise for London, where we arrived about 6 o'clock in the evening. Our booty was delivered to a broker whom we constantly employed. He was a Jew, and lived in St. Katherine's Row, near Tower-Hill, and his name was William Moses. There were also other brokers in different parts of England, with whom we had constant communication, and who were perfectly acquainted with our modes of acquiring property. After such a jaunt we thought it advisable to recruit ourselves by rioting on our spoils.

In a few days, it was concluded that I should go alone, and attempt to "touch" some gentlemen who frequented the plays at Covent Garden; this, considering my age and inexperience, was thought rather a bold stroke. Being villain enough to attempt any thing, I did not hesitate; but posted myself agreeably to direction. My efforts, however, were wholly unsuccessful, and I returned empty. The next night I was placed at London bridge, while Hyde stood at Black-fryars, and Wilson at Westminster. At half past 11 o'clock I met a Captain Duffield, and asked him the time of night. He told me. I said, "You know my profession; deliver or death." He stepped back to strike me with his cane; I cocked my pistol, and told him to deliver instantly, or death should be his portion. He then threw me his purse, which contained about 10 guineas, and a silver watch, which was valued by our broker at 6 l. Hyde, the same night, obtained about 40 guineas of Sir John Griffing. Wilson about 30 of a Mr. Burke; and each a watch, one gold, the other pinchbeck. The next day we saw advertisements, describing the robberies, and offering rewards for the perpetrators.

The next night, with little difficulty, I robbed Hugh Lindsly of 16 guineas, and a gold ring. Hyde, on the same evening, took from Lord John Cavendish about 20 guineas, and Wilson robbed William Burke of 11 guineas.

We now concluded to remain in London for a while, as *gentlemen of pleasure.*—The repeated robberies had furnished us with cash in abundance, and we indulged in every species of debauchery. We gambled very deeply at dice, cards, and billiards. Hyde and Wilson were very expert at this business, and would almost invariably swindle a stranger out of his money.

In March 1776, we went to the city of York, about 200 miles from London. Here we continued several weeks, waiting some favourable opportunities to rob at the plays; but none presented. We went from York to New-Market, to attend the famous races which took place about the first of June. There we found Lord Gore of Richmond, and Lord Tufton of

Sheffield in Yorkshire: We were much perplexed to invent the most advantageous mode of "touching" them. It was at length concluded to attack them at their lodgings, which were at an inn very large and greatly frequented by various classes of people. About 7 o'clock in the evening, while the attendants of those gentlemen were in the kitchens and stables, we entered the front door, and having bribed the porter with a few guineas, were immediately let into the room. Lords Gore and Tufton were sitting over a table at a dish of coffee, and reading news-papers. We instantly presented our pistols, and demanded their money, Lord Tufton delivered us one bank note of 100 l. and three others of 50 l. each. Lord Gore delivered us about 100 guineas, and two gold mourning rings. We quitted New-Market next morning, and went in the stage to York, where Wilson presented his bills for payment. Unfortunately for us, Lord Tufton, immediately after the robbery, dispatched his servant to the bank, with orders to stop those bills, if offered. The bills were accordingly stopped, and Wilson arrested, and sent to New-Market to be examined before a justice of the peace. Upon his examination he procured Hyde to swear that he was riding from New-Market to York with Wilson and that he saw him pick up a pocket book containing those bills. The coachman, having been previously bribed, swore to the same fact. Upon this testimony, Wilson was acquitted. I was not sent for as a witness at this examination, as I understood Lord Robert Manners was then in New-Market, and would probably attend the trial. The reason why I did not wish to meet his Lordship's eye, was, that on the night before we left London, I made a most daring attack upon him. He was walking unarmed, near Hounslow Heath, attended by his footman. I met him, presented my pistol, and he gave me 75 guineas, two gold watches, and two gold rings.—Hyde and Wilson were near at hand; but they did not discover themselves, leaving me "to play the hero alone."

In the latter end of June we again met at the old rendezvous in London and divided our plunder. The property which I then had on hand enabled me to live very freely for some months. My time was spent in the round of dissipation which was the necessary attendant upon so vicious a character, and which was tolerably well supported by the stock of cash in my own possession, and that of my broker.

I now resolved to quit this course of life which I had hitherto pursued with so much success. Accordingly I entered on board the brig Sally, as Cook, and made two voyages in her to Lisbon. Upon my return, after exhausting my pay, I made another voyage, in the Fanny, Capt. Sinclair, to Kingston, in Jamaica; which being finished in nine months, I again visited London, and concluded to relinquish the seafaring business for the present. At the old place of resort I became acquainted with one Haynes and Jones, both of Yorkshire. They were partially initiated in the science of *foot-pads*.

They soon proposed that I should resume my profession, and join them. My former mode of life, tho' singularly vicious, yet possessed many charms in my view. I therefore complied with their request; at the same time doubting, if they were possessed of sufficient courage and skill for companions to one who had served under experienced masters, and who considered himself at the head of the profession. Our first object was to assail the Newcastle stage, which would be in Tottenham-Court road at 8 o'clock in the evening. We were on the spot in season, and Mountain addressed them thus: "My Lads, 'tis a hazardous attempt—for God's sake make a bold stroke." Upon the arrival of the coach at half past 7 o'clock, four miles from London, I seized the bridles of the two foremost horses. Jones and Haynes went to the coach door, and said, "Deliver or death." Lord Garnick and several others were passengers: His Lordship said, "Yes, yes, I'll deliver," and instantly discharged a pistol at Jones, the contents of which entered his left shoulder: upon which he and Haynes made their escape. The coachman was then directed to "drive on"—He replied, "There is a man who yet holds the leading horses."—Lord Garnick then fired at me, but without damage; upon which I discharged my pistol at the coach, but without effect. Jones was so badly wounded, that Haynes and I were obliged to carry him into London upon our shoulders. We were soon overtaken by two highway men, who had assaulted Lord Garnick about 15 minutes before our engagement, one of whom was badly wounded. The next day we saw an advertisement offering a reward of sixty guineas for the detection of the robbers, and informing, that it was supposed three were killed. This specimen of the enterprize of my new associates convinced me, that they were not adepts in their *occupation*, and induced me to quit their society.

The business which now seemed most alluring to me, was that of *highway-men*. Considering myself at the head of the foot-pads, I aspired for a more *honorable* employment, and therefore determined to join my self to the gang of highway men, whose rendezvous were at Broad St. Giles, up Holborne, at the sign of the Hampshire hog, and kept by a William Harrison, a native of the Isle of Man. Harrison was the support, the protector and the landlord of this whole company. The horses and accoutrements were kept and furnished by him, and occasionally supplied to adventurers. He enquired my name, and finding that I was Mountain who was confederate with Hyde and Wilson, he readily admitted me to the fraternity. He asked if I dared take a jaunt alone; and finding me willing for any thing, he quickly furnished me with equipments proper for the expedition. Mounted on a very fleet horse, and prepared with proper changes of dress, I sat out for Coventry, about 90 miles from London. I made great dispatch in travelling, and about 10 o'clock the night after my departure, I met Richard Watts coming out of a lane about two miles from Coventry. I rode up to him, and enquired if he was not afraid of highway-men? He replied, "No, I have no property of value about me." I then told him I was a man of the profession, and that he must deliver or abide the consequences. Upon this he gave me his gold watch: I insisted on his money, and cocked my pistol, threatening him with instant death. He perceived that resistance and persuasion were equally unavailing, and threw me his purse containing 13 half guineas and some pocket-pieces. The gold watch was valued at 40 guineas. I then ordered him back down the lane, accompanied him thither, and fled with the greatest haste into an adjacent wood: Here I shifted my own and horse's dress, leaving them in a bye place, rode directly to a neighboring town, and there put up for the night. Thence I took my course for Newcastle in Devonshire, about 270 miles north of London, and thence to Warrington in Lancastershire. Here about 7 o'clock in the evening I met with a gentleman who appeared an object of plunder. I asked him the time of night; he drew his watch, and told me the hour. I observed "You have a very fine watch." He answered, "Fine enough." "Sir, 'tis too fine for you—you know my profession—deliver." He drew back; I caught his bridle with one hand, presented a pistol with the other, and said, "Deliver, or I'll cool your porridge:" He handed me a purse of 8 guineas, and a gold watch valued at 30l. sterling. To compleat the iniquity, and exhibit the extent of my villainy, I then took a prayer-book from my pocket, and ordered him to swear upon the solemnity of God's word, that he would make no discovery in twelve hours: He took the oath: I quitted him, and heard nothing of the matter till the next morning about 10 o'clock, when I saw a particular detail of the transaction in the news-paper.

Liverpool was my next stage. Here I tarried two days making observations for evening adventures. On the night of the second day I robbed Thomas Reevs of 6 guineas, and a gold watch worth about 30 l. sterling. To insult him in his distress, after committing the fact, I pulled off my hat, made a low bow, wished him good night, and sat out for Lancaster in company with the stage. It occurred to me, that riding as a guard to the stage would secure me against suspicion. Accordingly I accompanied it to Lancaster, and there put up at the "swan and two necks." Here I continued three days, waiting a favourable opportunity to exercise my profession. On the third evening at 8 o'clock, I stopped a Col. Pritchard, took from him a gold watch valued at 44 guineas, a purse of 30 guineas, 3 gold rings, and a pair of gold-knee buckles worth about 6 l. The knee-buckles appeared so tempting, I told Pritchard, I could not avoid taking them. At 11 o'clock I left Lancaster, and having rode about one mile from town, I stopped, pulled off my hat, and bid them "good-bye."

My course was now for Manchester, where I put up for about 24 hours at the "bull's-head." The evening following, about 11 miles from Manchester, I "touched" a Quaker. It was nearly 9 o'clock when I met him. I enquired if he was not afraid to ride alone. He answered, No. I asked him his religion; he replied "I am a Friend." I observed, "You are the very man I was looking for—you must deliver your money." He seemed very unwilling, and said, "Thou art very hard with me." I replied, "You must not *thou* me." He then gave me his plain gold watch, 6 guineas, and four bank notes of 20 l. each. I then presented a prayer-book, and demanded an oath that he would make no discovery in 8 hours: He refused an oath, alledging that it was contrary to his religion, but gave his word that my request should be complied with. I then dismissed him, returning the bank notes, and took a circuitous rout for London. The guineas which I obtained in this jaunt, I concealed and carried in the soles of my boots, which were calculated for that purpose, and effectually answered it. The mare I rode was trained for the business: she would put her head in at a coach window with the utmost ease, and stand like a stock against any thing. She would travel also with surprizing speed. Upon my arrival at Harrison's, (having been gone eleven days) I gave a faithful narrative of my transactions, and produced the plunder as undeniable proof. I never shall forget with what joy I was received. The house rang with the praises of Mountain. An elegant supper was provided, and he placed at the head of the table. Notwithstanding the darkness of his complexion, he was complimented as the first of his profession, and qualified for the most daring enterprizes.

Fatigued with such a jaunt, and fearing lest too frequent adventures might expose me, I determined on tarrying a while at home. My horse was given to another, and he directed to seek for prey. After one month's absence he returned with only 16 guineas, and was treated accordingly by the gang. He was inadequate to the business, and was therefore ordered to tarry at home, just to visit play-houses, & *sharp it* among people who might easily be choused of their property. Each took his tour of duty in course; some succeeded; others, from misfortune or want of spirit, were disgraced. One young fellow of the party was about this time detected at Guilford in Surry, tried, condemned and executed. He made no discovery, tho' we all trembled. A plan was now in agitation to dispatch two or three of the gang to Portsmouth, to attack some of the navy officers: It was finally adopted, and one Billy Coats, a Londoner, and Mountain were selected as the most suitable for the expedition. We mounted our horses on the next morning, and reached Portsmouth that day, a distance of more than 70 miles. We took lodgings at an inn kept by a rich old miser. We were soon convinced that he had cash in plenty, and that it "was our *duty* to get it;" but the difficulty was what plan should be concerted. At length, by a stratagem which was deeply laid and faithfully executed, we plundered the old man's house of about 300 guineas, and 50 l. sterling in shillings and six-pences.

There was a very great clamour raised the next morning. The house was surrounded with the populace. The old fellow was raving at a great rate for his loss of money. I was a spectator of this collection, and now perfectly remember the chagrin of the old man and his wife. We remained at Portsmouth two days, and then returned to London richly laden, and received the applause of our companions. The three following months I spent in frequenting ale-houses, defrauding and cheating with false dice, and practising every species of imposition which ingenuity could invent, or the most depraved heart execute.

In the beginning of June 1780, I joined the mob headed by Lord George Gordon. The mob was the result of a dispute between the Papists and Protestants. It was a matter of the most sovereign indifference to me, whether the rebellion was just or unjust: I eagerly joined the sport, rejoicing that an opportunity presented whereby I might obtain considerable plunder in the general confusion.—Lord Gordon represented to us in a speech of some length, the open attempts upon the Protestant religion, and the manner in which the petitions of the injured had been treated by parliament. He exhorted us all to follow him to the house of commons, and protect him while he should present, with his own hand, the parchment roll, containing the names of those who had signed the petition, to the amount of about 120,000 protestants. His speech was answered with loud huzzas, and repeated assurances of our zeal to support him and his cause. The whole body of us, in number about 50,000, left St. George's fields, and marched directly for the parliament house: We were in four separate divisions. A most tremendous shout was heard from all quarters, upon our arrival before both houses. Lord Gordon moved that he might introduce the petition; but the house would not consent that it should be then taken up. The mob became greatly inflamed: they insulted several members of the house of lords, who narrowly escaped with their lives. Several gentlemen of parliament reprobated the conduct of Lord George in the severest terms; and Col. Gordon, a relation of his Lordship, threatened him with instant death the moment any of the rioters should enter the house. At length, when the question was put in the house of commons, in defiance of the menaces of the mob, only six out of two hundred voted for the petition. The rioters now dispersed themselves into various parts of the city, destroying and burning the chapels of Roman Catholics and their houses. The five succeeding days were employed in demolishing the houses of Sir George Saville, in burning Newgate, and relieving about 300 persons confined in it, (some under sentence of death) in setting fire to King's-bench and Fleet-prisons, and in innumerable other acts of violence and outrage towards those who were in the opposition. The bank was twice assailed, but was too well guarded for our attempts. On the 7th day we were over-powered by superior force, and obliged to disperse. During the confusion, I provided for myself, by plundering, at various times, about 500 l. sterling.

After leading a life of such dissipation for five or six years, an incident occurred which caused me, for some time, to abandon my former pursuit, and settle down in tolerable regularity. I became acquainted with a Miss Nancy Allingame, a white girl of about 18 years of age. She was possessed of about 500l. in personal property, and a house at Islington.* It may appear singular to many, that a woman of this description should be in the least interested in my favor; yet such was the fact, that she not only endured my society, but actually married me in about six months after our first acquaintance. Her father and friends remonstrated against this connexion; but she quitted them all, and united herself to me. My whole residence with her was about three years; during which time I exhausted all the property which came into my possession by the marriage. We then separated, and she was received by her father.

In June 1782, having joined Hyde and Wilson, we determined to quit England, and see if the French gentlemen could bear "touching." We accordingly crossed at Dover, and at Dunkirk about 7 o'clock in the evening robbed a gentleman of about 200 French crowns. We then proceeded to Paris by the way of Brest. On the second evening after our arrival in this city, we robbed Count Dillon, on his return from the plays, of a gold watch and 12 French guineas. The next day, about 1 o'clock in the afternoon, we attacked Governor Du Boyer, at his country seat about four miles from Paris, and took from him about 200 l. in bank bills. Hyde and Wilson performed this, while I lay about 250 yards distant.

Dispatch in travelling, after such bold adventures, became very necessary. We immediately quitted Paris, and rode all night for Havre-de-Grace, where we arrived the evening of the next day. Here we found an advertisement, which prevented our changing the notes, and induced us to burn them.

Bayonne was the next object of our pursuit. At this place Hyde robbed two gentlemen in one night; Wilson one, and Mountain one—the whole of that evening's plunder amounted to about 500l. sterling. France now became dangerous, and therefore we pushed with all possible expedition for Spain, and arrived at Madrid, the capital, in a few days. The regulations of this city were such, that we were obliged to quit the object of our pursuit. The city was strongly walled in, and most scrupulously guarded. The gates were shut every evening at 8 o'clock, and every man compelled to be in his

*The reader will please to recollect, that Negroes are considered in a different point of light in England, from what they are in America: The blacks have far greater connection with the whites, owing to the idea which prevails in that country, that there are no slaves.

own habitation. After spending several months in rioting on our booty, we went to Gibralter. We bribed the Spanish centinel, and entered the British lines. We appeared before the English commander, General Elliott, and informed him we were Englishmen, and mechanics by profession. The fleet commanded by Lord Howe, arrived there on the fourth day after us. Gen. Elliott consented that we should enter on board the fleet as seamen. Accordingly I joined myself to the Magnificent of 74 guns, commanded by Capt. John Elverston; Hyde entered the Victory, Lord Howe; and Wilson a 74 gun ship, whose name I do not recollect. This was in the fall of the year 1782. I never saw Hyde and Wilson again till since the peace took place between England and the United States. I tarried on board the Magnificent about three months, during which time we had an engagement with the French and Spanish fleets. We drove them out of the Straits, sunk their junk ships with hot shot, and captured the St. Michael, a Spanish ship of 74 guns. The Magnificent sailed with the fleet for Spithead, where, directly after my arrival, I made my escape from her by bribing the centinel with 5 guineas, & swimming three quarters of a mile to the Isle of Wight. From this place I went to London by the way of Plymouth. The landlord at the old place of resort received me very cordially.

The business of robbing again solicited my attention, and in the fall of the year 1783, as I was walking in Wapping, in quest of plunder, I accidentally fell in company with my old companions, Hyde and Wilson. They had remained in the sea service ever since we left Gibralter. We concluded it adviseable to join ourselves to the gang at Harrison's, and resume our occupations. Holland now appeared an object worth attention. In November 1783, we went to Ostend, and thence to Amsterdam. On the road thro' Holland, we knocked an old Dutchman down, and took from him 1100 guilders. The next day about 4 o'clock in the morning, Hyde attacked a merchant, and obtained about 100 guilders; and the evening following, we robbed four gentlemen of about 150 l. sterling, and three silver watches of small value, we continued living very freely at Amsterdam 4 weeks, without effecting any thing: during which period we were preparing to assail a bank. At length, by the help of various instruments, we entered it about 1 o'clock at night. We found an iron chest which we could not open. We brought away two bags of gold, containing about 1100l. sterling. We buried them about 2 miles distant, and suffered them to remain there two months. The noise, relative to the robbery having by this time subsided, we took our money, entered on board a vessel bound for England, and were safely back in London in the spring of the year 1784. To invest our cash, & c. in real property, and quit a course of life attended with so much fatigue and hazard, was thought the most eligible plan. In pursuance of this idea, Hyde bought him an house and lot about 4 miles from London. My share was joined with Hyde's. Wilson purchased him a situation at Cherry-garden-stairs. Each kept an house for the reception of gamblers, swindlers and foot-pads.

The rioters who were concerned in Lord Gordon's rebellion were now daily arrested, tried and executed. Knowing myself deeply concerned in this mob, and supposing it probable that Mountain's turn might come next, I quitted London, went on board an European vessel, and made a voyage to Grenada. From this period till August 1789, I was employed as a sailor; during which time I made two voyages to the Coast of Guinea, and brought cargoes of Negroes to Jamaica; one voyage to Greenland; one to Leghorn and Venice; three to Philadelphia, and one to St. Kitts. Upon my return from voyages, I frequently went from Liverpool to London, and put up at Hyde's or Wilson's. In October 1786, we committed a burglary upon the house of General Arnold, who then resided in London. We entered his house about 2 o'clock at night, with a dark lanthorn, and, from a bureau in the room where the General and lady were asleep, we stole 150l. sterling in cash, and a pair of stone shoe buckles.

In the month of August 1789, I left New-York in the Briton, with a cargo of bread and flour owned by Mr. John Murray, jun. of New-York, and went to Bilboa in Spain. The vessel proved leaky, and was sold. Being discharged, I entered on board the brig Aunt, commanded by Capt. Thomas Moseley, and owned by William Gray, of Boston, sailed from Bilboa the 7th day of March, and arrived in Boston the 2d of May last. On the 14th of the same month I quitted Boston on foot for New-York. On my journey, at East-Hartford, I stole five dollars from the cabin of a sloop lying in Connecticut river. I was immediately apprehended, carried before George Pitkin, Esq. and adjudged to be whipped ten stripes. The sentence was executed forthwith, and I dismissed. This was the first time I was ever arraigned before any court. No event in my antecedent life produced such mortification as this; that a highway-man of the first eminence, who had robbed in most of the capital cities in Europe, who had attacked gentlemen of the first distinction with success; who had escaped King's-bench prison and Old-Bailey, that he should be punished for such a petty offence, in such an obscure part of the country, was truly humiliating. On the Saturday evening following I arrived at New-Haven. The Wednesday following, being the 26th of May, about two o'clock in the afternoon, I sat out for New-York: At the distance of one mile, I met the unhappy girl whom I have so wantonly injured. She was in company with an elder sister, and going into New-Haven. I began a conversation with them, and attempted, by persuasion, to effect my purpose. They were terrified at my conduct, and endeavoured to avoid me. Upon this I seized the eldest girl; she, however, struggled from me. I then caught the younger, and threw her on the ground. I have uniformly thought that the witnesses were mistaken in swearing to the commission of a *Rape*: That I abused her in a most brutal and savage manner—that her tender years and pitiable shricks were unavailing—and that no exertion was wanting to ruin her, I frankly confess. However I may attempt to palliate this transaction, there can be no excuse given for me, unless intoxication may be plead in mitigation of an offence. It was a most cruel attack upon an innocent girl, whose years, whose entreaties must have softened an heart not callous to every tender feeling. When her cries had brought to her assistance some neighbouring people, I still continued my barbarity, by insulting her in her distress, boasting of the fact, and glorying in my iniquity. Upon reflection, I am often surprized that I did not attempt my escape; opportunity to effect it frequently presented before I was apprehended. Yet, by some unaccountable fatality, I loitered unconcerned, as tho' my conduct would bear the strictest scrutiny. The counsel of heaven determined that such a prodigy in vice should no longer infest society. At four o'clock I was brought before Mr. Justice Daggett for examination. The testimony was so pointed, that I was ordered into immediate confinement, to await the approaching session of the Superior Court.

On the 5th of August last, I was arraigned before the Bar of the Superior Court. My trial was far more favourable than I expected. There was every indulgence granted me which I could have wished; and the court, jurors and spectators appeared very differently from those I have seen at Old-Bailey. The jury had little hesitation; indeed the most compassionate hearer of this cause could have only pronounced me *Guilty*. I beheld with astonishment the lenity of the Court, and am sure that in a country where such a sacred regard is had to the liberty of the subject, no man's life can be unjustly taken from him. On the Tuesday following, the Chief Justice pronounced Sentence of Death against me. I thought my self less moved with this pathetic address than either of the court, or any spectator; and yet, I confess, I was more affected by it, than by any thing which had previously happened in my life. On the next Sabbath I attended meeting. The address of the Rev. Dr. Dana on that day and the subsequent advice and admonitions which I have received from the Clergy of this and other places, were calculated to awaken every feeling of my heart. Much gratitude is due from me to those gentlemen who have exhibited such a tender concern for my immortal interest.

It now remains that I *die* a death justly merited by my crimes. "The cries of injured innocence have entered the ears of the Lord of Sabaoth, and called for vengeance." If the reader of this story can acquiesce in my fate and view me "stumbling on the dark mountains of the shadow of death," with composure, he will yet compassionate a soul stained with the foulest crimes, just about to appear unimbodied before a God of infinite purity.

*JOSEPH MOUNTAIN.*

*THE writer of the foregoing narrative assures the public, that the facts related were taken from the mouth of the culprit. In no instance has any fact been substantially altered, or* in the least *exaggerated.*

*On the 28th of September the writer applied to* Joseph, *to learn if he persisted in affirming the truth of the foregoing story. By the direction of the criminal his name was then set to this history, and he declared, in the presence of the subscribing witnesses, that it contained nothing but the truth.*

JOSEPH PECK.
SAMUEL PUNDERSON.

## Source Notes

*Sketches of the Life of Joseph Mountain, A Negro* was published first by Thomas and Samuel Green in New Haven immediately after Mountain's execution on October 20, 1790. Two more Connecticut editions with the same title soon followed: one printed by John Trumbull in Norwich, and another printed by Nathaniel Patten in Hartford. A fourth edition of the *Sketches* was published by the Boston printer Thomas Adams in his *Independent Chronicle: and the Universal Advertiser* (November 18, 1790). Under different titles, two more editions of the Mountain narrative were published: in 1791 Anthony Haswell printed the narrative as *The Life and Adventures of Joseph Mountain, a Negro Highwayman* in Bennington, Vermont; and in an edition without either a date or place of publication, the narrative was published as *The singular adventures, &c.* (the only known copy lacks the title page). Also, two German translations of the narrative were published in Pennsylvania: *Die Wunderbare Lebens-Beshreibung von Joseph Mountain, eines Negers* [The Surprising Life-Account of Joseph Mountain, a Negro] (Lancaster, no date) and *Das Leben und die Begebenheiten von Joseph Mountain, einem Neger* [The Life and Events of Joseph Mountain, a Negro] (Philadelphia: Charles Cist, 1791). After announcing that Mountain had been hanged in New Haven and advertising his robberies in England, France, and Holland, the Lancaster title page added: "Sehr wunderbare zu lesen, und Anzeigt wie tief die menschliche Natur fallen kan" [Very surprising to read, and indicating how low human nature can fall].

Although an anonymous work, the *Sketches* traditionally has been ascribed to David Daggett, the New Haven justice mentioned in the last part of the narrative. After holding Mountain over for trial, Daggett is believed to have interviewed the highwayman/rapist in prison, and from these interviews he wrote the narrative. In his *Biographical Sketches of the Graduates of Yale College*, Franklin Bowditch Dexter stated that "this anonymous compilation was prepared by Mr. Daggett" (Vol. 4, 262). In his *American Bibliography*, Charles Evans used brackets to indicate Daggett's anonymous authorship in four of the six editions (omitting the original New Haven edition, in which Mountain was listed as the author, and the newspaper edition printed in the *Independent Chronicle*). David Daggett (1764-1851) was an appropriate representative of the dominant social community. Throughout his long and active career, he was a lawyer, judge, politician, and law professor. Among his many accomplishments, he served as representative in the Connecticut legislature, as mayor of New Haven, as senator in Congress, and as Chief Justice of the Connecticut Supreme Court. In addition, he was one of the principal founders of the Yale Law School, where he lectured from 1824 to 1847. In addition to Dexter's "Sketch," see Samuel W. S. Dutton's *An Address At The Funeral Of Hon. David Daggett* (New Haven: A.H. Maltby, 1851) for further information concerning the justice.

While stressing the narrative's authenticity, an endnote in the original edition offered a glimpse of Daggett's composition process. After assuring readers that "*the facts related were taken from the mouth of the culprit*," the note stated that, three weeks before the execution date, "*the writer applied to* **Joseph**, *to learn if he persisted in affirming the truth of the foregoing story. By the direction of the criminal his name was then set to this history, and he declared, in presence of the subscribing witnesses, that it contained nothing but the truth*" (301). According to the narrative, no "fact" was "*altered, or* in the least *exaggerated*" in shaping the narrative; Daggett's role—the narrative insisted—was merely that of an amanuensis. Yet obviously the text was produced through the collaboration of the black criminal and the white justice. Daggett's words as much as Mountain's experiences shaped the narrative.

Also, to further exploit the sensation caused by Mountain's crime and execution, Thomas and Samuel Green published James Dana's execution sermon, which was delivered on "the day of the Execution" (*The Connecticut Journal* November 3, 1790): *The Intent of Capital Punishment* (New Haven, 1790). As indicated by the title, Dana indeed justified the use of "death by public justice" (5). According to Dana, the purpose of capital punishment was "to rid the state of a present nuisance—to prevent the extension of evil—[and] to reclaim or preserve those who have been, or might be in danger of being, seduced by examples of profligate wickedness" (5–6). Beyond Dana's extraordinary justification for execution, the sermon attracted readers because of Dana's lengthy "address" to Mountain. Such ministerial appeals were part of the elaborate ritual of death, but Dana's words were harsher than most. After acknowledging that God has the power to pluck some sinners "*as a brand out of the fire*," the minister focused on what he perceived to be Mountain's recalcitrance. Responding to what he called "the levity of your mind, during the first part of your imprisonment," Dana declared that Mountain had "by no means given the best evidence of true contrition" since his confinement (22).

Yet it was the highwayman's narrative more than his nature that seemed to bother Dana the most. In a paragraph intended to catalogue Mountain's crimes, the minister referred to the narrative several times, revealing his frustrations with the text's refusal to conform to genre conventions:

> If the history of your life, taken from your own mouth, and this day published, may be credited, you have been almost in all evil for sixteen years past; that is, ever since you were seventeen years old, and left your master's family. You have personally, and in the company with others, been guilty of high-way *robbery* in about twenty instances; of *burglary* once at least; of *theft* repeatedly; and for *rape* you are now to be executed. From robbery you have proceeded to *gaming*, *riot* and *debauch*, and from these to robbery. How many have you seduced? How many have you ruined in their character and estate? From early youth to thirty years you have lived in sloth, dissipation, lewdness and violence. . . . I say this on the supposition that you are such a person as you have now told the world. If your history [the narrative] is false, your depravity is equally manifest. For then, as you go out of the world, you mock at the most presumptuous sins. You boast of pretended valor as a villain, in the moment of death. . . . You still persist to affirm, that the history you have given of your life is true in every particular. You can reap no advantage from deceiving the world in which you are no longer to live. I shall therefore suppose that you have said the truth. (22–24)

In conclusion, Dana stated that if Mountain persisted on leaving behind "a character for skill and bravery as a thief or robber, a rioter in the spoils of your fellow-men," he would be committing a crime "more presumptuous than any or all your *great transgressions*" (24). Yet this was exactly what the robber-rapist did.

Newspapers throughout New England reported the rape, and a few continued to mention Mountain's later trial and execution. New Haven's *The Connecticut Journal*, of course, provided the most coverage, and its reports were reprinted by the other newspapers. Its first report (June 2, 1790) came shortly after the rape was committed, and it was the *Journal's* inflated rhetoric of indignation (with strong racial overtones) that was widely reprinted:

> Wednesday last, in the afternoon, a rape was committed on the body of a white girl, about 14 years old, by a transient negro, aged about 30. The infamous act was perpetrated about two miles from this city [New Haven], on Milford road, attended with circumstances too horrible to relate. The unhappy girl was with an elder sister, (coming to town) on whom he intended to commit his diabolical purpose, but she happily made her escape. The vile wretch was soon apprehended by some persons who were on the road, and is confined in our goal; being heavily ironed, it is hoped he will be secured, to receive the punishment justly due his villainy.

The *Journal's* report, which condemned and denounced as much as it reported, was reprinted in *The Connecticut Gazette* (June 11), *The Norwich Packet* (June 11), *The Boston Gazette* (June 14), and *The Independent Chronicle* (June 17).

On August 11, *The Connecticut Journal* mentioned Mountain's trial and conviction:

> Before the hon. Superior Court, now sitting in this City, one Joseph Mountain, a Negro, was indicted for a rape, committed on the 26th of May last, (as mentioned in this paper on the 2d of June) which fact being very fully proved, the jury immediately found him guilty; but his sentence is not yet pronounced. He says he was born in Philadelphia, and has liv'd in the family of his Excellency President Mifflin.

Other newspapers, such as *The Connecticut Gazette* (August 20), reprinted the *Journal's* account, while under its "New Haven" section *The Independent Chronicle* (August 12) offered: "A transient Negro man was brought to trial before the Hon. Superior Court, on Thursday last, for committing a rape on the body of a white girl of about 14 years of age, and was found guilty and sentenced to death."

On August 18, *The Connecticut Journal* followed up its trial account with the court's lengthy *Address to the Prisoner* upon passing sentence. This Address also was printed two weeks later in *The Connecticut Gazette* (September 3). Thus readers in Hartford as well as New Haven received an official assessment of both Mountain's malevolence and the court's kindness.

> On Thursday the 12th instant, Joseph Mountain, who had been indicted before the honorable Supreme Court, and found guilty of a rape, was brought into Court to receive his sentence, and being asked if he had any reasons to give, why sentence of death should not be pronounced against him, and having nothing to offer; the hon. Chief Justice, amidst a crouded audience addressed the prisoner, in a just, pathetic and forcible manner, and notwithstanding the aggravated circumstances of guilt which appeared, yet such were the sensations of a feeling heart, that the Judge could not pronounce the awful sentence without the most visible emotion; nor were those who heard, wanting in testimonials of sympathy, towards the poor unfortunate wretch.
>
> THE ADDRESS TO THE PRISONER
>
> YOU Joseph Mountain having been arraigned at the bar of this court, on an indictment of the grandjury of 18 respectable freeholders of this county, duly impannelled and sworn, who on their oaths did present that you Joseph Mountain, on the 26th day of May last at New-Haven, in the county of New-Haven, with force and arms an assault did make on the body of Eunice Thompson, of said New-Haven, a maid of thirteen years, and then & there against the mind and will of said Eunice, with the same force did feloniously ravish and have carnal knowledge of her body, against the peace and contrary to the form and effect of the statute in such case provided.
>
> To which indictment you have pleaded not guilty, and put yourself for trial on the country, and having the indulgence of your challenges, and pursued the same till you were satisfied, and having no further exception against the pannel then returned, they were duly sworn and charged, well and truly to try and true deliverance make between the state of Connecticut and you Joseph Mountain, the prisoner at the bar,

according to the evidence, and the laws of this state. You had counsel assigned you, learned in the law, and respectable in their profession, not only to advise and direct you in your trial, but to plead your cause and offer every reason and argument in your defence both as to law and fact; in which nothing was omitted which could be said or urged in your favor. After a most candid and impartial trial, the cause was committed to the Jury, who on full and deliberate consideration brought in their verdict that you Joseph Mountain the prisoner at the bar was guilty.

The crime which you are convicted, is of a deep dye, is very heinous in the sight of God and man, and in most if not all the civilized nations, punishable with death: It was by you committed with every circumstance of aggravation, and with a daring boldness and impudence, unheard and unknown, which with your after conduct, glorying in your shame, and even insulting the victim of your brutal lust, and with the most brazen affrontery, others of her sex who appeared to assist and console her in her distress, all discover in you the greatest depravity of heart, an uncommon boldness and hardiness in vice, and that savage and relentless cruelty which renders a person so abandoned as to be unfit for society, and unsafe to be at large among the human species; and has already subjected you to the punishment of death by the just laws of this state.

The female sex are weak and feeble in their frame, timid and unable to resist the force and strength of man, who was designed for their protection and defence against rapine and violence; but instead of protecting, you, regardless of the all-piercing eye of that God to whom even the darkest caverns are as the blaze of day, and in the light of the sun, wholly inattentive to human discovery, or the detection of your dark designs, meeting the harmless and innocent maid, tender in years, and in a way so frequented that she was unsuspicious of danger, urged on by worse than brutal lust, and more than savage barbarity, relentless to her cries, her shrieks, or her tears, with force and violence ravished her of what to a female is as dear as life, and which leaves her, (tho' an object of pity and compassion) to spend the remainder of her days in grief and sorrow.

Notwithstanding you have had no pity, and rendered yourself unfit for human society, and unworthy of life, yet we would extend to you every compassionate regard of which your situation will admit; and afford you, during the short remainder of life allotted you, every opportunity and advantage for the use of those means the gracious Author of our beings has instituted and directed for the salvation of your precious and immortal soul; and which we most sincerely wish you to improve with the utmost diligence and attention, as you must expect soon to appear before the awful tribunal of that Almighty Omniscient Judge to whom not only this, but all the numerous crimes and offences you have been guilty of, are perfectly known; and to whom the very thoughts and intents of the heart are manifest; and for which the most tremendous punishment awaits the finally impenitent and ungodly; and from which there is no way of your escape but by a sincere repentance, and a firm trust and reliance on the mercy of God through the merits, atoning blood, and righteousness of Jesus Christ the Saviour.

You will have the opportunity indulged you of attending the public worship on the Sabbath or Lord's-day in this place. There are a number of pious and instructive clergy in this city, who, we doubt not, will be ready to afford you from time to time all that advice, counsel, and instruction which your particular case and situation requires, and which you will do well to attend to, and to apply with continued and earnest prayer and supplication to Almighty God, against whom you have sinned, and before whom you must soon appear, for his pardoning mercy and grace, for the sake of Jesus Christ his Son, through whom alone mercy and forgiveness is to be obtained.

It now remains for me in behalf of this court, to pronounce the sentence of the law upon you; the solemn sentence of death!

This Court do sentence, and against you, Joseph Mountain, now at the bar of this Court, give Judgment, *That you be from hence returned to the prison from whence you were taken, and that from thence you be carried to the place of execution, and there to be hanged up by the neck, between the heavens and the earth, till you are dead, dead, dead, and the Lord have mercy on your soul.*

Wednesday the 20th of October next the above sentence is to be executed.

Mountain's "short remainder of life" was not extended by any sort of reprieve or respite, and his execution took place as scheduled. In the October 20 issue of *The Connecticut Journal*, the following notice was printed: "This day, between the hours of ten and 4, Joseph Mountain, a negro, is to be executed, pursuant to his sentence, for a Rape." One week later (October 27) the paper announced: "Wednesday last was executed Joseph Mountain, for a Rape. It is estimated that ten thousand people attended the execution." Ten thousand spectators must have encouraged Samuel and Thomas Green. Directly across from the execution announcement in the next column they inserted an advertisement calling attention to their narrative and its sensational story:

SKETCHES of the Life of
*Joseph Mountain*, a Negro,
WHO was executed at New-Haven, on the 20th
Day of October instant, for a Rape committed
on the 26th Day of May last, to be sold at this Office

(*The writer of this history has directed that the money arising from the sale thereof, after deducting the expence of printing, &c. be given to the unhappy girl, whose life is rendered wretched by the crime of the malefactor.*)

At the bottom of the same advertisement the Green brothers announced the publication of their second Mountain text:

IN the Press, and on Saturday next will be published,
Dr. DANA'S SERMON,
At the Execution of *Joseph Mountain.*

True to their promise, the following week (November 3) the Greens inserted an advertisement announcing the publication of Dana's sermon:

This Day is PUBLISHED,
And be sold by the Printers hereof,
(*Price 9d single, & 6s per dozen*)
THE INTENT OF CAPITAL
PUNISHMENT.
A DISCOURSE delivered in the City of New-
Haven, October 20, 1790: being the day of
the Execution of Joseph Mountain, for a RAPE.
By *James Dana*, D. D.
Pastor of the first church in said city.

Mountain is discussed in Richard Slotkin's essay, "Narratives of Negro Crime in New England, 1675–1800."

THE

# CONFESSION, &c.

OF

# THOMAS MOUNT,

Who was executed at Little-Reſt, in the State of Rhode-Iſland, on Friday the 27th of May, 1791, for Burglary.

MIDDLETOWN:
Re-Printed by MOSES H. WOODWARD,
For ISAAC RILEY, & Co.

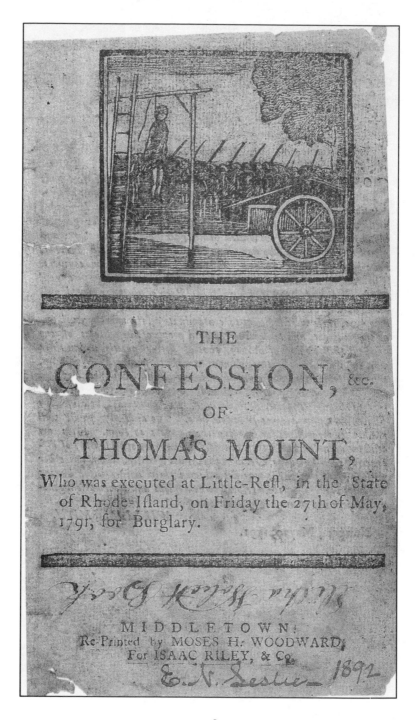

[ THOMAS MOUNT ]

# *The Confession, &c. of Thomas Mount*

[ 1791 ]

## *To the PUBLIC.*

SOME years ago there was in England a company of foot-pads and highway-men, connected together under certain laws and regulations, having a language (and books printed in that language) peculiar to themselves, called the Flash Company,—a similar gang of plunderers has infested the United States ever since the late war; and almost all the persons who have been hanged of late in North-America, have belonged to this company. Of this company are two convicts, *Thomas Mount* and *James Williams*, now lying in Newport gaol under sentence of death, for burglary. Both of these are noted villains, as well by legal evidence as their own confession; and were there no others, these were sufficient to contaminate all the unwary youth upon the continent, and to deprive the good people of these States of one of the highest blessings of heaven, that of sitting quietly under their vine and under their fig-tree and none to make them afraid. *Williams*, whether from artifice or an inferior degree of guilt, has not divulged the Flash proceedings near so fully as *Mount*, whose information, therefore, is the subject matter of the following sheets; and this is the cause why *Williams*'s name occurs so seldom here. The discerning public will readily see my motives for handing these papers to them. From my constant attendance upon these convicts, perhaps my opportunities of discovering their language, & c. are equal, if not greater, than any other persons; and the public may depend upon their authenticity, having committed to writing their respective confessions and informations generally before one or more competent witnesses.

WILLIAM SMITH.

*Newport, May* 20, 1791.

## The voluntary Confession of *Thomas Mount*.

I THOMAS MOUNT, now under sentence of death in the gaol of Newport, and to be executed agreeable to my sentence, at Little-Rest, on the 27th of this month of May—in bodily health and sound mind, and full of sorrow and regret for my wicked life, in sincerity and truth make the following confession:

My parents Samuel Mount and Mary Dobbs, lived in Middletown, in East-Jersey, where I was born some time I believe in 1764. My father, for the benefit of his family, removed to New-York when I was about four or five years old, where I and my brothers were put to school; they, viz. Adam and Joseph, now living in good repute in New-York, profited in their studies—I played truant, hated learning and every sort of good instruction. Upon Sundays especially was fond of doing mischief, such as robbing orchards, and spreading my wicked example among all the boys I could get acquainted with.—I began to despise my parents and to count every thing they said to, or did for me, as beneath my regard; and having never learned to know my duty, either towards GOD, or towards man or myself, I despised all religion; and at the age of ten or eleven, quitted my parents, who often told me I should one day come to an evil end, and went to sea on board one Capt. Hammond bound for Antigua; thence to Statia, Nevis, St. Kitts, Santacruz, Sanctakes, Savannah.—At Savannah I left him, and went on board the Florida brig bound for Jamaica; then I left him and went to live with one Mr. Kennedy in Kingstown, with him I lived about five or six weeks, then left him and got aboard of a sloop Capt. Alboy, and returned in her to New-York. In 1775, the war breaking out, I quitted my parents again, and listed with Capt. Palmer, and went with him to Albany, thence to Fort George, thence to Ticonderoga, thence to Crown-Point, thence to St. John's, thence to Montreal, thence returned to Albany, and being sick was dismissed. As soon as I recovered, I listed again, and went to Fort-George, where I remained five weeks, and was dismissed on account of my youth, so returned to live with my parents at Newyork. Not relishing the good rules and advice of my parents, again I left them and went to live with one John Minor, at Stonington-point, with whom I remained six or seven months; when he was drafted to go with the militia—I proposed to go in his stead; accordingly went, and at Groton, near New-London, availing myself of the privileges of a militia man, I listed in the continental army under Col. Huntington, and accompanied him to Denbigh, when the British troops landed and burnt it.—At Valley-Forge, in Pennsylvania, I deserted the American, and went over to the British army, then lying in Philadelphia. In a few days after this, I and two companions broke into a soap-boilers's store (this is my first act of theft) and stole some soap. When the British troops left Philadelphia, I came along with them through the Jersies, to New-York, thence to Staten-Island, where I broke open a store in the night soon after our arrival, and took a large quantity of goods, and about twenty dollars in cash, and the night following I broke into the same store and took a larger quantity of goods than I had done the former night. Determined to desert for fear of discovery, I and two of my companions confined the corporal that commanded the patrole, and so we escaped and went off to the American army, into the Jersies.—With my uncle Joseph Cox, at Embley's-Town, who married my father's sister, I remained some weeks; but soon wearied of this too quiet sort of life, I left my uncle and went to Philadelphia, where I entered on board a schooner, Capt. Strong, bound for Cape-Francois, from whence I returned safe to Philadelphia; and in about four weeks after my return, I entered again on board the same vessel, and then run off with the advanced pay, and entered on board the St. James, Capt. King, and cheated him of a month's advanced pay; next entered on board the Plow brig, Capt. Browster, with whom I went to sea, and in 24 hours were taken by the Cyble frigate, carried to New-York and put on board the Jersey prison-ship, from whence in about eleven or twelve days I escaped to New-York, where I entered on board the Macaroni privateer, and cheated the Captain of four guineas the advance money.—In a day or two after this I entered on board a schooner, received the advance money and made off with it. Next I was apprehended by the British regiment (the fourth battalion of Jersey volunteers) to which I formerly belonged, and was brought before a court-martial, but received no punishment on account of my youth. Under no restraint, and already hardened by the escapes I had made, I determined to double my diligence, if possible to arrive at the head of my profession; accordingly, next stole a watch from one Mr. Kelly; next broke open a store belonging to Mr. Kizek; next stole another watch; next stole a gilt-case watch; next stole a gold watch; next stole a large bag-full of English boot and bend leather; next in company with one William Flanegin, in the evening, the shop door standing open, stole a piece of corduroy about thirty yards; in Queen-Street, a few days afterwards, I went into a shop in the day time, and stole a paper of worsted stockings; and a few days after out of a shop in Hanover-Square, I stole a piece of linen about twenty-five yards; about a week or so, after this, I stole another piece in Broad-Way; next, in the night time, I and one John Delavan knocked down a sailor, and took his money—I knocked him down, but Delavan took the money and run off with it from me. The regiment now removing to Newtown, on Long-Island, I went with them, and in a few days after our arrival, I and one Henry Milton stole two horses and rode off with them to Brookland, and then let them go; next day after we came to Brookland, we were apprehended and carried back to the regiment and tried for desertion: Henry Milton was acquitted, and I sentenced to receive 500 lashes; but the day before my punishment commenced, I broke out of the guard-house, and escaped to the east end of the island, but there was taken up by Col. Thompson's light-horse, and carried to Huntington, thence under guard to Jerico, there committed to the care of one of the Yougers to carry me to the regiment.—The Youger's pocket I picked, as he sat by me in the waggon, and threw all his papers down on the road within five or six miles of Jamaica; some time after we came out of the carriage, at Jamaica, I told him that I saw the driver pick his pockets and take all his papers and throw them down on the highway about five or six miles from hence.—Seeing the waggon at some considerable distance, the Youger, desiring me to follow him, pursued after the waggoner, that instant I took a contrary direction and so escaped. I went down as far as South-Hole and then got over in a trading boat to the main, and travelled towards New-Haven, there one day went into a shop and stole out of a drawer a small quantity of cash; next day, out of another store, I stole from the cash-box five or six crowns and dollars with two French guineas; same day, in the afternoon, I went into another shop and stole about ten pounds in silver and one English guinea. Leaving this place, I set off for Philadelphia, where I listed into Col. Myland's light-horse, the fourth regiment of dragoons: soon after this peace took place, and I quitted the army entirely. Immediately after my leaving the army, I broke open a continental store and stole two pair of boots, and a parcel of shirts; a few days after I stole a piece of calico, thirty yards, in company with James Dawson; some little time after this, I stole from a kitchen door a silver tankard belonging to Mr. Penrose,—it was instantly missed; Dawson had cut it up, but one of the Captains of the garrison intercepted it, and Dawson and I were taken up and tried for the theft; he got 25 lashes, and I 100 lashes for the theft, and 25 for giving the court saucy answers. No sooner was this account settled, but I proceeded in my old way, and stole three large silver spoons from Mr. Joseph Carson, in Water-Street; next day or so, in the evening, I went into an apothecary's shop and took his cash-box, containing about ten pounds; near a week after this I went into a shop in——street, and took another piece of calico; some days after I was taken up for a debt I owed to Mr. Carson and put in goal; whilst in goal, the woman to whom I and Dawson had sold the calico, which I stole from Mr. Pool, was apprehended, having on a gown of it, informed that she bought it of me, accordingly I was tried for theft and received 21 lashes, and sentenced to imprisonment for court charges of fine and restitution money; the very second day after I broke goal and escaped, I picked the pocket of one Haggaty of about three or four dollars and two depreciation notes of about sixty pounds each; leaving Philadelphia, I went to Burlington and there passed the notes; thence went to Newyork, and lived with my brother Adam about one or two months at the baking business; here I got acquainted with John Lipton, and we broke open a hen-roost one night and stole a parcel of fowls; next day leaving New-York, we went upon Long-Island, thence to Ostend, and so on to New-London; upon the road Lipton stole a watch, but the owner missing it pursued us, and we in a very cowardly manner gave it up to him. We journeyed to Sagg-Harbor, thence crossed over to New-London, and from thence to Boston; there the first day of our arrival, we stole a few articles, such as shoes, and other wearables; but finding Boston no proper place for us then, on account of the alarms about stolen goods before our arrival, we set out to go back to New-York. Having travelled about 12 or 14 miles from Boston, in the night we broke open a store that stood upon the road, and took some cash and twenty-five pair of womens' shoes, a large quantity of nutmeg, and a gun; and travelling along with our booty, we came up to a waggon with a trunk of goods tied on it, standing at a tavern door, we broke open the trunk, and taking out of it a large quantity of chints, laces, silk, and cotton handkerchiefs, we left in their stead the shoes and gun; our next step was to secure our flight, by taking two horses out of the stable at the same place, and rode the remainder of the night, and in the morning turned them off, whilst we retired to the woods during the day; and when night came on we pursued our journey toward Worcester; but hearing a waggon behind us, we went out of the road a little till it should go past us, we fixed our eye upon it and saw one man only in it, and he seemed to be asleep; the waggon soon stopt, we suppose at the owner's house, straightway we made up to it, robbed the sleeping man of all he had, about four or five dollars, and left him sound asleep to pursue our journey, selling our goods after the best manner we could, pretending to be speculating sailors, till we arrived at New-York. Soon after our arrival at New-York, we listed with the troops destined for the Ohio expedition; the second or third night after our enlistment, we broke open a dwelling house belonging to Mr. Hyde, where Lipton formerly lived, and took a silver watch, a guinea, some small money, and a silver stock buckle; a few nights after, being informed by one Millar, whose right name was Copy Gelly, that there was money in a house close by Mr. Lither's ship-yard, Millar, Lipton, and I broke into this house, and took a watch, a pair of silver buckles, but were discovered just as we were ready to seize upon the money, yet we escaped. Having now received the bounty and our clothes, we deserted the regiment, and we three, viz. Lipton, Millar and I, went out about five or six miles from New-York, and there Millar went down a chimney and stole a watch, and handed it to me through a window. Our next route was towards New-Haven, and within about four or five miles of New-Haven, we broke into a dwelling house where a physician lived, at the sign of the ball, here we took some money and departed; thence to Hartford, here we listed with the troops going against the Indians with Capt. Hart; we received the bounty money, and in two or three days deserted. Lipton chose to remain a little while at Hartford; Millar and I set off for Boston. Within about four miles of Providence we broke into a dwelling house and stole some silver spoons, then straight to Providence; and the very same night broke into a dwelling house near Mr. Sterry's house and took a large silver spoon and a quantity of clothes; and the next day leaving Providence, set out for Boston: here we went to board with Mrs. Ritch, and when ready to leave her, we stole from her a pattern of a silk and cotton jacket, and set off for Dedham, where we broke open the dwelling house of Mr. Newell, and stole a large quantity of dry goods, for which we were apprehended and tried, and being found guilty, received 30 lashes, I was put upon the gallows one hour with a rope round my neck, and sent to Castle-William for three years. After about eighteen months confinement, in a foggy day I escaped from thence by swimming three miles, and just as I was approaching the wharves a boat took me up, with an intention of delivering me up to the Castle, from whence they supposed I had escaped; a little after we were on shore, and being favored by the darkness of the night, I run off from them. Next day I arrived at Providence, and got into employ with one Capt. DeWolf, late from Guinea; soon left him, and set out for Norwich Landing, where I fell in with an old companion, Archibald Taylor (since executed in Boston) and next day setting out for Boston, upon the road we robbed a woman of a gold earlock and a silk handkerchief, and used her very ill besides; a few miles further on the road, I stole a gold ring and a tortoiseshell silver-mounted fan, in Plainfield; here we changed our minds, and returned to Norwich Landing, where I stole a surtout; the first night after our return we broke into a store belonging to Mr. Devitt, and took about seventy or eighty pounds worth of dry goods; took the goods along and set off for New-London, and within two or three miles of that place, hid the greatest part of them in Mr. Parson's barn among the hay: at New-London we were both apprehended on suspicion, I having the art of representing myself innocent got clear, but my companion was confined in goal. Being set at liberty, I went to Mr. Parson's house, where I staid two or three days, and set off one evening towards New-York with part of the goods, which I disposed of by the way. As soon as my money was spent, in New-York, I left that place and set off to go back to Mr. Parson's for the rest of the goods; at Milford I got a companion to go with me, one John Delavan, we found the goods just as I had left them, and set out with them to New-Haven, where we tarried a few days; in the mean time Delavan received from me a part of the goods for his trouble; and making free to steal more of them made off with them to his house at Milford. In a day or two after Delavan left me, having sold the rest of the goods to different people, I and one Harry M'Cormic hired a boat to carry us to Milford; we run her ashore among the rocks, and before morning she stove all to pieces: from hence walking to Milford, I called upon Delavan, made him deliver up to me such goods as he had not sold. Leaving Milford, M'Cormic and I sat out for New-York, where in two or three days we fell in with another of our companions, George Gardiner (from Greenock, a famous key-maker.) Just before leaving New-York, where M'Cormic staid behind, I called on my brother Adam and received about four dollars from him; prepared for our journey, we then set out for Philadelphia, where next day after our arrival, Gardiner and I opened a barber's shop in Water-Street, with a false key, and stole razors, tooth-drawers, &c. next day I stole some paper money; some days after fell in with John Lipton and Daniel Kalaghan; by agreement we four set out for Baltimore, upon our way thro' Charleston, there, with a false key, opened a store, and took about twenty pounds worth of goods; we carried them as far as Susquehanna ferry and there hid them, and pursued our journey. At Bushtown we attempted to break open a store, but were discovered, yet we escaped. Arrived in Baltimore, we fell in with our old friend Holmes, and on the third day after Holmes and I went to fetch the goods we had hid at Susquehanna ferry; we found them as I left them, and returned selling them by the way. In Baltimore I stole a watch and a surtout out of a house; a few nights after we broke open a house and stole a large quantity of clothing and a piece of broadcloth. Gardiner and Kalaghan chose to remain in Baltimore, whilst I and Lipton should set off for Annapolis and sell the goods we had upon hand: at Annapolis Lipton was apprehended for breaking open the store in Baltimore and imprisoned. Before I left Annapolis, to mend my luck, I stole some black ribbon and a few more trifles. Again Kalaghan joined me, and another companion (I cannot remember his name.) We three set out for Alexandria, where I fell in with James Brown; he and I one day stole some silk handkerchiefs and a beaver hat; next day Gardiner and Stewart joined us; they had fled from Alexandria where they broke into a shop and had taken a large quantity of goods, and hid them; next day they went for the goods they had hid, and we all four in company set out for Dumfries, where I and Stewart were apprehended and all the false keys found with us. Gardiner and Brown escaped; Stewart and I were thrown into Dumfries gaol, and thence carried to Alexandria. We were tired, and nothing found against us, nevertheless we were all sentenced to lie in gaol a year and a day, or get some one to be surety for our good behaviour. In the second week of our imprisonment we broke gaol: at Wilmington, on our way to Philadelphia, we broke into a dwelling house and stole a great many things, next day were apprehended and sent to

Newcastle gaol, from whence in two or three weeks, we escaped. Arrived at Philadelphia, I left Stewart and took another companion, one Griffin, passed some counterfeit Newyork money, stole some handkerchiefs, a beaver hat, a surtout, and two shawls, from different shops; next, in company with Griffin and one Fogg, in the night time, broke into a store and took cheese, sugar, coffee, and several other grocery goods. Fogg was apprehended, Griffin and I escaped, and quickly leaving Philadelphia, we set off for Newyork: on our way, at Perthamboy, we stole some black silk handkerchiefs. Arrived at Newyork, Griffin, John Taylor and I broke into a store belonging to Mr. Ford, and took a large quantity of shoes, tea, cherry-rum, &c. next day, for this transaction, we were all apprehended and tried; I got clear, my companions were branded, getting the benefit of clergy, and so were dismissed. Then Ford swore his life against me, and got me shut up in prison about eight or nine months: I got out upon condition of quitting the place in twelve hours, and returned to Philadelphia, where, next day after my arrival, I stole a piece of chints and a piece of calico, from a store in Market-street; a few nights after I and David Griffin, and one Logan, a tailor, in Irishtown, broke open a dwelling house in Walnut-street, and stole a large quantity of dry goods; next day I and Griffin were apprehended, the goods found where we had hidden them in a church then building; I and Griffin were committed to gaol; next day after our imprisonment, a man appeared who swore highway robbery against me, which I was innocent of. After being confined about eight weeks I broke out, and in company with George Williams and Daniel Kalaghan set off to pass through the Jersies; upon our way stole some money about two dollars, from a man into whose house we had gone to rest ourselves; and in Allentown we attempted to break open a store, but did not succeed; thence to Middletown, crossed over to Long-Island; thence to Huntington; thence to Norwalk, where we three broke open a schooner and stole some clothes; on the same night broke open a store belonging to Squire Lockhart in Norwalk, from whence we took about seventy or eighty pounds in goods and some silver buckles, and about two pounds in cash; next day we were apprehended and tried, first for robbing the schooner; I and Kalaghan were found guilty and received 10 lashes apiece, Williams got clear; and then we were all three committed to Fairfield gaol, and tried for breaking open the store, I took all the blame upon myself and cleared the other two, and received the punishment 35 lashes and five years imprisonment. Eight or nine days after my whipping broke out of gaol, and I, Kalaghan, Kennedy and Williams set off for Norwich Landing, with an intention of breaking open a store, but did not succeed. Upon the way we stole some shirts and trowsers, and when we parted, Kalaghan and Kennedy took the road for Providence, Williams and I to Norwich Landing; at a dance in Norwich

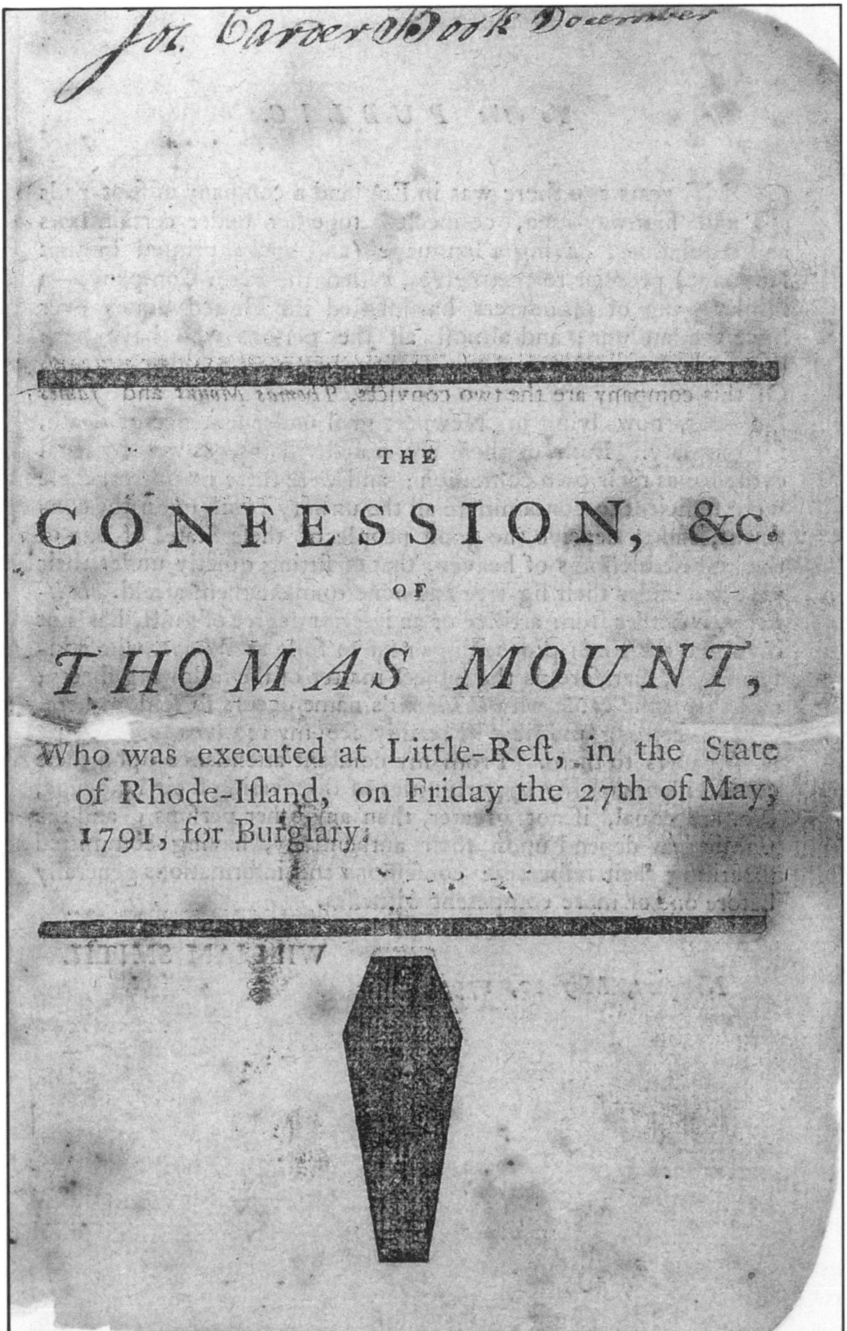

THE

CONFESSION, &c.

OF

*THOMAS MOUNT,*

Who was executed at Little-Reſt, in the State of Rhode-Iſland, on Friday the 27th of May, 1791, for Burglary.

Landing I took a silk cloak from a young lady, and sold it about two or three miles from Pockatanock bridge, and then set off for Providence; here I staid and wrought a week or two with Mr. Brown under the name of Charles Minor; then leaving Providence I set off for Boston, where I fell in company with James Williams for the first time of our connexion. I stole some buckles, and then, in company with Williams, set out for Newbury-Port, there I broke open a schooner and took out of her some clothes, some chocolate, some tobacco, and a bottle of rum: Williams stood upon the wharf and helped to take the things; we then set off for Portsmouth, and on the way I stole an axe and sold it for a pair of shoes. At Portsmouth I left Williams, and returned to Newbury-Port, there I fell in company with one Mr. Farrington, a gentleman thief: next night we two broke open a dwelling house, and took some silk gowns and womens apparel out of it; there I got apprehended on account of robbing a brig in Portsmouth, having part of the goods with me that were taken out of her by Williams, I was confined two or three days in gaol and then liberated. Leaving Newbury-Port I set off for Boston alone, where I broke open a schooner and took a parcel of clothes out of her; from thence returned to Providence, where I fell in company with John Hitchcock. Leaving Providence in a few days, we two set off for Norwich Landing, there we attempted to break open a store, and while I was lifting up Hitchcock in at the window, the gentleman of the house alarmed us and we escaped: from thence we went to New-London, where we broke open a store and took some money twenty or thirty shillings, and some cotton and silk handkerchiefs, &c. and then set off for Newport and sold some of the goods in Newport; here Hitchcock and Weathers broke open a store belonging to Mr. John Hadwen; for this I was apprehended and committed to gaol for two or three days, then was cleared, and set off for Hartford, upon the way I attempted to break open a house in Stonington, but being discovered I fled out of town, to Hartford, thence returned towards Providence; upon the way broke open a dwelling house in Connecticut, and stole some silver and pewter spoons, a hat and a tankard. Carrying the goods with me I arrived at Providence and sold them; here I worked with Mr. Brown a week or two under the name of Charles Minor; then I stole a pair of shoes out of Mr. Rogers's store where I had gone to receive my pay; next I went to Nancy Smith and told her I was a fortune-teller, and repeating several things that I had heard of her, she thought I was really a fortune-teller; then I proposed to marry her, and she approved of my offer; then I said I wanted to tell Miss Sally Brown's fortune, but could not in her father's house lest it should offend him, and asked whether it would be agreeable to bring down Sally Brown to her room; but this I could not do unless I was disguised; accordingly I desired her to give me some clothes for the purpose; she gave me a cloak and a surtout, but my plan was to run off with them. All this while I was aboard the Washington, Capt. Donalson, and Mr. Nightengale, as he thought he knew me aboard the Alliance frigate, but was not the purser, trusted me with money in advance. Leaving Providence with the advance money, I set off for Boston, there I took some shawls; from thence I went to Newbury-Port, where I fell in company with a young sailor going to visit his friends, carrying some handkerchiefs and shawls, we walked together about 14 or 15 miles, and at night we put up at Mr. Lovet's tavern betwixt Newbury-Port and Portsmouth: in the night I got up and robbed him of all he had, I took about four or five dollars in cash, a piece of calico, and two or three shawls, a pair of new stockings, a pair of new shoes, a pair of new buckles, a pair of new trowsers, a new shirt, and a beaver hat, a cotton and silk jacket, and a silk striped jacket, a pot of sweet pomatum, two books and two letters, and a parcel of oranges; from thence I went to Boston by the way of Exeter; arrived in Boston, I fell in company with Robert Tresson and Thomas Sherridan, where I took one or two shawls, and set out from Boston to go to Connecticut, about ten miles from Pomfret, Tresson and I attempted to rob a house, but were disappointed; then on we went to Pomfret, where we all three were concerned in robbing a waggon, and took two pieces of home-made bearskin, and on the same night broke open a blacksmith's shop, and got some tools wherewith to break open a store belonging to Lemming Grosvernor, took about 110 pounds worth in goods, and about two or three dollars in cash, then set off for Norwich Landing; about two miles from Norwich Landing, one Mountseer lives who is known to this sort of business, there we got apprehended, and sent to Windham gaol; Sherridan turned evidence against us, and we were tried and found guilty, and I received 40 lashes and to be imprisoned six months, Tresson 30, and to be imprisoned three months: within the first two months of our imprisonment, Robert Tresson, William Stanton, Gershom Palmer and I, being all in one apartment, broke gaol, Tresson, Stanton and I went to Voluntown, there Stanton left us, and Tresson and I went to Boston, where I stole two patterns of silk jackets. Here meeting with William English, one of our company, we three set off for Portsmouth; there we attempted to rob a store, but a fire breaking out in the town at that instant, prevented us; hearing the fire called we ran to where the fire was, there Tresson stole a jacket from Oliver Whipple, Esq. in the pockets thereof were a forty pound note of hand, a penknife, and a comb; next day we three were apprehended on suspicion of setting the house on fire, but were acquitted; then I set off alone for Kennebunk, in Massachusetts, eastward of Portsmouth, and there broke open a store belonging to Messrs. Condy and Clark, and stole a large quantity of dry goods and escaped 70 miles, and then was apprehended, in consequence of an advertisement, and committed to Old-York gaol, from whence after three weeks I broke out and set off for Portsmouth. The next night after my arrival at Portsmouth, I broke open the house of Mr. Shadwick, the gaoler, and stole some money and a quantity of mens and womens clothes, and gave Tresson, (whom I found here in prison) part of the money and two saws, and then set off towards Newbury-Port: next morning Tresson called the gaol keeper and told him that it was I that robbed him, and had given him two saws and a dollar in money wherewith to effect his escape; then the gaoler sent a pursuer after me, who apprehended and carried me back to Portsmouth gaol, from thence I was carried to Exeter for my trial: upon Tresson's evidence I was found guilty, but received no punishment by reason that I promised to inform of all those persons who received stolen goods, and how the house was set on fire; and therefore the court adjourned one month, and I carried back to Portsmouth gaol; but before the month was expired I broke gaol and set off for Boston, and fell in company with Joseph Kelly who had two coats and jackets he had stolen to bear our expences to Newport. We set off for Newport, and immediately upon our arrival, Kelly stole a pair of silver buckles from Mr. ——— a Jew, and I stole three or four black silk handkerchiefs from Mr. Wickham; next I and Kelly broke open a cooper's shop to get tools to break into Mr. Wickham's store, but daylight coming on we could not complete our business. No body pointed out the store to us, I had been in it the day before. Then leaving Newport Kelly and I went up to Mansfield, and there we parted; there I broke open a store belonging to Mr. Gilbert, and took out a quantity of goods, to the value of about twenty pounds, and with these goods set off to Voluntown to one Mr. Stedman's a receiver of stolen goods; there I again met with Kelly, and getting some money of Stedman for some of the goods, I returned to Providence, where I got playing cards with a countryman, cheated him of some money and two dressed sheepskins: there Kelly recommended me to one Lewis who supplied us with tools, and then Kelly and I set out to break Mr. Rogers's store, and had almost completed our business; but being alarmed by two or three men, made our escape, and took a couple of horses and rode almost to Voluntown, and then turned them off. At Voluntown we staid one day, and the next we fell in company with James Williams, who told me he was going to Providence to get on board Mr. Brown's India-man; I asked him to go with me the way of Stonington, and he consented; so Williams, Kelly and I set off to William Stanton's (we turned Kelly off telling him that two might keep a secret, but three could not) then Williams, Stanton and I set off for Hopkington with an intention to break a store, but did not succeed; but Williams and Stanton took a dozen pair of stockings off a fence.— Upon our return to Stanton's, I held the horses at the bridge, Williams and Stanton broke open a mill, and took all the meal and corn they could find, and we carried it to Stanton's house: Stanton next day sent some of the corn to Rowse Babcock's for rum. Next night Stanton, Williams and I set off to break into Joseph Potter's store; I broke open a mill and took a crow-bar out of it, and went to the door and broke it, and we all three went in, I first, and they following. Being most forward in this business, I lighted a candle and handed down the goods, about seven hundred dollars worth, and some money two or three dollars, and carried them to Stanton's house, where we divided them into three parts, and cast lots. Williams and I took our shares; after giving Stanton out of my share eight or nine pounds worth of goods for a mare, and hiding the goods under two corn stacks and under a barn, about five miles from Stanton's house, we set off for Voluntown, there were apprehended, and brought back to Hopkington, where Stanton, I and my wife were tried for breaking open the mill; Stanton's wife and Williams were admitted as State's evidence; accordingly I was sentenced to receive 20 lashes and my wife 10 (though she was innocent).—I paid the fine by giving up part of my clothes, then committed to Newport gaol, and tried for breaking Potter's shop, found guilty, and received the sentence of death—And the Lord have mercy on me.

*To the above Confession I here add my last Speech and Dying Words.*

*The* LAST SPEECH *and* DYING WORDS *of* THOMAS MOUNT, *published at his own Desire, for the public Good in general, and for that of his Comrades in particular.*

WHEN I see that every attempt to break gaol is unsuccessful, and that every effort to prevent my suffering an ignominious death, is like to be fruitless, I Thomas Mount, in conformity to the custom of publishing a last speech or dying words, for the benefit of my survivors, do hereby declare this to be my *last speech and dying words*.

And first—I pray that the Lord may have mercy upon me, and that all good people may pity and pray for me; and that my shameful end may deter others from those actions which have brought me to this dreadful hour.

Secondly—I desire to be truly penitent for my crimes, both against the laws of GOD and the laws of men; and to believe that Divine goodness hath thus arrested me in my career of wickedness, for his glory and my everlasting good. I desire to be more resigned to my sentence than I fear I am. So great has been my propensity to stealing, even from my childhood, that were my days prolonged, 'tis more than probable I should get into my old way again. I am horribly afraid to die; and yet confess I deserve not to live: but yet am certain, that the mercy of government in pardoning thieves, is no mercy at all to them, for every pardon they get hardens them so much the more in their villainy. The only way to reclaim *one* thief, is either to banish or hang all the *other thieves* and all the *receivers* of stolen goods; for so long as there are *receivers* and *thieves* living and at liberty, however penitent *one thief* may be the hour he receives his pardon and freedom, yet whenever he gets abroad among his old acquaintances, they will wish him joy of his escape from the gallows; they will get drunk with him; they will carry him to the places of general rendezvous, where the women and liquors are all in common, and with relating their wonderful escapes from justice, with the stimulating songs of his comrades, with the artful behavior of the scandals of their sex, he becomes ten-fold more a child of the devil than he was before.

Thirdly—Nothing corrupts young fellows more, than idleness and bad women, who are the first seducers to all evil, and if their extravagancies are not gratified to the full, become our betrayers: and therefore, as a dying man, would intreat all young men to get married and settled at some honest calling as soon as possible.

Fourthly—At my desire, the language and songs of the American Flash Company are published, to inform the world at large how wicked that company is, and how necessary it is to root them up like so many thorns and briars which if suffered to remain would destroy the rising crop of young fellows throughout the Continent. The whole of the secrets concerning this business, the names of the persons concerned in carrying it on, whether as thieves or receivers, or setters on, or suppliers with tools wherewith to break out of gaols, or into houses, to a good friend of mine when under sentence of death, I have communicated; at the same time taking his promise that he will transmit the same to the Governors of the United States of America immediately after my decease, that they may be of general utility to this country.

Fifthly—I have communicated likewise to this gentleman, the various ways of discovering thieves and house-breakers, so that in future it will be next to impossible to practice the thieving business without detection: And as all thieves are great cowards (for the bark of a dog will make them run) I would advise every honest man who wishes to preserve his property, to remember the rules I have communicated, and to act upon them; if he does, there is no great chance of being robbed, or having his house broke. Likewise I would submit it to the judgment of our rulers, whether it would not be proper to fine every man who was robbed on the high-way, provided only two thieves attacked him, because he did not defend himself; for the heroism of *one* honest man is, or ought to be, sufficient to make *two* thieves run.

Sixthly—As a dying man, a debtor to my country, and desirous of making all the compensation in my power, I further make known how any man of the least common sense may discover a thief,—by his often looking back—turning quick up lanes—standing to gaze at signs—and stopping to enquire for the houses of persons who do not live in the place—going into shops and giving the merchant a deal of unnecessary trouble in calling for a sight of one thing and another, and of twenty more, without buying one article. If a thief appears in the day time, you never see him without his rogue's face on; look at him pretty sharply, and you will see how suspicious and timorous he looks; take him by the hand, it feels soft, and your touch makes him shrink, you may perceive his hand nervous; but in nothing is this nervousness more perceptible than, if he takes a pen at your desire, to write with—it will therefore be to ask all suspected persons to write, and their hand will instantly tell upon their heart.

Seventhly—I must complain to the public of the receivers, or fences as we call them in the Flash language,—they are our *setters on*, and they cheat us confoundedly; we seldom receive from them more than a tenth part of the value, and must take it in what pay they please, and when they please; and by getting us drunk with our whores, every now and then, they generally steal from us all they can come at, and then set us to fighting with one another about the goods they had taken. These receivers being in league with our whores, make them very extravagant in their demands upon us, who, after treating them with the best of our spoils, if we do not promise quickly to get them more, threaten to inform against us.—In one word, a thief or highway-man is a pitiable animal; he risks his life every adventure he engages in, and all the recompence he gets for his pains, is the treachery of his whores and comrades, and last of all an ignominious death. Though at any time we take a large quantity of goods, we cannot sell them to any account; and after giving hush-money to some, paying a comrade for his help (for we hire one another on such-like expeditions, as breaking a shop or house, or way-laying the stage-coach, & c.) and gratifying our pretended friends with presents, we have seldom or never enough to buy decent clothes, wherein to assume the character and appearance of honest men and quit bad company, had we ever so much mind for it.

Eighth—When I look back upon a company of thieves, with their whores, met after some house or shop-breaking match, full of plunder, and recollect the scenes of cursing, singing, dancing, swearing, roaring, lewdness, drunkenness, and every possible sort of brutish behavior, I detest myself for having so often been one in such companies.—Under these circumstances we are very liable to be apprehended: and therefore, good people and bad people, thieves and honest men, take warning by my fate, and mind my advice; for if ye get into the way of thieving, nothing can cure you but the gallows.—I never heard of a thief that was reclaimed but one, and that under such circumstances as never can be the lot of any other thief to the end of the world.

Pray for me good people—I am wicked, and there are many others in the United States perhaps as wicked as myself; I pray they may depart from their wickedness, before their cup of iniquity becomes full, and they entail upon themselves the death I am going to suffer. It is but justice that such as have lived like wolves and beasts of prey, should die like dogs, and not like men.

And the Lord have mercy upon me—farewell.

*One day, in a frame of mind more devout than ordinary, I composed the following* LAMENTATION, *which I desire may be published exactly as I have dictated it, as a conclusion to my last speech and dying words.*

ALL ye good people who are assembled here this day,
Let my shameful end a warning be to you I pray,
Behold a dying victim who for his sins doth pardon crave,
Who once liv'd in good credit among his friends both fine and brave.
Thomas Mount it is my name,
And to my shame cannot deny
In New-Jersey I was born,
And on Little-Rest now must die.
Of robbing I own that I guilty be,
O may my dear Redeemer from further torments set me free,
Through all this country 'tis well they know my name;
From Boston to Newyork 'tis well they know my fame;
From Newyork to Philadelphia, from thence to Charlestown,
So basely I've behav'd roving up and down;
From Charlestown to Baltimore I quickly have set out,
For robbing of a merchant I was obliged to scout;
For robbing of another man I closely was pursued,
And my faithful comrade Lipton was taken on the road;
From thence to Newport gaol, which is the truth of my song,
So here I lie dismal bound down in irons strong.
Come all ye young men a warning take by me,
Love your wives, and mind your work, and shun bad company;
Quit gaming, and fine whores,
Pay off your tavern scores,
For they'll be staring at your daring,
When you can spend no more.
My wife pities my misfortune, alas! both night and day;
My comrades take good council and go no more astray:
I tried hard myself for to clear,
My relations will shed many a tear,

My wife she cries and tears her hair,
Oh! go I must, and the Lord knows where.
I hope my soul to heaven may flee,
And there remain to eternity:
Hoping that Christ will receive my soul,
And pardon my sins which are many fold.
Now on my dying day,
Pray for me all ye standers by,
(My friends do not parade
With sad and mournful tragedy.)
May the GOD of mercy grant me full pardon for my sin,
Open the gate, good Lord, and let a penitent sinner in.
(Signed) T. M.

*The Flash Company in London (of which* Mountain, *lately executed in Connecticut, was a member) had a language peculiar to themselves, and books printed in that language; Mount says he never saw any of those books, but Williams confessed to the publisher of these papers, that he had seen them in London, and one of them in the possession of a* J. S——rs, *in Jacksonborough, South-Carolina.—This language has been taken notice of in some British magazines, but little information communicated concerning it; and therefore, to gratify the public, the following dictionary of the Flash language (so far as could be obtained from Mount and Williams) together with several Flash songs, and the oath they administer to flats (as they call the novices in the art of thieving) when they are admitted into the Flash society, are added.*

## THE FLASH LANGUAGE.

A man, *a cove*
A woman, *a blowen*
A young woman, *a young blowen*
A young lad, *a young cove*
A house, *a ken*
Play-house or fair, *garf*
Master of the house, *cove of the ken*
Mistress of the house, *blowen of the ken*
Son, *young cove of the ken*
Daughter, *young blowen of the ken*
A gentleman, *a swell*
A lady, *a fine blowen*
A child, *a kinicher*
Hands, *dads*
Eyes, *peepers*
Head, *nanny*
Nose, *mugg*
Mouth, *mamma*
A hat, *a kelp*
A wig, *a busby*
A coat, *a tog*
A knife, *a chive*
A pair of pistols, *a pair of pops*
A sword, *a lash*
A crow-bar, *a gentleman*
A thief, *a prig*
A gambler, *a sharp*
A blanket or sheet, *a spread*
A bed, *a dause*
Dry goods, *chattery*
Cards, *broads or flats*

A pocket-book, *a reader*
A note of any kind, *a screen*
Ribbons, *dobbins*
Bread, *pinum*
Butter, *a spread*
Cheese, *caz*
Victuals of any kind, *grub or peck*
Rum, *suck*
Drunk, *sucky*
A bottle, *a glaze*
Sugar, *pellock*
Tobacco, *weed or funk*
Tobacco smoke, *blast of stumer*
Thief's girl, *blowen spenie or mush*
To take, *to hobble*
To lose, *to sweet*
A gaol, *a quod or a quæ*
A gaol-keeper, *a quod or quæcall*
A constable, *a horney*
A sheriff, *a trap*
A judge, *a beeks*
A clergyman, *a dull-gown's-man*
The law, *pattur*
The devil, *the crimson cove*
Hell, *the crimson ken*
The moon, *Oliver's leary*
The sun, *Phœbus*
A fit night for stealing, *a good darky*
A town, *a wile*
A vessel, *a barkey*
Lewd women, *cats*
A coach, *a rattle*
Flats, *country people*
The highway, *bonny-throw*
A jacket, *a javin*
A shirt, *a smisk*
Breeches, *kicksees*
Stockings, *leg-bags*
Boots, *quill-pipes*
Shoes, *crabs*
Buckles, *latches*
Cash, *lowr*
A watch, *a trick*
A guinea, *a quid*
A dollar, *a wheel*
Money of any kind, *bit*
Bad money, *blue bit*
Passing bad money, *ringing blue bit*
Gold in plate of any sort, *ridge*
Silver plate of any sort, *wedge*
Coppers, *maggs*
Silver spoons, *wedge feeders*
A horse, *a pred*
A horse-stealer, *a prednapper*
A sheep, *a wooly bird*
Picking pockets, *diving*
A snitch, *one that turns evidence*
A drag, *one that robs a waggon on the highway*

## FLASH PHRASES.

Peter, (a watch-word) *somebody hears us; also an iron chest where cash is kept*
Lea, (another watch-word) *look who comes*
Nose the cove, *watch the man and see where he goes*
Go weed the cove, *go speak to the man*
Stow your weeds, *hold your tongue*
I am spotted, *I am disappointed, some-body saw me*
Let us sterry, *let us make our escape*

Rumble like a miza, *wash my clothes*
Knuckling, *picking of pockets*
Doing the cove of a trick, *taking a gentle-man's watch*
A snow rig, *Stealing clothes out of doors*
Taking chattery upon the lift, *taking goods in the day time*
The evening or morning sneak, *goods taken early in the morning or late in the evening*
A scamp, *robbing a gentleman on the highway*
A dub, *opening a door with a false key*
Cracking a ken, *breaking into a house*
Open a glaze, *going in at a window*
Flying the lue, *going up or down a chimney*
Knocked down upon the crap, *condemned*
Turnips, *acquitted*
Naptatees, *a man to be flogged*
Knocked down upon the slum, *a place of confinement or castle*
I have done the cove out and out, *I have killed a man*
I have queered the quod, *I have broke prison*
I'm in slangs, *I'm in irons*
I'm napping my bib, *I'm crying*
Ready to be topped, *going to be hanged*

## THE OATH, AT THE ADMISSION OF A FLAT INTO THE FLASH SOCIETY.

THE oldest Flash cove taking the *Flat* by the hand, asks him if he desires to join the Flash Company. The *Flat* answers, yes. The Flash cove (head man) bids him say thus:—I swear by—that to the Flash Company I will be true—never divulge their secrets, nor turn evidence against any of them—and if a brother is in distress, that I will hasten to relieve him, at the risk of my life and liberty—and if he suffers, endeavor to be revenged on the person or persons who were the means of bringing him to punishment.—After taking the above, or a similar oath, the *Flat* receives a *pall,* i.e. a companion, and they two are sent out upon some expedition.

N.B. By the confession of Mount and Williams, it appears the Flash Company have spread themselves all over the continent, from Nova-Scotia to the remotest parts of Georgia—that the principal seaport towns are their places of general rendezvous—and that the number of the society at present, are from about 70 to 80, males and females. They have receivers in the principal towns of each State, who not only receive the stolen goods, but point out shops and houses for them to break into and plunder.

§ *Sometimes they swear by* GOD, *and sometimes by the* Devil: *when they use the name of* GOD, *they swear by the Old Cove, who knows all things*; *and when by the* Devil, *by the Cove of the Scarlet Ken*!

## FLASH SONGS.

### *A Highway-man's Flash Song.*

COME all ye roving scamping
blades,
That scamping take delight,
That go out on the bonny throw
Upon a darky night;
With pops into your pockets,
And lashes in your hand,
We'll ride up to the Diligence,
And boldly bid her stand.
By stopping of the Diligence
Put Jervis in a fright,
Who said I'll have your body hung
Before to-morrow night.
I said, ye gallows rogue
Haul in your bridle reins,
Or else a leaden bullet
Shall pierce your bloody brains.
Then to the inside passengers
Straightway we did repair,
To do them of their lowr,
It was our only care.
We dunn'd them of their lowr,
And thought it all our own,
We bid them a good darky,
They roll'd the road to town.

### *Another Highway-man's Song.*

I'LL sport as good a pred away
As any boy in town,
I'll trot her fourteen miles an hour,
I'll back her ten to one.
She's up to all the cross roads,
And never makes a stand,
Here and there, and every where,
We ride with pop in hand.
Next to my blowen spenie
I'll go without a doubt,
And if I meet a swell-cove,
I'll do him out and out.

### *A Pickpocket's Song.*

I AND my blowen to the garf
Straightway did repair,
We tripp'd the green flyers,
One two three pair of stairs.
She's flashing to the miz,
Then I do her lose,
She does them of their tricks,
And then we go to Snows.
Day-light being over,
And darky coming on,
We'll all go to the Flash-ken,
And have a roaring song.

### *A London Ken-cracking Song.*

COME all ye scamps both far
and near,
Listen awhile and ye shall hear,
How five young lads, who in
their prime,
Were all cut off before their time.
Up Ludgate hill we did set out,

Upon the crack ye need not doubt,
Scarce in bit, and low in sack,
Sir Robert's ken we meant to crack.
When to Sir Robert's ken we came,
Says Harry Jones, "as true's my
name,
With iron chisels and crow-bars too,
To's iron Peter we'll soon break
through."
And when his Peter we did burst,
His golden chain I hobbled first;
The next, it was a diamond ring,
This was doing quite the thing.
With active hands and tongues full
still,
With wedge and bit our sacks did
fill;
But when call'd for to be try'd,
The fact we all bore, I deny'd.
Frank being cast, to's mush did say,
With other prigs ne'er live I pray;
Jack Brim was there, Lyons the Jew,
Who turned snitch on lads so true.
There was Franc Finis, a hearty
blade,
Isaac Barton besides my dad,
Charley Johns, Bill Thompson too,
Five cleverer lads ye never knew.
Come all young lads a warning take,
Your honest trades pray don't
forsake,
For if ye do, ye'll rue the day
That e'er you scampt upon the lay.
Would'nt it grieve your hearts to see
Five clever lads hung on a tree,
Taking their leave, and last farewell?
I hope in heaven their souls may
dwell.

*A Song made by a Flash Cove the Evening before his Execution.*

MY blowen came here t'other night,
She fetch'd us a jorum of diddle,
To the prisoners it gave great
delight,
And we hopp'd it away to the
fiddle.
But our trade of diving doth fail,
My blowen has chang'd habitations;
For now she pads in the gaol,
And laughs at the flats of the
nation.
But at length the dull-gown's-man
comes in
And tips me soft tales of
repentance,
When on him I do cast my brow,
I care not one fig for his sentence.
By th' gullet I'll be ty'd very tight
To-morrow:—my blowen pray for
us,
My peepers will be hid from the
light,
The tumbler shoves off, so I *morris*.

*A Song, how a Flat became a Prig, then a Ken-cracker, and lastly got hanged.*

By Newgate steps young *Chance*
was found,
And brought up near St. Gile's
pond,
The truth I tell, deny it who can,
Saucy, lowring, Bilingsgate man.
At twelve years old as I've been
told,
This youth was sturdy, stout and
bold,
He learn'd to swear, to curse, to
fight,
And every thing but—read and
write.
He daddles clean, he'll slip between
A croud, a clout he'll nap unseen,
And home straightway the prize
he'd bring,
The ken-crackers roar'd "Jack's just
the thing."
But when he grew to man's estate,
Jack's mind ran on something great,

He napp'd a pred, went out on the
scamp,
For longer on diving he scorn'd to
tramp.
Strutting in park was all his pride,
With a flaming whore stuck by his
side,
And in a club Flash songs would
sing,
And the Flash-ken roar'd "Jack's
just the thing."
His man'al exercise he's been
through,
Both bridewel, pump, and horse-
pond too,
His back has oft-times felt the
smart
Of tibben and strings, at the tail of
a cart.
But that was no matter, he stood as
the pattur,
He gammon'd the twelve, and he
work'd in the water,
A pardon he got from a gracious
king,
And ken-crackers roar'd "Jack's just
the thing."
With black cockade, and hat for
war,
With bludgeon strong as iron bar,
To head a mob, Jack ne'er would
fail,
To rob a church, or crack a gaol.
A victim he fell to his country's
laws,
He died in no religious cause,
Ken-cracking caus'd the blade to
swing,
And "Jack tuck'd up was just the
thing."

*Mount's Flash Song upon himself.*

COME ye prigs, and scamps full
bold,
I'll sing you of a lad of fame,
Who in Newyork town once did
dwell,
And Thomas Mount it is my
name.
As I was going out on the scamp,
Void of any dread or fear,
I was surrounded by the traps,
And to the quod they did me
steer.
And when I come into the quod,
Captain R——ds did me know,
Tommy come tip me the bit, he
said,
And I'm the cove, that'll bring
you thro'.
Indeed, kind Sir, I've got no bit,
And this all your traps do know,
I had not been two hours in
town,
Before they prov'd my overthrow.
Ram'd into his closest gaol,
I had some bits, his traps well
know,
I sent some bits to fetch me suck,
And then to cracking we did go.
And now I've crack'd the quod
again,
Away to thieving I will go,
Gardiner went to fetch me tools,
Away to —— we did flow,
We dunn'd him out of all he had,
And then to Lovelies we did
steer,
For to whet the bit ye know,
And in the ken we hobbled were.
Again they brought me to the
quod,
The quæcall said, "you ne'er shall
go,
Hand me down large heavy irons,
On Thomas Mount a pair must
go."
When the quæcall shut me up
I did not break my heart with
woe,
I broke my slangs, then crack'd

the quod,
Again to thieving I did go.
*Chorus.* To Thieving and cracking,
To scamping and napping,
Of Coves with praddles
Of kens with daddles,
And away to thieving I will go.

## Source Notes

*The Confession &c. of Thomas Mount* was published first in Newport, Rhode Island, by Peter Edes following Mount's execution on May 27, 1791. Three more editions followed within a brief period of time. The second was printed and sold by Thomas and Samuel Green in New Haven, and the third was "Printed by Moses H. Woodward for Isaac Riley, & Co."; both of these editions were dated 1791 (title page). The undated fourth edition was "Printed and Sold by J. Melcher" in Portsmouth, N. H. (title page). The copy text used in the anthology is taken from the original Edes edition.

Mount's narrative was introduced by a preface "*To the PUBLIC,*" which was signed "William Smith" and dated "*Newport, May* 20, 1791." According to this preface, both Mount and his fellow burglar, James Williams, belonged to a "gang of plunderers . . . [that had] infested the United States ever since the late war." Smith further claimed that this "gang" resembled "a company of foot-pads and highway-men" known as "the Flash Company," which was organized "under certain laws and regulations" and which had "a language (and books printed in that language) peculiar to themselves." Smith's claim, one of the very first accounts of organized crime in America, must have shocked readers, particularly since he added that "almost all the persons who have been hanged of late in North-America, have belonged to this company." Consequently, Smith justified his "handing these sheets" to the public as an attempt to reveal "the Flash proceedings" and thus warn readers of the threat posed by the anti-world of the burglars. In order to quell skepticism, Smith declared that, due to his "constant attendance upon these convicts [Mount and Williams]," he had ample "opportunities of discovering their language, &c." and that readers could "depend upon their [these papers'] authenticity" (309).

In view of his station, readers were likely to believe Smith. He was not only in a position to attend the "two convicts," but he also was in a position of respect and prestige. William Smith (c. 1754–1821) was an Episcopal clergyman who, at the time of Mount's imprisonment and execution, was the minister of Newport's Trinity Church. Moreover, at the same time he attended Mount in prison, preparing him for death, he also was preparing *The Convict's Visitor* (Newport: Peter Edes, 1791), an eighty-five page book of "Prayers, Lessons, and Meditations, with suitable Devotions before, and at the Time of Execution" (see the advertisement included below). According to the preface Smith, as he began ministering to the condemned burglars, discovered a need for a devotional tract that would "communicate the 'glad tidings of salvation' to those 'who sit under the shadow of death' " (i). Using what he termed "the antient Way of Liturgy," he developed a series of dialogues and dramatic roles appropriate for any "*Minister*" and "*Convict*" in similar situations of impending execution. Divided into a progressive sequence of "PENITENTIAL OFFICES," Smith's manual offered model prayers and confessions that included fill-in-the-blanks for specific names and stage directions alerting the participants as to how the roles should be acted out. In prescribing exact forms and patterns, the minister intended to formalize the process of public death, allowing condemned criminals the opportunity to earn divine mercy through ritualized performance. Whether in dialogue, prayer, meditation, or confession, Smith provided exact words for "dying penitents" to adopt, and by adopting the rhetoric of the minister, they in turn adopted the standards and perspectives of society at large. Through ritual and rhetoric, the self was exchanged for salvation.

Certainly Smith was concerned with repressing Mount's criminal nature. In concluding his preface, he declared his desire that "the following devotions" might be speedily corrected and printed so that "they might be put into the hands of *James Williams* and *Thomas Mount*, now lying under sentence of death in the goal of Newport." His words were dated: "*Newport, Wednesday, in Passion Week*, 1791" (ii).

For biographical information concerning Smith, see the *Dictionary of American Biography* , IX, 358–59.

Outside of Newport, Mount's narrative probably attracted a lot more attention than the notices printed in the newspapers. Other crimes and criminals, such as David Comstock's trial and execution for murder, gained more notice than Mount both in and outside of Rhode Island. *The Providence Gazette*, however, included short notices of his trial (April 9) and execution (May 28). A somewhat lengthier account of his sentence and crime appeared in the April 16 issue of *The Providence Gazette:* "At the Superior Court in South-Kingston, last week, Thomas Mount, and ——— Williams, were tried for a Burglary, in breaking open a Shop contiguous to the Dwelling-House of Joseph Potter, of Westerly, last December, and taking from thence a Quantity of Goods—found guilty, and received Sentence of Death, to be executed on the 27th of May next." A few scattered notices were reprinted elsewhere (*The Boston Gazette*, April 25). Despite the lack of extensive newspaper coverage, Louis P. Masur stated that Mount was "the most notorious bandit in post-Revolutionary America (7). As evidence, Masur quoted one newspaper account that claimed Mount was "the most hardened villain that ever disgraced a gaol." According to this report, when asked to reform, Mount replied: "No, no that is impossible. Tommy Mount must be hung for a thief" (60).

Within Newport, however, the papers printed more revealing accounts of the burglar. In the April 16 issue of *The Newport Herald*, both Mount's trial and his response upon conviction were mentioned:

> At the Honorable Superior Court of this State which convened the last week in the county of Washington, Thomas Mount and James Williams were convicted of burglary, and were sentenced by the court to be executed in South Kingstown on Friday the 27th of May next.
>
> We are informed the prisoners who were capitally convicted in Washington county, appeared unconcerned until they were found guilty by the jury—at this moment their fortitude forsook them, and Mount, after lamenting his vicious life, entreated the court to grant him a long time to prepare for death.

Mount's entreaty had little effect; he was executed on schedule.

*The Newport Herald* also included a notice concerning Mount's less-than-repentant activities while in jail awaiting execution (April 30):

> On Monday night last the prisoners under sentence of death in the gaol in this Town, attempted to make their escape—On examining them and searching the room next morning, a saw, knife, gimblets, flints, steel, tinder &c. were found concealed, which were conveyed to them through the vault, by Mount's wife—who has since been taken up at Bristol, brought to this town, and committed to prison.

In the same issue, Peter Edes, publisher of *The Newport Herald* as well as the Mount/Smith *Confession* and Smith's *The Convict's Visitor*, inserted an advertisement for the latter Smith production:

> *In the Press, and in a few Days will be published and for Sale, by the Printer hereof,*
>
> The Convict's Visitor:
>
> Or, Penitential Offices, (in the antient Way of Liturgy) consisting of Prayers, Lessons, and Meditations, with suitable Devotions before, and at the Time of Execution.
> By WILLIAM SMITH, A. M.
> Rector of Trinity Church in Newport.
>
> Penitent—LORD, *remember me when thou comest into thy* KINGDOM!
>
> JESUS said unto him, "to-day shalt thou be with me in PARADISE.["]

This advertisement ran throughout the next month.

The longest account concerning Mount was published after his execution in *The Newport Mercury* on June 2, and then two weeks later in *The United States Chronicle* (June 16):

> On the 27th Ult. was executed at Little Rest, Washington County,

according to his Sentence for Burglary, *Thomas Mount*, in the 27th Year of his Age.—

An excessive and ungovernable Levity of Mind seems to have been the leading Characteristic of this unfortunate Man:—Endowed with uncommon Agility of Body, and a large Share of Greatness of Mind and Strength of Memory, he was certainly designed by the Sovereign Creator to fill some *useful* Station in Life.—During his Imprisonment, under Sentence of Death, twice did he attempt to escape, and his last Effort was so well planned, and so near taking Effect, that it failed rather from unaccountable Absence of Mind at the critical Moment, than through any Defect in the Contrivance; which induced him (a few Hours after the Detection) to say to the Rev. Gentleman [Smith] who attended him and others, "I have broke every Prison in which I hitherto have been confined—but defeated twice—in this I see the Hand of God."—

However variegated the Crimes of his former, a striking Uniformity marked every Hour of the last 4 or 5 Days of his Life:— Having spent the Whole of the last Night he was in Newport Gaol in Prayer—about 8 next Morning, in the examining Room, he acted his Part well, in one of the most affecting Scenes the Spectators had ever beheld—when on bended Knees and in each other Embraces, Mr. Reed and he mutually forgave each other with strong Cries and Tears, and the Kiss of Charity, preparatory to his receiving the Sacrament of Baptism. —Passing over many Things relative to his Behaviour while in the Prison at Little-Rest, and during the Interval of his leaving the Prison, and going to the Place of Execution, suffice it to be remarked, that, firm to the last, his Mind averted from sublunary Things and steadfastly fixed on God, and ascending up to Heaven in Holy Extacy of Prayer, he declared his *Willingness to be offered up a Sacrifice to divine and human Justice,—he forgave all Men in hopes of finding Forgiveness with God*—and after he was turned off—he was distinctly heard to breathe his last in Prayer—"Lord have Mercy upon me—Lord have Mercy upon me—Lord"—here he was suffocated, and quickly after this his whole Frame became convulsed—and his Soul prepared to forsake that Body which by being so long the Seat of Sin, had fallen under the Curse of the Law.

Multitudes mourned and bewailed him—no Triumph over his melancholy End disgraced the Feelings of Humanity—for the Space of a Quarter of an Hour, Nothing was to be heard but Prayers, intermixed with Sighs and Groans. Every Face displayed the Signs of being affected with the Solemnities of his Death, and the most tender Sympathies of Woe trickled down almost every Cheek.—The Body, put into a Coffin with much brotherly Compassion, was deposited, with these Words pronounced over the Grave—"With stern Voice the Law proclaimeth *cursed is every One that hangeth on a Tree*;"—but the Voice of the Gospel with Words of *Grace* and *Truth* comforteth Man by proclaiming, "*he who believeth in Jesus though he die yet shall he live again*." The deceased professed *this* Faith and *this* Hope—and according to his Repentance, Charity, Faith and Hope, in Jesus, be it unto him.—Therefore we commit his Body to the Earth, Dust to Dust, Earth to Earth, Ashes to Ashes—hoping that the Lord may have Mercy on him."—

"*There is more Joy in the Presence of the Angels of God over ONE SINNER that repenteth, than over NINETY and NINE just Persons, who need no Repentance!*"

# The Confeſſion and *DYING WORDS* of SAMUEL FROST, Who is to be Executed this Day, October 31, 1793, for the Horrid Crime of MURDER.

I WAS born at Princeton, in the County of Worceſter, and Commonwealth of Maſſachuſetts, on the 14th day of January, 1765. My father's name was John Froſt, he had four ſons the eldeſt of whom died when he was nineteen years old—two of my brothers are yet living. My mother is dead; I always regarded her, and ever thought my father had no affection for her, and that he uſed her ill; this induced me to kill him, which deed I executed on the 23d of September, 1783, as we were digging a ditch together; I knocked him down with a handſpike, and then beat his brains out. I was apprehended and committed to goal in Worceſter, and tried before the Supreme Court, and was acquitted contrarily to my expectations.

My mother died when I was about fourteen years old, and I always ſuppoſed her death was occaſioned by the bad treatment ſhe received from my father. He was very churliſh, and was void of all affection for his family.

After I was acquitted, and got releaſed from goal, I went and lived with Mr. George Parkis; afterwards with Mr. John Gleaſon, then with Mr. Phinehas Gregory; after living with them, I went and lived with Mr. Ezekiel Sawin, then went a ſecond time to Mr. Parkis, after this I lived with Mr. Jeſſe Fiſher, and then with Mr. Rice. All theſe people lived in Princeton. Whilſt I lived with Mr. Rice, I arrived at twenty one years of age; I left Mr. Rice, and went to live with a relation, Mr. Benjamin Wilſon, where I tarried about two or three weeks, and then went to Capt. Eliſha Allen's, where I lodged one night. From Capt. Allen's I went and lived a ſhort time with Mr. Solomon Parker, and then with ſeveral other perſons, but was only a little time with each—then I went to live with Mr. Ephraim Oſgood; I left him and went to the houſe where I formerly lived with my father, and tarried there about five months, in the year 1786; but receiving an affront, being told to do ſomething againſt my inclination, I went off without taking leave, and took to the woods—I wandered about for three days and nights: In the day time I kept in the woods, and at nights went to farms and lodged in barns, unperceived. In the woods I got and eat berries, and gathered apples in orchards, and on them I lived during the three days and nights.

Being tired of living in the woods, I went to Fitzwilliam, to the houſe of Benjamin Wilſon, my relation, beforementioned, who had removed from Princeton to that place. I arrived there on the 22d day of Auguſt, 1786, at breakfaſt time. I was very hungry and eat heartily.—I tarried here until the 5th day of September, the ſame year.

Soon after this time a number of people were going to Worceſter, to ſtop the ſitting of the Court—they aſked me to go with them, and treated me. I wanted to ſee what they would do, and went with them as far as Holden—at this place, ſtopping at Davis's tavern, I went out to pick ſome apples to eat; after which I laid down on the ground and went to ſleep—when I awoke, I thought I was doing wrong to go with thoſe people to ſtop the Court, and would not go with them any further. I left them and went to Princeton—there I met with more people going to Worceſter for the like purpoſe—they gave me ſome drink. I left them, and went to Mr. Stephen Merrick's where I lodged that night. I then worked for ſeveral perſons for a few days; and on the 11th day of September, 1786, I went and lived with Capt. Eliſha Allen—who took me becauſe it was the deſire of a number of people. It was town meeting day, and I went to the meeting.

I lived with Mr. Allen ſome time—when chooſing to go away—I went off at a time when I was ſent to paſture with the cows—I was gone almoſt three days, living as I could—I ſpent three coppers whilſt I was gone, and went almoſt as far as Boſton—then I returned to Capt. Allen's again. I went off ſeveral times afterwards, and was abſent ſometimes a longer and ſometimes a ſhorter time, but did not get any thing by going away but flogging when I returned. Conſidering myſelf as a ſlave, I have thought I had as well die as live as I did.—I had a ſmall eſtate and wanted to work on that, but I could not.—Mr. Allen had the care of my eſtate, and I ſuppoſed was paid for my living with him out of it. I thought ſeveral times I would kill him, and then thought I would not.—At length, on the 16th day of July, 1793, I effected it thus—Capt. Allen was going to ſet out cabbage plants, and ordered me to go with him, and to get a hoe; he went to the ſpot for planting, and I after the hoe; when I returned with the hoe, I found him ſtooping to fix a plant—I then thought it would be a good time to put my deſign in execution, and accordingly went up to him and gave him a blow with the hoe on his head, and repeated it. When I was about giving the third blow, he ſaid, "Forbear Sam, you have done enough." I made no reply, but continued repeating the blows until I ſuppoſed he was dead. I had beaten his head ſo as it had made a large hole in the ground and his brains came out. After I had finiſhed him, I went into the woods not far diſtant, where I remained four days, living on berries, &c. Whilſt I was in the woods, I heard the voice of the people who I ſuppoſed were after me; I heard them call me—but they did not find me; at length I was tired of being in the woods, as it was hard fare—came and loitered about a houſe where I had formerly lived, and was diſcovered by ſome of the family, who took me into the houſe and gave me ſome victuals, and ſecured me. I was then brought to Worceſter gaol again, and now ſhall certainly be hanged.

I declare that I had always a great averſion to ſtealing and telling lies, and think them to be great crimes.—I always meant to tell truth, and never ſtole, excepting taking a few apples from orchards may be called theft.

*The foregoing account was taken from the mouth of* Samuel Froſt, *in priſon.*

## ACCOUNT *of* SAMUEL FROST.

SAMUEL FROST was certainly an extraordinary character—his mind was evidently not formed altogether like thoſe of other perſons.—He thought it no great crime to kill ſuch as he ſuppoſed treated him very ill—and did not appear to have a juſt conception of the heinous crime of Murder.—His education appears to have been very indifferent, but his natural capacity in many reſpects ſeemed to be equal to perſons in general, whoſe minds have not been cultivated. He had high notions of honeſty, and appeared much offended when his honeſty was ſuſpected.—He appears alſo to have been a perſon who regarded truth; and he valued himſelf upon his probity and ſincerity.—One ſtriking proof of his diſlike to falſehood appeared when he was indicted before the Supreme Court—he plead guilty—he was told that he might plead not guilty, was urged ſo to do, and was remanded to priſon, in order that he might conſider of the plea he had made, and retract it, &c. yet notwithſtanding on his being again brought into Court, he perſiſted in pleading guilty. He was ſenſible of favours granted him, and expreſſed his gratitude for them—Yet, he had a moſt ſavage heart which nothing could meliorate, and he would talk with the ſame calmneſs and compoſure of the horrid Murders he had committed, as though the perſons who fell a ſacrifice to his fury, had been of the brutal creation. He could read and write, and often was found, whilſt in priſon, reading in the Bible--yet he ſhewed no ſigns of contrition eſpecially for the unnatural murder of his father. Notwithſtanding he read the Bible, he was not fond of converſing with the Clergy, and in general of the many who viſited him, few of them could get him to talk with them. He went two ſundays to meeting after his ſentence, but more through perſuaſion than inclination; and though urged refuſed to go again.—On the firſt Sabbath that he attended divine ſervice he appeared to be offended with the miniſter, becauſe he mentioned the murder of his father. Froſt ſaid he did not like to be twitted of that—that it was an old matter, and was ſettled long ſince.--On being aſked by the High Sheriff if he wiſhed to have a ſermon preached on the day of his Execution, he anſwered that he did not care any thing about it--he ſaid he would attend to the ſermon on condition that he might not be brought back to priſon, but be carried from the meeting houſe to the place of execution.

He had been known to ſay, that his killing Capt. Allen was rather more than he ought to have done--and that he would, if it was not done, ſtay ſeven years firſt. He was a moſt dangerous perſon to ſociety.--On being aſked if he had his liberty, if he would kill any other perſon, he anſwered there was one more he believed he ſhould. He told ſome perſons who viſited him one day, that he believed his father and Allen had a very tough time of it—Being aſked why he thought ſo, he ſaid he had been beating his head againſt the walls of the priſon, in order to know how they felt whilſt he was killing them.

He appeared to have a very confuſed idea of a future ſtate—ſuppoſed he ſhould go to Purgatory—and ſaid he believed the Devils wore large black wigs—and many other ſuch chimerical expreſſions of folly and abſurdity he uttered reſpecting a future exiſtence.—He did not appear pleaſed that the time of his execution was fixed at ſo diſtant a period—he wiſhed, he ſaid, to have it over a fortnight ſooner. On the whole, as a man, he was ſavage—void of all the finer feelings of the ſoul, and deſtitute of the tender affections of filial love and gratitude—He appears to have been a being caſt in a different mould from thoſe of mankind in general, and to be the connecting grade between the human and brutal creation.

The above will enable the reader to form ſome idea of his rational faculties.

He was about five feet four inches high, rather ſlenderly built, and very ſtrong. He had a peculiar way of toſſing or twitching his head, and his countenance was very unpleaſant.

Printed and ſold at Mr. THOMAS's Printingoffice, in *Worceſter*. Price 6d. Alſo, A Poem on the Occaſion. Price 3d.

[ SAMUEL FROST ]

# *The Confession and Dying Words of Samuel Frost*

[ 1793 ]

I WAS born at Princeton, in the County of Worcester, and Commonwealth of Massachusetts, on the 14th day of January, 1765. My father's name was John Frost, he had four sons the eldest of whom died when he was 19 years old—two of my brothers are yet living. My mother is dead; I always regarded her, and ever thought my father had no affection for her, and that he used her ill; this induced me to kill him, which deed I executed on the 23d of September, 1783, as we were digging a ditch together; I knocked him down with a handspike, and then beat his brains out. I was apprehended and committed to goal in Worcester, and tried before the Supreme Court, and was acquitted contrarily to my expectations.

My mother died when I was about fourteen years old, and I always supposed her death was occasioned by the bad treatment she received from my father. He was very churlish, and void of all affection for his family.

After I was acquitted, and got released from goal, I went and lived with Mr. George Parkis; afterwards with Mr. John Gleason, then with Mr. Phinehas Gregory; after living with them, I went and lived with Mr. Ezekiel Sawin, then went a second time to Mr. Parkis, after this I lived with Mr. Jesse Fisher, and then with Mr. Rice. All these people lived in Princeton. Whilst I lived with Mr. Rice, I arrived at twenty one years of age; I left Mr. Rice, and went to live with a relation, Mr. Benjamin Wilson, where I tarried about two or three weeks, and then went to Capt. Elisha Allen's, where I lodged one night. From Capt. Allen's I went and lived a short time with Mr. Soloman Parker, and then with several other persons, but was only a little time with each—then I went to live with Mr. Ephraim Osgood; I left him and went to the house where I formerly lived with my father, and tarried there about five months, in the year 1786; but receiving an affront, being told to do something against my inclination, I went off without taking leave, and took to the woods—I wandered about for three days and nights: In the day time I kept in the woods, and at nights went to farms and lodged in barns, unperceived. In the woods I got and eat berries, and gathered apples in orchards, and on them I lived during the three days and nights.

Being tired of living in the woods, I went to Fitzwilliam, to the house of Benjamin Wilson, my relation, beforementioned, who had removed from Princeton to that place. I arrived there on the 22d day of August, 1786, at breakfast time. I was very hungry and eat heartily.—I tarried here until the 5th day of September, the same year.

Soon after this time a number of people were going to Worcester, to stop the sitting of the Court—they asked me to go with them, and treated me. I wanted to see what they would do, and went with them as far as Holden—at this place, stopping at Davis's tavern, I went out to pick some apples to eat; after which I laid down on the ground and went to sleep—when I awoke, I thought I was doing wrong to go with those people to stop the Court, and would not go with them any further. I left them and went to Princeton—there I met with more people going to Worcester for the like purpose—they gave me some drink. I left them and went to Mr. Stephen Merrick's where I lodged that night. I then worked for several persons a few days; and on the 11th day of September, 1786, I went and lived with Capt. Elisha Allen—who took me because it was the desire of a number of people. It was town meeting day, and I went to the meeting.

I lived with Mr. Allen some time—when choosing to go away—I went off at a time when I was sent to pasture with the cows—I was gone almost three days, living as I could—I spent three coppers whilst I was gone, and went almost as far as Boston—then I returned to Capt. Allen's again. I went off several times afterwards, and was absent sometimes a longer and sometimes a shorter time, but did not get any thing by going away but flogging when I returned. Considering myself as a slave, I have thought I had as well die as live as I did.—I had a small estate and wanted to work on that, but I could not.—Mr. Allen had the care of my estate, and I supposed was paid for my living with him out of it. I thought several times I would kill him, and then thought I would not.—At length, on the 16th day of July, 1793, I effected it thus——Capt. Allen was going to set out cabbage plants, and ordered me to go with him, and to get a hoe; he went to the spot for planting, and I after the hoe; when I returned with the hoe, I found him stooping to fix a plant—I then thought it would be a good time to put my design in execution, and accordingly went up to him and gave him a blow with the hoe on his head, and repeated it. When I was about giving the third blow, he said, "Forbear Sam, you have done enough." I made no reply, but continued repeating the blows until I supposed he was dead. I had beaten his head so as it had made a large hole in the ground and his brains came out. After I had finished him, I went into the woods not far distant, where I remained four days, living on berries, &c. Whilst I was in the woods, I heard the voice of the people who I supposed were after me; I heard them call me—but they did not find me; at length I was tired of being in the woods, as it was hard fare—came and loitered about a house where I had formerly lived, and was discovered by some of the family, who took me into the house and gave me some victuals, and secured me. I was brought to Worcester gaol again, and now shall certainly be hanged.

I declare that I had always a great aversion to stealing and telling lies, and think them to be great crimes.—I always meant to tell the truth, and never stole, excepting taking a few apples from orchards may be called theft.

*The foregoing account was taken from the mouth of* Samuel Frost, *in prison.*

## ACCOUNT *of* SAMUEL FROST.

SAMUEL FROST was certainly an extraordinary character—his mind was evidently not formed altogether like those of other persons.—He thought it no great crime to kill such as he supposed treated him very ill—and did not appear to have a just conception of the heinous crime of Murder.—His education appears to have been very indifferent, but his natural capacity in many respects seemed to be equal to persons in general, whose minds have not been cultivated. He had high notions of honesty, and appeared much offended when his honesty was suspected.—He appears also to have been a person who regarded truth; and he valued himself upon his probity and sincerity.—One striking proof of his dislike to falsehood appeared when he was indicted before the Supreme Court—he plead guilty—he was told that he might plead not guilty, was urged so to do, and was remanded to prison, in order that he might consider of the plea he had made, and retract it, &c. yet notwithstanding on his being again brought into Court, he persisted in pleading guilty. He was sensible of favours granted him, and expressed his gratitude for them—Yet, he had a most savage heart which nothing could meliorate, and he would talk with the same calmness and composure of the horrid Murders he had committed, as though the persons who fell a sacrifice to his fury, had been of the brutal creation. He could read and write, and often was found, whilst in prison, reading in the Bible—yet he shewed no signs of contrition especially for the unnatural murder of his father. Notwithstanding he read the

Bible, he was not fond of conversing with the Clergy, and in general of the many who visited him, few of them could get him to talk with them. He went two Sundays to meeting after his sentence, but more through persuasion than inclination; and though urged refused to go again.—On the first Sabbath that he attended divine service he appeared to be offended with the minister, because he mentioned the murder of his father. Frost said he did not like to be twitted of that—that it was an old matter, and was settled long since.—On being asked by the High Sheriff if he wished to have a sermon preached on the day of his Execution, he answered that he did not care any thing about it—he said he would attend to the sermon on condition that he might not be brought back to prison, but be carried from the meeting house to the place of execution.

He had been known to say, that his killing Capt. Allen was rather more than he ought to have done—and that he would, if it was not done, stay seven years first. He was a most dangerous person to society.—On being asked if he had his liberty, if he would kill any other person, he answered there was one more he believed he should. He told some persons who visited him one day, that he believed his father and Allen had a very tough time of it—Being asked why he thought so, he said he had been beating his head against the walls of the prison, in order to know how they felt whilst he was killing them.

He appeared to have a very confused idea of a future state—supposed he should go to Purgatory—and said he believed the Devils wore large black wigs—and many other such chimerical expressions of folly and absurdity he uttered respecting a future existence.—He did not appear pleased that the time of his execution was fixed at so distant a period—he wished, he said, to have it over a fortnight sooner. On the whole, as a man, he was savage—void of all the finer feelings of the soul, and destitute of the tender affections of filial love and gratitude—He appears to have been a being cast in a different mould from those of mankind in general, and to be the connecting grade between the human and brutal creation.

The above will enable the reader to form some idea of his rational faculties.

He was about five feet four inches high, rather slenderly built, and very strong. He had a peculiar way of tossing or twitching his head, and his countenance was very unpleasant.

Printed and sold at Mr. THOMAS's Printingoffice, in *Worcester.* Price 6d. Also, A Poem on the Occasion. Price 3d.

## Source Notes

The first narrative published concerning Samuel Frost was published by Isaiah Thomas shortly before Frost's execution on October 31, 1793: *The Confession and DYING WORDS of SAMUEL FROST.* At the same time, Thomas also exploited Frost's notoriety by publishing *A POEM. On the EXECUTION of SAMUEL FROST.* Both broadside texts were published in Worcester, and both made use of the same execution engraving that Thomas had printed on at least three previous occasions (see above note on Johnson Green). Thomas' *Confession* sold for six pennies and his *POEM* sold for three pennies. After the execution, Thomas published a third Frost publication, the final sermon preached by Aaron Bancroft to the prisoner before he was taken to the gallows: *The Importance of a RELIGIOUS EDUCATION Illustrated and Enforced* (Worcester, 1793). A fourth Frost publication was "Printed and sold by Henry Blake & Co." in Keene, N.H., shortly after the execution (title page). This edition combined both of the two original Thomas texts in one broadside: *The Confession and Dying Words of SAMUEL FROST.* The copy text used in the anthology is taken from the original *Confession* printed by Thomas.

Frost's strange behavior attracted notice both in the newspapers and in his narrative. When he was executed, the November 11, 1793, issue of *The Boston Gazette* included the following report:

> WORCESTER, November 6.
>
> On Thursday last Samuel Frost was executed in this town, pursuant to his sentence, for the murder of Capt. Elisha Allen, of Princeton, on the 16th day of July last. This man, just ten years before he murdered Captain Allen, killed his father, for which horrid crime he was tried, but acquitted by the jury, who supposed him insane. Before execution a Sermon was preached by the Rev. Aaron Bancroft, to a very large audience. The criminal was present. After which he was carried to the place of execution. He shewed few or no signs of penitence. On being asked by the High Sheriff if he wished to say any thing to the spectators, he answered that he had not much to say—he would not have them follow him. The High Sheriff repeatedly asked him if he wished his execution delayed? He answered, as often as asked, No!—as he was to go (that was his expression) it had better be soon over. The scaffold dropped, and this uncommon murderer was launched into eternity.—It is tho't the number of spectators were about 2000.

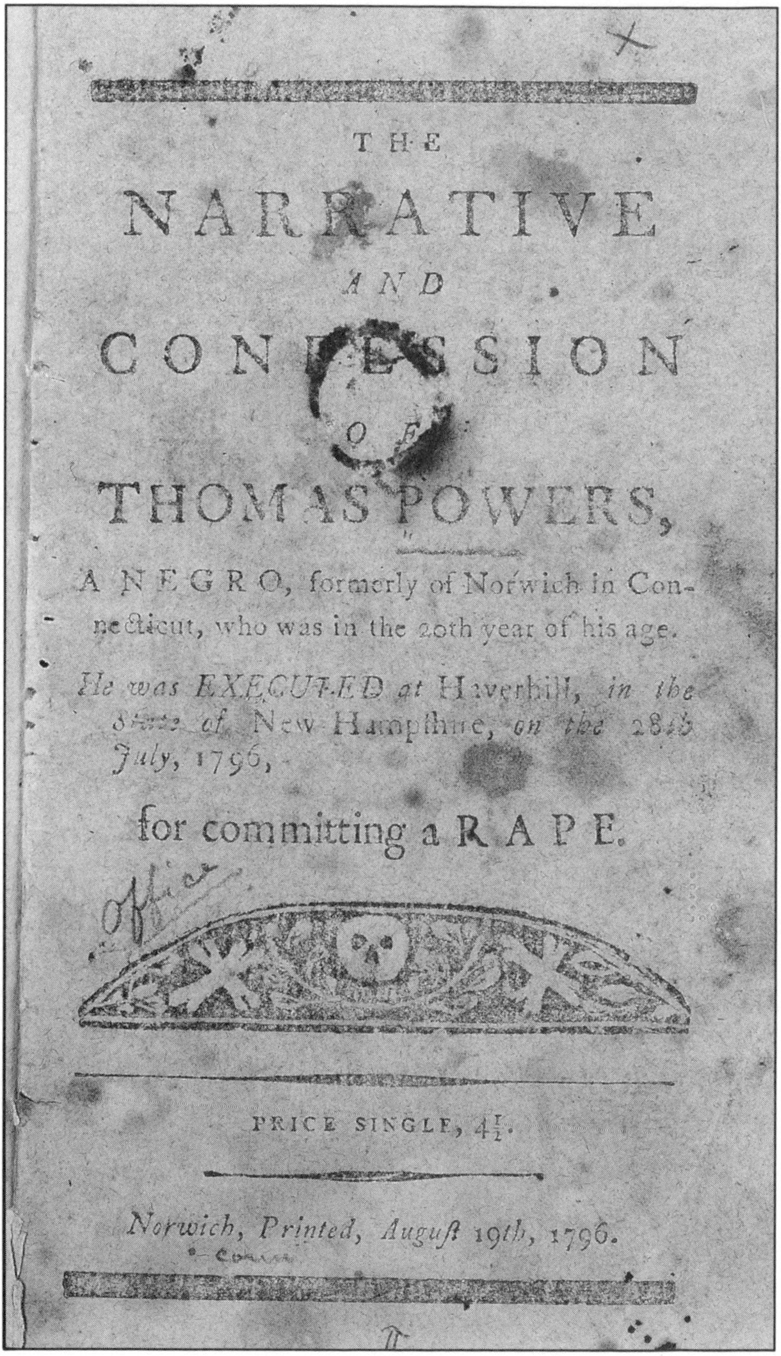

THE

NARRATIVE

AND

CONFESSION

OF

THOMAS POWERS,

A NEGRO, formerly of Norwich in Connecticut, who was in the 20th year of his age.

*He was EXECUTED at* Haverhill, *in the State of* New Hampshire, *on the 28th July*, 1796,

for committing a RAPE.

PRICE SINGLE, $4\frac{1}{2}$.

*Norwich, Printed, August 19th*, 1796.

[ THOMAS POWERS ]

# *The Narrative and Confession of Thomas Powers, a Negro*

[ 1796 ]

I THOMAS POWERS, was born in Wallingford, in Connecticut, September 15th, 1796 [1776]. My father's name is Thomas Powers; and my mother before marriage was Prudy Waterman. I was the second and youngest Son of my father, with whom I lived, till I was two years old. He then put me out to live with Mr. Moses Tharp, of Norwich, (Conn.) where I resided one year, and then returned to my father, who, being a very pious man, endeavored to instruct me in my several duties, to God, to my parents, and to all mankind; as far as my young and tender mind was capable of receiving any virtuous impressions. But I was naturally too much inclined to vice, to profit by his precepts or example; for I was very apt to pilfer and tell lies, if I thought there was any occasion.

When I was nine years old, I was put out to live with Isaac Johnson, of Lebanon, (Conn.) where I lived two years, and very early began the practice of villainy and debauchery. It was here I began my career in the gratification of that corrupt and lawless passion, which has now brought me to the threshold of eternity, before my years were half numbered.

Being one Sunday at home from meeting, with nobody but a young Negro woman, who lived in the house, she, enticing me to her bed, where she was sitting, soon taught me the practice of that awful sin, which now costs me my life; for which together with disobedience to my master, and many other villaneous tricks which I used to play upon him, he often corrected me, but to so little purpose that he dismissed me from his service.

Then I returned once more to my father, where I lived a few months, till he, not liking my behaviour, bound me out to Mr. Oliver Hyde, of Norwich, (Conn.) During my residence with him, who was a pretty kind master, I was taught to read and write a tolerable good hand; but being naturally vicious I improved my talents, (or rather misimproved them) to very bad purposes. I used to make a point of pilfering whenever I could; for when I saw an opportunity, the devil, or some other evil spirit, always gave me a strong inclination. I supposed it was because I was naturally inclined to be light-fingered; for I never hesitated to touch any thing that came in my way. Here too I played my pranks, with the young black girls about the streets; and indulged myself as freely as I could without discovery.

In the year 1789, I broke open a store in Norwich, (Conn.) owned by Mr. —— took a few articles of goods and fifteen dollars in Cash. In the next place, knowing my present master, Oliver Lathrop, to have on hand a large sum of money, I supposed that I might take about twenty dollars and neither of us fare the worse. I, however, soon repented of this bargain; for being discovered, I was forced to return the money, and take a few stripes on my back; but if I had received my just deserts I might possibly have escaped the fate, which now awaits me.

In the year 1793 I moved with my master from Norwich, in Connecticut, to Lebanon, in New Hampshire, where I soon run the length of my chain, and compleated my villany, committing a number of crimes, which black as I am, I should blush to repeat.

Before I removed from Norwich, (Conn.) I attempted to ravish a young girl, who was visiting in the neighborhood. For this purpose, I took an old sword, and went into the woods where I supposed she would return in the evening, and concealed myself in the bushes, where I waited till 12 o'clock; but as providence ordered it, she did not go home that night, and so escaped the snare I had laid for her.

On the 7th day of Dec. 1795, being at work with Mr. Gordon Lathrop, I agreed to meet him in the evening, at Thomas Rowels, to wrestle. Accordingly a little after sun down I sat out, without any evil intentions. I overtook a young woman, whom I knew to be——I passed on by her, a pretty good jog, till after a little querying with myself, and finding nothing to oppose, but rather the devil to assist me, I determined to make an attempt on her virgin chastity.—So I waylaid her, and as she came up, seized her with one hand, and her horse's bridle with t'other, she ask'd me what I wanted?—I told her to dismount and I would tell her. At the same time taking her from her horse, I threw her on the ground, and in spite of her cries and entreaties, succeeded in my hellish design. Then left her, and went to the place proposed, where I found my antagonist; but the evening being far spent, I returned to my master's house and sat down, as usual, to play chequers with the children.

It was not long before I heard people round the house, and was afterwards informed they were after me; but seeing me so lively at play, says the Esq. "It can't be Tom"—so they went away. I soon went to bed, but in about two hours, I was awaked from sleep by a number of people who entered my room, and called me their "prisoner."

I was confined, till next day, when I had my trial before Esq. Hough, who sentenced me to prison; accordingly I was immediately secured in Haverhill jail, on the 10th day of Dec. As we were passing by the place, where the crime was committed, I was questioned concerning the fact; but, I, like a hardened villain, as I was, denied every syllable of the truth, and had but little sense of my situation, till the key of the prison was turned upon me, when my feelings were such as no pen or tongue, can describe. On the fifth of April, after 4 months confinement, with the help of two of my companions we broke goal after three hours hard work. We went to the river, stole a boat, ran three miles down, and sent her adrift. One of my comrads, by the name of Bayley, went to his father's, where he procured some refreshment for us.—

From thence, we went to Capt. Frye Bailey's in Newbury, where we stole a horse, and went fifteen miles to Ryegate. On Sunday evening we arrived at St. Johnsbury, & took up lodgings in a barn. At twelve we took up our line of march, and returned to Barnet, where I parted with my companions; It being my object to go to Portland, and ship myself aboard of a vessel. I, however, missed my road and came back to Littleton where I enquired for Lake Champlain, and as I was going quite the other way, I was suspected of being a rogue, and I confess they had some grounds for their suspicion, as one of them was acquainted with me. I was, of consequence, immediately returned to my old lodgings in Haverhill. Here I was now hand-cuffed, and my arms pinioned; and put into the upper loft of the Prison: but on Sunday, the 4th day after my last commitment, I sawed of[f] my pinions across the grates of the prison; and with the help of a knife, got a piece of board, with which I pryed off the grate. I then went to work to cut up my blanket, into strips, and tying them together from the grate, I descended from the upper loft. As I passed by the grate of the lower room, I called to the prisoners below telling them, of my liberty but desired them to say nothing till I had got off; but Holmes swore he would stop me, if in his power, and immediately raised the Jailor.—I ran as fast as I could, after being almost spent with fatigue, in getting my liberty, and descending from the upper loft, with hand-cuffs on; and while they were looking for me in the most obscure places, near the Goal, supposing me to be there concealed; but I made my escape into the river road, and at break of day, I found myself at Capt. John Mann's in Orford. I then thought it prudent, to avoid discovery, to go back into the woods, where I lay till night.

I then proceeded on to Lyme, and broke into a blacksmith shop, to rid myself of my Hand-cuff's which in my travels, I found rather uncomfortable companions, and I suspected, in case of being seen and noticed, they would prove but a poor recommendation. However I could not succeed; so I went on to Gould's Tavern, and took a horse, which I rode about three miles; but not being able to get him any farther, I attempted to drown him to get my revenge; but could not easily succeed, and I left him to shirk. I then proceeded on to a smith's shop on College Plain, where I made another fruitless attempt to get my hands at liberty. When I got into the edge of Lebanon, it was day light; so I wandered about in the woods till evening, when I went to Mr. Quimbe's shop in Lebanon and sawed, and twisted my hand-cuffs about two hours, and gave out being quite overcome for want of food. I then went to my master's house, looked in at the window, but guilt being my companion, I dared not enter. I then retired some distance from the house and sawed my cuffs across a rock, till by the help of a file, I liberated my hands, and went to Mr. T. Rowel's, whom I supposed to be a friend; But he, like most friends, in adversity, forsook me, and turned my enemy. For upon seeing how cold and hungry I was, he seemed to pity me, and told me to go to a certain barn, and he would bring me some refreshment; but instead of victuals, he mustered all the force he could to take me. Being however, aware of his treachery, when day light appeared, I fled to the woods, and lay there, where I suffered extremely with the cold. Upon seeing them come into the woods I lay down under a log, and as they passed along one of them trod on me, but did not perceive me. I then thought best to shift my course, and taking across lot, one of them saw me, as I ascended a little rise of ground, and hailed me. I pointed to a barn at some distance, and said, "he has just gone by the barn.—" which turned the attention of the whole that way; he then supposed me to be one of their party, as it was between day light and dark.

This gave me a little breath again, and I thought of trying to get some refreshment by milk, from a cow of my master's, as I had not eat or drank for nigh 4 days, but could not find her, where I expected. I however found some raw potatoes and eat of them freely. At last I took up a resolution to use my hand-cuff bolt, for my defence, and to go into the house; which I did, but found none but children round the tea-table, who where [sic] exceedingly frightened, and run away, all but a boy, who told me to take what I wanted, if I was hungry. I seized half a cheese, and half a loaf of bread, which was on the table, and ran off. I soon met a Mr. Colburn, who knew me, and told me to go with him, and nobody should hurt me adding that I should have any refreshment I wanted. I followed him home, and no sooner had we got there, than he sent to inform my pursuers. I stept to the door, and saw them coming over the hill—I started to run and Colburn struck at me, but I escaped and ran till I fainted and fell. His dog followed me, however, and barked till they came up and took me, as their prisoner.

The time of my trial was now come on, and instead of carrying me to

Haverhill, I was carried to Plymouth, where I immediately had my trial before the Hon. Superior Court, and was sentenced, very justly, to death. At first, upon hearing my sentance, it had no impression on my mind—for my heart was hardened beyond description. After a little reflection, however, I fainted, and could not speak for some time.—At length I came to myself, and desired to see the young Lady, whom I had injured. This she refused, but said she, would receive any message I wished to send to her. I then set down and wrote a confession of my crime, and of the justness of my punishment. I begged pardon, most sincerely for the injury, I had done her. She sent me for answer, that she could forgive me, and hoped that God would do the same. I was then conducted to prison and bound with irons. During my residence here under sentence of death, I have not been wholly insensible of my pitiable situation; as my master as well as the divines who have attended me, have ever endeavored to impress me with a sense of a state of future happiness or misery to which I was destined; but the secret hope of making my escape, and, the jollity of countenance that appeared in most of my spectators; did in some measure banish the idea of death from my mind. The ninth of June, a number of Doctors made application to me for my BODY, for DISSECTION, after my execution; to which I readily consented for the small sum of ten dollars, thinking it might afford me a comfortable subsistance while here, and my BONES be of service to mankind after the seperation of soul and body, which must shortly take place, and at which time may I receive forgiveness of all mankind, and of my God, before whom I must appear through the merits of a Redeemer.

*Finis.*

## Source Notes

In his *American Bibliography*, Charles Evans listed four Powers narratives, only one of which is still extant: *THE NARRATIVE AND CONFESSION OF THOMAS POWERS, A NEGRO* (Norwich, Conn.: John Trumbull, 1796). On the title page of this edition, Trumbull mentioned that, although Powers "*was* EXECUTED *at* Haverhill [New Hampshire]," he was "formerly of Norwich in Connecticut," a fact which obviously was exploited by the printer to arouse reader interest and which revealed his marketing strategy. Also, the title page stated that Powers was executed "*on the* 28*th July*" and that the narrative was published less than a month later on *August* 19*th*." Despite the celerity of Trumbull's narrative response, it seems likely that an earlier edition was published. The first edition listed by Evans was *THE DYING SPEECH OF THOMAS POWERS (WRITTEN BY HIS OWN HAND)*; this broadside edition supposedly was "Printed and sold by Nathaniel Coverly" in Haverhill. According to Shipton and Mooney, who prepared the Readex series of the Evans bibliography, the New Hampshire Historical Society at one time had a copy of this text. Moreover, in the July 28 issue of Coverly's newspaper, *The Grafton-Minerva*, which was printed in Haverhill and which included a notice of Powers' execution, an advertisement for THE DYING SPEECH appeared:

> This day published, and to be sold, by the Printer hereof, Price 9d. The Dying Speech of Thomas Powers, (written by his own Hand), to which is added, a letter from a black woman, sent to him while under sentence of Death: Also—an affecting letter delivered to him on Tuesday morning, previous to his execution.

The second edition listed by Evans was *THE LAST WORDS, AND DYING SPEECH OF THOMAS POWERS*; based upon a newspaper advertisement, Evans determined that this edition was "Printed by Alden Spooner" in Windsor, Vermont. Shipton and Mooney could find no other verification for Evans' entry other than the Spooner advertisement. The third spurious edition Evans included was *THE NARRATIVE AND CONFESSION OF THOMAS POWERS*, which was listed as being "Printed by Dunham and True" in Hanover, N.H. Unable to find further evidence of publication, Shipton and Mooney decided that this edition merely was "assumed" by Evans from an advertisement. However, as Powers awaited execution in the summer of 1796, three newspapers printed the same disclaimer which referred to "*several very* different *Dying Speeches . . . in circulation*" concerning Powers, stating that the condemned man "*himself condemned the one printed at Hanover, as false and libellous*" (see below for full reference).

In all likelihood, the model Trumbull used for the Norwich text was the Coverly edition printed in Haverhill. The copy text used in the anthology is taken from Trumbull's edition.

Although no copy of the DYING SPEECH is available, Nathaniel Coverly's commercial interest in the Powers case indeed can be documented. Shortly after the execution, he printed Noah Worcester's *A SERMON DELIVERED AT HAVERHILL, New Hampshire, July 28, 1796, at the EXECUTION OF THOMAS POWERS* (Haverhill, 1796). While introducing his text, Worcester drew attention to the dramatic spectacle of death and to the anxiety that surrounded it:

> We are convened this day to be spectators of a most solemn and affecting event, the launching of a mortal vessel from the land of probation into the boundless ocean of eternity, and endless retribution, never to return. And whether it will depart, freighted with the love of God, penitence, faith, and the joys of pardoning grace, as a vessel of mercy, prepared unto glory; or freighted with pride, impenitence, unbelief, and the guilt of unpardoned sin, as a vessel of wrath fitted to destruction, is, to us, a matter of dreadful uncertainty. (5)

Later, during his address to the "UNHAPPY FELLOW MORTAL," Worcester again emphasized the same "dreadful uncertainty" (17). After conventionally reminding Powers that he was "soon to appear before another tribunal" at which his soul would "be decided for eternity," the minister offered the rapist two alternatives: either he could pattern himself after the Penitent Thief to whom Christ promised paradise, or he "could spend his last moments in *railing* rather than *praying*" like the Impenitent Thief (18, 19). Heaven or Hell, salvation or damnation. Moreover, in order to heighten the drama even more, the minister told Powers that "a multitude of invisible angels, good and evil are now hovering about, waiting for your decisive choice" (20). Yet the minister offered both readers and parishioners a hint—the "dreadful uncertainty" was not all that uncertain. Worcester already had indicated the direction of the condemned man's soul; already he rhetorically had linked "the boundless ocean of eternity" with "endless retribution." And even before he called upon Powers to make his "decisive choice," he already had described how the young black man had chosen to live:

> You have proved yourself to be by nature, a child of wrath, by being a child of disobedience. You have been a lover of pleasure more than a lover of God; by yielding to the temptation of Satan, and indulging your own vicious inclination, you have paved the way to an infamous death. (17)

Interestingly, Worcester's sermon and Powers' narrative shared rhetorical similarities, especially concerning statements of (self-) castigation. Echoing (or adopting) the minister's words, the rapist admitted that he was a disobedient child and fond of physical pleasure. He further admitted that he was "naturally vicious" and unable to resist indulging his evil inclinations (see pages 328–29 from the narrative).

Several area newspapers printed notices of Powers' crime, conviction, and execution. The first notice, mentioning the rape, was published by Dunham and True on December 21, 1795, in *The Eagle: or, Dartmouth Centinel*:

> A RAPE
>
> Was committed last week, in Lebanon, on the body of Sally Messer, [by] Tomas Powers, a Mullatto, from Connecticut. N.B. *The gentleman has gone to Jail!*

The next notices appeared in both *The Eagle* and the *Courier of New Hampshire* on June 6, 1796:

> Last Wednesday the Superior Court finished their last session, holden at Plymouth. During which several Criminals were tried and convicted . . . . and one *Thomas Powers* a Negro, from Norwich in Connecticut, for a RAPE, committed at *Lebanon*, in this State, who was convicted and sentence of Death was passed upon him accordingly: he will be *Hung* at Haverhill, on the 7th of July next. This last Trial was conducted with great solemnity and decorum, and before a large and respectable con-

> course of Spectators. The Honorable Judge OLCOTT, after pronouncing sentence of Death, addressed the Criminal, in a short but pathetic speech, exhorting him to Repentance, and recommending him most fervently to the mercy of the supreme Judge of the Universe.
>
> The Criminal manifested a stoical insensibility, during the whole trial. (*The Eagle*)

A few days later, on June 14, *The New Hampshire and Vermont Journal* reprinted the above notice.

The next notices were printed in early July and concerned a short reprive that was granted to Powers. On July 12 the *Courier of New Hampshire* simply informed readers that a "REPRIEVE" had been granted to Powers "by the Executive until Thursday the 28th inst." But a day earlier in *The Eagle* the same news had caused some mirth:

> The EXECUTION
>
> Of THOMAS POWERS, who was condemned to be hanged the 7th ins. is defered by a REPRIEVE for 21 days; he will probably be Executed on the 28th instant.
>
> (N. B. A Vast *Concourse of both Sexes*, assembled upon this occasion, from all quarters, anticipating the pleasure of *novel* amusement:—but what was the disappointment, on the News of the *Reprieve!*
>
> A Wit present, noticing the *chopfallen* countenance of the *Multitude*, observed, that instead of a *Reprieve* of the *poor Prisoner*, he should have tho't they were all *to be hanged*. However, the *Innkeepers* snickered in their sleeves, and plied the *Punch bowl*, till each went his way in better *spirits*, tho' "with a flee in his ear."—Tis supposed the concourse will be much greater—*next time he is hanged*; as many more would have gone, but they chose not to see him die—*but once*.)

The same account was printed a month later in *The Oracle of the Day* on August 4.

On July 26, the *Courier of New Hampshire* printed the first of several notices warning readers to beware of spurious "Dying Speeches":

> TOM. POWERS
>
> Is to be executed at Haverhill, N.H. on Thursday next.—It is a curious circumstance, that several very different Dying Speeches of his are in circulation, and offering for sale. He has himself condemned the one printed at Hanover, as false and libellous.—How many others may be of that character, is best known by those who have a hand in making them without consulting the criminal.

The *Courier*'s printer, George Hough, is not known to have printed a Powers text of his own, and his jab at other printers ("*those who have a hand in making them*") might have been motivated by a disapproval of those who sought to exploit Powers purely for profit. Since he mentioned Hanover, he might have been referring to John Dunham and Benjamin True. According to the full title listed in Evans, the

Dunham and True text was published before the execution and, if so, was in circulation during July: *THE NARRATIVE AND CONFESSION OF THOMAS POWERS, WHO IS TO BE HUNG AT HAVERHILL, THE TWENTY-EIGHTH OF JULY, FOR A RAPE.* If the two printers indeed were responsible for the NARRATIVE, then they implicated their own text as being "*false and libellous*" (which ironically might have increased its promotion and sales). In the August 1 issue of *The Eagle*, Dunham and True reprinted the above notice of the *Courier*'s warning. This same notice also was reprinted in *The Salem Gazette* on August 5.

In addition to printing a warning about what was possibly their own publication, Dunham and True also included several other interesting notices concerning Powers in the August 1 issue of *The Eagle*. Since Powers had been executed previously on July 28, the newspaper included a short announcement of the execution:

> TOM. POWERS
>
> Was executed at Haverhill, last Thursday in pursuance of his sentence, for a Rape.

The printers, however, were unwilling to allow Powers to rest in peace. At the bottom of the same page they included a humorous piece announcing a jailbreak (perhaps written by the same "Wit" who observed the spectators' disappointment when the reprieve was given):

> BROKE GOAL
> and Ran Away!!!
>
> Last Night from Haverhill, a Mulatto man named Thomas Powers, he was of a midling stature, straight and well built, of a *Pallid* countenance, by reason of enduring the pain of execution for the crime which he was condemned. Had on when he went away, nothing save,
>
> "The Sable Coffin,
> He moved off in."
>
> From several circumstances, 'tis suspected he has gone towards *Antipodes*. Whoever will discover the road he has taken, over-haul him, and bring him back to the SURGEONS, by whom he was recommitted immediately after his execution, by writ of mandamus, (the habeus corpus act being suspended,) and who are now waiting his return, shall have fifty cents reward, but no charges paid.—In behalf of the Medical Corps—
>
> QUIMBO QUACKY *Jun. Secretary*
> *Haverhill July* 29, 1796

With far less levity, Haverhill's newspaper, *The Grafton-Minvera*, published at least two notices concerning Powers. In the June 30 issue the paper reported:

> On Sunday last the unhappy criminal who is under sentence of death, for a rape, and who is to be executed the 7th of July next, was conducted

> from the Gaol to the Meeting-House in this Town [Haverhill], where at his own request he was permitted to attend Divine Worship, and a suitable and well adapted discourse on the solemn occasion, was delivered by the Rev. ETHAN SMITH, from *2 Cor. v: 20, Now then, we are ambassadors for Christ, as though God did beseech* you *by us; we pray* you *in Christ's stead, be ye reconciled to God.*
>
> The prisoner behaved with the greatest propriety and solemnity, during the whole performance of Divine Service. He was observed to be very thoughtful and attentive, before and afternoon, and appeared to give the strictest attention in particular, at the time the Throne of Grace was addressed in his behalf.

On July 28 *The Grafton-Minerva* stated:

> Thursday, July 28, 1796. This day will be executed, pursuant to his sentence, Thomas Powers, a mulatto man. The Company of Light Infantry, commanded by Capt. John Montgomery of this town [Haverhill], and a detachment of the Light Horse from the town of Plymouth are, at the request of the High Sheriff to attend the execution. Particulars in our next.

Unfortunately, the next issue of the *Grafton-Minerva*, containing the "Particulars," is not extant. However, on August 8 the paper advertised Worcester's execution sermon:

> Now in the Press,
> *and will be published the 25th inst.*
> A SERMON, delivered at
> *Haverhill*, New-Hampshire, at the
> Execution of
> THOMAS POWERS,
> *Who* was Executed for a RAPE
> committed at *Lebanon*, Dec. 7th, 1795.
> By
> *Noah Worcester*, A. M.
> Pastor of a Church at Thornton.

The *Courier of New Hampshire*'s final notice was somewhat anticlimactic. On August 2, at the very bottom of a page filled with European and domestic news, it simply reported: "*Tom Powers was executed at Haverhill on Thursday last.*"

Powers is also discussed in Richard Slotkin's essay, "Narratives of Negro Crime in New England, 1675–1800."

# *Works Cited*


*An Account of the Pirates, with divers of their Speeches, Letters, &c. And a Poem Made By One of them: Who were Executed at Newport, On Rhode-Island, July 19th, 1723*. [Newport?], 1723.

Adams, Eliphalet. *A Sermon Preached on the Occasion of the Execution of Katherine Garret, an Indian-Servant, (Who was Condemned for the Murder of her Spurious Child.) On May 3d. 1738. To which is Added some short Account of her Behaviour after her Condemnation. Together with her Dying Warning and Exhortation, Left under her own Hand*. New London: T. Green, 1738.

Ahlstrom, Sidney E. *A Religious History of the American People*. New Haven: Yale University Press, 1972.

Bancroft, Aaron. *The Importance of a Religious Education Illustrated and Enforced. A Sermon: delivered at Worcester, October 31, 1793, occasioned by the Execution of Samuel Frost, on that day, for the Murder of Captain Elisha Allen, of Princeton, on the 16th Day of July, 1793*. Worcester: Isaiah Thomas, 1793.

Baym, Nina. *Novels, Readers, and Reviewers: Responses to Fiction in Antebellum America*. Ithaca: Cornell University Press, 1984.

Bercovitch, Sacvan. *The American Jeremiad*. Madison: University of Wisconsin Press, 1978.

Bethke, Robert D. "Chapbook 'Gallows-Literature' in Nineteenth-Century Pennsylvania." *Pennsylvania Folklife* 20 (1970): 2–15.

Billias, George A. *Law and Authority in Colonial America*. Barre, Mass.: Barre Publishing, 1965.

Bosco, Ronald A. "Lectures at the Pillory: The Early American Execution Sermon." *American Quarterly* 30 (Summer 1978): 156–76.

Brown, Herbert Ross. *The Sentimental Novel in America, 1789–1860*. Durham: Duke University Press, 1940.

Brown, Richard D. *Knowledge Is Power: The Diffusion of Information in Early America, 1700–1865*. New York: Oxford University Press, 1989.

———. *Modernization: The Transformation of American Life, 1600–1865*. 1976. Prospects Heights, Ill.: Waveland Press, 1988.

Burke, Peter. *Popular Culture in Early Modern Europe*. New York: Harper and Row, 1978.

Butler, Jon. *Awash in a Sea of Faith: Christianizing the American People*. Cambridge: Harvard University Press, 1990.

Campbell, John. *After Souls by Death are separated from their Bodies they come to*

*Judgment. Asserted in a Sermon Deliver'd at Worcester, November 24th, 1737. Being the Day of the Execution of John Hamilton, alias Hugh Henderson. (With his Confession and Dying Warning.)* Boston: S. Kneeland and T. Green, 1738.

Chamblitt, Rebekah. *The Declaration, Dying Warning and Advice of Rebekah Chamblitt A Young Woman Aged near Twenty-seven Years, Executed at Boston, September 27, 1733*. Boston: S. Kneeland and T. Green, [1733].

Chandler, Frank. *The Literature of Roguery.* New York: Burt Franklin, 1958.

Chandler, Peleg W. "Trial of Mrs. Spooner and others before the Superior Court of Judicature, for the murder of Joshua Spooner, of Brookfield, Massachusetts, 1778." *2 American Criminal Trials.* (1844): 1–58.

Chapin, Bradley. *Criminal Justice in Colonial America, 1606–1660.* Athens, Ga.: The University of Georgia Press, 1983.

Checkley, Samuel. *Mr. Checkley's Sermons to a Condemned Prisoner.* Boston: T. Fleet, 1733.

Cockburn, J. S., ed. *Crime in England, 1550–1800*. Princeton: Princeton University Press, 1977.

Colman, Benjamin. *It is a Fearful Thing to Fall into the Hands of the Living God. A Sermon Preached to some miserable Pirates July 10, 1726. On the Lord's Day, before their Execution*. Boston: John Phillips and Thomas Hancock, 1726.

Cohen, Daniel A. "In Defense of the Gallows: Justifications of Capital Punishment in New England Execution Sermons, 1674–1825." *American Quarterly* 40 (1988): 147–64.

———. "A Fellowship of Thieves: Property Criminals In Eighteenth-Century Massachusetts." *Journal of Social History* 22 (1988): 65–92.

Cowie, Alexander. *The Rise of the American Novel.* New York: American Book, 1948.

Dana, James. *The Intent of Capital Punishment. A Discourse Delivered in the City of New-Haven, October 20, 1790. Being the Day of Execution of Joseph Mountain, For a Rape*. New Haven: T. and S. Green, 1790.

Dargo, George. *Law in the New Republic: Private Law and the Public Estate*. New York: Alfred A. Knopf, 1983.

Davidson, Cathy N. *Reading in America: Literature & Social History.* Baltimore: The Johns Hopkins University Press, 1989.

———. *Revolution and the Word: The Rise of the Novel in America*. New York: Oxford University Press, 1986.

Davis, Lennard J. *Factual Fictions: The Origins of the English Novel.* New York: Columbia University Press, 1983.

Delbanco, Andrew. *The Puritan Ordeal.* Cambridge: Harvard University Press, 1989.

Dexter, Franklin Bowditch. *Biographical Sketches of the Graduates of Yale College* 4, July 1778–June 1792. New York: Holt, 1907.

*Dictionary of American Biography.* New York: American Council of Learned Societies, 1935.

Dow, George Francis, and John Henry Edmonds. *The Pirates of the New England Coast, 1630–1730*. Salem: Marine Research Society, 1923.

Dunton, John. "Letters." *The Puritans A Sourcebook of Their Writings*. Eds. Perry Miller and Thomas H. Johnson. 1938. New York: Harper and Row, 1963. 414–25.

Dutton, Samuel W. S. *An Address at the Funeral of Hon. David Dagget, April 15, 1851*. New Haven: A. H. Maltby, 1851.

Eliot, Andrew. *Christ's Promise to the penitent Thief. A Sermon Preached the Lord's-Day before the Execution of Levi Ames, Who suffered Death for Burglary, Oct. 21, 1773. Age 22*. Boston: John Boyle, 1773.

Elliott, Emory. *Power and the Pulpit in Puritan New England*. Princeton: Princeton University Press, 1975.

———. *Revolutionary Writers: Literature and Authority in the New Republic, 1725–1810*. New York: Oxford University Press, 1982.

Elliott, Mabel. "Crime and Frontier Mores." *American Sociological Review* 9 (1944): 185–92.

Erikson, Kai. *Wayward Puritans: A Study in the Sociology of Deviance*. New York: Wiley, 1966.

Evans, Charles. *American Bibliography: A Chronological Dictionary of All Books, Pamphlets and Periodical Publications Printed in the United States of America from the Genesis of Printing in 1639 Down to and Including the Year 1820*. New York: Peter Smith, 1941.

Faber, Eli. "Puritan Criminals: The Economic, Social, and Intellectual Background to Crime in Seventeenth-Century Massachusetts." *Perspectives in American History* 10 (1977–78): 81–144.

Faller, Lincoln B. *Turned to Account: The Forms and Functions of Criminal Biography in Late Seventeenth- and Early Eighteenth-Century England*. Cambridge: Cambridge University Press, 1987.

Ferguson, Robert A. *Law and Letters in American Culture*. Cambridge: Harvard University Press, 1984.

Fiske, Nathan. *A Sermon Preached at Brookfield March 6, 1778. On The Day of the Internment of Mr. Joshua Spooner, Who was most barbarously murdered at his own Gate, on the Lord's-Day Evening preceeding, by three Ruffians, who were hired for the Purpose by his Wife*. Boston: Thomas and John Fleet, 1778.

Fitzroy, Herbert William Keith. "The Punishment of Crime in Provincial Pennsylvania." *Pennsylvania Magazine of History and Biography* 60 (1936): 242–69.

Flaherty, David H., ed. *Essays in the History of Early American Law*. Chapel Hill: University of North Carolina Press, 1969.

Fliegelman, Jay. *Prodigals and Pilgrims: The American Revolution Against Patriarchal Authority, 1750–1800*. Cambridge: Cambridge University Press, 1982.

Fobes, Peres. *The Paradise of God Opened to a Penitent Thief, in Answer to his dying Prayer to a dying Saviour, considered and improved in a Sermon; The Substance of which was delivered at Taunton, November 11, 1784. Upon the Day of the Execution of John Dixson, for Burglary, Age 24. With an Appendix, on the Nature and Enormity of Burglary. And a Sketch of Dixson's Life*. Providence: Bennett Wheeler, 1784.

Foucault, Michel. *Discipline and Punish The Birth of the Prison*. Trans. Alan Sheridan. New York: Pantheon Books, 1978.

Franklin, H. Bruce. *The Victim as Criminal and Artist.* New York: Oxford University Press, 1978.

Freidman, Lawrence M. *A History of American Law.* New York: Simon and Schuster, 1973.

Foxcroft, Thomas. *Lessons of Caution to Young Sinners. A Sermon Preach'd on the Lord's-Day Sept. 23, 1733. Upon the affecting Ocassion of An Unhappy Young Woman present in the Assembly under Sentence of Death.* Boston: S. Kneeland and T. Green, 1733.

Genovese, Eugene D. *Roll, Jordan, Roll: The World The Slaves Made.* New York: Pantheon Books, 1974.

Gilmore, Grant. *The Ages of American Law.* New Haven: Yale University Press, 1977.

Gilmore, William J. *Reading Becomes a Necesssity of Life Material and Cultural Life in Rural New England, 1780–1835.* Knoxville: University of Tennessee Press, 1989.

Green, Samuel Swett. "The Case of Bathsheba Spooner." *5 American Antiquarian Society Proceedings (New Series).* (1889): 430–36.

Greenberg, Douglas. *Crime and Law Enforcement in the Colony of New York, 1691–1776.* Ithaca: Cornell University Press, 1974.

Hall, David D. *The Faithful Shepherd A History Of The New England Ministry In The Seventeenth Century.* Chapel Hill: University of North Carolina Press, 1972.

———. *Worlds of Wonder, Days of Judgment: Popular Religious Belief In Early New England.* New York: Alfred A. Knopf, 1989.

Hambrick-Stowe, Charles E. *The Practice of Piety Puritan Devotional Discipline in Seventeenth-Century New England.* Chapel Hill: University of North Carolina Press, 1982.

Harris, Michael. "Trials and Criminal Biographies: A Case Study in Distribution." *Sale and Distribution of Books from 1700.* Eds. Robin Myers and Michael Harris. Oxford: Oxford University Press, 1982. 1–36.

Haskins, George L. *Law and Authority in Early Massachusetts.* New York: Macmillan, 1960.

Hay, Douglas, Peter Linebaugh, John G. Rule, E. P. Thompson, and Cal Winslow. *Albion's Fatal Tree: Crime and Society in Eighteenth-Century England.* New York: Pantheon Books, 1975.

Henderson, Hugh. *The Confession and Dying Warning of Hugh Henderson, Who was Executed at Worcester for House-Breaking Nov. 24. 1734.* Boston: 1737.

Henretta, James A. *The Evolution of American Society, 1700–1815: An Interdisciplinary Analysis.* Lexington: D. C. Heath, 1973.

Heimert, Alan. *Religion and the American Mind: From the Great Awakening to the Revolution.* Cambridge: Harvard University Press, 1966.

Hindus, Michael S. *Prison and Plantation: Crime, Justice, and Authority in Massachusetts and South Carolina, 1767–1878.* Chapel Hill: University of North Carolina Press, 1980.

Hirsch, Adam J. "From Pillory to Penitentiary: The Rise of Criminal Incarceration in Early Massachusetts." *Michigan Law Review* 80 (May 1982): 1179–1269.

Hobsbawm, E. J. *Bandits*. New York: Dell, 1971.

Horvitz, Morton J. *The Transformation of American Law: 1780–1860*. Cambridge: Harvard University Press, 1977.

Hull, N. E. H. *Female Felons: Women and Serious Crime in Colonial Massachusetts*. Urbana: University of Illinois Press, 1987.

Jordan, Winthrop. *White Over Black: American Attitudes Toward the Negro, 1550–1812*. Chapel Hill: University of North Carolina Press, 1968.

Konig, David Thomas. *Law and Society in Puritan Massachusetts Essex County, 1629–1692*. Chapel Hill: University of North Carolina Press, 1979.

Lane, Roger. "Crime and Criminal Statistics in Nineteenth-Century Massachusetts." *Journal of Social History* 2 (1968): 156–63.

Lawson, John D. "The Trial of Bathsheba Spooner, William Brooks, James Buchanan and Ezra Ross for the Murder of Joshua Spooner, Massachusetts, 1778." *American State Trials*. (1914): 175–201.

Lazenby, Walter. "Exhortation as Exorcism: Cotton Mather's Sermons to Murderers." *Quarterly Journal of Speech* 57 (1971): 50–56.

Losche, Lillie Deming. *The Early American Novel*. New York: Columbia University Press, 1907.

Lovelace, Richard F. *The American Pietism of Cotton Mather: Origins of American Evangelicalism*. Grand Rapids, Mich.: Christian University Press, 1979.

MacCarty, Thaddeus. *The Guilt of Innocent Blood Put Away. A Sermon, Preached at Worcester, July 2, 1778. On Occasion of the Execution of James Buchanan, William Brooks, Ezra Ross, and Bathsheba Spooner, For the Murder of Mr. Joshua Spooner, Brookfield, On the Evening of the first of March preceeding. Together With an Appendix, Giving Some Account of those Prisoners in Their Last Stage*. Worcester: Isaiah Thomas, 1778.

McDade, Thomas M. *The Annals of Murder*. Norman: University of Oklahoma Press, 1961.

Macfarlane, Alan, and Sarah Harrison. *The Justice and the Mare's Ale: Law and Disorder in Seventeenth-Century England*. Cambridge: Cambridge University Press, 1981.

Marcus, Gail Sussman. "'Due Execution of the General Rules of Righteousnesse': Criminal Procedure in New Haven Town and Colony, 1638–1658." *Saints & Revolutionaries Essays on Early American History*. Eds. David D. Hall, John M. Murrin, and Thad W. Tate. New York: W. W. Norton, 1984. 99–137.

Masur, Louis P. *Rites of Execution: Capital Punishment and the Transformation of American Culture, 1776–1865*. New York: Oxford University Press, 1989.

Mather, Cotton. *Call of the Gospel Applyed, unto All men in general, and unto a Condemned Malefactor in particular. In a Sermon Preached on the 7th d. of the 1st m. 1686. At the Request, and in the Hearing of a man under a just Sentence of Death for the horrid Sin of Murder*. Boston: R. P[ierce], 1686.

———. *Diary of Cotton Mather*. 2 vols. New York: Frederick Ungar Publishing, 1957.

———. *Magnalia Christi Americana*. New York: Arno Press, 1972.

———. *Speedy Repentance urged. A Sermon Preached at Boston, Decem. 29. 1689. In the Hearing, and at the Request of One Hugh Stone: A Miserable Man Under a just Sentence of Death, for a Tragical and Horrible Murder. Together with some Account concerning the Character, Carriage, and Execution of that Unhappy Malefactor. To which are Added, certain Memorable Providences Relating to some other Murders; & some great Instances of Repentance which have been seen among us*. Boston: Samuel Green, 1690.

———. *Warnings from the Dead. Or Solemn Admonitions Unto All People; but Especially unto Young Persons to Beware of Such Evils as would bring them to be Dead.* Boston: Bartholomew Green, 1693.

Mather, Cotton, [and Benjamin Colman]. *The Sad Effects of Sin. A True Relation of the Murder Committed by David Wallis, On his Companion Benjamin Stolwood: On Saturday Night, the first of August, 1713. With his Carriage after Condemnation; His Confession and Dying Speech at the Place of Execution, &c. To which are added, The Sermons Preached at the Lecture in Boston, in his Hearing, after his Condemnation; And on the Day of his Execution, being Sept. 24. 1713*. Boston: John Allen, 1713.

Mather, Increase. *The Folly of Sinning, Opened & Applyed, In Two Sermons, Occasioned by the Condemnation of one that was Executed at Boston in New-England, on November 17th. 1698*. Boston: B. Green and J. Allen, 1699.

———. *A Sermon Occasioned by the Execution of a Man found Guilty of Murder: Preached at Boston in New-England, March 11th 1685/6. (Together with the confession, Last Expressions and Solemn Warnings of that Murderer, to all Persons; especially to Young Men, to beware of those Sins which brought him to his Miserable End.)* Boston: John Dunton, 1686.

———. *The Wicked mans Portion or, A Sermon (Preached at the Lecture in Boston in New-England the 18th day of the 1 Moneth 1674. when two men were executed, who had murthered their Master.) Wherein is shewed That excesse in wickedness doth bring untimely Death*. Boston: John Foster, 1675.

Mather, Samuel. *Christ sent to Heal the Broken Hearted. A Sermon, Preached at the Thursday Lecture in Boston, On October, 21st. 1773. When Levi Ames, A Young Man, Under a Sentence of Death for Burglary, To Be Executed on That Day, Was Present to Hear the Discourse*. Boston: William M'Alpine, 1773.

Hillis Miller, J. "Narrative." *Critical Terms for Literary Study*. Eds. Frank Lentricchia and Thomas McLaughlin. Chicago: University of Chicago Press, 1990. 66–79.

Miller, Perry. "Errand into the Wilderness." *Errand into the Wilderness*. 1956. New York: Harper and Row, 1964. 1–15.

———. *The New England Mind: From Colony to Province*. 1953. Boston: Beacon Press, 1961.

Minnick, Wayne C. "The New England Execution Sermon, 1639–1800." *Speech Monographs* 35 (1968): 77–89.

Mitchell, W. J. T. ed. *On Narrative*. Chicago: University of Chicago Press, 1980.

Moody, Samuel. *Summary Account of the Life and Death of Joseph Quasson, Indian*. Boston: S. Gerrish, 1726.

Morgan, Edmund S. *Visible Saints: The History of a Puritan Idea.* 1963. Ithaca: Cornell University Press, 1982.

Murrin, John M. "Magistrates, Sinners, and a Precarious Liberty: Trial by Jury in Seventeenth-Century New England." *Saints & Revolutionaries Essays on Early American History.* Eds. David D. Hall, John M. Murrin, and Thad W. Tate. New York: W. W. Norton, 1984. 152–206.

Nelson, William E. *Americanization of the Common Law: The Impact of Legal Change on Massachusetts Society, 1760–1830.* Cambridge: Harvard University Press, 1975.

———. *Dispute and Conflict Resolution in Plymouth County, Massachusetts, 1725–1825.* Chapel Hill: University of North Carolina Press, 1981.

Neuburg, Victor E. "Chapbooks in America Reconstructing the Popular Reading of Early America." *Reading in America.* Ed. Cathy N. Davidson. Baltimore: The Johns Hopkins University Press, 1989. 81–113.

———. *Popular Literature: A History and Guide.* New York: Penguin Books, 1977.

Parker, Patricia L. *Early American Fiction: A Reference Guide.* Boston: G. K. Hall, 1984.

Patterson, Mark B. *Authority, Autonomy, and Representation in American Literature, 1776–1865.* Princeton: Princeton University, 1988.

Petter, Henri. *The Early American Novel.* Columbus: Ohio State University Press, 1971.

Pettit, Norman. *The Heart Prepared: Grace and Conversion in Puritan Spiritual Life.* New Haven: Yale University Press, 1966.

Phelan, James, ed. *Reading Narrative: Form, Ethics, Ideology.* Columbus: Ohio State University Press, 1989.

Pope, Robert G. *The Half-Way Covenant: Church Membership in Puritan New England.* Princeton: Princeton University Press, 1969.

———. "New England Versus the New England Mind: The Myth of Declension." *Puritan New England.* Eds. Alden T. Vaughn and Francis J. Bremer. New York: St. Martin's Press, 1977, 314–25.

Powers, Edwin. *Crime and Punishment in Early Massachusetts, 1620–1692.* Boston: Beacon Press, 1966.

Rankin, Hugh. *The Golden Age of Piracy.* New York: Holt, Rinehart, and Winston, 1969.

Rediker, Marcus. *Between the Devil and the Deep Blue Sea: Merchant Seamen, Pirates, and the Anglo-American Maritime World, 1700–1715.* Cambridge: Cambridge University Press, 1987.

———. "'Under the Banner of King Death': The Social World of Anglo-American Pirates, 1716–1726." *William and Mary Quarterly* 3rd ser. 38 (1981): 203–27.

Richetti, John. *Popular Fiction before Richardson.* Oxford: Clarendon Press, 1969.

Ritchie, Robert C. *Captain Kidd and the War against the Pirates.* Cambridge: Harvard University Press, 1986.

Ritz, Wilfred J. *American Judicial Proceedings First Printed before 1801: An Analytical Bibliography.* Westport: Greenwood Press, 1984.

Rothman, David J. *The Discovery of the Asylum: Social Order and Disorder in the New Republic*. 1971. Boston: Little, Brown and Company, 1990.

Schwartz, Bernard. *The Law in America: A History*. New York: McGraw-Hill, 1971.

Scott, Kenneth. *Counterfeiting in Colonial America*. New York: Oxford University Press, 1957.

Scott, Harold Richard, ed. *The Concise Encyclopedia of Crime and Criminals*. New York: Hawthorn, 1961.

Sewall, Samuel. *Diary of Samuel Sewall 1674–1729*. 3 vols. New York: Arno Press, 1972.

Sharpe, J. A. "'Last Dying Speeches': Religion, Ideology and Public Execution in Seventeenth-Century England." *Past and Present* 107 (1985): 144–67.

Shipton, Clifford K. *Sibley's Harvard Graduates*. Cambridge: Harvard University Press, 1933.

Shurtleff, William. *The Faith and Prayer of a dying Malefactor. A Sermon Preach'd December 27, 1739. On Occasion of the Execution of two Criminals, Namely Sarah Simpson and Penelope Kenny, and in the Hearing of the Former*. Boston: J. Draper, 1740.

Slotkin, Richard. "Narratives of Negro Crime in New England, 1675–1800." *American Quarterly* 25 (1973): 3–31.

Smith, Carl S., John P. McWilliams, Jr., and Maxwell Bloomfield. *Law and American Literature: A Collection of Essays*. New York: Alfred A. Knopf, 1983.

Smith, William. *The Convict's Visitor: Or Penitential Offices (In the Antient Way of Liturgy) Consisting of Prayers, Lessons, and Meditations; With Suitable Devotions Before, and at the Time of Execution*. Newport: Peter Edes, 1793.

Snow, Edward Rowe. *Pirates and Buccaneers of the Atlantic Coast*. Boston: Yankee Publishing Co., 1944.

Stillman, Samuel. *Two Sermons: The First from Psalm Ch. 19. 20. Delivered the Lords-Day Before the Execution of Levi Ames. Who Was Executed at Boston, Thursday October 21. For Burglary. Age 22. . . . The Second From Proverbs XVII. 25. Preached the Lords-Day after his Execution; and designed as an Improvement of that awful Event, by Way of Caution to others*. Boston: John Kneeland, 1773.

Stout, Harry S. *The New England Soul: Preaching and Religious Culture in Colonial New England*. New York: Oxford University Press, 1986.

Suleiman, Susan R. and Inge Crosman, eds. *The Reader in the Text*. Princeton: Princeton University Press, 1980.

Thomas, Isaiah. *History of American Printing in America, with a Biography of Printers, and an Account of Newspapers*. Albany: Joel Munsell, 1874.

Tompkins, Jane P., ed. *Reader-Response Criticism*. Baltimore: Johns Hopkins University Press, 1980.

———. *Sensational Designs: The Cultural Work of American Fiction, 1790–1860*. New York: Oxford University Press, 1985.

Towner, Lawrence W. "True Confessions and Dying Warnings in Colonial New England." *Sibley's Heir: A Volume in Memory of Clifford Shipley*. Ed. Lawrence W. Towner. Boston: The Colonial Society of Massachusetts, 1982. 523–39.

Ulrich, Laurel Thatcher. *Good Wives: Images and Reality in the Lives of Women in Northern New England, 1650–1750*. New York: Alfred A. Knopf, 1982.
Walker, Samuel. *Popular Justice: A History of American Criminal Justice*. New York: Oxford University Press, 1980.
Webb, John. *The Greatness of Sin improv'd by the Penitent as an argument with God for a Pardon. A Sermon at the Thursday Lecture in Boston, October 17th. 1734. Preach'd in the Hearing of John Ormesby, and Matthew Cushing, Two Condemned Malefactors on the Day of their Execution, The One for Murder, and the other for Burglary*. Boston: S. Kneeland and T. Green, 1734.
Weis, Frederick Lewis. *The Colonial Clergy and the Colonial Churches of New England*. Lancaster: Society of the Descendants of the Colonial Clergy, 1936.
Wiebe, Robert H. *The Opening of American Society: From the Adoption of the Constitution to the Eve of Disunion*. New York: Alfred A. Knopf, 1984.
Willard, Samuel. *Impenitent Sinners Warned of their Misery and Summoned to Judgement. Delivered in Two Sermons: the former on the Sabbath, Nov. 6. the other on the Lecture following, Nov. 10, 1698. Occasioned by the Amazing instance of a Miserable Creature, who stood Condemned for murdering her Infant begotten in Whoredom. To which are subjoyned the Solemn Words spoken to her, on those Opportunities. Published for the Warning of others*. Boston: B. Green and J. Allen, 1698.
Williams, Daniel E. "Puritans and Pirates: A Confrontation Between Cotton Mather and William Fly In 1726." *Early American Literature* 22 (1987): 233–251.
———. "Behold a Tragic Scene Strangely Changed into a Theater of Mercy: The Structure and Significance of Criminal Conversion Narratives in Early New England." *American Quarterly* 38 (Winter 1986): 827–47.
Williams, John. *Warnings to the Unclean: In a Discourse From Rev. XXI. 8. Preacht at Springfield Lecture, August 25th, 1698. At the Execution of Sarah Smith*. Boston: B. Green and J. Allen, 1699.
Williams, William. *The Serious Consideration: A Sermon Preach'd at Cambridge, September 15, 1738. On Occasion of the Execution of Philip Kennison, For the Crime of Burglary*. Boston: Thomas Fleet, 1738.
Winthrop, John. *Winthrop's Journal: History of New England, 1630–1649*. Ed. James Kendall Hosmer. 2 vols. New York: Charles Scribner's Sons, 1908.
Worcester, Noah. *A Sermon Delivered at Haverhill, New Hampshire, July 28, 1796, At the Execution of Thomas Powers, Who was Executed for a Rape, Committed at Lebanon, on the 7th of December, 1795*. Haverhill: N. Coverly, 1796.
Zanger, Jules. "Crime and Punishment in Early Massachusetts." *William and Mary Quarterly* 3rd ser. 22 (1965): 471–77.

# Index